The Answer Within:

A CLINICAL FRAMEWORK
OF ERICKSONIAN
HYPNOTHERAPY

The Answer Within:

A CLINICAL FRAMEWORK OF ERICKSONIAN HYPNOTHERAPY

by

Stephen R. Lankton

and

Carol H. Lankton

BRUNNER/MAZEL, *Publishers* • New York

Library of Congress Cataloging in Publication Data

Lankton, Stephen R.
  The answer within.

  Bibliography: p.
  Includes index.
  1. Hypnotism—Therapeutic use. 2. Erickson,
Milton H. I. Lankton, Carol H., 1950–   . II. Title.
RC495.L34   1983   616.89′162   82-20637
ISBN 0-87630-320-3

Copyright © 1983 by Stephen R. Lankton and Carol H. Lankton

Published by
BRUNNER/MAZEL, INC.
19 Union Square
New York, New York 10003

MANUFACTURED IN THE UNITED STATES OF AMERICA

10 9 8 7

We wish to express our deepest appreciation as we dedicate this book to the late Milton H. Erickson, M.D.

"I invent a new theory and a new approach for each individual."

Milton H. Erickson, M.D.,
personal communication, November, 1977

CONTENTS

ACKNOWLEDGMENTS

Most of all we thank our clients, trainees, and sponsors who have helped us investigate, learn, and share. We also want to acknowledge the recognition and sense of encouragement which we receive from all the persons currently sharing and developing ways to teach Dr. Erickson's work ethically and accurately, especially to Jeffery K. Zeig, Ph.D., and the Milton Erickson Foundation, Inc.

We would like to thank The Boston Family Therapy Institute for allowing us generous access to their extensive film library and Dr. Frank Maple and the University of Michigan School of Social Work for the personal assistance and equipment necessary to research the many hours of videotape that eventually became a part of this volume.

Thanks also go to Susan Barrows and Dr. Reid Wilson for their editorial candor. And special appreciation goes to Joe Byrne for his support and frequent assistance with the technology that helped make this book a reality.

And finally, this acknowledgment section would not be complete without a grateful mention of the many hours of personal and professional attention that Dr. Erickson and various members of the Erickson family gave to us, often free of charge.

PREFACE

"Leave a trail of happiness . . ."

On March 25, 1980, in Phoenix, Arizona, Milton Erickson died. He had become a mentor, guru, father, artist, teacher, friend and trainer for many of us. He had become a legend, a mystery, and a miracle for some of us. Many people lamented that they had put off seeing him and studying with him and that his death made it impossible for them to ever have that unique experience.

Milton Erickson pioneered the clinical use of hypnosis in a way that no other person has done. He published over 150 articles on hypnosis, co-authored six books and there are at least 10 books about him. He founded the American Society of Clinical Hypnosis in 1957 and edited the *American Journal of Clinical Hypnosis* from 1958 to 1968. He hypnotized over 30,000 people all over the world in conducting research and treatment. His work in hypnosis has resulted in the "discovery" and clinical use of many techniques and theories now used both in and outside of hypnotic settings. In many cases he used techniques that inspired others to write about and imitate his work. Some of his techniques, such as paradox, metaphor, therapeutic double binds, and symptom prescription, are now well-known and frequently used in nonhypnotic therapies.

The purpose of this book is to illustrate the clinical aspects of Erickson's work, rather than overemphasizing the mechanical aspects. We present here the structure of much of Erickson's hypnotherapy work, especially his use of embedded metaphors. Overall, we emphasize techniques only in the context of understanding the actual logic of treatment in an Ericksonian style. Whether we are dealing with the microdynamics of voice tone or the macroscopic level of clients' life development, we focus on Ericksonian interventions within multiple embedded metaphors and strategically used trance phenomena.

Erickson was well-known for his wit. His creative wit blossomed everywhere —in his treatment, his teaching, his child-rearing, in the frontispieces of books he signed, in his greetings and even in a wedding "ceremony" he conducted for us. At that time he said to us, "Leave a trail of happiness . . . and look forward to the days when you can look back." Another one we like is: "Don't give up any of your faults; you'll need them to understand your spouse's!" Time after time you may hear of his one-liners, which are both thought provoking and entertaining. Several come to mind now. "Into every life some confusion should come—also some enlightenment." And since this preface is written on the very anniversary of his death, we recall his "good recipe for longevity: Always be sure to get up in the morning . . . and you can insure that by drinking a lot of water before you go to bed."

His wit often led him to make points with anecdotes. He noted, for example, that if we place a narrow wooden plank on the ground each of us could walk it. But if it were raised 200 feet in the air, who then could walk it? How easily the same task becomes difficult because "ideas, understanding, beliefs, hopes, and fears all impinge easily upon performance in the state of ordinary conscious awareness—disrupting and distorting even those goals which may have been strongly desired" (Erickson, CP IV,* p. 55). When the logic behind that quote is turned into its converse we find the secret of Erickson's work: Change the frame of reference of the conscious mind and appeal to the necessary historical unconscious resources each person has experienced and automatized.

His approach to people was the same as his approach to himself: Teach the mind to concentrate on the countless learnings, potentials, and resources that lie within. But more important, perhaps, are the values of life he taught and lived. Professionally, we like to say he "did his homework." Many young (and old) clinicians like to attend workshops hoping to get quick skills and rapid talent transfusions. But professionals must work methodically and "do the homework" in order to become proficient and effective clinicians.

Perhaps it is our culture's ultimate dilemma—balancing specialization and cooperation. The professional person is often split into two people—the private and the professional person. Erickson, however, was not "on" and "off."

---

*For bibliographic conciseness, we are using CP in the text to refer to The Collected Papers of Milton H. Erickson on Hypnosis. Volume I: The Nature of Hypnosis and Suggestion; Volume II: Hypnotic Alteration of Sensory, Perceptual and Psychophysiological Processes; Volume III: Hypnotic Investigation of Psychodynamic Processes; Volume IV: Innovative Hypnotherapy. Ernest L. Rossi (Ed.). New York: Irvington, 1980.

He was always Milton H. Erickson. A large part of his life was dedicated to being an outstanding hypnotist and he was committed to earnestly and vitally doing the preparation he needed to do in order to learn what he needed to know. Perhaps most of all, he had learned how to learn in all situations. He conveyed to us a real joy about learning that could be noticed frequently.

His eyes would twinkle several times a day at the delight of an ambiguity he had observed, a pun he had made, a good-humored joke he had casually led you into, a charming remark. He frequently laughed and smiled throughout his teaching and therapy sessions. Even when shouting to have someone quiet the dog, there seemed to be that alertness to detail and readiness to learn. So, "doing homework" is not meant to imply drudgery in the usual sense. Erickson did his homework by holding certain principles and attitudes. We have illustrated these in the first part of this volume.

He was also a farm boy willing to put forth the hard labor, commitment, and time required for achieving certain goals. As a brief example, Erickson on one recorded occasion worked with a psychotic man hospitalized in Michigan. The man only spoke "word salad" to others and consequently he was not "getting through" to anyone on the staff. Erickson recorded, transcribed and then laboriously learned to emulate the word-salad speech patterns of the client. He actually learned to sound like the client. Several days of verbally interacting with the man while using the word-salad eventually resulted in the client's saying, "Talk sense, Doctor" (Haley, 1967, p. 502)! And he did.

Another example of the work that Erickson put forth involves constructing an induction. He didn't just "wing it" from a notion that mumble-jumble would create the desired trance state. He wrote an induction 30 pages long and then polished it down to 15 pages and then to eight pages, then five, three, and finally down to one-and-a-half pages. When finished, his induction was well thought out, poignant, and powerful. That's doing your homework!

Erickson said that he invented a new theory for each individual. He was the most congruent person we ever met with regard to his conviction that everyone be treated as an individual. It may seem like a paradox that Erickson's style was distinctive and yet his approach different for each person. That was something that fascinated us and attracted us to the careful study of Erickson's work. It may be that his range of interventions was far broader than the casual investigator of his work is aware.

Before he was confined to a wheelchair, he often made very active interventions which were related in numerous stories. Many are too long to share adequately in this introduction but can be briefly illustrated with the following abridged versions. For example, "Big Bertha" used to periodically destroy the forensic hospital room where she was under observation. On one occasion Erickson instructed the staff to enter the room and destroy it themselves at the first sign that she was about to destroy it. When they did, Big Bertha became tearful and requested to talk to Erickson (she knew he was "behind it"). This was the first time she had requested help rather than becoming violent; furthermore, she had torn her room apart for the last time. On another occasion there was the man whom Erickson took shopping and taught to buy lace panties for his wife. On still another occasion Erickson went to the home of a young girl who had become obsessed with the size of her feet. She believed they were utterly too large and she withdrew from social contact, school, friends, and church, retreating to her room. Erickson came to her home on the pretense of treating her mother (who was feigning illness at his instruction). The little girl became interested in his care for the mother and was asked to fetch some warm towels. When she returned with them Erickson turned and carefully stomped on her feet. The girl looked up with a mixture of shock and anger, only to be greeted with Erickson's mildly scornful shout—"If you would grow the damn things big enough for people to see them then I would not have stepped on them!"

These stories tell of the commitment and daring that Erickson was known to exhibit. There was also a loving side. There were, for example, the many clients and trainees whom Erickson saw without charge. There was the young woman who had had such a deprived background that he invented a fantasy person for her unconscious. Week after week he helped her meet the imaginary "February Man" in hypnotic trance, as a way of building the continuity of a loving relationship that she could come to accept unconsciously. The "February Man," though imaginary, was a person, like Erickson himself, who loved her personal achievement and her joys and also shared in comforting her sorrows (Erickson, *CP* IV, p. 525). He told us that one of his sons came home from school and asked what he thought about the teacher's admonition that "beating a shoe on a desk is not a very good way to get attention." Erickson asked, "Does it work?" to which his son replied, "Yes, it works every time." Erickson said he replied, "Then it's a very good way to get attention!"

Erickson was, however, as elusive as a guru or a Zen master. Just when we thought he would be sympathetic he was tough and vice versa. One time when I (S. L.) thought I'd found a proper moment to tell him I had a lot of affection for him he replied, "You have too much!" And then at another time when he was relating case stories in training and I was listening intently, distracted from any thought of getting something for myself, he captured my gaze and, with more sincerity than you can imagine, imprinted on my mind the words, "You are as unique as your fingerprints. There will never be another one like you in all the world. And you can't change your fingerprints and you can't change that!" He would answer the phone and hang up without the customary "hellos" and "goodbyes" and yet he was thoroughly able to officiate as master of ceremonies, such as the time we had him say words of wisdom for our marriage.

He was one of a kind. He loved life and he was hopeful of the human condition. And he had an ever ready sense of humor. Immediately after the wedding words, we entered his office and he picked up a large chunk of what looked like granite, stating that "since you climbed Squaw Peak, you'll be interested in seeing this." With that introduction, he suddenly hurled the "rock" at me (C. L.), much to my surprise. Then, even more to my surprise, I discovered it to be weightless—foam rock or nerf granite. As he chuckled over my reaction, no words were spoken and yet a clever message was sent—don't take anything for "granite." It was a message that primarily amused me at the time but, as with many messages from Erickson, took on a greater meaning over time, hitting me, as it were, with more impact. For instance, I realized only after his rather sudden and unexpected death that I had left his office that day still taking for granted that I would see him again at the upcoming Ericksonian Congress in 1980.

Despite his limiting physical handicaps, Erickson grew larger and reached further than any of us. The only difference between weak people and strong people is the ideas they embrace. Milton always stretched his mind for a new way, a creative angle to accomplish what he intended to do. His greatness began in the realm of imagination and with the idea that within each of us is an incredible untapped potential. He found and built those potentials in himself from childhood and redoubled his effort after the personal difficulties brought on by his bouts with polio. He helped tap that potential in his patients and trainees with the use of paradox, therapeutic binds, anecdote, hypnosis, and its related phenomena. But finally, Milton was a venerable man with an extraordinary commitment to an outstanding idea.

After he died many of us found ourselves separating the ideas, theory, or the approach from the man. Since Erickson was always "on," his approach was an integral part of his total personality. But his techniques and treatment interventions and overall approach are available for others to learn and use as part of their own particular style. Once, when we asked for his definition of hypnosis and prepared to take notes of his studied answer, he replied: "It's concentrating on your own thoughts, values, memories and beliefs about life." We wrote that down, expecting that a more "scientific" version would follow. But there was no more. His short definition seemed slightly inadequate at the time but later came to mean more and more until it now says far more than any well chosen psychological "jargon." The right time to question Erickson about exactly what he meant by that and many other notions about therapy was forever postponed by his death. The answers we have and the meanings we create are all that remain. He gave us a great deal in his own special way.

One of his children told us once that as he grew up "my father gave to me so much year after year until one day I realized I wasn't ever expected to give anything back." I think many of us have seen that side of Erickson and have that same feeling. We sincerely hope that you, the reader, will find much of Erickson's work a gift that is meant for you to use and enjoy as you study this and other works of explanation and inquiry. There were never any "strings attached" to what we were given by Milton and there are no strings attached to your reading, studying, training, and learning of his approach. We do, however, hope that you approach this volume and hypnotherapy work with your clients with a sense of professionalism. Be reminded that Erickson worked most of his career to give a positive connotation to clinical hypnosis, despite the ever present influences of television and stage entertainment that vainly used the name of hypnosis for personal aggrandizement, profit, and false power.

In this volume about Erickson's clinical approach, we have emphasized the diagnosis and treatment planning aspects because we think there already exists enough written copy about the mechanics of his work. There is an imbalance in favor of a reductionistic and mechanical view of the microdynamics of Erickson's linguistic work. While we support such an approach in general, we believe there is a great need to examine and make available to others the treatment planning and clinical orientation that gives rise to and justification for the use of such cunning linguistics and uncommon therapeutics.

Our special emphasis in this volume is the use of the multiple embedded metaphor as a modality to deliver unique interventions designed on the basis of the diagnostic assessment. We begin with a brief discussion of the history of hypnosis in order to properly frame the context in which Erickson's work emerged. Chapter 2 discusses Erickson's attitude and principles of treatment. His unique approach to formulating interventions has given rise to the conception of special values and priorities with clients. We relate only those principles about which he gave us his agreement. It is our firm belief that these principles can be a guide in shaping clinicians' thinking about their clients and in formulating the interventions which best represent the Ericksonian approach.

Chapter 3 addresses the diagnostic considerations that parsimoniously describe Ericksonian approaches. Chapter 4 describes dramatic theme metaphors and introduces the multiple embedded metaphor with a representative example from Erickson's work. Here, too, we discuss the diagnostic formulations for metaphoric detail and outcomes that we believe best encompass Erickson's style. We provide supportive theory and substantiating case material from Erickson's work regarding this theory. Chapter 5 details aspects of Erickson's conscious/unconscious dissociation inductions. Included here is our discussion of indirect suggestion and therapeutic binds. Chapter 6 discusses fine points of strategically using trance phenomena and retrieving experiential resources. Repeatedly we relate these to the overall context of the multiple embedded metaphor. Thanks to the Boston Family Institute we have included several case examples from "nonhypnotic" family therapy. These illustrate strategic uses of trance phenomena and facilitate additional investigation and understanding of trance phenomena in the context of both hypnotic and nonhypnotic therapy.

Multiple embedded metaphor is elaborately illustrated in Chapter 7, with three entire case transcripts and discussions of the work and the results. Chapter 8 looks at self-image thinking and other work that is directed at changing unconscious emotional conflict. Again, this is done in the context of the multiple embedded metaphor. Chapter 9 concludes with a discussion of terminating therapy.

We sincerely hope that you will make significant gains from this volume, which is about the work of a great man. Buddha once said that great men are like mountains—they can be seen from a distance. And with mountains, there are always those who climb and create paths for others to follow. Perhaps we have created such a path with the magic that is in us, but in the Ericksonian tradition we remind you that the magic in us is less than the Buddha in you. We trust that your learnings will stay with you. "And," as Erickson would say before he embarked with you on a hypnotic journey, "my voice goes everywhere with you, and changes into the voice of your parents, your teacher, your playmates and even the voice of the wind and the rain. . . . "

Part One
BACKGROUND
AND DIAGNOSIS

1 THE HISTORICAL FRAMEWORK

HISTORY OF THERAPEUTIC HYPNOSIS

This brief historical review offers a perspective on hypnosis that Erickson emphasized in several of his lectures. We feel that it is an appropriate glimpse into the particular angle of history that we wish to highlight. In particular, the many derogatory myths and foreboding associations to hypnosis have been the logical outgrowth of its history and the prevailing "scientific" attitudes that existed when hypnotic phenomena were first studied. There has been, from time to time, much discouragement regarding the use of hypnosis or its long-term effectiveness and its general advisability. As we shall outline in this volume, we agree with Erickson's thoughts about these skepticisms. We trace these attitudes through historical events in order to put them in proper perspective.

Although hypnosis has been a cultural phenomenon in many cultures for many centuries (witness the temples of sleep in early Babylonian times in southern Mesopotamia), our modern story seems to begin about the time of the American revolution:

1773—Mesmer (1734–1815), an Austrian physician in Vienna, began promoting the idea of animal magnetism. He noticed that some of his patients seemed to be helped when magnets were passed over their bodies. He "found" that the patients could benefit from being near a tub of circulating water with magnetized rods. Some of the patients would have states of crisis or convulsions that ended in unconsciousness. When these patients aroused, they were often improved. Soon he discovered that he could produce the same result by only touching the patients; subsequently he came to the conclusion that he possessed a fluid which he could store up and transmit to others—animal magnetism.

1784—A team from France, including Ben Franklin, Antoine-Laurent Lavosier (a chemist), and Joseph Guillotin from the French Academy (who later got "a head" in another line of business!), set out to study Mesmer. They declared Mesmer a fraud; animal magnetism was mere imagination. Soon the entire matter became associated with mysticism and quackery. Phineas Quimby (1802–1866), a "mental healer," came to Portland, Maine and further associated Mesmerism with spiritualism, thereby further discouraging serious scientific investigation of suggestive phenomena connected with Mesmer's observations (Alexander & Selesnick, 1966, p. 129).

1841—James Braid, a Scottish surgeon, attached the term "hypnotism" to the techniques of eye fixation and suggestion. It came from the Greek "hypnos" (sleep) and referred to the sleeplike state in which a subject is responsive to a variety of external stimulations. Braid noticed that individuals seemed to suspend the normal judgment which inhibited behavior and to be capable of apparent sensation in accordance with the hypnotist's suggestion, even when it was at odds with their normal perceptual response. Even memory could be altered (Braid, 1846).

At the same time James Esdaile, using a similar technique in Calcutta, began to achieve publicity for his Mesmeric techniques. He soon resorted to using the term "hypnosis" to more adequately depict the techniques and responses. He was successful doing such procedures as leg amputations with the techniques.

1886—Bernheim (1895) and Liébault experimented with similar techniques in their practice in Nancy, France, and attracted attention of a Paris professor of neurology, Jean-Martin Charcot, and the soon-to-be-famous Sigmund Freud, in Austria. Although there was some disagreement among these men regarding the causes and the credits for the phenomena, the controversy created awareness of the phenomenon called, at times, Mesmerism, hypnosis, and suggestive therapeutics.

1890—Freud heard about the work of Bernheim and Liébeault and went to Nancy, France to study with them. Their work consisted of progressive relaxation and direct suggestion. Freud believed that he could use these techniques with his clients suffering from neurotic disorders. Freud was, however, to play a larger role in destiny. He was, at that time, developing his theories of the unconscious and attempting to isolate more advantageous therapeutic tools for uncovering repressed unconscious material "from" the unconscious. Hypnosis for Freud was only a temporary departure from his approach of free (albeit expensive) association (Alexander & Selesnick, 1966, pp. 188–191).

1896—Freud published the papers on hysteria and also denounced hypnosis. His denouncement was for several primary reasons: 1) Not everyone seemed to be hypnotizable with this approach. 2) Symptoms seemed to recur. 3) Repression was increased by the suggestions. 4) The transference relationship was sometimes dramatically altered by outbursts of joy or anger from the patient (Brill in Freud, 1938, pp. 8–9).

At first glance it would seem that hypnosis, at this time, had received a fatal blow. However, many others continued to experiment with it in various ways and locations around the world: Pavlov in Russia, Pierre Janet in France, Morton Prince in the United States, as well as others in the U.S. who followed the earlier works of Phineas Quimby, including his well-known follower, Mary Baker Eddy. Despite the increase in scientific investigation, however, hypnotic phenomena still carried associations to Mesmerism, occult mysticism, and sensationalism.

1933—Clark Hull, an American behaviorist, included an entry on hypnosis and suggestibility in his text by the same name, which presented the pioneering experimental approach he helped develop with Milton Erickson. Otherwise, there was little professional investigation of hypnosis during this period. Hypnotism (or Mesmerism) did, however, appear in the entertainment media and was associated with "forces of darkness." Hypnosis, from the Greek "hypnos," lent itself easily to such an association, not only because sleep happens in the darkness of night and is accompanied by dreams and sometimes nightmares beyond one's apparent control, but also because of historical and mythological connections with the Underworld. Hypnos was a Greek god, the son of Night and the father of Morpheus (dreams). Hypnos and his brother Thanatos both were said to live in the Underworld. Hypnos was not malevolent, however; he was benevolent, as he brought rest to the weary souls trapped in the Underworld, often fanning them to sleep with his wings or soothing their pain with a touch of his wand. But, as it turned out, the fine points of his mythological employment were overshadowed in history by his association to the Underworld, Thanatos, and the forces of darkness. And so it remains in the minds of many today.

1956—The American Medical Association dedicated a journal to the medical uses of hypnosis. However, outside of a few universities, hypnosis had not been seriously investigated.

1957—The American Society of Clinical Hypnosis was founded by Milton H. Erickson (1901–1980), who edited its journal for a decade and published cases of clinical hypnotherapy dating as early as the 1930s. His style was distinctly different. Instead of using progressive relaxation and direct suggestion as had been done for the last 100 years, Erickson demonstrated a style which eventually came to be known as utilization and indirect suggestion.

Erickson studied the effects of communication and hypnosis even as a child and taught his approach throughout his graduate school years. His work was often shrouded in mystery and professional criticism because he did not automatically value the psychiatric beliefs of his time: insight for repressed unconscious material, time-consuming "working through," and noninvolvement of the therapist in analysis of the transference phenomenon. He supported and promoted brief therapy, family therapy, use of hypnosis with amnesia, active and paradoxical intervention by the therapist, encouragement rather than confrontation, and utilizing resistance from the client (Erickson & Rossi, *CP* III, p. 74; IV, p. 97).

During his lifetime Erickson authored 150 journal articles, worked with over 30,000 patients, authored or co-authored several books, worked closely with a few therapists, and is credited with the development of certain techniques, such as structured amnesia, confusion technique, pantomime induction, my friend John technique—to name only a few.

1980—The International Congress on Ericksonian Approaches to Hypnosis and Psychotherapy was attended by 2,000 clinical psychotherapists. This congress was, therefore, the largest gathering of clinicians to honor and study the work of a single individual therapist. Since that time, the demand for thorough and precise training in Ericksonian techniques has been great.

Since Erickson had no theory of personality, but rather had a theory of intervention, many psychotherapists find that his approach is not easily learned or understood. Consequently, many may fall victim to that aspect of human nature which is inclined to attribute old myths to that which they do not understand.

Despite this apparent liability, Erickson's influence is thought by many to equal Freud's. Whereas Freud can be thought of as the Einstein of theory, Erickson will likely be acknowledged as the Einstein of intervention. There are several features that typify an Ericksonian approach. Among these are:

1) indirection—the use of indirect suggestion, binds, metaphor, and resource retrieval;
2) conscious/unconscious dissociation—multiple level communication, interspersal, double binds, multiple embedded metaphors; and,
3) utilization of the client's behavior—paradox, behavioral matching, naturalistic induction, symptom prescription, and strategic use of trance phenomena.

INDIRECTION

To briefly conceptualize Erickson's early work, we quote a 1941 paper.

Concerning the techniques of the induction of hypnotic trances, this is a relatively simple matter requiring primarily time, patience, and careful attention to and consideration for the subjects, their personalities, and their emotional attitudes and reactions. Properly, there is no set form or pattern to follow, just as there is no set form for a good bedside manner. One needs the respect, confidence, and trust of a subject, and then one suggests fatigue, a desire for sleep and rest, an increasing feeling of sleep and finally a deep sound restful sleep (*CP* III, p. 15).

It is important to remember that Erickson's approach grew and developed over many years. In this earlier quote we see his attitude and also a sketch of his early induction techniques. In 1941 he relied upon repetition and suggestions of "sleep." Later he moved entirely (or almost entirely) away from this style, but his attitude toward the client remained unchanged and became more integrated into his treatment style throughout his career.

Later, in 1973, for example, he said, "People come for help, but they also come to be substantiated in their attitudes and they come to have face saved. I pay attention to this and I'm likely to speak in a fashion that makes them think I'm on their side" (Haley, 1973, p. 206). The same attitude of respect and acceptance for the client can be seen here as in the previous quote 30 years earlier. However, the difference is evident as Erickson continues:

Then, I digress on a tangent that they can accept, but it leaves them teetering on the edge of expectation. They have to admit that my digression is all right, it's perfectly correct, but they didn't expect me to do it that way. It's an uncomfortable position to be teetering, and they want some solution of the matter that I had just brought to the edge of settlement. Since they want that solution, they are more likely to accept what I say. They are very eager for a decisive statement. If you gave the directive right away, they could take issue with it. But if you digress, they hope you will get back, and they welcome a decisive statement from you (Erickson in Haley, 1973, p. 206).

This contrasting position of extreme indirection typifies the later years of Erickson's work. It represents the foundation for his use of metaphors, indirect suggestions, binds, and naturalistic induction. He moved further away from the direct suggestion and relaxation of Bernheim, Charcot, and Freud's era and developed a manner much more consistent with his deeply respectful attitude about people, problems, and the unconscious. He stated to us person-ally that "it is not necessary to repeat the same suggestion over and over."

This attitude toward his clients and this style of indirection created a turn of events in the historical course of hypnotherapy and psychotherapy in general. Erickson was well aware that his orientation was a complete departure from the archaic approach of the late 1800s. Even in 1941 he was keenly aware that his approach was different:

> Psychologists are beginning to discard the old belief that hypnosis transforms a person into some strange, passive, dominated new crea-ture. Instead they are beginning to realize that hypnosis can be used and should be used to elicit the natural and innate behavior and reactions of the subject, and that through such a measure human behavior can be studied in a controlled and scientific manner (*CP* III, p. 18).

UNCONSCIOUS AND CONSCIOUS

Erickson was aware, too, of the difference in his concept of the uncon-scious. Before continuing this explanation of Erickson's approach we would like to present what Erickson said about the unconscious in his later years:

> Weitzenhoffer (1960) has convincingly presented the view that the term "unconscious" in contexts such as we have used here is not the same as Freud's "unconscious." Our use of the term "unconscious" is similar to its usage with finger signaling and the Chervreul pendulum (Cheek & LeCron, 1968) where Prince's (1929) definition of subcon-scious or co-conscious as any process "of which the personality is un-aware" but "which is a factor in the determination of conscious and bodily phenomena" is more appropriate (Erickson & Rossi, *CP* I, p. 424).

We find the Ericksonian view of the unconscious to be compatible with the contemporary understanding of the unconscious held by various theories of operational personality (Burton, 1974). The unconscious is thought to be a complex set of associations. The degree of "out of awareness" between these patterns varies due to many factors: unique personal history, intensity of learning, subtlety of experience, and social sanctions placed upon knowing and experiencing. What remains in a person's repertoire of experiences are automatized, unconscious patterns which regulate, calculate, modulate, and otherwise guide the routine conduct of even the most disturbed human being.

"The overlay of neuroticism, however extensive, does not distort the central core of the personality, though it may disguise and cripple the manifestations of it" (CP I, p. 146).

These automatized resources are associations of perception-experience-behavior with varying degrees of unconscious functioning (CP I, p. 453). They may frequently be patterns of experience that cannot be accurately conceptualized within our customary worldview. For example, we hardly have the vocabulary for discussion of our inner experience to the extent present in some other cultures. "Sanskrit has about 20 nouns which we translate into 'consciousness' or 'mind' in English" (Tart, 1969, p. 3). Consequently, Erickson, unlike Freud (1938, p. 482), was not often interested in helping clients achieve insight with which to engage in controlling unconscious-directed ideas.

It may be considered by many that everything done in, by, to, or for the body at an unconscious level is either maintaining health, prohibiting it, or promoting it. In any case, it affects the person's experience in the world. And it is, therefore, a communicational event. The mere observation of the general manner in which people conduct themselves as total beings in the world may be said to result in an intuitive judgment about their lives in many ways. The common wisdom in such judgment is expressed colloquially by the use of such jargon referred to as "vibes" (as in "I didn't like her vibes," etc.).

Accordingly, Erickson said: "All the forms of body language can be understood as systems of ideomotor signaling" (Erickson & Rossi, 1981, p. 119). Whether all this unconscious communication can be noticed and then understood in context by any observers is a matter of cultural, societal, and personal learning. Much unconscious experience, then, remains nonverbally expressed. That statement does not preclude the possibility that some unconscious behavior is, in fact, not expressed at all. But in that case, how would science or psychology even know of its existence or activity at all? Consequently, Erickson's conception of the unconscious covers a broad range of possible human experience.

The ability to articulate such out-of-awareness experiences depends upon variable factors. Most experiences defy the dominant hemisphere's attempt to verbalize all of their particular components. The manner of expression or the verbal capacity is limited to a linear and digital mode, in contrast to the global, comprehensive experience actually lived. "If we translate the terms 'conscious' and 'unconscious' into 'dominant' and 'nondominant' hemispheres, we may have the neuropsychological basis for describing a new hypnotherapeutic approach" (Erickson & Rossi, 1979, p. 247). We return to this topic again in "flow of induction" in Chapter 5.

UTILIZATION

The final distinction could be conceptualized as the utilization approach whereby clients are not thought of as resistant. Instead of considering the client resistant if s/he failed to comply with the mode of conduct necessary in therapy, Erickson shaped the therapy to the client. He often seemed to eliminate any potential resistance by using it in the therapy. He wrote: "If they bring in resistance, be grateful for that resistance. Heap it up in whatever fashion they want you to—really pile it up. But never get disgusted with the amount of resistance. . . . Whatever the patient presents to you in the office, you really ought to use" (Erickson in Erickson & Rossi, 1981, p. 16).

Keeping in mind certain ideas about human behavior can either limit or expand the available behavioral options. Erickson kept in his mind the idea that individuals know more than they think they know. Change is a matter of initiating new and creative responses to the environment. He was willing to be flexible with other people so they could find their personal and unique adjustments to their situations.

"A small percentage of individuals exist who get 'others' to react to them in the widest range of possible behaviors and who can utilize a wide range of appropriate reactions. Most individuals tend to train 'others' to react to them within a narrowed range of behaviors, and in turn show a restricted set of favored reflexes" (Leary, 1957, p. 109). Erickson's flexibility and tolerance for unique individual differences probably allowed him to facilitate helpful changes in many individuals and families. He held attitudes toward others that permitted his formulation of the unique interventions that were his hallmark. We devote the next chapter to examining and illustrating those attitudes.

2 PRINCIPLES OF TREATMENT: THE ATTITUDINAL FRAMEWORK

Learning to make Ericksonian interventions is a precise task comparable to mathematics or, if the precision of mathematics seems too severe as a comparison, we might say the task is as precise as tuning an automobile engine. While not as exacting as mathematics, it does require that proper tools be applied in specific ways. The concept of "principles," however, at first seemed to be associated with resolutions, abstract statements, and hopelessly vague notions about proper procedure. Dealing with Erickson's work in terms of principles struck us as awkward and inappropriate.

But we are endorsing the use of "principles" in the same way that a computer programmer might use the concept of an algorithm program. If the programmer wanted to explain to a person exactly how to climb to the top of a mountain, the programmer would need very detailed and accurate information about where to turn left and when to turn right and how to grab on there and not somewhere else. The programmer would have to have privy to the actual facts of the terrain before giving the instruction.

By contrast, if the programmer used an algorithmic program, s/he would only have to tell the person something akin to "Go up and up and up." This algorithm would allow the person to get to the top with no prior knowledge of the terrain. The person would only need to know about the operations of turning and grasping, etc. Later, of course, the algorithm could be specified and the detailed answer would constitute a strategic program for future climbs up that exact same mountain in the exact same way. (That, of course, would only work if the mountain did not change in any way!) It is clear that the algorithmic program is like a principle. And the principle, like the algorithm, allows novel and creative approaches to a problem while maximizing the probability of reaching the goal.

The goal here is establishing an attitude toward the client and the process of change that is conducive to generating and using the types of treatment interventions typical of an Ericksonian approach. We have combined 11 treatment principles from several sources which, if incorporated in the therapist's belief system, make the Ericksonian approach possible. One of the most perplexing aspects of Erickson's work is the nearly total absence of a uniform

11

theory of personality which would account for the often startling and dramatic changes that he documented; nevertheless, these principles do constitute a theory of intervention. They are:

1) People operate out of their internal maps and not out of sensory experience.
2) People make the best choice for themselves at any given moment.
3) The explanation, theory, or metaphor used to relate facts about a person is not the person.
4) Respect all messages from the client.
5) Teach choice; never attempt to take choice away.
6) The resources the client needs lie within his or her own personal history.
7) Meet the client at his or her model of the world.
8) The person with the most flexibility or choice will be the controlling element in the system.
9) A person can't not communicate.
10) If it's hard work, reduce it down.
11) Outcomes are determined at the psychological level.

INTERNAL MAPS

People operate out of their internal maps and not out of sensory experience. The first principle acknowledges that each individual perceives the world from the unique vantage point of his or her own frame of reference (Korzybski, 1933). A first step in therapy is ascertaining something about that "map" from which the client is operating. Erickson stated: "We always translate the other person's language into our own language" (Erickson in Zeig, 1980, p. 64). Will therapy primarily work to "edit" and alter limiting aspects of the map which seem to either prevent desired behaviors or automatically produce unpleasant feeling states and unwanted behaviors? Or will therapy work to expand and elaborate the existing map to provide new experience and behavior? Answering those questions can be an ongoing process throughout interviewing, diagnosing and actual treatment. Keeping this principle in mind serves to enhance the sensory experience of the therapist going about the task of tailoring interventions that will compatibly expand or alter the client's map.

An ingenious intervention is wasted if the client rejects it. Have you had the experience of relating a joke that really amused you and then getting a hurt, offended, or opposite response from your audience? In situations such as those the different frames of reference are obvious. When we speak to large groups, it is almost certain that someone there is depressed; someone feels like he is a failure; somebody else feels as if he had better get a divorce; somebody thinks she had better hurry up and get married; somebody else is worried about her pregnancy or the one she's not having, etc. Everyone walks into the room with perceptions that are out of context. The way that those perceptions are associated produces feelings and behaviors that are out of context as well. Erickson would customarily say in his inductions, "You make your own sense out of my words. My voice can turn into the sound of a friend or a stranger, someone from your past, your own voice, . . . " as a way of making certain that he validated the person's own experience and internal map.

BEST CHOICE

People make the best choice for themselves at any given moment. This is not to say that a person always makes the best choice that anybody could have made. It does say that, given a person's particular frame of reference and history of learning, even a "problem" behavior or feeling is the best choice the person has learned to make in a particular circumstance. If a person can be confident in the bathtub but cannot be confident in front of groups, then it is not because s/he is resistant or has an investment in not succeeding. Rather, in Erickson's belief system, it is because the person has not learned the association mechanisms to pull that confidence into the foreground when it is desired.

The idea of making the best choice is incompatible with ideas of "resistance." Erickson's attitude toward his clients reduced any apparent resistance. We find support for this systemic view of resistance in Upham's definition (1973, p. 86): "Resistance is defined here as client behaviors motivated by discomfort aroused by lack of congruence between the expectations of the practitioner and those of the client regarding help or regarding their reciprocal roles." While this is highly speculative, it seems to be consistent with Erickson's statement of attitude that "sick people do want to try; usually they don't know how" (CP IV, p. 60).

Consider the following example. An exceedingly attractive, 23-year-old woman came for therapy and approached the entire situation in what could be termed a histrionic manner. She regularly flipped back her long hair, crossed her legs carefully in such a way so as to slide her nylons together, and made rapid angular movements of her head. Her appearance suggested a sophistication that turned out to be noticeably lacking during conversation with her. With regard to social interaction skills she was actually very impoverished. For teaching purposes we characterize her as someone who doesn't know how to say: "That's a nice looking jacket you've got on. I love your smile. What a nice haircut. Where'd you get that thing around your neck?" That is, she didn't know how to make small talk. She didn't know how to sit beside someone and feel a constellation of proprioception that she would call "comfort."

If she sits in a cafeteria displaying that kind of histrionic behavior, more than one young college man is going to approach her, sit down beside her and begin talking to her. She was very anxious about how to behave in those situations. If an interested man suggested a date or put his hand out to touch her she would probably become so anxious that she would jerk away, maybe even accusing him of being an impudent beast with only one thing on his mind, etc. Now, some therapists, transactional analysts for instance, might describe this interaction as a woman playing a transactional game of some kind, setting up a con in order to collect a familiar bad feeling and advance her life drama.

We disagree with that theory of motivation and suggest that she did not know another response and how to be comfortable with it, generate it or use it during such a demanding situation as courtship. The apparent game payoff, then, is only the logical result of finding herself extended beyond her individual comfort zone of interpersonal behavior. She would have been fine if the man in question only used flirtation, as she did, as a method of light social contact. But if he went beyond that and interpreted her behavior in the framework of sexual "come-on," he was likely to request interpersonal behavior from her that was beyond her range of learned comfortable responses, outside the comfort zone of her self-image. Whenever that happens, a person's best choice of problem-solving, emergency or avoidance behavior will be elicited. We believe she wanted to feel fine, to the extent that she knew what "fine" feels like. Taking the angle that people make the best choice for themselves often requires updating old theories and explanations.

THEORIES ARE NOT THE CLIENT

The explanation, theory, or metaphor used to relate facts about a person is not the person. This principle refers both to the therapist's theory, which may need to be revised to fit a particular client, as well as to clients' explanations or theories about themselves. In fact, most clients come to therapy with more explanations than you want to hear about why they can't get the change they want (i.e., 'That's just the way I am. I've always been that way").

Erickson was well-known for therapeutically "bypassing" conscious mind associations, believing that the conscious mind primarily contains biases, limiting beliefs, and rigid patterns of perceiving (*CP* III, p. 90). He was also known for inventing a new theory for each client he met. Margaret Mead once commented that Erickson never solved a problem in the same old way if he could think of a new way—and he usually could (Erickson, personal communication, August, 1977).

So the explanation is not the person and often an explanation only helps the client focus more on the way of being stuck. Think for a moment about the kind of explanations you give yourself. For instance, you might wake up in the morning and say to yourself something like this: "This is going to be another rotten day. I have all those unfinished projects and I don't know why I can't finish those projects. I remember my father never really finished many projects. In fact, I remember that once when I was trying to build that birdhouse and he broke the wood and never bought any more wood. That made me feel bad years ago. In fact, I feel bad like that a little now, just thinking about it." If you should continue with such a line of thought, you will create an outcome by telling yourself how you are stuck. With yourself and with clients, we suggest it is better to use internal memory to retrieve resources rather than explanations.

Jones, in a treatise on the "self-fulfilling prophecy" aspects of theory (1977), comments that theories of mental health practitioners may sometimes hurt the client. This same phenomenon often occurs in family life and so reminds us of the pervasiveness of the potentially harmful effects of attributions and seemingly harmless theories.

RESPECT ALL MESSAGES

Respect all messages from the client. "An attitude of empathy and respect on the part of the therapist is crucial to ensure successful change" (Erickson & Zeig, *CP* IV, p. 336). There are, of course, many messages sent simultaneously during communication. There is always a psychological level message in addition to the social level message (Lankton, Lankton, & Brown, 1981). There are both verbal and nonverbal components to consider. Responding appropriately (with respect) to messages sent requires first being attuned so as to notice the more subtle elements of a communication—the voice tone, gestures, facial expressions, breathing, order of imagery, right to left congruity, etc.

The following example is particularly useful in illustrating this principle. A woman and her husband came for therapy, the husband complaining that his wife was not affectionate enough. When the wife was asked what she wanted to accomplish in the session, she responded: "There are some things we can't talk about." As she said this she simultaneously thrust her hands over her genital area. Now we could respond to the message but not respect it by saying something like, "Oh, you mean we can't talk about sex," or "I notice that as you told me that you didn't want to talk about some things, you covered your groin. Is there any relationship between the two acts?" Either of those responses would demonstrate a lack of respect for her verbal message. She knows far better than we do that to talk about sex in front of her husband is not wise at this point. She does not want to open that cateogry when she has already exhausted all of the resources she can think of to solve the problem.

Since we had noticed the message, we wanted to respond to it in some way, either metaphorically or possibly in the same channel in which it was sent, that is, by visually specifying ambiguous word-language. Capitalizing on the client's momentary disorientation experienced from the shock of the new interview, Carol turned to her, repeated her gesture, and fixated her conscious attention with words: 'The things we can't talk about here (*hands in lap*) are things which you both will be able to work out at the appropriate time and place (*moving hands out of lap and gesturing toward both of them*)." We then proceeded with ambiguous verbal language and visual specification through a range of subjects to find out what she *did* want to talk about and learn. We mentioned a range of various concerns that "people" come to therapy to change and when one of us finally said, " . . . they want to understand those factors in the relationship which are important" (while making a gentle fist motion in a rhythmical pounding over the heart area), she nodded her head quite vigorously "yes." Just how much of this communication passed the threshold of excitation necessary for her to be conscious we did not know and did not need to determine. What was important was that we showed respect for the communications she presented by valuing them enough to use them in our further information-gathering.

Erickson was certainly a master of perceiving and responding with respect in clever and touching ways. One group of his students, discussing and arguing about the range of Erickson's perceptual skills, set up a test by turning a very small figurine of an owl on its side where it sat on a very crowded shelf in the back of the office. They waited expectantly, wondering if Erickson would notice the small alteration and, if he did, how he would respond. He said nothing about it all day and apparently hadn't noticed it. At the end of the day, as the students were filing past his wheelchair to leave the office, Erickson casually remarked, "Oh, by the way, that other thing you want me to mention, I don't give a 'hoot' about!"

TEACH CHOICE

Teach choice; never attempt to take choice away. This follows logically from the second principle that people will make the best choice for themselves. Erickson said:

When you understand how man really defends his intellectual ideas and how emotional he gets about it, you should realize that the first thing in psychotherapy is not to try to compel him to change his ideation; rather, you go along with it and change it in a gradual fashion and create situations wherein he himself willingly changes his thinking (Erickson & Zeig, *CP* IV, p. 335).

We occasionally encounter clients who want us to help them get rid of some part of themselves, that part that they perceive as causing them trouble. In essence, they want our help in taking a choice away. But since we believe that people will automatically make the best choice, once it is available, we prefer to spend therapeutic time teaching new associations and choices. This leaves the client's old choice still available in the event that it or parts of it become the "best choice" in some future situation. Teaching choice certainly involves expanding a client's map or limiting frame of reference to include behaviors, thoughts, and feelings that may previously have been unavailable, at least in a particular context.

Consider those clients with suicide on their minds. Some approaches insist that the therapist extract a pledge from those clients in specific words that they will under no circumstances kill themselves. If the contract is not secured, therapy will not begin. The rationale is that a change might precipitate the suicide. In response to such theories we usually relate one of the several well-known "suicide" cases treated by Erickson.

One very sad and woeful woman approached him asserting that she planned to commit suicide in three months because of how miserably she had been treated and how unfortunate her life had been in every way. Erickson very emphatically reiterated her sad story and agreed with her that "people have treated you badly and you are perfectly justified in thinking about ending your life, but let me ask you this—how much money do you have in the bank?" It happened that she had an ample amount of money in savings. Erickson suggested that it would be a "damn shame" for her to die and leave all that money to those people who had treated her so badly all those years. Why not, he suggested, take a portion of that money and spend it in the way he directed to have a "last fling." She agreed, since it was only a further way to "give up" and go "down hill." Actually, of course, she was then assisted, step by step, in learning to take care of herself, to increase her social skills and her involvement in various areas. He instructed her to spend some of the money at a department store and consult with the saleswoman and cosmetician about flattering clothes and makeup. He had her buy a new car, take a vacation, get dancing lessons with the money, etc., until finally, when three months had passed, suicide was the farthest thing from her mind—she was far too busy living (Erickson in Haley, 1973, p. 71).

RESOURCES LIE WITHIN

The resources the client needs lie within his or her own personal history.
This is a statement about potentialities. Erickson repeated to clients and students again and again that "your unconscious contains a vast storehouse of learnings, memories and resources," and then he would proceed to prove it to them by telling common stories about growth, development, childhood experiences, and "automatic" skills until they had retrieved from their own histories a personal meaning of his story and with it a resource experience. As Zeig stated, "it can further be assumed that the patient has resources in his personal history that can be used to effect change" (Erickson & Zeig, *CP* IV, p. 337).

Since Erickson treated each client as an individual, he did not always go about retreiving resources in a conversational way. Often he would surprise, challenge, and sometimes shock a resource into the foreground. (See example following discussion of the next principle.) Erickson believed that the potential for every resource is inherent in the person by virtue of being alive; the therapist's job is to help the client maximize these resources in order to accomplish the desired changes. Simultaneously, we are minimizing our role to the extent that we help the client learn to associate to his or her own resources at those times when it will be beneficial to do so. This is so essential that we have devoted an entire chapter to the topic of resources.

MEET CLIENTS AT THEIR MODEL

Meet the client at his or her model of the world. We refer, with this principle, to subsuming the client's belief system and matching the behavior offered as an initial rapport-building phase of treatment. "Initially, Erickson meets the patient where the patient is" (Erickson & Zeig, *CP* IV, p. 336).

The idea of building rapport in this manner is anything but new. We find reference to the same in Romans 12: 15–16:"Rejoice with them that do rejoice, weep with them that weep. Be of the same mind one toward another." In a more recent reference, Scheflen writes, "Participants in parallel postures are likely to show synchronous movement; they puff on cigarettes at the same time, use similar facial expressions, direct their gazes coordinatively, sometimes say the same things, and gesture alike . . . In general, people in parallelism and synchrony are acting as a social unit. In psychoanalytic terms, they are said to be 'identified'" (1973, p. 146).

Occasionally, when we teach this principle, someone objects about the infeasibility, absurdity, or danger of matching aggressive, depressed, or bizarre behavior. At that point we stress that the principle refers to *meeting* the client at his or her model of the world, not living or staying there. The goal is to teach choice and rapport is a necessary first step in all but the most unusual cases (Truax, 1966).

Erickson's ability to meet clients at their model of the world by matching their physical posture was somewhat hampered by his inability to be mobile in his wheelchair, so he would "meet" with metaphor and by matching the syntax and words of clients. For example, there is the previously mentioned case of the psychotic man in the state hospital in Michigan who only spoke in a "word salad." To "put one foot in the client's world," Erickson recorded the speech, transcribed it, and learned to speak it. When the man spoke to Erickson in word salad Erickson answered, as best he could, in a similar word salad. Erickson made certain to match the behavior for equal lengths of time. The dialogue between them continued for several weeks and in conversations ranging in length from a minute to several hours. Finally, after a particularly grueling session lasting more than six hours, the client began the next session with two sentences of word salad and then a request to "Talk sense, Doctor." Erickson replied, "Certainly, I'll be glad to. What is your last name?" "O'Donovan," he replied, "and it's about time somebody who knows how to talk asked. Over five years in this lousy joint" (Erickson, in Haley, 1967, p. 502). He ended with two sentences of word salad. Thereafter Erickson and the patient would begin with one sentence each of word salad, speak normally, and terminate with one sentence each of word salad until the client was discharged.

The next two examples from Erickson's work illustrate several principles operating sequentially and simultaneously. The first one is about a young couple who came to Erickson stating:

> Our problem is most distressing and destructive of our marriage. Because of our desire for children we have engaged in the marital union with full physiological concomitants each night and morning for procreative purposes. On Sundays and holidays we have engaged in the union for procreative purposes as much as four times a day. We have not permitted physical disability to interfere. As a result of the frustration of our philoprogenitive desires, the marital union has become progressively unpleasant for us, but it has not interfered with our efforts at procreation; but it does distress both of us to discover our increasing impatience with each other. For this reason we are seeking your aid, since other medical aid has failed (Erickson, in Haley, 1973, pp. 164–165).

Erickson met them at their model of the world by repeating their very stilted statement of the problem almost verbatim and offering them an opportunity for therapy that would be risky and require a shock of a psychological kind. He then left them alone to discuss the matter. (He later stated to us, "I couldn't bear to be in the room while those two talked it over!")

They concluded that, because of the extreme frustration they had encountered, they would take the risk involved in receiving the shock. Erickson again repeated that very difficult language, restating their problem in their words and then instructed them to prepare for the shock. He stated that he was about to administer it and that when he did they would know it and were then to leave the office immediately without speaking and to go directly home. They agreed. He said, "Now hang tightly to the bottom of your chairs, because I'm now going to give you the psychological shock. It is this: for three long years you have engaged in the marital union with full physiological concomitants for procreative purposes at least twice a day and sometimes as much as four times in 24 hours, and you have met with defeat of your philoprogenitive desires. Now why in the hell don't you fuck for fun and pray to the devil that she isn't knocked up for at least three months. Now please leave!" (Erickson, in Haley, 1973, p. 166).

They left immediately and speechlessly as well! Three days later they phoned to say they had driven directly home with their heads just filled with all kinds of strange and unusual thoughts and desires. They were in such a state of agitation, they reported, that by the time they reached the house they could hardly wait to get inside and they couldn't wait to get to the bedroom. They disrobed in the living room and three months later she was, in fact, pregnant. So, very clearly, Erickson met them at their model of the world and then with his strategic use of vulgarisms elicited resources or experiences associated to those "thoughts and desires" which had perhaps been prohibited by original socialization. He therefore provided new experiences and a possible map for new choices once he had their full cooperation through rapport.

This is a very unusual example, of course, and we don't advocate such tactics be used indiscriminately as a method of imitating Erickson's retrieval of resources. Chapter 7 deals in detail with resource retrieval. Here we are stressing the importance of meeting clients at their worldview and of recognizing that resources do lie within.

The second example involves a recalcitrant nine-year-old boy brought in by his mother. She reported that he was, for instance, writing on the walls, calling her names, not eating properly, not going to bed when asked, not getting up for school, getting in trouble at school, and more! The mother was a college graduate and highly embarrassed about her inability to control her son.

She brought him to Erickson with the warning that the boy threatened to "stomp" the office. Erickson sent the mother away with instructions to return in the square root of four hours. We speculate that this transaction was designed to let the child know indirectly that grownups can communicate in ways that children cannot. We also imagine that the mother then left to look up square root and confirm her idea about when to return. As soon as the mother left the boy stomped the floor with his foot. "I assumed a look of astonishment, commenting that the stomp was far better than I had expected of Joe, but I doubted if he could keep it up. I said that Joe would soon weaken, and then he would discover that he couldn't even stand still." After about 30 stomps Joe found that he grossly overrated his ability to stomp and Erickson "patronizingly offered the privilege of just patting the floor a thousand times, since he really couldn't stand still and rest without wiggling around and wanting to sit down" (Erickson in Haley, 1973, p. 219). The boy was exceedingly still for the remainder of the two hours, at which time his mother returned. Erickson requested the boy to "do exactly as I tell you." The boy agreed. "Show your mother how hard you can still stomp the floor." The boy stomped. "Now, Joe, show her how stiff and straight you can stand still" (Erickson in Haley, 1973, p. 220). He did so. Then Erickson instructed them both to leave the office and not discuss the incident again. That was the end of the boy's recalcitrance.

This case appears elsewhere in an article entitled "The Identification of a Secure Reality" (*CP* IV, pp. 507–515). Erickson didn't structure that secure reality with any element or ability other than those from the boy's own personal history. The boy's unconscious had the necessary resources to control himself. The goal was to meet him at his model of the world (challenge), and utilize all messages from him, with respect for his behavior, in order that he retrieve for himself and successfully utilize that control.

FLEXIBILITY

The person with the most flexibility will be the controlling element in the system. We appreciate the logic of this cybernetic principle. The city that has the most railroad tracks, telephone lines, freeways, etc. is the controlling metropolis. The family member who has the most behavioral flexibility will be the controlling element there, even if that "flexibility" means getting sick and somatizing in the middle of the grocery store. The therapist with the most flexibility will be able to meet more clients at their unique models of the world and will be able to gain rapport more rapidly with a wider range of clients. Furthermore, such flexibility will foster or tolerate a greater range of risk-taking or change as new or creative behaviors are generated.

Every therapist has limits. Erickson occasionally failed to exhibit the needed flexibility and the necessary packaging for his communications. Of attempting to communicate with a particular client Erickson said, "I couldn't do it. I tried

—first by being very gentle and then by telling her the straight truth. . . . When I saw that gentleness had failed, I presented her with the harsh truth. She couldn't take that either" (Erickson in Zeig, 1980, pp. 284–285). Nevertheless, Erickson demonstrated considerable flexibility in his ever changing approach to clients. We have seen how he could speak word salad, be gentle, be insulting, be clever, be subtle, be a doctor, or be a friend in order to find the right approach for each client.

CAN'T NOT COMMUNICATE

A person can't not communicate. This refers to the fact that even if clients are not overtly communicating verbally, they are still sending messages nonverbally (Watzlawick, 1964). And the client always has internal responses. That is, a client can be expected to respond to verbal and nonverbal stimuli by either searching across internal experience in an attempt to find meaning for the incoming communication or by actually retrieving related images or internal representations which *do* create a personal meaning. When an image is retrieved, that image will guide performance or behavior. The behavior may be very subtle, such as a breathing shift, a slight nod of the head, a grimace, or muscle tonus shift. These subtle behavioral responses are herein referred to as "ideomotor behavior." It is very important for the therapist to notice these responses and be guided by them.

It is, of course, important to be guided by verbal responses as well, even if they are not exactly the responses you would have desired. Erickson was lecturing on hypnosis once when a man in the back of the auditorium stood up and denounced hypnosis as a fraud and Erickson as a charlatan. In the utilization tradition, Erickson noticed the persistence of the heckler, and chose his words so that they were sure to be contradicted by the heckler. The heckler was told:

> . . . that he had to remain silent; that he could not speak again; that he did not dare stand up; that he could not again charge fraud; that he dared not walk over to the aisle or up to the front of the auditorium; that he had to do whatever the writer demanded; that he had to sit down; that he had to return to his original seat; that he was afraid of the writer; that he dared not risk being hypnotized; that he was a noisy coward; that he was afraid to look at the volunteer subjects sitting on the platform; that he had to take a seat in the back of the auditorium; that he had to leave the auditorium; that he did not dare to come up on the platform; that he was afraid to shake hands in a friendly fashion with the writer; that he did not dare to remain silent; that he was afraid to walk over to one of the chairs on the platform for volunteer subjects; that he was afraid to face

the audience and to smile at them; that he dared not to look at or listen to the writer; that he could not sit in one of the chairs; that he would have to put his hands behind him instead of resting them on his thighs; that he dared not experience hand levitation; that he was afraid to close his eyes; that he had to remain awake; that he could not remain and go into a trance; . . . that he dared not go into deep trance, etc. (*CP* I, pp. 192–93).

Here again we see Erickson meeting the client at his model of the world and giving a challenge right back to the man when a challenge was offered. Then he introduced a new element which resulted in the heckler's walking toward him, "cooperating" by resisting him at his suggestion. Flexibility is certainly obvious in this example. In fact, this outcome was only possible because Erickson was comfortable being flexible. He realized that no "different" response from a person is not failure but rather behavior to utilize. He questioned, "What response *did* I get?" rather than "Why is this man resisting?" Here is yet another example of Erickson using a theory of intervention and change instead of a theory of personality to form his interventions.

Other therapists will determine for themselves the range in which they can be comfortable with these principles of intervention, such as being flexible in matching behavior. We refer you to the section on self-image thinking as an aid in effectively expanding the comfort zone you have for new and uncommon behaviors such as those espoused by these principles.

REDUCE TO COMPONENT BITS

If it's hard work, reduce it down. This is both a training principle and a treatment principle. We frequently promote the idea, humorously, that Custer could have won if the Indians had come over the hill one at a time. In the same way, even complex tasks are manageable if taken one step at a time, in component pieces.

Juggling is a complex task that seems impossible if one attempts to learn it by starting with three balls. However, if the task is divided into component skills and the aspiring juggler begins with one ball and develops a perceptual and motor program for that piece or skill before gradually adding more and more skills the goal becomes attainable, even though the task is still as complex. When we teach the principles and skills described in this book, we create many exercises designed to develop familiarity and confidence with each component part of an overall diagnosis, treatment plan, and treatment approach. This book is written in a similarly progressive manner and we recommend that readers attempt to become proficient with various new aspects of this Ericksonian approach, step by step, in stages.

But perhaps this principle is most applicable to intervening with clients and helping to expand their maps to include skills and behaviors which were previously "too complex or difficult." When a client who has been socially withdrawn and naive is led, for example, to "make a decision to get close to significant others," this is only a beginning. Often, therapists tend to operate on the belief that helping a client realize how s/he was struck or why s/he developed a particular destructive pattern will automatically produce the freedom to follow through on a "decision" to reverse that pattern and achieve those new and desired patterns. But knowing why someone had difficulty learning motor skills as a child really will not provide the detailed instruction, coaching, reinforcement, modeling, and so on needed to learn the skills now.

Similarly, a client "deciding to get close to others" (men, women, etc.) probably won't know the first thing about what psychological processes should be initiated to "get close." As in the analogy above there is a distinction between initiating juggling and successfully carrying out the many steps involved in mastering it, so, too, in deciding to get close to others, there is a distinction between the formation of the goal and the ability to initiate and carry out the chains of behavior and experience to fulfill it.

Erickson was thorough, methodical, and patient in working with those clients who needed to learn complex tasks at their particular rate of speed. There is a case in which a severely obese woman (in excess of 250 lbs.) called Erickson stating that she was just a "plain fat slob" and so ugly and pitiful that he probably wouldn't want to see her but that she hoped hypnosis could help her. Erickson insisted that he see her right away and when she arrived he invited her in courteously. She refused to enter and Erickson stated that as he looked at her he had to stop and do some careful "rethinking" because he realized that no amount of courtesy would get through to this woman. It was not part of her frame of reference to be treated courteously and she did not trust it. In fact, the woman had been treated atrociously by her parents, who exiled both her and her sister to the garage for most of their childhoods, throwing food out to them and reminding them that everyone would be better off if they just died. The sister and both parents had died before this client approached Erickson for therapy. After quickly "rethinking," Erickson remarked to the woman:

> You haven't told the truth. I'm going to say this simply so you will know about yourself and understand that I know about you. Then you will believe, really believe, what I have to say to you. You are not a plain fat, disgusting slob. You are the fattest, homeliest, most disgusting horrible bucket of lard I have ever seen, and it is appalling to look at you. You have gone through high school. You know some of the facts of life. Yet here you are, four feet ten inches tall, weighing between two hundred and fifty and two hundred and sixty pounds. You

have got the homeliest face I have ever seen. Your nose was just mashed into your face. Your face is too damned spread out. Your forehead is too hideously low. Your hair is not even decently combed. And that dress you are wearing—polka dots, millions and billions of them. You have no taste, even in clothes, your feet slop over the edges of your shoes. To put it simply—you are a hideous mess. But you do need help. I'm willing to give you this help. I think you know that I won't hesitate to tell you the truth. You need to know the truth about yourself before you can ever learn the things necessary to help yourself. But I don't think you can take it. . . . Maybe you can learn to go into a hypnotic trance. . . . I'd like to have you go into hypnosis. It's an opportunity to say a few more uncomplimentary things to you. Things I don't think you could possibly stand to hear when you are wide awake . . . (Erickson in Haley, 1963, p. 116).

In this case, Erickson demonstrated his flexibility by meeting the client at her model of the world to gain remarkably rapid rapport. The "things" her conscious mind could not bear to hear initially were that she did have resources, was worthwhile, and could change. In the first session, Erickson included in the trance a posthypnotic suggestion that she go during the next week to the library and look through National Geographic magazines until she found just how hideously some women can distort themselves and still get husbands.

He followed this suggestion with amnesia for the instruction and the reason behind the instruction. This was the first of many small steps in the direction of helping this client eventually achieve a sense of self-worth and social skill. Over several months of treatment he led her through a series of such gradual steps that they were not overwhelming. But the end result was quite noticeable. The woman lost 150 pounds, learned to groom and value herself, and finally married a man who thought himself quite lucky to get her. The detailed treatment of "Harold" in Chapter 8 provides a lengthy example of therapy by component bits.

OUTCOMES AT PSYCHOLOGICAL LEVEL

Outcomes are determined at the psychological level. This is one of the three rules of communication described by Eric Berne (Berne, 1966, p. 277; Lankton, Lankton, & Brown, 1981). It refers to the fact that there are several simultaneous levels operating in any communication and that when the social level message (usually in words) says one thing and the psychological message (usually reflected in voice tone, use of gesture, or emphasis) indicates something else, the psychological message, outside of awareness, will be the determinant of the outcome. We use this principle to help ourselves be mindful and purposeful about our psychological level communication as therapists and also in diagnosing, evaluating, and responding to all messages being sent by the client, as will be shown later.

An important facet of psychological level communication is related to understanding how metaphor and indirect suggestion facilitate therapeutic changes in the client's experience without his or her consciously being able to explain the problem in the therapist's terms or to say exactly what happened. Erickson said that hypnosis per se doesn't effect a cure, but that cure is accomplished by a reassociation of the client's experiential life (CP IV, p. 38).

This conception of change insures that the therapy work will keep on task, directing therapeutic effort and energy where it will do the most good: associating needed experience. The idea of reassociation is also in distinct contrast to the idea of "insight." After reviewing research by Truax and others, Albert Bandura wrote about insight: "It is evident from the results of interpretive approaches that a therapist who leads his clients to believe that insight will alleviate their behavioral malfunctioning is unlikely to accomplish the changes he implies" (Bandura, 1969, p. 103). Similarly, Erickson stated that: "insight into the past may be somewhat educational, but insight into the past isn't going to change the past." (Zeig, 1980, p. 269).

Bandura and behavior modifiers seemed to part theoretical company with Erickson regarding the selection of interventions. Bandura concluded, "cognitive and affective modifications can be achieved more successfully through planned behavior change than through attempts to alter internal events directly" (Bandura, 1969, p. 91). In sharp contrast, the Ericksonian approach employs metaphors to help expand a client's choices. In our opinion, Erickson's approach seems very logical, based on Bandura's own research. Bandura, researching modeling and no-trial learning, showed that "when a person observes a model's behavior, but otherwise performs no overt responses, he can acquire the modeled responses while they are occurring only in cognitive, representational forms" (Bandura, 1969, p. 133). Examining Erickson's work in this light, we find that he frequently presented clients with models they could follow by means of metaphor (Campos, 1972).

Erickson utilized imagery and ideomotor feedback in communicating at the psychological level. "The utilization of imagery in trance induction almost always facilitates the development of similar or related more complex hypnotic behavior" (CP I, p. 141). We expect that the ideomotor signals indicating the client's participation are indicators of acquiring modeled behaviors through covert rehearsal. The Ericksonian approach uses metaphor and indirect suggestion to gain rapport, retrieve resources, and link those resources to previous stress signals or typical stimuli in the client's environment. And we do this at the psychological level rather than exclusively at the conscious level. The client finds that, for some unknown reason, when a situation is encountered that had previously been difficult, "something" clicks; a new idea, feeling, or behavior comes to mind, rendering the situation less threatening or even enjoyable. The conscious mind is then free to examine and concentrate upon more enjoyable, adaptive, and appropriate experience.

The use of even simple multiple embedded metaphors to change the temporary framework of conscious awareness makes a convenient modality in which to organize psychological level communications. Chapter 4 addresses the background and use of metaphor for helping clients build cognitive maps for new behavior, while Chapters 7 and 8 address the use of multiple embedded metaphor to help the client change severely inhibiting and conflictual maps and experience and unconscious emotional conflict. The next chapter deals with assessing the unique situation, the unique family, the unique client, the unique map of the world, and developing a treatment plan in keeping with these principles.

3 THE DIAGNOSTIC FRAMEWORK

A SYSTEMS AND TRANSACTIONAL APPROACH

It is not surprising to find at the heart of Erickson's work a diagnostic framework that beats to the rhythm of today's systems and communication theories. Erickson formulated and used a relationship and family approach before it was fashionable. Moreover, his approach was rooted in the awareness that people operate from internal maps which include internalized objects and guides. He conceived of an approach that related these ideas. Tracing the lines of thought that have influenced our conception of diagnosis reveals that Erickson's work has been quietly in the background of various theory builders for decades. It is now firmly established in the psychotherapy profession that communication between individuals creates and maintains experience. Erickson stated that "mental disease is the breakdown of communication between people" (CP IV, p. 75).

Most modern therapists are well aware of the dynamic interplay between social pressures and personal psychodynamics. We will refer to that relationship as transactional or communicational theory. But Erickson worked with those ideas before they were introduced into common awareness and before they had names. Few others shared his controversial views, though pioneering works by Alfred Adler and later by Harry Stack Sullivan also predate the widespread understanding of these concepts as they now exist. These pioneers contributed to theoretical linking between intra- and interpersonal aspects of human behavior. Perhaps greater consciousness about the importance of the transactional nature of personal difficulties was stimulated by the widely read work of Jay Haley, Gregory Bateson, and the group generally referred to as the Palo Alto group of communication theorists.

Bateson, as a major contributor to various emerging theories of biology and transactional and systems analysis, brought knowledge of Erickson's work to Haley, who had been influenced by the work of Sullivan and Thomas Szasz (Haley, 1963, p. 1). Haley then used Erickson's work to demonstrate the relationship of such communications as therapeutic binds, paradox, metaphor, and multilevel metacommunication to symptoms and changes in relationships of couples (especially) and families.

Haley made it clear that the relationships between people and their psychiatric symptoms could be profitably analyzed from a communicational point of view. He, like Szasz, illustrated that this communicational, interactional, transactional point of view was much different from the then prevailing historical conception of mental disorders. In relation to that prevailing medical model Erickson was a heretic and a maverick. Widespread knowledge and acceptance of his work had to wait until other early pioneers such as Bateson, Adler, Szasz, Haley, Watzlawick, Satir, Berne, and Perls had sensitized professional consciousness about transactional and communicational frameworks. Where Bateson, Adler, and Szasz linked the intrapsychic and the interpersonal with theory, Erickson did so with techniques.

The difference between the old and new frameworks takes on the magnitude of a paradigm shift in science. This major shift in conceptualizing has, in fact, followed or accompanied changes in other fields. It is beyond the scope of this book to relate the factors in other sciences that are responsible for creating this paradigm shift. We are concerned here with the nature of the transactional view.

Bateson wrote of this paradigm change:

> The difference between the Newtonian world and the world of communication is simply this: that the Newtonian world ascribes reality to objects and achieves its simplicity by excluding the content of the context. . . . The theorist of communication insists upon examining the metarelationships while achieving its simplicity by excluding all objects (Bateson, 1972, p. 250).

He went on to explain:

> This world of communication is a Berkeleyan world, but the good bishop was guilty of understatement. Relevance or reality must be denied not only to the sound of the tree which falls unheard in the forest but also to this chair which I can see and on which I am sitting. My perception of the chair is communicationally real, and that on which I sit is, for me, only an idea, a message in which I put my trust (Bateson, 1972, p. 250).

Certainly Erickson worked from an implicit understanding that a client's rules of conduct or map of the world of experience guide his or her behavior. He took care to get a detailed report of the client's map before assuming that

.his conception was correct and proceeding on that basis. Later in this section we examine his case of a young woman who vomited on her date because of instructions she carried unconsciously. Her map of the world about dating was obtained from her mother many years earlier before the mother died.

The case is exemplary because it demonstrates how Erickson carefully and gradually elicited and suggested changes in the young woman's map so as to respect her need to save face. Operating from her own map of the world, she was making her best available choice as she attempted to live safely according to her personal understanding about how to do that. Erickson approached that case as if there was a conflict created between her inadequate internalized map and the demands of the real world. He did not approach the case from a model that implied genetic predisposition or volitional intention to create anxiety.

This case also demonstrates, by his use of the transactional paradigm, the value he placed on relationships. In the course of treatment the woman did not further alienate herself from her internalized "mother"; rather, she transformed her "relationship" with her deceased mother in a creative and adaptive manner. The case illustrates the relationship between social network and therapeutic changes in a person's internalized map of the world. By adjusting the internalized map, Erickson improved the client's relationship with her social network without damaging the relationship with her mother that she experienced as an internal "event." Adjusting the map expands the client's comfort zones as it enhances the client's self-image.

The case exemplifies Erickson's original approach, in which he related psychodynamics and the social network. He helped create changes in both by first changing the internal map of experience. He found many parallels and much correspondence between these different dimensions: cognitive, emotional, interpersonal, social, physiological, behavioral, and historical. He worked in a unified way, whether he first intervened at the social level (visits to a restaurant) or used hypnotic trance to correct inadequate experiential maps of the world (in the case of the vomiter). An artificial isolation of the individual from the social network did not occur with Erickson's diagnosis and treatment.

As R. D. Laing has demonstrated, each person's influence on the experience of others is often ignored even by transactional theory. This is true for no other reason than a lack of the required language of experience: "We need concepts which both indicate the interaction and inter-experience of two persons, and help us to understand the relation between each person's own experience and his own behavior, within the context of the relationship between them" (Laing, 1967, p. 48). Although Erickson did not use his career to develop the necessary conceptual language Laing wrote about, he did develop a systemic approach that does not artificially separate intrapsychic and interpersonal experience. He utilized the interconnectedness of each level of inner and social experience.

The readiness of the professional community to be influenced by Erickson's work is not due solely to his own efforts. While Erickson was developing these ideas, other family therapists were following similar lines of thought from different theoretical roots. James Framo, for instance, concluded:

> Family transactional findings suggest further the momentous prospect that the intrinsic nature of psychopathology, usually seen as solely the outcome of insoluble intrapsychic conflict, may have to be recast and broadened as a special form of relationship event which occurs between intimately related people (Framo, 1972, p. 271).

Framo arrived at a conclusion surprisingly similar to one Haley had written about earlier: "In recent years there has been a shift in psychiatry and psychology from an emphasis upon the processes within an individual to an emphasis upon his relationships with other people" (Haley, 1963, p. 3). Framo had developed this line of thought by following object relations theorists such as Fairbairn. Both of these theorists considered the socializing and communicating process the mechanism by which one develops, inherits, decides upon, or otherwise incorporates unique psychological and behavioral problems and potentials. About that, Framo wrote:

> The implicit or explicit irrational assignment of roles in the family — role being defined as a pattern or type of behavior which a person builds up in terms of what significant others expect or demand of him—reflects unconscious attempts by the parents to master, reenact, or externalize their intrapsychic conflicts about these powerful human needs, derived from relationship experiences in the family of origin (Framo, 1972, p. 274).

Erickson was continually interested in a person's degree of role differentiation and attainment (Haley, 1973). He not only worked with the intrapsychic aspect of a personality but also turned the client back into the social network with new choices regarding roles. He included a wide range of psychological components in this shaping of roles, components such as perception, emotion, attitudes, expectations, behaviors, etc. He worked at a speed determined by the client's developing attitudes of curiosity, interest, enjoyment, pride, aggressiveness, and so on. He systematically retrieved resources for the role being developed and associated them with the client's anticipated future life experiences. In this way self-image thinking and role expectations were simultaneously changed.

ETIOLOGY OF THE SOCIAL MAP

Let us digress for a moment and examine the relationship of pathology to social interaction. Assume, hypothetically, that a child is raised by parents who do not care for children and who are frightened, both by the child and by the world, and consequently are hostile to both. By the time the hypothetical child becomes school age s/he will have internalized a map of a hostile world. The map of the world will include models of the hostile behaviors that were displayed by the parents. The map may also include unique roles, emotions, or behaviors developed by the child. Perhaps these include autistic withdrawal. As the child with these behavioral choices interacts, s/he shapes behaviors, expectations, and perceptions of others. The eventual behaviors are based on the original internalized objects or map.

Soon the hypothetical child emerges from hypothetical grammar school. The teen will have learned "comfort zones" or types of behavior and places for interaction that tend to insure certain familiar inner experiences. The psychologically abused child will have turned into a young man or woman with a limited repertoire of choices. S/he will probably not go to social functions that demand more than a modicum of cheerful and courteous interaction. S/he will be unlikely to enter student government or clubs. And, if the distrust and dislike for others is great enough, s/he may develop some (logical) symptom which keeps others away or provides a convenient (and symbolic) excuse to avoid those situations that bring discomfort.

Failing to gain subtle social skills that come via peer interaction, the teenager will become increasingly less equipped than his or her peers. The increased pressure of high school will be experienced, resulting in anxiety about remaining in school with the demand for increasingly sophisticated social behavior, as well as anxiety about leaving high school.

This hypothetical example, not uncommon, is a ripe situation for various deviant behavior. Parents, some peers, teachers, store owners, neighbors, etc. come to expect that the person they do not trust is, in fact, not trustworthy. The social network will "request" abnormal behavior. The teenager, not knowing how to acquire the symbols of status and the means of livelihood needed, may comply and engage in illicit means to acquire the goods.

When others act as if they do not like him or her around, s/he makes sense of those actions according to his or her internal map. In this imaginary case, the map says: "People don't like me or want me. My best choice is quiet withdrawal." By the time the hypothetical youth reaches the late teens social demands (from television, media models, peers, etc.) beg that the individual consider courtship and marriage. But the youth may not find the resources to be confident around others. If s/he cannot initiate the experience of enjoying others, being tender toward others, or taking emotional risks with others, the chances for violent or autistic behavior further increases.

Finally, autistic withdrawal or violence is recognized as deviant. Such behavior does not even give the pretense of coping with the biological and social demands the youth faces. The hypothetical person, now a young adult, may come into the mental health system via the local psychiatric ward—schizoid and suicidal or hostile and violent. Then, along with many others, s/he may become a chronic client in the community health structure.

Over the years s/he may make the rounds: inpatient, day treatment, salvation army, local community mental health center, social services, outreach programs, manpower programs, alcohol programs, and so on. The individual can become stabilized in an environment that s/he only partially helped to create. And can we conclude that this client at 40 years of age is resistant when s/he fails to follow advice, show up for appointments, and so on? The person simply learned to perceive, act and experience a particular map of the world and failed to learn how to use resources within the self that could result in an enjoyable and successful life.

Now while this is a hypothetical scenario, the story is true enough to ring a bell with nearly every reader. We have been using it to illustrate the range of historical variables that affect people and by means of which each person co-creates his or her world. We might, then, imagine that the entire process of psychopathology or growth is cyclical:

1) The conduct of the primary caretakers permits certain behavior and experience in the child.
2) Role assignment is perceived and learned by the child.
3) Incorporated objects and incorporated relationship affects from the family become the child's inner reality and inner guiding map for the assigned roles.
4) Guided to varying degrees by the internal map of "reality," the individual has expectations of others that train others to act in certain roles (others who are not able to conform to the reciprocal role arrangements are avoided).
5) The growing individual selects and interacts with others, building a social network in accordance with the internal map of expectations and options.
6) The social network grants various sanctions to the person.
7) Mate selection is accomplished within the range limited by social sanctions and status.
8) The person in turn raises children in accordance with beliefs, perceptions, experiences, and behaviors which have been repeatedly verified in his or her unique world.

AN EXPERIENTIAL MAP

A question occasionally arises when we mention the notion of "family mapping" (Laing, 1972, p. 117). Is the social map only cognitive or is it also simultaneously a biological and psychological experience for the person? We answer that the map is very much a bodily event, as well as a perceptual, behavioral, and a cognitive experience (Lankton, 1980b). According to Framo, "these internal objects are not just fantasies but become subidentities and part of the structure of the personality" (1972, p. 274). Since these internal experiences, personality structures, and so-called subpersonalities themselves have been associated with the performance of role demands and the occurrence of emotional affects learned in the family of origin, it is no wonder to find that they have been mentioned in literature from William James to Roberto Assagioli, who wrote: "The functions of an individual, in whom various psychological traits are not integrated, form what we consider to be subpersonalities" (1965, p. 75).

We prefer to avoid debates over semantics and labels. The theorists have observed the behavioral and psychological differences in a person's behavior from one moment to the next and have noticed that sets of behaviors which seem distinguishably different have equally different associated inner experience. Whether we call these associations of inner experience and behavior "traits," "roles," "subpersonalities," "ego states," "parts," or "resources," the label refers to gross motor characteristics, idiosyncratic nonverbal language, perceptual components, cognitive components, rule-governed associations, and motoric, digestive, and vegetative differences. We refer to all of these parts as the client's map.

The case study of the woman who vomited on her boyfriend made the vegetative and metabolic component of her map dramatically obvious! Alterations in the client's mood, muscle tonus, level of energy and so on make it apparent that the internal experience or map, which is altered solely as a result of communication, is not "just cognitive" but has profound bodily aspects as well.

SYMPTOMS AND THE MAP OF THE SOCIAL NETWORK

Erickson believed that "maps," or rules for recombining experience, are so automatized that they become unconscious and the experiences and perceptions attached to them become automatized. Since the map is rarely in a person's conscious awareness, it is not scrutinized and updated with the passage of time. It is, instead, reinforced by the outcomes of the person's selective behavior and perceptions. Symptoms are generally the result of the client's making the best choice among options determined unconsciously by those associations available in his or her map. Erickson wrote: "The development of neurotic symptoms constitutes behavior of a defensive, protective character. Because it is an unconscious process, and thus excluded from conscious understandings, it is blind and groping in nature and does not serve personality purposes usefully" (CP IV, p. 149). He explained that the hostile and resistive client is being hostile and resistive as an interpersonal defense (CP I, p. 298).

Often it is the symptom that the client presents when entering therapy. To assess the function of the symptom we examine both individual and social or environmental factors. Brief therapy, as developed by Erickson, was concerned with the likelihood that some clients are not suited for lengthy treatment despite their need for considerable change. He consequently recommended several alterations of the symptom, depending upon individual and environmental factors. His assessment included the client's position in the family and broader social network, available resources, personality traits, and the current value of the symptom in the system. Perhaps differences between the transactional and medical-psychiatric paradigms seem insignificant; however, with regard to the treatment of symptoms, it makes a considerable difference whether therapy attempts to uncover conflicts to resolve a symptom or teaches clients to tap the resources they need to change their involvement in the social world.

Researchers have also contributed information that supports these theoretical contentions. Cartwright and Zander explain evidence regarding communication and role differentiation in task oriented groups: "The type of role which may be developed is prescribed in part by the communication restrictions; the time at which the roles emerge also is determined in part by the same communication restriction" (1968, p. 516). Erickson's work fits snugly with the growing need for social and systems oriented developments in theory and clinical practice. His approach is increasingly recognized as the clinical community increasingly turns to the transactional, relational, and communicational orientations.

As mentioned, this approach has been the reference point for therapeutic use of communications such as binds and paradox and their potent effect on communication in family therapy. Pathological binds, by the same token, involve communications of a similar structure which profoundly affect the experience of children in schizophrenogenic homes. Erickson's examples constitute the "flip side" of effects created by the negative bind. The multidimensional diagnosis of the client system offered in this work leads to treatment plans and interventions that are similar in structure to those experiences which socialize and shape the individual's map of the world and self-image.

Our conception of the transactional nature of internal experience and so-

cial role demands takes us into a broad realm of behavior, including digestive, muscular, respiratory, gross motor, mental imagery, preconscious family mapping, feelings, and emotions. Diagnostic information comes in many
channels and the treatment plan is designed to therapeutically influence the
various arenas of a client's life. These vary, of course, with the individual and
the situation. We illustrate with several cases throughout this book, using the
same parameters with varied symptomatology.

PARAMETERS OF THE CLIENT-SYSTEM

Erickson operated from the proposition that a complete diagnosis includes
a treatment plan and vice versa. That is, diagnosis should result in an operational set of interventions. Assessing the client in several areas is intimately
connected with developing the treatment plan. There are six major parameters that Erickson seemed to consider in his cases. These are:

1) The structure of the family system and social network.
2) The stage of family development.
3) The developmental age/task of the individual(s).
4) The availability of resources, whether directly or only indirectly re-
   trievable.
5) The flexibility and sensitivity of each member for the other in areas
   of perception, cognition and meaning, and behavioral role and emotion.
6) The verifiable function of the symptom in the current life of the client
   or family.

Consider the previously mentioned case of the young woman who became
violently ill during a much anticipated date with a young man. The case is
titled: "The Successful Treatment of a Case of Acute Hysterical Depression
by a Return Under Hypnosis to a Critical Phase of Childhood" (CP III, pp.
122–142). The woman, 23 years old, was referred for therapy by her family.
To summarize, her mother had died when the client was 13. Before her death,
she had instructed her daughter severely regarding sexual contact with boys.
The mother's death prevented her from ever presenting more adequate instructions for sexual conduct and courtship. This set of instructions, attitudes, and roles was incorporated in the client's map, although she did not
consciously remember her mother's instruction.

At the beginning of treatment, this information was not yet known to Erickson. What he did know was that this 23-year-old woman was facing social
and peer pressures of courtship. She was inadequately equipped for those
role behaviors needed by the young adult:

> When young people graduate from the juvenile to the adult status, they enter a complex social network that requires a variety of kinds of behavior. . . . This adventure involves many factors: the young people must overcome personal inadequacies, they must be able to associate with people their own age, they must achieve adequate status in their social network, they must have become disengaged from their family of origin, and they require a society stable enough to allow the steps of courtship to go to their completion (Haley, 1973, p. 65).

This young woman's withdrawal after her mother's death accounted for some of her deficient learnings regarding social conduct.

It was known that after a period of social withdrawal this young woman succeeded in living an apparently normal adulthood. However, normal young adulthood includes courtship and eventually terminates at the phase of marriage and its consequences (or the decision not to marry and those consequences). At that time in her life she had no obvious difficulty, at least not until the night she came home violently ill from the aforementioned date. Her roommate reported that she was extremely upset, sobbing and talking about how nasty, terrible, and disgusting she was.

She refused, however, to discuss, with either her roommate or family, the event or the problem, except to rule out any possibility that foul play was involved. She sought psychiatric help and soon improved enough to return to work. Personally, however, she continued to be depressed and withdrawn. When she withdrew from therapy and became suicidal the family asked Erickson to become involved. She had, by this time, become difficult to approach on the subject of her problem. Any attempt to work with her resulted in a relapse of her illness, including vomiting. She would become ill at the mention of psychiatrists, dates, the incident that night with her roommate, men in general, or sex specifically!

The family and roommate knew she had to receive treatment. As is the case with any client, psychological symptoms and deviant or pathological behavior would continue to increase until the social and biological demands of her growth were abated or until she gained the needed map of experience and performance to live more productively. Until she learned to generate the psychological processes she needed to adapt satisfactorily and creatively to courtship and questions of marriage, she would continue to exacerbate her difficulty by avoiding interaction with others in her social network.

Erickson acknowledged the family's expressed concerns and the woman's safety when he decided to accept this case. This case represented an uncommon treatment contract for him and he was therefore compelled to discuss it. He remarked that he would have to approach the work "completely without her cooperation, either conscious or unconscious, without raising

the least flurry of anxiety, . . . and most important of all, without her feeling
that the therapist was directing his conduct toward her at all" (Erickson &
Kubie, *CP* III, pp. 125–126).

In an attempt to take the necessary historical information, Erickson consulted her entire social network, including her family, relatives, a man involved, several involved psychiatrists, and the roommate. Erickson intervened on behalf of the family system and the extended social network. The
social system, as well as the individual, can be viewed as a system with many
interactive parts. Each part can be framed as an ally or as a problem. "We find
that the energies and talents of people can be focused to provide the essential
supports, satisfactions, and controls for one another, and that these potentials are present in the social network of family, neighbors, friends, and associates of the person or family in distress" (Speck & Attneave, 1973, p. 7).
Likewise, Erickson employed the roommate as the identified patient to get the
client in his office for the ostensible purpose of helping in her roommate's
therapy.

The social network can be used not only for gathering information, but
also for intervening. Erickson got the woman to come for therapy, ostensibly
as an aid for the therapy of her roommate. Erickson began the therapy by offering paradoxical definitions of her role in the therapy. He instructed her to
be attentive to the hypnosis of the roommate because, he suggested, she
might want to try hypnosis for herself at some unspecified time. By using the
roommate, Erickson appealed to the resources available in the social network
to help create a situation in which needed personality traits could be evoked
for treatment.

As the real client listened, Erickson carefully interspersed hypnotic commands and made certain to speak in rhythm with her breathing and bodily
movements. These extremely indirect techniques were successfully employed
to establish hypnotic trance. The client's response to an intervention is itself
diagnostic information. The real client was adaptive. We could say that a
strength in this client was her readiness to go out of her way or subjugate her
own wishes to help someone in need. Judging from the interpersonal responses she manifested with the roommate, one could observe that she was
quick to follow the modeled behavior of others, that she would be a good
subject for trance, and that she was a person who could learn by modeling.
Thus, Erickson indirectly won her over as a willing trance subject.

She was also given much reassurance and protection for her involvement
in the trance. She was to continue the trance only if she thought the conditions were permissible. Again, judging from her social compliance in the session, we might speculate that this young woman, as a child, learned to readily
subjugate her own needs to the needs of others. This was a diagnostic clue.
With such a diagnostic clue offered in the session as a result of Erickson's

probing, the origin of the woman's internal map of "proper" conduct was suggested: the relationship with her mother and compliance with her mother's wishes. We see, then, the multifaceted approach with the social network: history, intervention with the roommate, and assessment based on role and conduct in the network.

Consideration of the developmental age (and associated "tasks") of an individual was a significant feature in Erickson's diagnosis for several reasons. One outstanding reason for assessing the developmental age is the need to "meet the client at his or her model of the world" and establish rapport. This joining principle applies to the therapy even in an ongoing manner. As stated before, the therapist is only *meeting* the client there, not staying. Following empathic matching appropriate to the client's demonstrated "age," Erickson would direct the client's associations in accordance with the treatment plan. But the treatment plan was also based on the age of understanding displayed by the client, and each new intervention was also directed to current developmental age. The associations trailing from each intervention are more successfully conveyed when such matching of frameworks occurs. Assessing the age of the individual's psychological development allows matching to occur more realistically.

The psychological age of this individual guided Erickson's choice of metaphoric content and age regression. Knowing that this 23-year-old woman was operating as a withdrawn young teenager made it possible to predict that she would likely be intellectually curious about a query Erickson posed to her in trance dealing with dating (whereas a younger child might be less inclined to be curious about *that* subject). The knowledge that she was operating developmentally at about the level of a 13-year-old helped greatly in knowing which resources she might have available and where her problematic map of conduct might lie.

The assessment of developmental age also pointed to the pathway of change. Most young teenagers need to learn several skills in coping with their developing sexuality. They need, for example, to exert control over their sexual impulses and thoughts; they need the use of such skills as negative hallucination (concentration) to assist them in attending to social requirements during libidinally exciting moments. Also, they need to have confidence in social contact, perhaps gained in previous developmental growth. They must learn to experience that confidence and the associated ease in the new variety of activities their peers and overseers prescribe. They must learn to create and follow their own internal rules as their increased mobility takes them farther and farther from the immediate supervision of their caretakers. The age assessment of the individual is the vehicle that facilitates the therapist's investigating these resources and working in these areas.

Using her social network behavior and interpersonal behavior as a guide,

Erickson assessed her developmental age as early teens. Then he secured her participation in developing age regression to that time of her life and investigated the map of social conduct she incorporated then. He also helped her develop amnesia as an aid in the examination, respecting her difficulty in consciously dealing with these matters (as reported by the roommate).

She was asked to disorient with respect to time and place and to regress to some significant event between the ages of 10 and 13 years old. She was asked to speak about everything she had been told about sex. She replied with a long list of instructions including: "Girls mustn't let boys do anything to them. Not nice. Nice girls never do. Only bad girls. It would make mother sick, etc." Parenthetically, the client's mother had died during intercourse, as had another mother-substitute. Erickson commented that the same thing might happen to the patient. "It is a child's passive acceptance of logic from the image with which it has become identified" (Erickson & Kubie, CP III, p. 130).

It was apparent that she had learned to be especially adaptive in her childhood and she adapted to information that did not now assist her with normal social development and pressures of living. While this adapting was the basis for the growth of her psychoneurosis, it was also a strength and a resource to be utilized in the therapy. The therapy consisted of six sessions which we could summarize as follows: Erickson accepted and restated to the client's satisfaction the beliefs and attitudes of the parent introject. He offered only the slightest implication that those were rightly the mother's instructions to her at *that* age and it makes one wonder what she would have said to the client at various ages if she had lived longer. In subsequent discussion the client displayed total amnesia for what she had said in trance but was conscious of a curiosity about certain sexual practices, such as kissing.

Erickson utilized the trances to build a framework for the client's understanding a positive interpretation of the mother's behavior and discussed at length the normal biological and concurrent psychological changes that occur as a girl ages. He was careful to answer her only in the most general manner to allow her to make her own choice regarding the rules she would now expect her mother to have given her at different ages. And she did form her own opinions. At the beginning of one later session, she announced that kissing was great sport.

Later, she commented about her therapy that "I appreciated my mother's careful instruction of me when I was just a little girl" (CP III, p. 133). This statement from the client articulately reflects the degree of acceptance of her past and the pride and self-image enhancement which she gained. Thus she aquired a new map of behavior but she was able to continue her great respect for her mother. Again, this outcome, especially in such a potentially difficult case, illustrated the value of respecting all the client's communications and helping her save face.

Erickson was careful to move to new areas of conflict for her only after she displayed willingness, interest, and curiosity to continue. Moreover, he built associations to experiences of enjoyment, love, appreciation, safety, objectivity and self-regard into personality traits that were used to assist her in making what he has called a "reassociation in the client's experiential life" (*CP* IV, p. 38).

Using interventions aimed at her age of development, he helped evoke those experiences which permitted her to have new or modified perceptions of her experience, her roles, and the situations in which she would find herself. These resources were employed both to aid in the comfortable and curious investigating of her mother's early instructions (induction of the hypnosis) and to motivate the search for and acquisition of new and appropriate modes of behavior (utilization of the hypnotic trance phenomena). Using her available resources was a necessary part of the interview management and the treatment outcome itself and, hence, was part of the diagnostic assessment.

> In this way I could give the patient a general review of the development of all the primary and secondary sexual characteristics: the phenomenon of menstruation, the appearance of pubic and auxiliary hair, the development of her breasts, the probable interest in the growth of her nipples, the first wearing of a brassiere, the possibility that boys had noticed her developing figure and that some of them had slapped her freshly, and the like . . . modesty, the first stirrings of sexual awareness, autoerotic feelings, the ideas of love in puberty and adolescence, and the possible ideas of where babies came from. This again was done slowly and always in vague general terms, so that she could make a comprehensive and extensive personal application of these remarks (Erickson in Haley, 1973, p. 81).

Thus, we have a direct connection from diagnostic considerations to the treatment plan. The client's mother had been unable or unwilling to give appropriate elaboration for her daughter's sexual development. The resources in the map from her mother (avoiding sex, getting physically ill, etc.) were the most easily accessible experiences she had associated with the context of sexual conduct. Erickson gave her understandable examples of various behaviors and attitudes that provided elaboration on experiences she needed to understand. His summary illustrates the somatic, behavioral, interpersonal, psychological, and physical aspects to which he referred in order to be certain that he was being relevant to her psychological world of 13. This is an example of Erickson's approach of diagnosing the age of development and available resources and then designing the treatment plan to include speaking to the client with age-appropriate metaphors and anecdotes.

As we have briefly mentioned in discussing the resources of the client or client-system, the availability of such resources is often the basis for decisions regarding the extensiveness of the treatment that will be undertaken. Erickson was practical. He wrote: "In attempting such modified psychotherapy the difficult problem arises of what can really be done about neurotic symptomatology where the realities of the patient and his life situation constitute a barrier to comprehensive treatment" (*CP* IV, p. 149). When clients are so impoverished or there is such disorganization in their experience that they are not likely candidates for extensive psychotherapy, then therapy must be modified. Erickson named various brief therapy goals, such as symptom substitution, symptom amelioration, symptom transformation, and corrective emotional response.

Part of the initial and ongoing assessment of the client must include considerations of how much is realistically achievable. In the preceding case, the therapy goals might best be categorized as "corrective emotional response" brief psychotherapy. Additional cases which follow illustrate how resources can be made available to the client and just what type of resources can be co-created in therapy. In all cases, however, the assessment of the difficulty or ease of co-developing the resources with the client is translated directly into the treatment planning. Decisions about the length of therapy and the manner in which to proceed with resources are derived from such an assessment. This woman's case is a monument to Erickson's belief that the needed resources lie within the client's personal history. Certainly, the woman developed her own new understandings and experiences and she did so despite what seemed at first to be an impoverished sexual understanding and an unwillingness to learn from others.

The client's flexibility as a communicator in the various roles s/he plays is another important factor to consider. Questions used in assessing this variable involve the client's perceptions of others: Does the client always view others in the same way? Always one up? Always friendly? Always as hostile? Never as sad? Hurt? Happy? The client's cognitive flexibility is equally important: Others may be seen both smiling and frowning but either activity may be comprehended as "sneaking around behind the back." The client just discussed may have perceived sexual conduct among others but always interpreted it by her particular map of the world to be "dirty" and "sickening" conduct. This type of inflexibility would, of course, hinder the ties in her social network and limit the interactions and social sanctions she might enjoy.

The final consideration in the flexibility of the client to other members of the social system includes the client's behavioral and emotional flexibility.

This relates to the interpersonal reflex patterns mentioned earlier (Leary, 1957). Erickson's client had gotten herself into an inflexible position. She vomited in the dating context or even when dating was mentioned!

Sensitivity and flexibility toward others are considered important in the treatment plan. Within the multiple embedded metaphor modality of treatment, the therapist creates a special opportunity for treating problems that arise from deficits in these areas. Even in this case of corrective emotional brief therapy, Erickson dealt with this important element by orienting the patient into her social network with a pre-shaped map of the world that allowed her new social adjustments in keeping with her social role demands, as well as her biological urges and her internal map of relationships and meanings.

This turned out to be much to the client's satisfaction. She dated, became engaged, and married the man with whom she had the ill-fated date earlier. About a year later she came into Erickson's office and reported that married life was all that she could hope for and that she was looking forward to motherhood. Of the client's summary, Erickson related: ". . . she had gained an entirely new understanding of many things, and that this new understanding had made it possible for her to accept the emotion of love and to experience sexual desires and feelings, and that she was now entirely grown up and ready for the experiences of womanhood" (*CP* III, p. 140).

It may seem odd that Erickson not only consulted with the client's social network but also employed it as a resource in the sessions. Actually, on many occasions he took the social network as his client and the identified client, the symptom carrier, remained the hub of the activity. Speck and Attneave have defined the social network as: "the nuclear family and all of the kin of every member. But it also includes the friends, neighbors, work associates, and significant helpers from churches, schools, social agencies, and institutions who are willing and able to take the risk of involvement" (1973, p. xxii). While that list seems to include about everyone known to the identified client, we believe it is consistent with those authors to stress the key word in the definition: "involvement." The real or imagined involvement of family members may be a factor in the client's difficulties and anxieties and, to wit, those authors add: "Our experience is that in some instances the entire social network causes and perpetuates pathology, scapegoating the individual and/or family" (p. xxii).

In this case it is clear that the client's dead mother, or at least her introjected image, people in the social network who reminded her of the mother, the boyfriends and other eligible males in her life, her roommate, employer, and others played a part in her symptoms of somatizing and withdrawing.

The inner connectedness of the social network and the members' roles, emotions, attitudes, and thoughts has been researched extensively by social scientists Cartwright and Zander (1968). The individual's sense of identity is in many ways shaped and maintained by the social network (Erikson, 1963); the same is true for the interpretation of experience (Laing, 1967, 1972), and the sense of destiny (Berne, 1966). Any systemic explanation must account for the importance of elements in a chain of events, which, although circular in nature, might be shown to begin and proceed as follows:

1) Social cues induce an internal search.
2) Internal search produces various experiential resources.
3) Ideomotor identification (including emotion, gestures, etc.) feeds back indicators of the person's map of experience.
4) The social network is joined and co-creation (in whatever form has been learned or devised) begins.
5) The social network selectively carries and transmits the information received.

For our purposes here the reader need only be alerted to the logic of this inter-relatedness so that a better understanding can be had regarding the enormous complexity of material that Erickson could both derive and help create with a client during a series of hypnotherapy sessions. We will tie all of these diagnostic factors to the treatment plan using multiple embedded metaphors in the chapters that follow.

Clients bring their problems with them and act them out over and over. They induce others to perform certain roles with them. The display of problems is noticeable not only through the transference phenomena, but also through the client's patterns of perceiving. Even though the entire social network may not be available to the therapist, many indicators of the social network become evident by assessing the client. As in the case above, when the client was interacting in the office she would, as everyone does, concentrate on internal experience to search out specific words and experiences. People seem to have only a finite amount of consciousness available for attending. This limited amount of consciousness can quickly become absorbed in attending to experience brought into the office in the troubled client's internal map. This inward attention accounts for the search phenomena which we discuss in the next few chapters.

Observing these phenomena, Erickson might well have asked himself these questions: What experience is that client searching for? Did she find it or something else? Is her experience out of context or incongruent? What does the expression on her face and in her voice invite in different social situations? Why did or didn't she terminate the inner search for instruction and get some aid from others? Who did the client turn to when and if she did stop the internal searching? How was social contact first made? What experience was brought to the social interface? What did she selectively perceive about the person(s) with whom she connected? These questions presuppose a type of systemic thinking that links together several factors—the internal structure of the personality, the family or social structure, the types of transactions received from the network, and the sequence of inner experiences.

Consideration of these six diagnostic parameters may prove to be time-consuming. Each diagnosis will be approached differently depending on the client and the situation. The broad range of approaches Erickson took in so many cases demonstrates a well balanced fluency in each of these modalities. He saw clients in state hospitals, in his own office, and sometimes in the client's home; at times he and his wife, Betty, would even go with a client to a restaurant. He went shopping with clients, had them sleep out on his lawn over several nights, had them climb Squaw Peak behind his Arizona home. He conducted therapy with individuals and families alike, and used waking state and trance states for the duration of therapy sessions. His keen observation of details allowed him to assess the social life and styles of individuals in their families even when he was limited to seeing only a single member or marital couple. Also, his ability to use the formula and principles just described provided a noticeable measure of feedback and rationale for helping the client shape social perceptions and associate to the resources needed in the social network after therapy.

Finally, the current role the symptom plays in the client's family or social system must be considered. Too often therapists tend to fit the client to the theory rather than inventing a new theory for each client as Erickson recommended. Principle three from Chapter 2 emphasizes that the theory is not the client. There is always the tendency to selectively perceive facts that fit one's worldview. But Erickson believed that clients will make better choices when better choices are successfully taught. This, of course, includes the option of acting with the symptomatic behavior. In either case, he depended on the client's assistance in providing necessary information to make those decisions: "The patient can be relied upon to fit the jigsaw together and, in point of fact, should have joint responsibility with the therapist for doing so" (Erickson & Rosen, *CP* IV, p. 110).

For the client just discussed, one might speculate, from a medical-psychiatric framework, that social pressure increased her oedipal anxiety; that her symptom resulted from the ego creating massive measures of hysterical conversion to protect her from the thoughts she internalized from her mother; and that her ego was taking massive measures of denial to protect her from the thought that she had aggressive and competitive feelings about her mother. Since the introjection of her mother would have inhibited the expression of her sexual energy, there would also be complications due to the possibility that her aggressive wishes against her mother somehow resulted in her mother's death. All this speculation presupposes a perverse motivation of the client.

Erickson warned against such use of psychoanalytic frameworks and against projecting any theory onto the client. Instead, his assessment of the symptom's function related to the current and real gratification or anxiety experienced by the client. The vomiting was prescribed behavior from the woman's mother. Both the vomiting and the social withdrawal seemed to establish a negative re-inforcement paradigm. That is, if she avoided the dates, she avoided the sick-ness and the prohibited behavior prescribed in her map. Erickson's view was that she chose the best option she could from those available to her. Her socialization had not taught her how to mobilize and use the resources of con-fidence, curiosity, pleasure with kissing, etc., and her symptom signaled her need to gain experiential choices which were becoming increasingly remote in her maladapted social withdrawal. About the here-and-now "value" of symp-toms, Erickson wrote:

> Symptoms and even syndromes, when emotionally based, may subserve the repetitive enactment of traumatic events; may reproduce, instead, specific life situations; may satisfy repressed erotic and aggressive im-pulses; or may at one and the same time constitute defenses against, and punishment for, underlying instinctual drives (Weisman, 1952). They may mask schizophrenic reactions or hold suicidal depressions in check (Rosen, 1953a, 1953b). They may serve all these functions concurrently, or none of these, or any specific one or combination of them (*CP* IV, p. 103).

In the case just discussed we have illustrated Erickson's transactional use of the social network as a device not only for gathering historic information but also for conducting the therapy. Also, his help in expanding the woman's map of what she could expect from herself sexually included the shaping of her social perceptions and her expectations of what others (men) would be perceiving, feeling, and thinking. Erickson seemed to be keenly aware that he was participating in the process of co-creating, with the help of the client's available unconscious resources, that world in which she lived.

Beginning therapy with a good treatment plan and getting the client en-gaged in it comprise a major part of any treatment. To further elaborate the previously discussed parameters, we now present two first sessions with two different clients from the standpoint of our diagnostic considerations and treatment planning.

A CASE OF STOMACH ULCER

David was a young physician from the Midwest who sought help for a stom-ach ulcer. He was 34 years old, father of five children, married quite happily, with an excellent reputation in his social network for being fair, honest, and, above all, hardworking. He was accustomed to working 16 hours a day, six days a week. When he told us of his ulcer it was the first time he had spoken of the problem to another person other than his wife. None of his colleagues knew of his frequent pain.

His usual method of responding to the ulcer pain was denial. When he entered the office and was seated he introduced himself and got right to business. "Well, what I want to do is, well, I have an ulcer." When asked how he cared for the ulcer he replied that sometimes he did not change his schedule at all and only occasionally would he drink milk. When asked if he relaxed he replied, "No, it seems like I can't afford to. I know that I should but I just don't." When asked if he ever relaxed he said only occasionally after playing handball. He quickly added that he would like to play handball more often.

We immediately noticed in his self-presentation a regular incongruent laughter whenever he spoke of his difficulty. He was somewhat hyperactive and nervous in the session but his activity was concentrated upon the task at hand. He therefore gave the appearance of being alert and well controlled. To the average observer he might seem alert and "sharp" or "keen," highly helpful and quite friendly. We observed him, with his nervous laugh and tension, as anxious and somewhat counterphobic.

We also saw him as someone who had developed a great deal of personal strength. He was intelligent, responsible, socially graceful, capable of caring, and alert. Also, he displayed a sense of humor other than the incongruent laughter mentioned above. We "sized him up" as a man with many resources, easy to communicate with, and relatively flexible in his dealings with others. His relationship to others was, however, lacking in at least one obvious area: He could display managerial, responsible, and competitive behavior but not dependent behavior.

We speculated from his history (e.g., not revealing his ulcer, heavy work load, incongruent nervous laugh, and his pattern of denial) that he was not comfortable with his dependency needs. The early picture of our treatment plan was shaped around these variables. He could make use of a map of conduct that allowed him to easily, and with psychological comfort, associate to resources of relaxation, interpersonal dependency, and those experiences we might call "pride" in his body. If he were to gain nothing more than new access to these resources, he could change his self-presentation, become sensitive to his body, and respect the messages it would continue to send regarding his degree of stress. He could "surrender" to his dependency needs and rely upon his very capable spouse for support at those times. Just how the various scenarios for his possible new lifestyle would be conducted remained a mystery to us.

In the first several minutes of the first interview this much was ascertained about David and tentatively planned. We were told that his ulcer began about five years ago. We inquired as to the age of his children and found that the youngest had just turned five. The clinical picture was even more understandable. It is no small job for a couple to raise four children and for one of them to complete a medical degree and establish a respected job in the community. David had apparently developed his ulcer simultaneously with the birth of his youngest child. He was not aware of this coincidence and we did not intend to bring it into his awareness (at least not yet). If we were to make this connection conscious for him we would co-create with him the association of two consciously unassociated events: his daughter's birth and the lack of gratification for his dependency needs. Since he was apparently uncomfortable with those needs, a heightened awareness of how his daughter's presence in the family evoked those very needs could only be iatrogenic. Insight could possibly lead to unnecessary conscious resentment. David had been unable, in the reality of his daughter's birth, to rely upon his own inner phenomena and gain the sense of relaxation and security he needed. One might further inquire about his psychological experience at the time of discovering the pregnancy. Did he suppress anger or fear?

We are reminded that cure does not come through insight but rather through a reassociation of the client's experiential life. Regardless of the deficit in functioning that resulted in the ulcer, there was a certain unconscious pattern that he could rely upon to produce it. Therapy could help him use the same mechanisms to initiate his needed inner or social resources instead of the ulcer. The resources he needed would be those he failed to initiate at the time of the ulcer's onset (and probably during childhood). David provided a simple example of the difficulty a client may have in actually verbalizing what those needs and resources were. There were several reasons for this: the onset of the problem was years ago; he had practiced suppression of the incident; he currently had a self-image that required excluding dependency needs from awareness. Consequently, we would not spend several treatment sessions in the process of discovering the exact multiple meanings carried by the onset of the problem. We assumed that his learning to make the adjustments that he needed to make five years earlier and needed to make at the time of the therapy would be more than sufficient.

Before continuing with his treatment plan, we want to contrast the logic of this approach with the traditional psychiatric approach. From the history David shared it seemed very likely that six years ago he was unable to consciously postpone the gratifications he personally desired. His resources for delayed gratification had seemed exhausted by the hard work he had done in medical school, marriage, and the births of and attention to the first four children. He explained wistfully that he and his wife had planned to take a special trip to Hawaii. In that way he might have created for himself the sense that he had arrived at adulthood successfully. He could have taken pride in himself and fortified his confidence. The entire experience might have served as a reinforcement, self-created, for the delay of gratifications he had endured.

Instead, he discovered that his wife was pregnant. His plans changed. His income was in jeopardy of being too small, and the trip to Hawaii, symbolizing his passage into full manhood, was postponed. He had good reality-testing and knew he had to work more to increase his income and support a larger family. As a result he apparently taxed his ego mechanisms by reviving those ways of thinking and behaving that created rage during various earlier deprivations. But, he did not consciously keep the rage in mind—it would do no good. He began defensive measures using the mechanisms of denial and suppression. He was somewhat angry at his wife and new baby and he used a conversion mechanism to feign joy and happiness while silently bearing his frustration and fears. In the act of defending he could forget about his "childish" plans and work hard to increase his responsibilities and his income. As a result, his own needs for gratification were even less fulfilled. The ulcer, a result of organ dysfunction, was the first obvious somatic sign of unresolved internal conflicts for this man.

Before summarizing the traditional psychoanalytic approach, we apologize that due to our brevity here we will make some unfortunate overgeneralizations. These are included only to highlight the possible differences in approach.

In the tradition of psychoanalytic psychotherapy, the therapy would be oriented toward uncovering his early childhood adjustments that produced the experience of rage toward his caretakers. He would be expected to gain insight about this and thereby realize that his suppressed anger at his wife and baby was actually only an expression of inadequately defended rage toward his mother (probably) or father. This insight would be expected to result in a diminution of some "bad feelings" toward them and perhaps result in making him closer to his wife and child—if (and this is a big if) he has the intellectual capacity to use the insight.

If the client is willing to stay in therapy and gain this insight, he would then be asked to "work it through." This therapy would amount to a small degree of age regressing, "staying with" the rage and experiencing, as one does in these situations, that the world is not destroyed by his rage. With acceptance of the rage the mechanisms of repression would no longer be needed. Thus, the defensive measures could be stopped. The pain of the ulcer would be expected to stop as well, because it is a symptom created from the failure of the defensive measures. When the defense is not needed and is not used, the ulcer will not emerge.

Since the above scenario reflects the historical foundation of most therapeutic approaches, we imagine that the reader can recognize the departures
from custom taken by the Ericksonian approach. Ericksonian therapy, for instance, will not usually investigate historical scenarios for the sake of developing insight. We think that, rather than developing insight, clients need to
learn to use unconscious potentials that will connect their needs with the personal and social resources necessary for gratifying them.

As clients, even unconsciously, associate to needed mechanisms in therapy, the conscious mind undergoes a change. This change is not insight about
the existence of childhood remnants but rather the gaining of a new framework for understanding current and future circumstances. With respect to
the inner conflict and rage mentioned above, that client will no longer create
it, since appropriate inner associations previously too complex or difficult
will be used instead. The mechanisms for defense will no longer be needed in
the original way. Lastly, his conscious mind, both during and after therapy,
will remain alert to current life considerations and not those of the previous
years.

Let's return to David's actual diagnosis, treatment, and social situation.
We had obtained in the first five minutes of the interview initial impressions
and historical information which provided our initial understanding of several diagnostic parameters. One important consideration was his apparent age
of development. We had been surprised to learn that David was 35 and that
he was a physician. He seemed much younger, perhaps in his early to middle
twenties. One of his major and striking features was his humorous and somewhat adolescent manner. We speculated regarding developmental age that he
was operating as a teenager. This impression further supported the picture of
a man whose situational adjustments to adulthood were stressful. This was a
man who needed to regain some discarded aspects of his functioning and the
place where he "left off" in his development of these resources was probably
adolescence.

He was articulate and responsive to us in our questioning. Due to his social
accomplishments and his adolescent manner, we recognized that he had
many personal resources to draw upon and eliciting them would not be exceedingly difficult. Consequently, therapy would not be as difficult as with
some others. David no longer needed to work feverishly to develop his career. He had the proverbial ball rolling. In the world in which he lived, the
next few years were likely to involve the emergence of needs in the area of adjustment to adolescent children. He would need to teach them, through interaction with them, as large a variety of roles as possible. He would have to tolerate their dependency needs and not view them as in competition with his
own. And he would be adjusting to the reality of a large family—including

enjoying them for the long maturation process ahead. The extent to which he was unprepared to make those adjustments gracefully and creatively was the extent to which his personal "pathologies" were communicated to others and would be learned by his children (Berne, 1966; Haley, 1973; Laing, 1972). These general statements depict a vague sketch of his social system's next developmental stages.

In summary, the considerations have included his social network, his flexibility and sensitivity to members of it, and the stage of development of the family system. His age of developmental functioning was consistently reminiscent of adolescence and he had a plethora of resources to draw from. With this information we turned to the treatment contract of helping him with his ulcer, taking these additional factors into account. After all, his ulcer only existed in a matrix of such internal, external, and social influences. Bodily symptoms speak an existential language: The ulcer spoke for the whole person as it communicated. It did not simply ask relief from the pain; it asked for this man and his social network to evolve to the level of functioning where joy and gratification are possible. Our client, however, like most individuals and families, didn't ask for joy and comfort. Clients don't usually seek such goals because they don't believe they can even get free of their problem, much less hope for more. One might speculate that, in fact, the inability to solve the problem was due to the limited scope in which the problem was framed.

Our tentative plan was to use a naturalistic induction and multiple embedded metaphor to structure interventions which would be designed to associate the social cues he received, as well as the first signs of symptomatology, to various resources. We would begin with the tension and anxiety that he displayed and utilize that to lead naturalistically to trance and trance phenomena.

The trance phenomenon that seemed a most relevant resource was dissociation. It could be useful for two important reasons. The concentration and focus that he displayed indicated an ability to become quickly absorbed which would facilitate dissociation. Also, dissociation would be relevant for our purposes since it would allow him to develop relaxation. We knew he thought he could not take time to relax. So the possibility of using dissociation to help him improve his conscious frame of reference about relaxation was an attractive prospect in our plan. He clearly could use relaxation but he did not believe he could afford to relax. It would be necessary for the metaphoric content to offer a new frame for the importance of relaxation.

He needed both a reason to use relaxation and a way to associate to it. His lack of this resource probably accounted for the high muscle tonus and active tension in his self-presentation. His personal experience of relaxing in the trance and the offering of a new frame of reference about relaxing could perhaps be combined to produce both a reason and a way to experience relaxation that would be compatible with his lifestyle. Then we could use relaxation in some social context to bridge the way to understanding other tender experiences two people can share. These tender experiences, involving parasympathetic dominant chemical sets, could provide the groundwork for discussing social exchanges in which one receives attention or caretaking from others. This discussion could be the channel for getting David on the track of accepting his dependency needs in the context of his real life. His real social network offered the opportunity to express a range of dependency-related needs. Sensitizing him to the social cues that indicated an opportunity to express some of these new behaviors would be part of the job of our treatment.

* *Tension and concentration→ Will be used to develop trance*
* *Trance→ Will be utilized to develop dissociation*
* *Dissociation→ Will facilitate the development of relaxation*
* *Relaxation← Will be triggered at first indications of ulcer*
* *Relaxation→ Will further be used as a vehicle to accept dependency
  needs*
* *Dependency resources→ Will be associated to social cues*

The above outline illustrates our basic plan at the end of the first discussion of his situation. We examined our thinking for how this pattern of overall treatment could be approached. Did we want to have a session of one hour in length for each item? Did we want to work at accomplishing some of each item during each session? How many sessions did we think we would need? These questions remained partially unanswered, of course, until we interacted with the client in real time and discovered how he responded to our interventions. It would make a big difference, for example, if he could not easily develop trance or if he developed some unexpected reaction to the relaxation response. For instance, simple conditioning could have produced the ulcer by creating a situation in which he had a great deal of signal anxiety as soon as he began to relax.

Another consideration involved his associations to the metaphors we selected. Metaphors have a great effect upon the client's unconscious search process and provide ongoing diagnostic information, as will be discussed in the next two chapters. Any of these elements can change a treatment plan. The therapist must be able to change with the information received during the sessions.

David's self-image thinking treatment is explained at greater length in Chapter 8. At that point the reader will be better equipped to follow our thinking in the use of metaphor, trance phenomena, and direct symptom work. For now, discussing the general plan of treatment is our goal. An initial decision in treatment planning involves the selection of metaphor(s) or some other verbal delivery of information. In choosing to use metaphor we are greatly influenced by the client's needs. In David's case, he had a very prejudicial attitude toward relaxation and the use of metaphor could provide a new framework for him to consider it. A framework free of the constraints of his present map of the world, provided by metaphor, would also allow him new associations to the resources he developed in trance. For these reasons we decided to outline and use metaphor for portions of the work.

It is not crucial for Ericksonian therapists to use metaphors. Even Erickson did not always use them. We decided upon an approach to David's symptom that might directly inhibit its occurrence in favor of the relaxation response. For this we would present a version of Erickson's confusion technique that we refer to as a "scramble." The resulting confusion would make it comparatively more difficult to simply "turn on" the usual course of conflict mechanisms that result in the ulcer symptom. Thus, the choice of relaxation would be one that was comparatively more attractive than his associations to mechanisms of denial.

The amended treatment plan was as follows:

Tension and Concentration → Trance

This was consistent with meeting the client at his model of the world and respecting his anxiety and tension as his current best choice. Rather than expect him to use progressive relaxation at our suggestion and thereby come to speak our language, we asked him to do exactly what he was doing and develop trance in his own unique way. Our initial metaphors were presented to appeal to the concerns of an adolescent. In this way we could appeal to the age of development and increase the likelihood that David would understand fully and develop resources when presented. We chose, in this case, a metaphor of an adolescent delivery boy. This particular delivery boy had problems of an interpersonal nature. We modified the true story to say that the delivery boy had trouble with his fifth delivery. The delivery boy's subsequent development and learning was, of course, planned as a vehicle for David's learnings.

Trance → Dissociation

The metaphor of the delivery boy provided a context for developing the trance phenomenon of dissociation. An idea from our common everyday life experience came to mind. People can frequently be observed developing dissociation as they ride in automobiles, trains, buses, and airplanes, whenever they prolong staring out of a window beyond which the world is effortlessly passing. Apparently the effect results from the disparate experiences of the body gliding away while farmers toil in fields, cows bend to drink, trees sway in the wind, and the world, in general, dances to the beat of a different drummer. To satisfy this need we formulated a scenario in which someone did ride on a bus trip. This also provided a logical framework for David to examine, without usual prejudice, the idea of "leaving the driving to someone else." If he could find relevance in the use of dissociation he should certainly be able to find a personal memory of such an incident in his past and therefore be able to dissociate in the revivification of that memory.

*Dissociation → Relaxation

While dissociated a person is very amenable to suggestions for increased relaxation. In this case we would not have to spend much time developing memories of relaxation. We knew that he would know and understand the experience of a teenager who had finished a sporting event, for example, or the experience of relaxation a child in the Midwest gets after mowing the lawn on a warm summer's day. We could help him employ the memories of lying on his back, looking up at the clouds float by, smelling the fragrance of newly cut grass, enjoying sounds of chirping birds, and feelings of breeze, etc. to achieve relaxation.

*Relaxation ← At First Indications of Ulcer

We intended to offer some type of confusion to help stall the usually automatic and rapid chain of events that began to occur somatically at the onset of the physical signs of the ulcer. We discuss the protocol for such work directed entirely at the symptom in Chapter 8 (p. 331). We planned to either illustrate in quotes embedded within a metaphor or simply explain to him directly how he might successfully employ confusion on his behalf. In place of the confusion we would suggest that he experience relaxation instead. This is the logic of offering a worse alternative to the client, a common strategy used by Erickson. In this strategy the choice of continuing the symptom was available but the price the client had to pay was higher than that for choosing the more therapeutic option. Since David did not want to "waste time," we illustrated the difference between these alternatives (searching with confusion for the symptoms vs. triggering relaxation) as a matter of time conservation. Would he rather waste time going through the many steps leading to his symptom or save time and go directly to relaxation? Paradoxically, he learned to "waste time" relaxing in order to save time!

*Relaxation→ To Accept Dependency Needs

We planned, in the multiple embedded metaphor modality, to return to one of the previous metaphors as we progressed in the treatment. In this case, mentioning the boy who mowed the lawn and experienced relaxation afterwards would allow further elaboration of tender feelings and the related ability to "lie back" and let someone else be in control. We related general events in the lives of teenagers as they grow and learn about different roles they can play in life. Such experiences as taking turns riding in the front of a canoe and enjoying the relatively effortless ride while the partner in the back is primarily responsible for steering could provide the link to enjoyably accepting a "passive" role. Tangents about pushing each other in swings or playing on a ball team and enjoying the rest while another team member "goes in" for you would sensitize him to those situations in his own life when he could enjoy allowing someone else to do something for him, even something he was capable of doing for himself or for them at another time. These various experiences, consistent with his adolescent developmental age, were related until David displayed through ideomotor signals that he identified with some such memory.

*Dependency Resources→ To Social Cues

We planned to link the experience of comfortable dependency and vulnerability retrieved in the previous situation to social contexts via self-image thinking. We could use the original delivery boy format and illustrate how a boy like that unconsciously makes use of such prior learnings as those we have outlined as he copes with his chores. We expected that we could relate the associations of making rounds as a doctor to making deliveries as a teen. Also, a teen attempting to become a man was similar to David's dilemma of coping with his rapid passage into adulthood, fatherhood, and professional roles. Again, the notion of the "fifth delivery" provided an opportunity to elaborate his map about the issue of his fifth child without alerting his consciousness. His conscious mind could be free to enjoy his pleasant experience around his daughter, rather than his memories of unpleasant associations.

Finally, David was reoriented from trance with general suggestions for the use of his unconscious learnings and reassociations. This amounted to posthypnotic suggestions to link his search for resources to the cues in his social network where he would need them. In this case David needed them in his current family situation. The delivery boy metaphor allowed an excellent vehicle for that type of association.

Of course, trance maintenance operations and reassurances are always included in planning as an ongoing part of treatment. Additional factors include particular applications of inductions, as well as nonverbal and indirect suggestion. We will illustrate treatment planning with another case before examining these elements of multiple level communication in detail.

THE CASE OF A CHILD ABUSER

A child abuser in Michigan was referred by the Protective Service branch of the Department of Social Services for psychotherapeutic treatment. The family walked in, led by the 17-year-old daughter, who had the appearance of a magazine cover girl. She was dressed to the hilt and wore heavy makeup. Since this was a therapy interview instead of a disco dance, her inappropriateness was quite obvious, so much so that we simultaneously thought to ourselves as she walked through the door and seated herself: "She certainly has a long way to go!"

When we turned to look back, the mother was making her way through the door. Her appearance was very much the opposite of the daughter's. The predominant color about this woman was brown. She was not well groomed, her hair was tousled. She was at least 50 pounds overweight and her dress resembled a gunny sack. Seeing these two in such juxtaposition immediately led to the idea that sexuality was the theme for issues and problems in this family. The girl was overacting her developing sexuality and the mother had misplaced any sexual appeal she might have had. She seated herself directly in front of us and assumed a posture of one who has "tried everything and nothing works."

A moment later the father walked in. He was a different story! He marched through the door and then pranced back and forth across the office. *Big* was the first impression. He began almost shouting: "You better teach that girl some respect! I've tried everything I can do and nothing works! I try to tell her what's right but she does what she damn well pleases. She doesn't listen to me so I brought her here so maybe you could teach her some respect!" He stopped talking and stood still, looking at us with one hand on his hip and one pointing at his daughter.

In that moment I (S. L.) remembered something Erickson had told me about being powerful with clients and not "pussy-footing around." Erickson's approach was to match clients and meet them at their model of the world. In this way he was less likely to create an interference to communication in the session, and he reduced the percentage of "resistant" clients. I instantly stood up and assumed the same posture as this client. I looked him in the eye from a distance of about 14 inches and said: "Let me get this straight— you want me to teach your daughter some respect, right?" I demanded!

He paused for just a fraction of a second and then, without changing his intensity, gave a rapid purposeful head nod and said: "That's right!" Then, walking across our office in a manner similar to his, I spoke firmly, clearly, and distinctly, just as he had done. "You love her! You care about her! You tell her what's right and wrong . . . but she just goes out and does what she damn well pleases, right!?" He firmly and eagerly added: "That's right!"

I continued: "You tell her what's right. You care for her and you want her to do the right things because you do. But if she goes and does whatever she wants to do . . . then what'll happen, right?" Again, he supplied a firm "Right." I had said what he said and had almost repeated it verbatim with the exception of one slight alteration. I added the notion that his motivation was positive. I said he loved her and he cared about her and he agreed! I had framed his behavior in a positive light. I had not accepted it but I had immediately helped him save face. The faces of his wife and daughter indicated a lack of understanding about just exactly what was happening before them. They were waiting to get more information.

As far as my sentence structure was concerned I was working to systematically move my phrase about his love for her closer to the end of my sentences. I wanted it to be my final word and I wanted his emphatic "That's right!" to follow it. I finally said: "And if she never follows your advice she's never going to know that you love her, right?" He enthusiastically agreed again. "Then go ahead and tell her you love her," I concluded.

I watched him expectantly. He was searching for understanding. As he watched me I slowly lowered myself into my office chair and said softly, "It's as easy as when you sit down." We simultaneously nodded our heads toward his chair as the words were spoken. After a slight pause he slowly sat down. As he did so he said quietly, and much to our delight, "I guess that's what I need to learn."

That was the first intervention and the beginning of therapy. We had previously learned from Protective Services that the incident resulting in child abuse was the daughter's returning home from a date 25 minutes later than her curfew. But we also knew quite a bit about this family from our observations in these first few minutes.

Further questioning confirmed what our senses had already revealed. The family system was structured around the husband and wife and their 17-year-old daughter. The father was authoritarian, employed in a blue collar job, had a high school education, and was in his early forties. He did not frequently meet the public and was not very flexible or tolerant in his dealings with others. He was dominating in the family.

The mother and daughter were in conflict. The mother considered herself hardworking. She received little or no appreciation from her husband. The daughter was becoming isolated from the family. The daughter was the family member most in contact with the world outside of the family. Problems and needs in this family were most likely handled by appealing to repression by authority instead of discussion and feedback.

The most interesting and striking element to us was the stage of development of the family system. The daughter was exhibiting difficulty adjusting to her new sexuality. She was experimenting with her role as a woman and she had many things to learn. The family was reacting to her experimentation and learning with tension and fear. One look at the poorly groomed mother, overweight and sloppy, revealed that this woman had not developed much of a positive self-image. It was as if sexuality itself was an issue in this family. The mother did not try to exploit any of her sexual appeal and the daughter was overdoing it. The father was threatened by the daughter's developing womanhood. The problems in this family would not soon be over.

If the daughter continued to test her "teen-angel" wings, she could expect her parents to push her right out of the home. The father's anger and violence, having served as her model of a man's behavior, probably had left her in need of new and more adequate learnings about how men may really act. As these factors continued to interplay, the tension in the home would increase. The likely outcome of the situation was that the daughter would leave home soon, looking for "love." She would probably use pregnancy as the crowbar to pry herself away from the rigidity of this family. In other words, what the parents feared (or perhaps secretly wished) was just what was likely to happen: the daughter's sexual behavior would lead to early pregnancy and more problems.

When the daughter left home, either as we predicted or some other way, the mother and father would be left together. Alienated from one another but alone together, they would be spending considerable time together. They could make this adjustment with joy and curiosity or with anger and insecurity. They did not seem to get along very well at the time of the therapy contact, and without the daughter to fight about they would probably find that they had little in common. Two things were certain: The daughter would soon leave home and the nuclear family would be restructured.

The strong erotic element in this family was the immediate problem. If the father (and mother?) had his way about it the daughter would have ceased her attempts to be attractive and sexy. The problem would, through repression, be over. However, that strategy seldom works as well as the users wish. Attempts thus far to use repression as the mechanism for control of growth and development in this family had only made matters worse.

People's behavior represents the best choice they have available for themselves at the time. This married couple emitted evidence of their poor self-images and their fear of sexuality. The map of the world they taught the daughter in this regard was as impoverished as the one they held. The conflict over sexual matters was a highly charged issue that would probably play a key role in this young woman's behavior for many years to come. Her behavior might best be explained as her attempt to adjust her self-image and personal map of the world. The social and biological pressures of her age engaged her to resolve conflicts about her erotic feelings and prepare herself for courtship and marriage stages of development. It was a credit to this girl that she was aware, perhaps unconsciously, that repressing her sexual development would not be an adaptive choice. Her rebellion was an apparent attempt to find an adjustment not for the present but for the world she would enter in the future.

It was a credit to the daughter that she was attempting to stay in the home, be a good citizen, and work with the family as a unit. Her cooperation and strengths were going unnoticed in the shadow of these concerns over her womanhood. So we saw in the presenting picture a graphic display of the problem which existed at the unconscious level in this family.

The family structure and stage of development were stereotypical. The insensitivity and inflexibility of the members in relation to one another were apparent. The role of the symptom in the family was clearly understandable as well: repress, even with violence, the sexual impulse that no one in the family understood.

We considered the father to be the major client in this system for initial treatment. Regarding his developmental age, we had been given some cryptic information when he stomped around our office like a large four-year-old shouting: "Give me my truck! You tell her to give me my truck!" He was narcissistically self-centered and insensitive to the feelings of others. As far as available resources were concerned, he would be most able to develop those which took into consideration his apparent psychological age.

The treatment situation was complicated by his original presentation of the daughter as the problem carrier. You will recall his opening gambit: "You better teach her some respect. . . ." However, in response to the energetic joining behavior he had finally stated: "I guess that's what I need to learn." He thereby defined the treatment contract to include his learning something as well. We wished to take advantage of that momentum. Using the diagnostic information gathered thus far, we began to structure the therapy session, as outlined below. Our initial treatment plan pivoted around the father's need for a new and more appropriate map for his feelings, conduct, and the relationship a man could have with his daughter—and eventually with his grandchildren.

* *Accept his presenting behavior → Reframe it*
* *Use his fixated attention → Offer trance*
* *Trance → Elaborate upon the reference frame*
* *Trance and new frame → Various resources*
* *Link resources → Understand his daughter*
* *New view of daughter → New sense of self*

If this plan could be carried out, his therapeutic gain would be an enhancement of the relationship with his daughter. He would actually learn to observe his daughter afresh and appreciate the many good qualities he was overlooking.

Finally, we would pre-frame the daughter's inevitable departure from the home as a sign of his success and not a sign of failure. This would appeal to his child-like narcissism and allow him to save face. The daughter would be allowed to leave home at a more relaxed speed and her departure would not be as violent. She would not have to "burn bridges" and alienate her family in order to leave. Consequently, her accomplishments of early adulthood could be made with less conflict. If the father's self-image was enhanced, rather than damaged, by the daughter's leaving home, the situation between him and his wife would be more relaxed and conducive to fostering growth in their marriage.

Accept His Presenting Behavior → Reframe It

We had already begun accepting and placing his conduct in a different framework. I mentioned that his motivation for worrying about his daughter was love. He accepted and, in fact, willingly included himself in the treatment when a face-saving explanation was presented to him. It was as if he needed and eagerly sought a map of the world that would help make sense of his experience. His ready acceptance of our new map alerted us to consider this part of the unconscious treatment contract.

Use His Fixated Attention → Offer Trance

He thoughtfully had suggested that perhaps he needed to learn to show his love to his daughter. This was an excellent entry point into trance. He was in search of an understanding of love and tender expressiveness. Our next response was, "All right, close your eyes, and we'll just say some general words about how to learn what we want to know," whereupon we began a trance induction related to learning from himself. The trance arrangement established a clever paradox: We were instructing him to learn from himself. The situation so structured allowed a great deal of protection for the client both consciously and unconsciously. It allowed him to be consciously protected from the implication that he might be "one down," that he might "have something to learn," or that he had been doing things wrong. Thus, it reduced his defensiveness interpersonally and prevented the occurrence of strong internal self-criticism from his own superego or internalized parent figures. Unconsciously, he was actually following the lead of our suggestions and therefore was not "on his own" with his own limited associations. The likelihood of his failure was greatly reduced. Because of the paradoxical arrangement of the trance, he could take all of the credit for his achievements in trance.

*Trance → Elaborate Upon the Reference Frame

At least two areas needed to be included here for his increased learning. The most important, perhaps, was his understanding of how to observe his daughter and not be threatened by her sexuality. The second area was related to the fact that she would soon leave home. He would have to modify the hold and control he attempted to exert over her conduct. He would have to give up control without coming to believe that he had been wrong in his earlier attempts to control. The resources retrieved would be aimed at helping him come to his own conclusion about letting go of his attempts to control her. He would be led to make up his own mind rather than be "told" what to do. This was accomplished within an elaborately altered framework begun with a metaphor about a gardener whose income suffered because he did not spend enough time with his plants. This is often the case in Ericksonian approach and in this case the benefits were especially apparent.

*Trance and New Frame → Various Resources

The resources needed in this case were of a simpler type than those in the previous case. They were similar in that the client needed to become accepting of his tender, erotic, and parasympathetic dominant feelings. They differed, however, in that the developmental age of the child abuser was that of a very young, perhaps four-year-old, boy.

This man was personally insecure about his present world and perhaps, too, about his role as a client. We began with a discussion of how a person gains a sense of security, starting with how a child comes to know security. For example, a child learns to have a sense of security from finding that the toys he put in the toy box at night are still safely in the box the next morning.

We watched to be certain that he could, in fact, identify with such lines of thought and experience. We intensified the sense of security by anecdotes dealing with similar childhood learnings.

One of the elaborations we used concerned a boy discovering the tenderness he has for a puppy. The logic behind the story was that adults learn from childhood experiences. That story was just a way of illustrating. The purpose behind telling it was to appeal to his four-year-old memory and understanding of what it is like to be sensitive and tender. The story concerned a boy on a hot summer day holding a puppy on his lap and discovering the puppy breathing, feeling the warmth of the animal against his skin. We went into great detail regarding the physiology and attitude of the boy, his sense of awe inspired by the delicateness of the life next to him. Thus we developed tenderness he could understand in a framework he could tolerate. This was the foundation of his tolerance for erotic feeling.

We helped him understand also the value and purpose in holding on to what he believed in and valued. With similar anecdotes aimed at an age-appropriate level of comprehension, we outlined how some children hold on to and try to control what they love. When his head nods indicated he was following us from his own experience, we further elaborated upon something he did not understand very well. We offered the idea of how a person notices, values, and uses his feelings of love, tenderness, risk-taking, and acceptance. As is customary in an Ericksonian approach, we frequently reminded the man that his understanding our stories meant that his unconscious already knew and had already acquired all of this knowledge by experience. He was therefore learning to learn from himself.

Link Resources → Understand His Daughter

While he remained in trance experiencing the childhood remnants of risk-taking, acceptance, and tenderness, we had an opportunity to further evaluate and diagnose his situation. His available resources, for example, were indicators of his childhood history. Ideomotor indicators kept us informed about his experience and his attitude about his experience. Whenever he reached a memory that was too painful to be of positive value, we took tangents from our direction to deal with this. We detail such tangents in the following chapters on induction and metaphor. When he finally had retrieved and could hold constant the pleasant feelings we spoke of, we pointed out how his perceptions were altered by those experiences and we asked him to open his eyes and remain in trance. In this way we were able to encourage him to view his daughter with "new eyes." We then associated perceptual cues from the daughter to his recognition of the pleasant experiences. We reminded him that harboring these perceptual memories would help him produce the feelings again and again, and, of course, that his unconscious could do it automatically. His conscious mind could be free to do other things.

Finding the good feelings triggered by thoughts of his relationship with his daughter was the same learning we had just discussed: The child learns confidence and security as a result of finding the toys in the toy box the next morning. We communicated with him to the extent that we could monitor his personal experience. Indeed, he had not noticed very much about his daughter. He took pride in realizing, at our direction, that his daughter cared about him enough to come to the therapy; she was quiet and pleasant during the session; she was accepting of his experience; her face reflected signs of compassion, interest, and concern for his feelings; he had done a fine job in raising a girl who could be so mature and understanding; so many children today don't understand such subtle things about their parents; she reflected it in her face and posture; she had some of his features. We pointed out her facial and postural features, comparing and contrasting how she looked like him and how she had gained some personally distinct features.

This tactic allowed us to set up a therapeutic arrangement wherein he could safely recall and reexperience some of his erotic feelings. Furthermore, he was to have those feelings while observing his daughter. This new frame of reference was thereby intimately connected to his perception of his daughter and his subsequent cognitive interpretation. He had built a new map of experience for himself as a logical outgrowth of his own understandings. We had helped him build it firmly on his own experiences, give it meaning appropriate to his current life, and shape his perceptual mechanisms so that he could perceive these things again. His conscious mind could pay attention to the sense of pride he got from knowing his unconscious was taking care of things so well, or his conscious mind could pay attention to what he wanted to say to her. Likewise, his conscious mind could be free to listen and learn about her world and what gives her those feelings.

*New View of Daughter → New Sense of Self

He had been holding on to his daughter, controlling her, and pushing her out, all at the same time, pushing her away by his punitive actions but controlling her by his acts of repression. We therefore ended his first trance with a logic implied in anecdotes about how a person changes the way he holds on to his children. We began by agreeing with the importance of holding on to children and making them responsible human beings. Then we amplified the meaning and ramifications of holding on. First, one holds a baby in the uterus, then in the arms. As the baby grows, one must hold on by holding the child's hand and walking beside her. Then comes the need to hold on by voice alone because the child is growing. The child outside playing can be held by voice alone and the parents can be proud that they have been able to change the way they hold on to their child. Still later, the child becomes more mobile. The parents hold on by the values they have given the child. He could remember some of his daughter's features which indicated how his values had been conveyed to her. Ultimately, parents hold on to their children by holding the grandchildren. We described the various joys in this and how these memories (and even these anticipations) give parents that same sense of pride.

By offering him a way to change his understanding of holding on to and controlling his daughter, we enabled him to still respect his pre-therapy efforts. But he could now modify his approach to his daughter. He had received a reason, a way, and a rehearsal for his new role. We mentioned that his pride would eventually come from holding grandchildren, which is a common understanding in our culture. But this presupposes that his daughter is going to leave the home, date, marry, have sexual contact, and children. In other words, to enjoy his need to control his daughter and enjoy pride in so doing (both are an appeal to his narcissism), he has to get a grandchild. And to do that he must acknowledge that his daughter is developing sexually and even that she is eventually going to have sexual activity. In short, he can be proud that his daughter is a healthy, developing woman.

We concluded the first session with reminders to his daughter and wife of things they may have learned in the session. The father had been extremely attentive and kind to her today and they had both learned something about what kind of a man he really was. We underscored that the daughter's posture and looks were pleasing to her father.

We highlighted to the wife that she and her husband had some things to look forward to together in the next years to come, etc. In this way we continued the interventions into the family as a whole: The daughter's self-image and bodily image were enhanced; the wife and the husband were beginning to have a new basis for communicating and being married; the father and the daughter were changing their pattern of conflictual transactions in the family and opening a line of connectedness that was sure to reduce the daughter's isolation from the family.

Future sessions with the family were spent expanding the family's understanding of what it was like to have pleasant feelings with one another (as per his expressed contract). They found enjoyment in activities such as golf, lawn care (much to our surprise and delight), and eventually sitting home together with the girl's boyfriend, playing table games. Recently, this family has successfully and cheerfully helped the girl move into her own apartment across town. The father and mother celebrated their success as parents by "strolling" through the park near their home and reminiscing. There were no further outbreaks of violence after the first session; more importantly, the family did not only control their symptoms but also used the change to propel themselves into the next stage of family development as model parents!

In order to make the greatest application of these diagnostic considerations and treatment plans, we need to outline a number of facets, including the use of paradox; metaphor construction; indirect suggestion; trance induction, maintenance, and use; trance phenomena; and multiple embedded metaphor.

4 METAPHOR: THE COGNITIVE FRAMEWORK

PARADOX

In the previous cases we have made several references to the use of paradoxical interventions. We mentioned that it was paradoxical to teach the child abuser to learn from himself. We also described a paradox in the naturalistic induction with David: He was to use his tension to produce a trance of profound relaxation. There are many ways to build paradox and a number of therapeutic uses for it in Ericksonian approaches. It may seem odd, at first, that we are considering paradox as a saddle-mate of metaphor. But our logic will soon become apparent as we consider the use of paradox and metaphor to help the client shift frames of perceptual and cognitive reference.

Paradoxical commands have a particular effect on the listener. Even when trained to hear and understand paradoxical binds, one can suddenly find oneself in a moment of engagement from the effects of receiving paradoxical communications. The effect is suspension of normal frameworks of rule and logic and initiation of an internal search. Outward signs of the inner search include pupil dilation, flattened cheeks, increased skin pallor, lack of movement, slowed blink and swallow reflexes, and lowered and slowed respiration. Essentially, these are the signs of light trance—concentrated inner attention and decreased motoric output.

A paradox has been defined as a contradiction in conclusions that were correctly argued from consistent premises (Bateson, 1979, p. 23). Bateson discussed Erickson's work in one case: "When Erickson gives the signal, the subject hallucinates the hand moved, or hallucinates himself in a different place and therefore the hand was moved. This use of hallucination to resolve a problem posed by contradictory commands which cannot be discussed seems to us to illustrate the solution of a double bind situation via a shift in Logical Types" (1979, p. 223). It is of little wonder that the receiver of such communication is temporarily confused.

We use the term paradox and paradoxical bind to cover those types of formal arguments that Bateson has referred to above, as well as all therapeutic binds (brief and extensive) and the Ericksonian confusion techniques. In the latter case, the confusion is an essential paradox of a contextual nature. Typically, however, the paradox is a statement between these two extremes where the formal arguments of the paradox are implied or inferred rather than listed.

The "punchline" of the paradox may be all that the client hears. The rest is inferred and, of course, no matter which conclusion the client makes regarding the therapist's meaning, s/he realizes that the conclusion is logically inconsistent with some element in the line of thought that produced it! One example occurred during our wedding ceremony when Erickson said to us, "Don't give up any of your faults . . . you're going to need them to understand your spouse's." Still another example of the inferred logic is in the paradoxical command he next made: "And, look forward to the days when you can look back."

The moment of temporary confusion is not necessarily unpleasant, as the colloquial notion implies. In fact, it is often interpreted as a mild sense of well being. Think for a moment of the mild confusion of a joke and the delight that accompanies that brief experience. In a very similar manner the confusions of everyday life precede the brief "aha" experience in which old ways of perceiving are temporarily interrupted and the world is in that moment reorganized in a delightful way.

In general, the emotional affect that accompanies the "aha" is regarded as pleasant and the moment of preceding confusion does not hinder the person from having the pleasant affect or the seemingly heightened understanding. Likewise, the emotional reponse to the moment of confusion following the use of paradoxical binds does not predetermine or make unpleasant the affect that is subsequent to the use of paradox in therapy.

The client's conscious mind is temporarily overloaded by the illogical logic of the paradoxical communication and the first subjective mental state is confusion. During the moments of confusion, the client is in a process of mental search. Such mental search is an adaptive function and probably is best characterized by the concept of primary process activity. The high speed search is, according to experimental data reported by Erickson and Rossi (1979, p. 18), conducted at the rate of 30 items per second. As the conscious mind begins to search, so does the unconscious mind. Both hemispheres are engaged in the search experience.

Erickson, Rossi, and Rossi state that the effect of binds and double binds is to confuse the conscious mind with "mild quandaries" so that "choice is not easily made on a conscious voluntary level . . . and lead one to experience those altered states we characterize as trance so that previously unrealized potentials may become manifest" (1976, p. 63). We would simply apply the same explanation to paradox, a double bind of a special kind.

Several examples of paradoxical double binds are found in Erickson's induction with "Monde," a client who was hesitant to think highly of herself and was overly compliant in her interactions. One example which we have noticed has been frequently overlooked because it is characteristically subtle. It occurs in one of the first sentences to Monde as she is beginning to follow instructions to develop trance. Erickson said, "Not quite that fast Monde, . . . 'cause in the trance I will want you to do something of importance for you, and just for you" (Lustig, 1975). As Monde heard these words, Erickson could be sure that she would interpret them from a framework of someone who tries to please others, someone who is especially alert to the possibility of doing "wrong." Given this unique map of the world, the construction of the paradox was particularly personal.

Hearing the initial "Not that fast, Monde," she would question whether she was in the process of doing something incorrectly. For her, that was a very grave situation. In fact, her persistent sense of doing something wrong brought her to therapy. Erickson had spoken her language and captured her attention. It is likely that Monde, fixated and listening to the next part of that sentence (" . . . 'cause in the trance *I'll want you to* do something of importance"), would selectively hear the "I'll want you to" and ready herself to adaptively "do" the "something of importance" that Erickson was about to instruct her to do. But before she could identify and follow that instruction in her automatic fashion, an unexpected element was introduced—namely, that this "something" was to be of importance for *her*, and *just* for her. Furthermore, the something was unspecified and she suddenly found herself experiencing that moment of confusion, lack of muscle tonus, and lack of movement as she engaged in the search process to make meaning of his instruction. In so doing she would, paradoxically, have to please herself in order to please him.

Other varieties of therapeutic double binds include prescribing or encouraging the symptom. As we illustrated in the example of David, we prescribed the symptom of tension. David was instructed to experience his tension even more fully as a means of paradoxically developing trance and its inherent relaxation. We explained to him that his tension only served to illustrate that he would go into trance in his own unique way. He was instructed to review all parts of his tension in any order and discover in each part of his body just how he was developing trance. As he followed this first instruction he hypnotized himself quite adequately.

Encouraging the symptom to occur often involves the adjunct use of reframing (Chapter 8). By combining the two strategies the therapist can change the entire meaning of a situation with a "face-saving" positive attribution. Such was the case with the previously mentioned child abuser who, we said, was "trying to show his daughter he loved her." We paradoxically prescribed his attempts to hold on to and control his daughter. "Holding on" was redefined as a perfectly natural activity, albeit one which involved a natural progression of proper holding on. He was instructed to hold on by phone and eventually by holding her child (his grandchild). Thus, his abuse was reframed into holding on and then holding on was prescribed. He could save face and listen to us; what he heard was how to appropriately hold on to his daughter. Meanwhile, it must be remembered, we had helped him have the actual experiences of tenderness and security. Our words were not merely empty sounds but were related to real experiences.

There are several factors to consider in designing and delivering therapeutic paradoxical interventions. One factor involves the type of client who will benefit from such an approach. One simple formula has been suggested based on the fact that when people enter therapy they usually bring with them symptoms and/or goals. "When the more the client tries to avoid or get rid of the symptom, the more it occurs or the worse it gets, paradoxical intervention is probably appropriate. When the more the client strives to attain her/his goal, the farther away the goal seems to get, that is another indication for paradoxical intervention" (O'Hanlon, 1981). When it has been ascertained that paradoxical interventions are indicated, the following points are useful in constructing and delivering relevant paradoxical symptom prescriptions, reframing the meaning of the problem, and aligning resources necessary for change. These are:

1) Begin with verbal empathy and nonverbal matching.
2) Emphasize a positive interpretation of the problem.
3) Change the symptom with an unexpected alteration, "splitting," or addition to the way the problem is usually experienced.
4) Use anecdotes to retrieve resources and establish readiness to make the suggested alteration.
5) Deliver the paradoxical instruction in a one-down manner (or at least not one-up).
6) Deliver the paradoxical instruction either first or last in a therapeutic sequence.

In discussing these six requisite items, a few case examples will be useful. We begin with excerpts from Erickson's work with a retired couple. They entered therapy due to the husband's difficulty with phantom limb pain and the wife's problem with tinnitus (ringing in the ears).

They had been seen one time prior to this session. Joining and rapport had been accomplished in the first session such that "response attentiveness" (Erickson & Rossi, 1979, p. 104) was already well established and the need for nonverbal matching and verbal empathy was diminished. Therefore, when the wife began with the statement, "If we could lick that (the phantom pain), it would be wonderful," Erickson immediately responded with a simple: "All right." This was sufficient to imply the acceptance and empathy that had been established in the earlier interview. Then he continued, "Now I am going to give you a story so that you can understand better. We learn things in a very unusual way, a way that we don't know about" (Erickson & Rossi, 1979, p. 103). With this introduction, he briefly interpreted both problems as "things" that had been learned by the body automatically even though they didn't know how they were learned—or why. He also set the stage for their automatic use of learned relief mechanisms for those problems. Before prescribing the symptom and the relief mechanisms, however, he digressed on a tangential anecdote and brought into the foreground their awareness of the phenomena he would later suggest they use to alter their problems.

> In my first year of college I happened to come across that summer a boiler factory. The crews were working on 12 boilers at the same time and it was three shifts of workmen. And those pneumatic hammers were pounding away, driving rivets into the boilers. I heard that noise and I wanted to find out what it was. On learning that it was a boiler factory, I went in and I couldn't hear anybody talking. I could see the various employees were conversing. I could see the foreman's lips moving, but I couldn't hear what he said to me. He heard what I said. I had him come outside so I could talk to him. And I asked him for permission to roll up in my blanket and sleep on the floor for one night. He thought there was something wrong with me. I explained that I was a premedic student and that I was interested in learning processes. And he agreed that I could roll up in my blanket and sleep on the floor. He explained to all the men and left an explanation for the succeeding shift of men. The next morning I awakened. I could hear the workmen talking about the damn fool kid. What in hell was he sleeping on the floor there for? What did he think he could learn? During my sleep that night I blotted out all that horrible noise of the 12 or more pneumatic hammers and I could hear voices. I knew that it was possible to learn to hear only certain sounds if you tune your ears properly (Erickson & Rossi, 1979, pp. 103–104).

Having thus "warmed up" both clients to the idea of learning in ways they don't usually understand consciously, he delivered the paradoxical symptom prescription to the wife: "You have ringing in your ears, but you haven't thought of tuning them so that you don't hear the ringing." Thus, he accepted the ringing and suggested it was possible for her to keep it but simply not hear it. He "split" the occurrence of the sound into "having" and "hearing." He proceeded to relate various common examples of "tuning" oneself so that she could learn to hear the ringing or not at will. In this way he worked to align their own similar memories as convincing evidence that they already had and used the skills he was discussing:

> Now this matter of tuning yourself. I spent three months on the Mississippi River and I got invited into a home and I felt so cooped up after being out in the open. Getting into a room, everywhere you look, your looks come to an end. . . . And when I got back from that canoe trip, have you ever tried to sleep on a soft bed? You are miserable. I had learned to sleep on the ground, in brush piles, inside the canoe. My ribs fighting with canoe ribs. When I got home and had a mattress, that was torture. The Indians did not like, in the early days, the white man's bed. They wanted the ground to sleep on. They wanted comfort. Just nothing but sheer comfort. On the Tribal Eye program on KAET. Those nomads from Iran. How can they dress with all those petticoats? And be comfortable in the hot sun on those desert plains? And you can get so used to the ringing in your ears that you don't hear it. I grew up on the farm. I had to be away from the farm for quite some years before I learned the barn smell on your hands when you live on the farm. I never smelled it when I was on the farm. I had to be away from it for a long time before I discovered the barn smell (Erickson & Rossi, 1979, p. 105).

These anecdotes were common and real memories for the farm couple. He was speaking to their condition. When listeners make personal meaning of an anecdote and have the "idea," they will also demonstrate ideomotor response. Retrieving the understanding also brings the mental mechanisms and bodily phenomena into the foreground. The preceding anecdotes dealt with tuning auditory, visual, physical, and even olfactory senses in ways which could be automatically used by both husband and wife in the alleviation of their symptoms.

Though he had been ostensibly speaking primarily to the wife, the husband could be expected to benefit from the discussion of tuning, since his paradoxical symptom prescription was soon to follow. Erickson turned to him and asked where he felt the pain. The man responded that he felt it in his "foot which, of course, wasn't there." Erickson immediately responded with, "All right . . . " again accepting the difficulty and setting the stage for the forthcoming anecdote to establish readiness for the specific instruction:

> I had a friend named John. He was a psychiatrist, and we were visiting. He reached down and scratched his ankle. I said, "John, that really itches, doesn't it?" And he said, "Yes." We both knew it was a wooden leg. . . . " So you scratched it, how does your foot feel now?" He said,

"Good." . . . Because you can have good feelings in the foot, not just painful ones. . . . Now if you have phantom pain in a limb, you may also have phantom good feelings. And they are delightful (Erickson & Rossi, 1979, p. 106).

Thus Erickson prescribed the symptom as "go ahead and have phantom feelings," but altered or "split" the occurrence of the symptom by suggesting that phantom good feelings were also available precisely because he was "able" to have phantom pain. The client's response was simultaneously hopeful ("Oh, I hope so, Doctor") and incredulous that he could "tune" himself to experience pleasure instead of pain ("That I haven't had yet"). When Erickson countered, "But you can learn them," the client couldn't really disagree since he had just been identifying with numerous anecdotes about "learning to change sensory-perceptual experiences" (Erickson & Rossi, 1979, p. 107).

With regard to the last two points of designing paradoxical intervention, Erickson presented these symptom prescriptions in a one-down manner via metaphor and indirect advice. At no point in this phase did he authoritatively or directly tell either client how to behave. These interventions occurred as the initial transactions in a longer therapeutic sequence. The next phase involved formal trance inductions for both husband and wife. In that context Erickson directed a "reassociation" of learnings and automatized skills to occur at the first sign of their symptoms.

Since delivering the paradoxical instruction with a high pressure approach might easily arouse the client's resistance, Weakland, Fisch, Watzlawick and Bodin (1974) commented that a confused, ignorant stance on the part of the therapist seems to facilitate client compliance. As was just stated, the use of indirect advice through metaphor is another way to avoid being one-up and authoritative in giving the prescription.

Though Erickson frequently utilized this approach, he was also quite successful with other reported cases by setting up binding conditions prior to the paradoxical prescription, insisting that the client promise in advance that his directives would be followed without protest. We recommend this approach only for those particular situations where "high pressure" seems crucial and/or only for those clinicians with the degree of seniority, professional respect, and diagnostic acumen evidenced by Erickson.

It is neither necessary nor possible in every case involving paradoxical prescriptions to find all six points, but these six elements recur in various combinations when researching each case example and they are factors which contribute to the acceptance and success of this type of intervention. The first step of nonverbal matching and verbal empathy is a useful first move for gaining rapport in just about every therapeutic situation, but it is particularly important to have the kind of rapport this maneuver produces when instructing a client to do something which will be highly illogical from the current frame of reference. In the suicide case discussed in Chapter 2, Erickson's first move with the woeful, complaining woman was to empathize that she had certainly been treated so badly that it was perfectly logical and blameless of her to consider suicide. Having gained her trust rather rapidly in this manner, he then moved to the "alteration" phase in which he suggested it would be a damn shame for her to die and leave her money to those scoundrels who had treated her so badly—why not spend her money in a fashion he directed since she was going to kill herself anyway in three months? She accepted the alteration offered by the paradoxical "prescription" to have a "final fling," and of course did not follow through with her decision to kill herself, because through accepting the alteration she learned skills that quite sufficiently transformed her living.

In many cases, the positive interpretation element is intimately connected with the alteration element. The positive interpretation can often be the "logical" reason for following an otherwise illogical directive. For example, "Since your backache provides such an important feedback signal, why not experience it even sooner next time so that you can more immediately learn the valuable lesson it teaches you and monitor your activities accordingly" stresses the positive rather than negative aspect of the sensation. Or, as Erickson said, "that tired backache is a good pain—it means you've done a good day's work." Stressing the positive is a form of relabeling or reframing (Soper & L'Abate, 1977). Once a client has accepted that a behavior previously considered to be only negative is positive, there is a greater likelihood that an unusual sounding directive can be accepted and acted upon, paving the way for other experiences to be viewed from a different perspective and experienced differently.

Selvini Palazzoli, Boscolo, Cecchin, and Prata (1974, p. 433) declared themselves as allies of the family and approved the behaviors of the family members—particularly those members traditionally scapegoated—making them the family heroes, i.e., "By drawing attention to himself Giovanni has protected the whole family, and especially father and mother, from looking at themselves and how they behave." In another case the Milan group reported a martyr-like mother of a schizophrenic young boy who declared herself "changed" in an early session and no longer wanted to suffer. To this the therapists expressed concern over her premature change and described the importance of her suffering as a commendable virtue without which she would be at a severe loss (Soper & L'Abate, 1977, p. 14).

When operating in this way, the therapist is, in effect, accepting everything the client does as a positive, best choice. Creating a specific positive interpretation becomes very spontaneous, automatic, and sincere. Even if the positive intention is unspecified, it is at least assumed and communicated at various levels that this is the belief. Experiencing this attitude from the therapist, the client is likely to search for something useful in even the most bizarre sounding "alterations."

There are several dimensions along which we regularly create alterations. One involves the scheduling or timing of a problem. For instance, the problem can be experienced sooner, later, longer, shorter, on alternating days, more frequently, etc. Another is the location of the problem, whether it be the physical location of a somatic symptom or the geographical location where the problem takes place. Another is the intensity of the symptom. If a client can purposefully alter a symptom previously considered involuntary, a new measure of hope is realized. So even making a pain more intense, or having it at an unaccustomed time of the day, or having it move to a different part of the body will produce for the client a therapeutic sense of control over the symptom. It is then possible to either dispense with the symptom altogether or to use it positively as a signaling device that becomes an associative link to needed resources and preferred methods of responding to the situation(s) which had previously produced the symptom. In this latter case, especially, we think of paradox as a doorway to second-order change.

Adding a slight alteration to the symptom prescription can be accomplished with a simple addition of a previously unassociated behavior, as when Erickson told the young boy to go ahead and stomp the office (as he intended to do) as hard and long as he wanted *but*—he wouldn't be able to stand still once he had finished because he was just a little boy who would have to squirm and fidget. In this way, a resource "tag-along" was challenged when the boy accepted the symptom prescription. Also providing an example of the simple addition alteration was the previously mentioned suicide case in which the woman was convinced to spend her money learning to live —since she was going to kill herself anyway.

Another dimension of altering the problem which is frequently useful is the instruction to "split" the problem between its physical and psychological components. This involves a perceptual and/or qualitative change in the way the problem is experienced. For example, a person complaining of pain can be presented the paradoxical split between noticing the tension and noticing the pain. In this example, a split has been offered between the observation of the physical component (tension) and the psychological component (pain). Similarly a case of embarrassment over blushing resulted in the paradoxical directive to "continue, if you must, to experience sensitivity about the color change but enjoy the warmth." A split was thus designed between an embarrassing social component of the symptom and a pleasant sensation. The prescription was more specifically defined as "that embarrassing color" and "that surge of warmth." The resulting split and conscious confusion allowed for an entrance into the topic of enjoyment of erotic experiences in general and how one can use that knowledge to enjoy the warm surge "to which someone as lonely as you are is certainly entitled." The logic is only apparent in such a split and confusion ensues in the client's mind for a moment in an attempt to determine what is logical and what is not. This pause of confusion is a therapeutic opening which provides a pathway to change.

In an upcoming transcript with "Tracy" (see Chapter 6), we had induced trance and spoken of the "bad luck" that can come to a person. In this way we further satisfied the first requirement of establishing the empathic connection. Tracy had experienced severe headaches for 12 years since her son's violent death and had tried every explanation for her headaches, including "bad luck." Then we continued, "We don't know why things happen. . . . But enough bad luck can come one's way, you don't need to add to it. You'll always have a good supply of that. But you do need to add to the good luck and the good things that come your way." With this we had set the stage with "folksy" advice or a simple anecdote as advised in item four.

Item five involves presenting the suggestion, not one-up, but rather as an observation about "life" in general. In this equal or one-down manner we deal with item three, specifically, "splitting" her experience of the problem: "Some people think they have to wait for good luck; that they have no choice in the matter of being lucky. That's because they're not really thinking of luck as choice. (Nonverbally): Go ahead and notice your bad luck. (Verbally again): as that unique moment when preparation meets opportunity."

Tracy experienced relief from her headache for many reasons. The paradox did not provide a magical cure, but it did provide the opportunity to change her frame of reference about her "excuse" and other beliefs. Her temporary change of mind allowed us to help her develop her awareness of the resources which she needed. When you read that transcript, notice those interventions which elaborate item four and associate her to her experiential resources. Finally, having delivered the paradox at the beginning of this therapeutic sequence (item six), we arrive "at the door of opportunity and preparation" and then move to provide a link between retrieved resources and Tracy's situational cues in the therapy that follows.

As was just mentioned, we consider paradox to be a doorway to second-order change. We have introduced it toward the beginning of this book, preceding metaphor, induction and direct treatment patterns, in the same way that it is advantageously introduced toward the beginning in a therapy session, before "official" induction has signaled actual treatment. We see it as central to the basic framework of accepting whatever the client is doing, uti-

lizing and/or prescribing presenting behaviors, then making a slight alteration which will associate the client to internal resources and change the
"problem" into an "ally." It underscores the difference between Erickson's approach and the historical hypnotic approaches that rely upon relaxation to
begin therapy. Erickson, though he frequently elicits relaxation, begins with
the presented behavior, even if it seems resistant, and paradoxically pre-
scribes its continuance as his first step in therapy.

Paradox does not require hypnotic trance to be powerful and yet that "moment of confusion" we've spoken of certainly fixates attention on internal
processes, as the client searches to make meaning of the communication just
received. In this regard, a naturalistic "trance" has already begun. Whether
the trance is then deepened and utilized or whether a series of metaphors is offered in "nonhypnotic" style, the paradox has facilitated a state of readiness
to "listen with new ears," "see with new eyes," "feel differently," because no
previous framework adequately applies and a new frame has been offered.

To the extent that the metaphors provide readily understandable examples
of the paradoxical directive, the client will have a sense of the therapy being
relevant and valuable. For example, after instructing Monde (Lustig, 1975) to
"do something of importance for you and just for you," her search for meaning provided an opportunity for Erickson to induce eye closure and deepen
trance rapidly. She didn't know what was "of importance" for her; that, in
fact, was one of the problems that brought her to therapy. So Erickson assisted
her by encouraging her to recall something very nice that she hadn't
thought of for years. To stimulate her memory, he then began a discourse on
children discovering the world: " . . . Such as the time when you discovered
you could stand up and the entire world looked different. The world suddenly takes on a wonderful look when you stand up and are no longer creeping.
And, older, you bent over and looked at the world from between your legs
. . . " (Lustig, 1975). In this way Monde was able to respond appropriately to
the earlier directive to do something of importance for her. And, after all,
what could be more important than retrieving her own experience of wonder-
ment, curiosity, self-worth, etc.?

This paradox was presented to Monde at the beginning of her therapy session. It left her conscious mind in search and her unconscious more open to
the elicitation of resources in the session. Another approach with paradox is
to present the client with resources first and end the therapy session with a
paradox that, by its confusing nature, actually gives more meaning to the
metaphoric content that preceded it.

In Chapter 7 on multiple embedded metaphor is a complete transcript of a
client referred to as Dorine. She was a client who presented herself for treatment in a complaining, demanding, bitter, and incongruently angry way.

She stated she was "tired of being responsible for her own support" and resented that no one was volunteering for the job. Here, then, was a client who was socially isolated and who, by pushing people away, was likely to remain that way.

The therapy she received, while discussed more fully later, could be summarized here as a series of metaphors designed to help her put her past behind her and help her interact with others without the framework of bitter complaining. Finally, a paradox was presented to her at the end of the therapy session. We suggested that she not give up any of her faults (that kept her separated from others) because her faults would help her understand the faults of others. The more faults she had, the more people she could know and understand. The fact that she sensed faults in others (her bitter complaints) was then to be a sign that she was like them. Also, her deep sense of inadequacy was lessened to the extent that understanding her own faults was actually the reason she could have friends (rather than the reason to avoid others).

While she had a moment to think about that consciously, her search was likely to leave her only with the meanings implied in the previous metaphors. Those metaphors served as the basis for retrieving and organizing many experiences of both a positive and negative nature. Alternative conclusions after considering the paradox are summarized:

1) If she finds faults with others noticed by virtue of the fact that she, too, has faults, then she can't avoid others because she is superior.
2) If she notices her own faults and does not change them, she has the opportunity to notice that others also have faults and she is not worse than others. Thus, she can't avoid contact because she is inferior.
3) If she gives up her faults, she has no reason to defend against social contact. She won't be avoiding others as a defensive measure.

The metaphors used prior to the paradox were designed to help her sort and organize her resources so that she might be better prepared to meet others in her future. The paradox, by confusing her normal frame of reference (that she has faults and should stay away to avoid rejection—or that others have faults and she should stay away due to her superiority), opened the door to the change proposed in the previous metaphors. Here then, we find paradox equally effective when used at the very end of a therapeutic sequence.

As stated earlier, paradox is often introductory to and compatible with metaphor. The use of paradox opens access to a new frame of reference, and the use of metaphor provides associations to experiences of life that have previously been unused. We turn now to a detailed elaboration of several components of metaphor, and the use of metaphor to help tap into the storehouse of life's experiences. We discuss elements of drama in metaphor and introduce an overview of steps to create multiple embedded metaphors. We then examine each step separately, keeping in mind that people are only free to comprehend completely to the extent that they allow themselves to comprehend in part.

Now this matter of complete comprehension. . . . Looking over The Black Forest from the perspective of the airplane revealed only its vast scope. Having never explored that particular forest before, the naturalist could only speculate about the unique life forms he would encounter there. He did expect that he would find trees, shrubs and animals typical of other forests he had explored in his own country. But still he looked forward with excitement to the moment when, embedded in the heart of that enchanted forest, he would scarcely remember the total picture because his attention would be captured and delighted with his personal discovery of those unique life forms that he could only wonder about from the airplane. He knew that not seeing the forest for the trees would enable him to really see the forest in a way he would remember when next he surveyed it from the air.

HYBRIDS OF COMPARISON

Come, fill the Cup, and in the fire of Spring
Your Winter-garment of Repentance fling:
The Bird of Time has but a little way
To flutter—and the Bird is on the Wing

In *The Rubiyat of Omar Khayyam* (1952, p. 82), the concept of time and the idea of a bird are married to create a unique poetic image. Not only is the image alive and tangible but it is vibrantly compelling. Poetry kisses the senses and caresses the mind in an embrace created by both the lyric and the cortex. This love affair is created by simile, comparison, anecdote, and metaphor. A metaphor is a figure of speech that makes an implicit comparison between two unlike entities. You may recall that the use of "like" or "as," in making comparison, will create a simile. For the purpose of Ericksonian communication, we do not need to rigorously make distinctions between these figures of speech. Nor are technical differences between stories, anecdotes and metaphors of concern to us.

In this clinically oriented volume, we will consolidate these various forms in the category of metaphor. The distinction between simile and metaphor is not qualitatively different, since both make a leap from reason and prosaic comparison to a blending or fusion between two or more objects, processes, or experiences. Indeed, the metaphor often contains elements of both of the original items or situations that were blended together. In the "bird of time" metaphor, both the passing of time and the behavior of fluttering birds are suggested. This fusion or blend, then, ascribes to our conception of time other bird-like qualities (such as apparent randomness of direction and care-free movement) and produces a hybrid idea that did not previously exist.

These are compelling features of therapeutic metaphors used by Erickson —stories guaranteed to engage clients in a search for meaning and to engage them in a way that was valuable, in itself, because of the mental motivation that was generated.

FRAME CHANGES

The perceptual predisposition of clients presenting themselves for therapy is part of their problem. Clients usually seek to become clients when their manner of perceiving viable options has left all options exhausted, unbear-able, or unattractive. They either sense no change for their concerns or they sense changes that they do not desire. The exceptional client enters therapy to enhance already blooming personal growth. For the majority of clients, ther-apy is a necessity or a "last ditch effort" to gain relief from problems that are immediately threatening. Their perceptions about possible change are locked or obscured and helping them alter perceptions is at the foundation of change in psychotherapy.

Regardless of the therapeutic approach, whether behavioral, relationship-oriented, cognitive, or muscle-oriented, an alteration in the client's percep-tual predisposition must accompany the outcomes achieved, so as to provide altered expectations of upcoming situations and potential resources. Living is, after all, an interaction with the physical and social world, requiring that an organism sense and apprehend information such as food, energy, temper-ature, language, etc., and then behave appropriately. As that organism acts to survive, work, create, and enjoy, it must repeatedly apprehend informa-tion regarding the results of its activity and make further modifications.

For the psychotherapy client this may amount to the establishment of stimulus discrimination for a particular behavior. That could be the adjust-ment of parataxic or transference distortions in a relationship, perceptions creating cognitive consonance in a new cognitive framework, or perceptions of proprioceptive and affective constellations as new roles and feelings are ac-quired. These perceptions may be reducible to such observations and mem-ories as a child abuser seeing and hearing his child's cries instead of the screaming in his head from his childhood. But that's not all. He must change perceptions so as to apprehend the communication from his wife when it is a request for tenderness. And, too, he must perceive the experience of tender-ness and the muscle movements that provide biofeedback to him that he is in the role of a tender husband. All of these new perceptions and more must be associated into a framework or map of the world that he considers viable, ef-fective, and acceptable.

The Ericksonian approach requires that the therapist involve clients in therapy by appealing to the perceptual framework they bring into the office. Speaking the client's language, putting one foot in the doorway of the client's world, and utilizing the client's presenting behavior are the initial therapeutic tasks designed to engage the client by appealing to preexisting perceptions. The use of metaphor, following that beginning, blends new hybrids of mean-ing into that framework. The client's own mental activity creates a unique understanding of the hybrid, and in doing so, begins the process of change by altering perceptions. Nothing of the original thinking and understanding is surrendered. Instead, new associations, new meanings, and new understand-ings are gained, thus enriching rather than reducing the client.

Fixating attention and stimulating the client's own thinking are two gener-al goals. The use of metaphor is particularly compatible with the values and principles Erickson promoted: meeting clients at their model of the world; re-specting communications from clients; teaching choice instead of removing it; and developing experiential resources from "within." Whether therapy is structured with formally induced trance or naturalistically shared metaphor, the fixation of attention provides the means by which concentration can be heightened and the client can be prepared for the exchange of ideas and exper-iences.

This seems to present a paradox. How is it that attention and perception can be fixated and, at the same time, changes in perception facilitated? On the one hand it seems that the therapist thus capturing attention is stabilizing and reinforcing a perceptual set; yet on the other hand a framework is created that conveys the possibility of change. Stimulated by the enchantment of meta-phor, an unconscious search for meaning takes place. Erickson and Rossi speculated that this unconscious search occurred faster than conscious per-ceptions could observe (Erickson & Rossi, *CP* I, p. 457). The search engages more than conscious attention. Metaphors engage normal comprehension-making mechanisms of the mind more effectively than logical speech. While conducting a massive mental search for related associations, the mind brings together the common symbols and elements of a new perceptual framework by entertaining the metaphoric theme. The blending of the original percep-tual framework and the metaphoric framework only increase the number of associations that seem relevant. The presence of so many possible associa-tions creates the same effect on the mind as that produced by unconditioned stimuli: heightened attentiveness.

Perceptual alertness is increased by the addition of a new framework. Consciousness is partially engaged in investigating this new framework. Attention is thus held and yet change is also presupposed. The client's own thoughts, stimulated by listening to the metaphor, provide personal evidence that the character, the meaning, or the problem is changing. Since the new metaphor is a framework that is not identical to the client's original understanding, new options are conveyed. We should expect that these options will be different for each individual (even in response to the same or similar metaphors), since the hybrid ideas will be a result of a unique interaction with a particular individual's personal history.

These new options, tentatively formulated by the client, may be expected to precede eventual perceptual, behavioral, emotional, and social role changes, though the "comfort range" may also need to be expanded with systematic self-image thinking in order to accommodate such changes. We present the following examples, categorized according to specific changes, as an aid in creating treatment plans that offer more than mere random attempts to convey ideas to clients.

PERCEPTUAL CHANGES

Aesop's Fables are a favorite source of instructional material in our culture. One well-known story involves the little boy who cried "wolf." In this story a boy is entrusted with the chore of overseeing a flock of sheep. He enjoys crying out "wolf" as a predictable method of arousing the townspeople and securing attention. However, he calls wolf too often and the people of the town habituate to his false alarm. As the story goes, the boy eventually encounters the real wolf and when he shouts for help no one pays any attention to his pleas.

The story represents a cultural example of using metaphor to create attitudinal and perceptual change. The listener is expected to alter perceptions related to narcissistic, self-centered, immediate gratification to approximate the perceptions of the townspeople. Perception is thus changed from a personal to a societal frame of reference. The protocol for use of this method is: The protagonist's position is examined first from his or her own perspective and then from that of the other characters. Finally, consequences of each significant person's behavior are related to the perceptions each held.

The same approach works in therapeutic metaphors, though it is not necessary to crudely state the moral at the end, as was done in Aesop's children's stories. The storyteller does need, however, to examine the protagonist's position from two or more perspectives and eventually show how that attitude results in good or bad consequences. In that way the detailed portion of the metaphor highlights the attitudinal aspect of experience. As a result, clients will examine their own attitudes and be encouraged to consider different attitudes. They will have a heightened understanding of the relationship between attitude and behavior and consequently will be better prepared to create changes in attitude.

BEHAVIORAL CHANGES

The parable of the good Samaritan (Luke 10:30–37) has been told so often that the term "good Samaritan" is literally a household phrase. The point of the parable is that one should conduct oneself in a manner similar to the Samaritan who helped the unfortunate traveler and not like the priest or Levite who passed him by. No statistics describe the countless number of children who have altered their behavior as a result of hearing this parable in Sunday school, but we speculate, from personal observation of our clients, that behavior is frequently changed as a direct result of hearing such a metaphor.

The general protocol for designing metaphors to elicit behavior change involves describing the *motivation* of others in less detail (as compared to the first example of Aesop's fable) but detailing the *behavior* demonstrated and the results of the behavior. For instance, Erickson once described one of his colleagues and his wife, whom he had known since medical school. As the story goes, Tom and Martha invited him to go swimming at a lake adjacent to the hospital farm, but Tom was phobic: He wouldn't swim; feared promotion and responsibility; repeatedly postponed having children; and even bathed with a "lousy one inch" of water in the tub. Due to Tom's hesitancy the couple never had children and he eventually retired without ever advancing professionally (Zeig, 1980, p. 255). Personally relating the story to us, Erickson concluded: "And life went by. Tom never took the chance. He's dead now . . . and I'll bet he's sitting in the back row in heaven. And I pity the poor one who's sitting there with him. Either you take things when they come along or forever hold your peace" (Erickson, personal communication, December, 1979)! This story obviously includes a detailed consequence of the character's behaviors, and the behaviors themselves were elaborated at length before the consequence was shared.

We are interested in behavior change that results from hearing a story and yet our definition of metaphor is so broad that almost any alteration in a framework could be considered metaphor. Giving highway directions, for example, could be considered a model for the behavior of driving to some destination. Successful directions involve detailing particular behaviors at specific choice points with sufficient precision and elaboration so that the prescribed acts can be approximated by the listener.

But even more than with attitudinal changes, the storyteller's personal credibility influences the apparent validity of the metaphor's message. Consider receiving highway directions from someone who expressed them so improperly or so incongruently that following the directions was out of the question. It didn't even matter if they were correct because the perceived credibility (or lack of it) of the direction provider invalidated them. By contrast, many people have faithfully followed incorrect directions given by someone who seemed very believable. To favorably enhance personal congruence we recommend therapists use true metaphors whenever possible. Then even the most unbelievable stories can be told with the "courage of conviction."

Actually motivating a person to enact new behaviors is somewhat more difficult than getting him or her to simply consider a different attitude. Behavior change is influenced by several factors, including status of the storyteller, affective involvement, concern with the consequences, social pressures, and coping tendencies (Zander, 1968, p. 428). How these factors influence individuals depends on how they perceive themselves in comparison with others in their social network. Increased resistance or increased motivation can result as clients hear a new metaphoric framework detailed. The therapist must take these diagnostic features into account and engage, utilize, or paradoxically prescribe interfering perceptions and attitudes; otherwise, metaphors designed to elicit change may be as irrelevant as unsolicited highway directions.

AFFECT CHANGES

Another type of behavior change involves not motor behavior, but affective or emotional behavior. Who cannot recall those ghost stories of one's youth? A good ghost story would, of course, elicit shivers and fears on an emotional level. But also, a good ghost story would produce long-term avoidance behavior of certain "haunted houses," hillsides, and woods. The avoidance was created, often unconsciously, as a method to help suppress those fearful emotions.

Ghost stories provide an example of metaphors which stimulate an interplay between perceptual, behavioral, and affective alterations but emphasize the affective dimension. Non-ordinary perceptions, such as so-called experiences of extrasensory perception, can be the result of alterations that begin as unexplainable or undetected shifts in emotional affect. This unexplainable shift can be stimulated by listening to a story, a poem, a song, a metaphor, a movie, or a bizarre framework related by an acquaintance.

Readiness for non-ordinary perception—and this need not be arcane—is prefigured or preset as a result of unnoticed emotional shifts created by images in the story line. Alterations in affect alter the person's expectations about sensory information. Unusual sensory information may be accepted or sought to account for the emotional change which was not understood and which may not have even been noticed consciously. This phenomenon not only is therapeutically relevant but may also help explain a variety of unusual or psychotic perceptions of some clients.

Therapeutically, for example, an emotional shift might first be stimulated via metaphor, such as in the case of the child abuser who was told the emotionally moving anecdote about the puppy. Then, while experiencing emotions of which he was only vaguely aware, we asked him to open his eyes and examine his daughter. As he did, we could be certain that he was prepared for new perceptions—perceptions that would support his non-ordinary emotions. Thus we created an emotional shift upon which a perceptual change was built. Finally, both of these alterations were used to support a behavioral change. Since his emotional shift created a perceptual readiness for apprehending those things we pointed out about his daughter, our personal credibility and social status became less important variables in his subsequent behavioral change.

Many years ago one of the authors coordinated a crisis intervention center immediately adjacent to a theatre in which "The Exorcist" was first shown. The center was noticeably filled in the evenings by a large number of individuals with a novel crisis after watching the movie. Frightening movies in general and particularly "The Exorcist" elicited in certain viewers a fear that was not ordinary. Concurrent with the elicitation of fear and an altered readiness for perception, the viewer was presented with an explanation for the fear from a framework of demonic possession. The result for some unfortunate viewers was an alteration in perception that convinced them they were possessed.

While it is quite likely that those who believed themselves to be possessed were predisposed to certain thought disorders (although we did not have this information), results of exposure to "The Exorcist" are no less convincing. In fact, it would seem that the change in perceptions was accomplished by first matching and then utilizing, as it were, the perceptual predispositions of the affected viewers.

In therapeutic settings Erickson often told a metaphor about instructions he gave his parents when they retired from the farm: how he told them to go to many locations on the farm (fields, stoves, attics, porches, etc.), visit each one, reminisce, and "Say Goodbye!" In relating the story he had the opportunity to repeat the words "Say Goodbye!" as ambiguous commands, thus facilitating therapeutic grieving for those clients who needed to respond in that manner. This story is detailed in Chapter 8.

It is apparent that hearing this story would bring to mind associations of finality. A client inhibiting responses to finalities such as death and divorce would be moved to emotional catharsis via the alteration of frameworks. Here the formula for creating emotional change includes detailing the protagonist's relationship with things (or others) to which there is an attachment. Other alterations in the attachment (in addition to severing it) may be used to elicit different emotions. For instance, moving toward elicits erotic experience; moving against elicits aggressive experience; inability to move despite a desire to do so produces frustration; desire to move changing to necessity to move may transform frustration to fear; moving without knowing what results the movement will bring produces anxiety; movement into behavior which has been forbidden produces guilt. And so it goes with the production of affect via metaphor.

Detailing and emphasizing different parts of a metaphor can produce attitudinal, behavioral, and emotional changes, as well as perceptual predispositions which will reinforce those changes. Before applying these methods for creating those results to various therapeutic outcomes that correspond to the diagnostic assessment of the client, there is one final piece of preparation to be considered.

We have shown that self-motivated thought (searching), blending of hybrid ideas, and discovering myriad associations to metaphors eliminate the client's original perceptual predisposition. But there is another psychological component to Ericksonian metaphors which addresses the paradox of fixating attention while presupposing and stimulating change. That component is the element of drama. It seems that people are prone to surrender their original perceptual frameworks and withhold their biases and impressions for long periods of time when drama is present in a story.

DRAMA IN METAPHOR

Since the narrative mechanisms (written or spoken) that convey dramatic movement impart a sense of the character's history, the listener assumes an attitude of expectancy toward the material in the story. Metaphors employing those same devices suggest to clients what is taught by history and experience: "Things change in time." Dramatic interest is a phrase to describe this perceptual alteration or predisposition. Thus, creating drama in metaphor facilitates both fixation and a new framework in which change can begin. As the client, through unconscious processes, associates similarities of dramatic action in the metaphor with events in his or her own life, the hybrid becomes an internal map which contains elements from both.

In order to have a story we must have movement. Movement in a storyline creates drama. Experts on drama have agreed on at least three types of specific drama. These are mystery, suspense, and shock or surprise. Alfred Hitchcock offered a formula for creating stories characteristic of these three dramatic styles. It involves three factors: the character(s) in the story, the audience, and information about what is going to happen. When something happens that simultaneously surprises both the audience and the characters, "shock" has been created. When the audience knows that something is about to happen but the character(s) is unsuspecting, the situation is one of "suspense." "Mystery" is created when some characters in the story have information about something which is not yet known to the audience.

These dramatic elements can be added in various combinations to any story. Consider a hypothetical story: It begins as the audience overhears only a bit of a conversation between the main characters who are on board a boat. The conversation is well under way when the audience tunes in; since something is known to the characters that is unknown to the audience, there is an element of mystery which tends to bind the audience and fixate attention. As the action unfolds, more and more of the mystery is revealed to them until it is finally resolved. Mystery is resolved when the question "What?" is answered.

Meanwhile, if a large wave unexpectedly rises and knocks the hypothetical characters off of the boat, everyone is surprised. The audience's attention is now further fixated by shock as they await the aftermath of the unexpected wave and how its impact will affect the course of the already existing mystery. Shock immediately resolves its own drama. It reminds the observer that "something unexpected has happened and something else might happen." Therefore, it is implied that one should be alert for new clues and dramatic developments.

Suspense can be entered into the plot by giving the audience knowledge about an upcoming event that the characters have no way of knowing about. For example, if the audience glimpses a patrol boat making its way toward the characters capsized in shark-infested waters, an obviously suspenseful situation now exists. The audience becomes spellbound with the obvious need for closure on the important issue of the possible sea rescue. They have an opportunity to actively engage in probability thinking. Questions such as "Will the boat get there in time?" are essentially induced in the minds of the audience. The suspense continues until it is resolved with information or circumstances which answer the question: "When?"

Mystery, shock, and suspense are elements of drama which, woven into a story, facilitate active problem-solving by the audience. The attention of the audience or client is fixated on the story and becomes involved in it through personal mental engagement.

DRAMATIC THEME AND THERAPEUTIC OUTCOMES

In the course of producing drama, knowledge of the story ending or outcome is important. Placing clues about the ending in certain relationship to the listener creates the desired dramatic "holding." It is similarly beneficial to conceive of the desired therapeutic outcome. Psychotherapy and clinical hypnosis are broad fields containing many different approaches, "schools," and ideas about the "true" path toward change, but in any therapeutic situation we expect to find change occurring in one or more of the following six areas of a client's life. We propose these six areas as major arenas in which to measure therapeutic change, regardless of the type of treatment. In our own work we insist on evidence of change in each area before we consider treatment complete:

1) Bonding and age-appropriate intimacy.
2) Self-image enhancement.
3) Attitude restructuring.
4) Social role change.
5) Family structure change.
6) Enjoyment of life.

After coordinating information gathered from the initial diagnostic assessment, we question the kinds of changes a client might need to make in these six areas of personal development. Consider the complicated situation of the following case. Diagnostic information about the patient is presented in the order that it unfolded in the interview and is then related to the formation of dramatic themes for the metaphors which were subsequently told to her.

The client, a woman in her early sixties who was employed as a civil servant, articulately reported a physical problem that had been medically examined and found to have no physical or organic basis. She suffered from pain in her right hand which she associated with other disturbing feelings in her elbow and shoulder.

Her presentation of this problem was puzzling in that she described herself as procrastinating in getting medical help for it, yet stated that she had indeed consulted several medical sources in the past without getting assistance. She had been told that the problem was not severe enough or that she might need more extensive testing and she was concerned that she had not followed through properly.

We asked why she didn't wait until it became worse and get extensive medical help then. She said this was what she had planned but that she should take better care of herself in these matters, as she believed her husband would have done. She explained further that she had been separated from him for three years. The problem in her hand, by some coincidence, had also existed for three years. She believed the pain in her hand would cause difficulty in writing and signing her name.

She made no conscious connection between the three years of separation, the three years of pain in her hand, and the importance of signing her name for divorce papers and other legal matters. However, an important symbol of independence is one's valid signature. On the practical side, getting a divorce and taking steps in her own behalf would require signing her name and this was the one thing she thought would become increasingly difficult. When asked what would happen if she let the problem go untreated, she replied with disgust in her voice, "My husband would probably come and take care of me medically," then added, "but he would not give me any sympathy!"

So, the "meaning" of this problem became evident. She wanted some sympathy from her husband and she did not have the resources she needed in order to feel good or to want the divorce. Exactly what such "sympathy" meant to this unique individual was not yet known to us. It might have meant that she would finally get from her husband that which she had never gotten, perhaps recognition for effort expended. It could have been a sign that she had not yet ended her denial of the separation and its realities. It might have meant some kind of forgiveness and end to the separation. There were also other possibilities.

It was important to respect the dichotomy and incongruence between her conscious and unconscious thought processes. While her conscious mind continued to believe she had separated from her husband with her consent and desire, a portion of her unconscious energy was constructing a symptom that would hurt the most when she had to sign her name. Her conscious mind would find an answer for the difficulty in the framework of "procrastination and medical care," while her unconscious problem-solving mechanisms would continue to provide a unique adjustment to her problems of personal transition. We formulated metaphors to appeal to both parts "because his (sic) conscious mind cannot deal directly with the unconscious, the limitations of the conscious level are held in check until the unconscious can marshal a solution through some original problem-solving" (Erickson & Rossi, *CP* I, p. 422).

Even though she had presented only a small part of her entire situation, initial diagnostic assessment indicated a woman who believed she would be ultimately disappointed by the authorities if she sought help for her problem. In addition to this obvious theme, her unconscious mind could be depended on to work for solutions to the broader and more relevant issues of divorce and readjustment. These issues posed special problems for a person at her age, in the type of social network that she had, as well as the type of network and family connections she was likely to develop in her future.

Constructing a treatment plan for the multiple embedded metaphor modality requires first identifying several metaphoric themes that are relevant to the client's conscious and unconscious concerns. To do this, we review the six areas in which change is to be reflected after therapy. For this client at least six dramatic themes were selected, all of which would likely remain outside her conscious awareness. These are summarized as:

1) *Bonding and stabilizing age-appropriate intimacy.* Must get closure and distance from family members.
2) *Self-image enhancement.* Self-image must adjust to her being alone at her age, caring for self, and being proud of her abilities.
3) *Attitude restructuring.* Person who thinks authorities will disappoint her ultimately needs to change her attitude to trust that she can depend on others.
4) *Social role change.* She must learn to express her anger and channel part of it toward the task of taking good care of herself even if no one appreciates her.
5) *Family structure change.* Children raise families of their own and do not give as much to their parents. She must live alone or find a new mate or alternative lifestyle.
6) *Enjoyment of life.* Person seeks and finds satisfaction in retirement or develops career opportunities.

These metaphoric themes would be likely to address important aspects of this woman's general development of cognitive, emotional, and experiential options. But we would not discuss them with her without their being altered in some metaphoric way. Let's imagine just one element of her dilemma. She needs to be ordering her life to become satisfied with retirement or generate other options, regardless of her relationship with her husband. This and her adjustment to the divorce were surely the most stressing situations for her but she had "procrastinated" dealing with either of them.

We could begin by directly questioning her: "What are you doing about the bigger picture of . . . ?" While that might be appropriate, the result of that line of questioning would only reveal what we already knew—that she had not been consciously considering these problems and had "reasons" to explain her avoidance. We might instead begin with a simple metaphor: "I knew a client once who found satisfaction after retirement." But this crass approach could be worse than ineffectual because it would not respect the fact that she had been attempting to adjust in her world for years but had not included associations to retirement and satisfaction. That was not how she conceptualized her situation. Simply relating stories in this manner would surely arouse resistance and fracture the rapport and trust that had been developed. Furthermore, it would imply that her problem was far larger than she consciously considered it to be and this would constitute an unmerciful extra burden to add to her already heavy load. And, in her case, it would be interpreted as further evidence that authorities disappoint her and do not give her the sympathy she needs.

We would deal with what was important but would opt for introducing it in a more indirect manner. For instance, instead of talking about a person who is not finding satisfaction in retirement, we might metaphorically discuss aspects of a rose from bud to full bloom, eventually unfolding its petals, producing seed and being suspended in full beauty for the enjoyment of the environment and its owner prior to the final cyclical demise.

In that way, we would be addressing her upcoming retirement and other matters related to her stage of social development, but in a nonthreatening and metaphorical way. Metaphor provides an altered framework in which novel experiences can be entertained. The process of engaging in a career, developing competence, and then seeking and finding satisfaction in retirement is parallel to the evolution of a maturing rose. The bud begins its life taking in an abundance of nutrients. As it grows it soon blooms, revealing sexual parts. It produces a beauty which is pleasing to all who experience it and which also serves to attract insects to complete its propagation. Once its cycle has run its course, the rose, as a mature flower, having survived to bring pleasure and seed, dies proudly in order to assist the development of the new growth on the bush. It would be foolish and even embarrassing for a rose not to comply with this fate, as all its beauty lies in its conformity to the natural cycle of true roses. In some cases it is fortunate enough to be removed from the bush before it dies, so that its beauty can be shared with unexpected others while also making it possible for the bush to bloom even more fully.

Discussing that particular theme in symbolic and metaphoric fashion offered this client an opportunity to examine ideas related to finding satisfaction outside her normal framework of priorities. In this new framework she could think about the priorities of the flower, such as making seed, sprouting buds, and attracting the bee. While reordering priorities in the metaphor about the rose, she could also consider her satisfactions and the importance of fulfilling goals outside her current framework of dissatisfaction.

Looking at the themes related to therapeutic outcomes, we can translate them into metaphors by answering the question "What is this parallel or similar to?" Once translated, we can embellish them with elements of drama and various interventions in the context of multiple embedded metaphor. The following six metaphors were derived from the above outcome themes:

1) New distance between family members: An office puts up partitions between workers as the company gets larger and more mature.
2) Self-image changes: Bottle of wine improves with age when left alone.
3) Her attitude of disappointment in authority must turn to trust and hope: A child who hides from policemen, fearing they would disappoint her as her parents had done, examines her childish reasons in the course of growing up and comes to regard policemen as helpful.
4) Changing role and expressing new emotions: A young adult moving from one country to another has to learn to drive on a different side of the road and follow different customs; he needs to be assertive but not offensive.
5) Family structure changes as children begin to have their own families: An architect eventually learns that his buildings are his own only as he designed them, but when they were completed people moved in and used the buildings, making them their own and using them in ways far different from the way he might have planned.
6) Retirement: Rose bud grows to full bloom and death.

Once the dramatic themes have been outlined and metaphors sketched, decisions are made as to which portion will be most detailed. This emphasis will affect the client's learning to make perceptual, affective, or behavioral alterations. Specific drama is also included to hold the client's interest by considering the outcomes of the stories and deciding when and how they will be introduced to generate suspense, mystery, or shock.

The actual outcome, or story ending, of the metaphors is not nearly so important, therapeutically, as the stimulation of associations in the detailed portions within them. However, the choice of ending may be influenced by the client's "nature." A cynical person, for example, would not expect the rose to be proud of a final appreciative glance it receives from a passerby. In fact, the cynical person would fully expect an indignant demise of the rose by something such as a lawn mower blade. The therapist might then arrange the finale to surprise the normal frame of reference of the client in a gentle manner. A person who is overly optimistic might expect exactly the opposite, but the therapist might still choose the pleasant ending because of the good feeling and positive associations it would be sure to elicit.

In this case we chose the following six endings:

1) The office workers appreciate the walls between them.
2) Old bottles of wine are enjoyed in many ways: with two intimate friends, between lovers, among a group of acquaintances, at a family reunion, and to celebrate success.
3) The child becomes an adult who respects others because she ex-

amines her parents' inadequate responses, which are described in detail, and comes to see others as peers.

4) The young immigrant was so offensive he lived a lonely life but the client is reinforced for learning what he never learned.
5) The architect changes his attitude as he begins a design to insure his good feelings in the end.
6) The rose dies proud and its dried leaves find their way into an expensive potpourri because of their delicate and haunting fragrance.

Each of these metaphors could serve for developing behavioral, perceptual, or emotional change. It is only a matter of which part of the metaphor is detailed. At this phase of the book we are elaborating the components of complex multiple embedded metaphors, examining the bits and pieces needed in construction. So we need to share the strategy that provides a completed set of metaphors as the raw material for the treatment session. The following is a condensed outline of therapeutic strategy which we use repeatedly in arriving at a series of relevant metaphors for each client:

1) Listen to the problem as offered.
2) Guided by the six areas of desired outcomes, list dramatic themes that are part of the current and desired situation.
3) Construct metaphors that parallel those themes.
4) Design appropriate general outcomes.
5) Arrange the outcome to create suspense or mystery.

These metaphors can serve as the basis for several treatment sessions or for a single session, depending on many factors. They are the "stock" for the stew or the adhesive in the glue. As a primary track from which to take various tangents, these dramatic themes and parallel metaphors can form the basis for a major character revision. They could also be delivered so rapidly as to take only a single hypnotherapy session, which could, nonetheless, have signifcant impact on the client's life for months to come. Decisions about how to use these metaphors are made on the basis of the diagnostic considerations, available time, therapeutic goals, etc. This book, however, concentrates on the use of Erickson's multiple embedded metaphor as a treatment modality and we will therefore emphasize telling metaphors in this manner, in blocks of treatment often longer than a single hour. In telling these metaphors, tangents are frequently taken whenever therapeutically appropriate to elicit or intensify a feeling state or experience.

METAPHORIC TREATMENT: TRANSCRIPT

The next case illustrates several dramatic theme metaphors as they were actually told. A transcript of the entire session is presented. The case provides a good example because of its simplicity and the fact that the client ("Florence") made obvious and remarkable changes as a result of this single treatment session. Prior to the transcript we will briefly analyze the metaphors used in this case according to the present strategy.

Background and Context

Florence was a 30-year-old woman, who, as a result of going back to college, experienced much anxiety. She had a strong family system and appeared generally well equipped for her life changes, except for her noticeable lack of comfort with assertiveness. Again, dramatic themes were chosen by first considering the six areas of desired outcome: bonding and age-appropriate intimacy, self-image enhancement, attitude restructuring, social role change, family structure change, and enjoyment of life.

This client was aware of anxiety and lack of enjoyment only because of the flux in her life. She thought she was going through an uncomfortable stage in her life that would only be resolved when she graduated and changed employment! Indeed, she did not expect to feel competent, happy, and "balanced" for many years, and she did not seek therapy to accomplish those goals. She only wanted to eliminate the stress and frustration resulting from her role changes. From this brief overview we can demonstrate the logic used as possibly relevant goals were sketched.

1) *Age-appropriate intimacy.* She will emerge from her identity crisis when she learns that her ties to significant others will hold and her fears are in response to transition problems, not real threats to her family relationships.
2) *Self-image enhancement.* Her self-image will be sufficiently altered when her range of comfort includes a general coping style of the type needed to persevere as a hardworking student and a temporarily "less present" mother and wife.
3) *Attitude restructuring.* When her crisis is creatively resolved, the alteration of her attitude will be apparent in her ability to approach other minor challenges with an air of calm self-assurance.
4) *Social role changes.* Her social roles will reflect her integrated change when she displays leadership with assertiveness and decisiveness, as well as humility and willingness to cooperate.
5) *Family structure changes.* In this woman's case her family structure probably will not change during this period of adjustment, but her involvement and healthy dependency may increase.
6) *Enjoyment.* New enjoyment of the entire process was her conscious request. Of course, success in this area is an essential criterion in order for her conscious mind to accept that she has succeeded.

These dramatic themes were incorporated in a set of five metaphors. They are briefly summarized here so that they will be easily recognized in the transcript:

1) *Intimacy.* An unbalanced canoe results in spilling precious possessions that, for a while, are feared to be lost. They are not lost in the
end.
2) *Self-image enhancement.* No metaphor was designed for this; rather,
she was asked to consider her present situation in the framework of
her future successes.
3) *Attitude.* A story about a boat that continually tipped over and was
then righted by its passengers. It finally became a pleasant part of the
trip when the boat was topsy-turvy.
4) *Role.* A "humanistic psychologist" was not able to "deal with" seemingly hostile or aggressive communication. In the end his boat crashed
because of his hesitancy and rigid insistence upon a particular role.
5) *Family structure.* A computerized bathroom scale was purchased so
that the owner might undertake a plan for self-improvement. It was
not immediately helpful after all and, in fact, presented new difficulties. In the end a new but old-fashioned scale was accurate and it
taught a lesson about balance. The effect of using it was beneficial
and the user became healthier.

These metaphors were told in an embedded manner. Some begin and do
not end until others have been introduced and developed. Metaphors embedded one within another offer special benefits, which will be discussed in
Chapter 7. Briefly, they include using the structure specifically to: fixate attention, elicit trance phenomena, build resources in the client, associate experiences, and produce generative change. At this point we only present its
gross structure and its implementation in the treatment session which follows.

The client, as previously stated, was newly involved in a graduate program which required her driving to a campus 100 miles from her home (and
husband and four-year-old child) two days a week. She worked part-time as
a counselor in her own town as well. The therapy took place in a professional
training seminar which she had attended for several years. In this particular
session of the group, she had participated in learning activities prior to the
trance work, which served the purpose of establishing a learning framework
for the session. These activities were therefore readily available for utilization in the trance.

Specifically, she had: 1) completed a personality checklist inventory and
listed important instances of her life (both highly pleasurable and fearful) in
what resembled a legal "balance sheet"; 2) listed several future goals; and 3)
imagined herself as the "star" in a parade where friends and fans waved to her
from the sidelines, cheering their praise and acknowledgment to the sounds
of lively parade music. In this exercise, especially, she was observed to giggle
and respond with considerable pleasure, indicating her ability to respond

to suggestion, imagine vividly, and display ideomotor behavior. She said she had not officially experienced "trance" at the time this transcript begins.

*Client Statement of Problem

Discussing her problem prior to her statement here, she described in vague terms an unsettled feeling related to her new involvement in graduate school. She especially emphasized a need for "balance," stating that her life was operating as if a "wrench" has been thrown into the works, and that she needed for things to somehow "jell." When she was asked to summarize her problem and desired change for the group, she said:

> Basically the problem seems to be brought on by school and I'm feeling stress about not being with my family. Part of the frustration is trying to be an effective mother and wife while at the same time trying to be a good student and teacher and then continue my spiritual development. I don't want to give up any of them but would like to find a balance . . .

Florence's description, including the key words "balance," "wrench," and "jell," indicated her own metaphors for her situation. She used a mechanical framework to describe her life. The following outline summarizes the initial treatment plan, which was designed prior to the therapy to include and utilize significant aspects of her own metaphors. It was possible to follow the initial treatment plan in this case; however, it is important to remember that ideomotor behavior from the client can often provide new information during the course of the session, sometimes necessitating a departure from the original treatment plan to deal with emergent needs of the client. In the following transcript "F" refers to Florence and "C" refers to Carol.

* *Orientation and induction*
* *Dissociation and deepening*
* *Begin matching metaphor*
* *Paradox and resource retrieval*
* *Metaphor to retrieve firmness*
* *Metaphor to retrieve sexual associations*
* *Dream metaphor → Elicit confidence*
* *Boat metaphor → Direct sense of control*
* *Linking resources with self-image thinking*
* *Complete the matching metaphor*
* *Reorient to waking state*

*Orientation and Induction

C: Have you ever been in trance officially?

F: No.

C: Do you have any ideas as to how it will be?

F: My first reaction is that it may be scary.

C: Are there particular fears you have about it?

F: No.

C: I have a lot of reassurances I could give you, especially in regard to any specific fear.

F: Well, you could just give me one or two of those.

C: OK. Well, one thing I'll tell you that's very reassuring is that even though you haven't thought about being in a trance before, you *have* experienced *trance*. It is really only a way to *become very relaxed* and to *learn from yourself*, make new associations, become familiar with yourself at a different level. It's not a level you're totally unfamiliar with because you experience it in dreams at night and in daydreams during the day. So, if you're ready, I'd like you to begin by placing your legs flat on the floor. Take a potential load off your leg. Legs can become very heavy and perhaps one of the dangers of trance is discomfort from crossed legs. So, take whatever measures necessary at the outset while you're still mobile to *get comfortable*. And I would suggest you just place your hands flat on your thighs. You'll certainly be able to move should this position become uncomfortable but it's not necessary to move, not necessary to talk; in fact, it's not necessary to do anything.

You might find it helpful in the beginning to find some one spot to gaze at, and I imagine as you do we will both notice an increasing comfort as we become familiar with each other in this mutual contact. Now it's not necessary to *close your eyes* though it's certainly an option and you can *close your eyes* whenever you want to, thus making it possible to blot out the visual stimuli of the room so that you can more fully *imagine in words and pictures and feelings those ideas that come to mind* in response to my words. I'd certainly like to reassure you that you needn't be oblivious to what I say. I expect that you will *hear everything* I say though your conscious mind may not be particularly interested. It's reassuring to know that *your unconscious mind is* interested in *making new associations*, always on the lookout to *learn something new* in your best interest.

This session began with a typical orientation to trance, emphasizing fixation and reassurances of safety, comfort, and relaxation. Italicized words or phrases were spoken more softly than the surrounding text. Rationale for both the type of induction used and voice tone shifts toward soft will be explained in the next chapter. Because the entire therapy session is presented here, the overall length of the session can be compared with the length of the metaphors. The session lasted 75 minutes. Each story was, therefore, approximately 15 to 20 minutes long. The same was true for the induction and the dissociation and deepening to follow.

*Dissociation and Deepening

C: And like I said before, you've been in trance before, though I don't expect you've really thought about it in that way. Imagining that parade this morning you were able to *have a good feeling* (client smiles and straightens shoulders in ideomotor identification response) and I think it would be an excellent idea for you to follow that good feeling into another trance because your ability to *imagine* is all that's necessary for you to *have a very personal learning* and come to a new understanding. Now your conscious mind may not be able to verbalize just what your unconscious mind understands.

Now I know one thing. Your conscious mind is most likely interested in what I'm saying while your unconscious mind is automatically taking care of all those minor adjustments necessary to insure your comfort. Your conscious mind can wonder about what I'm doing and what structure I'm following, perhaps analyzing images your unconscious presents to you in response to my words. And that's a fine thing for a conscious mind to do. So just *relax*, more and more, and perhaps it will be easier to think in terms of just relaxing one twentieth of the way with each count as I count backwards from 20, 19, with each breath, that's right, just noticing and letting go of any residual tension. And one thing you can do is to become increasingly aware of the *comfort, safety,* 17, and *security* of the trance. And most important, be aware that you can *trust your own unconscious* mind to provide your own answers and personal meanings in response to my words; 16, 15, that's right, and those little unconscious movements, jerks, simply imply that your body is relaxing, allowing any tension to dissipate, 14, 12, 10, 6, 4, 1.

And have that same feeling of being washed clean that's identified when walking at the edge of the sea. You could almost *hear that gentle lull* of the ocean that allows you a fresh vantage point, perhaps a new interpretation of those problems which seemed so important but can now be remote as you stroll along thinking and feeling (tear rolls down from left eye). And sometimes, being appreciated can cause a tear to fall or the memory of times when you haven't been appreciated in the manner you deserve. Because there are different kinds of tears, tears of joy, tears of maturity. So *experience those tears and learn.*

And it doesn't really matter what depth of trance you reach. Instead I'd like you to concentrate on developing that depth of trance that *you* think you want or *may want* to *deal with a psychological problem.* You may deal with the psychological problem you've discussed or you may be surprised to *discover* that you deal instead with *learning something else* totally unexpected. Now as I continue to talk, your conscious mind may wonder why I choose the stories I tell and be entertained while your unconscious mind pursues its habit of doing something relevant though unknown to you.

Induction continued in the above paragraphs, emphasizing that she follow the recently retrieved delightful "parade-feeling" as a method of going into trance. In response to her movements and her tears, the trance was ratified, deepening was begun, and an anecdote about walking by the ocean was introduced. This was done in an attempt to help her dissociate from any uncomfortable images which might be stimulating her tears. Several reassurances were offered about depth of trance, the nature of unconscious resources, and permission for her conscious mind to analyze and wonder about the "real" meaning without disturbing her unconscious processing of symbolic and personal meaning.

Deepening of the trance and dissociation between conscious and unconscious functioning are quite important and are discussed in the next chapter. The induction and ratification of the trance were complete and treatment framed as a metaphoric comparison could begin. The matching metaphor was introduced about the purchase of a frustrating pair of bathroom scales. Care was taken to use the client's own key words such as "balance" and "wrench" while mentioning her fears of being undependable to her family and indecisive about her change in lifestyle which began about six months earlier:

Begin Matching Metaphor

C: Now about six months ago, a close friend of mine bought a new, modern, digital scale; she was tired of the old-fashioned model. She wanted one that she could really depend on to know exactly what her weight was. She expected that the new, computerized model could do the job. But no sooner had she gotten that scale home than she realized that every time she stood on the scale it reflected a different weight, reflecting changes in weight far more rapidly than her weight could actually change. It was as if it had a wrench in its works. It was as if it just couldn't make up its mind as to what the accurate reading really was. And that was such a hassle, as you can imagine. My friend was interested in watching her weight, interested in keeping a particular balance within a particular range. And every time she got on that scale, she got results that couldn't be depended upon. And it was infuriating, time and time again!

The above metaphor served an introductory function. It contained the same key elements, themes, and relationships that Florence had used to describe her problem. Because of that, we call it a matching metaphor. We use this term exclusively for the metaphor that is placed in the beginning slot, following induction and appealing to the similar dramatic theme as that consciously presented by the client. In Florence's case the concern was an emotional one and related role changes were important. She was worried about school and the role she would play. Her emotional state was foremost. The metaphor similarly concerned the emotional issue of being unable to trust and rely upon something (the scale) and the indirectly related role the protagonist was seeking by attempting to improve herself.

Elements of suspense were created with such lines as "She expected . . . but no sooner. . . . " Emotional attention was fixed and a slight alteration of her framework was added. In "real life" Florence was not suspenseful about the "story of her life." She was not waiting, as it were, to find out how she "turned out." In fact, such an attitude would have been almost guaranteed to reduce her anxiety and inspire creativity. Instead, she felt anxious about her life as if it would continue forever and as if her anxiety did not itself create some effect on her progress.

In this introductory metaphor she actually heard the elements of suspense. The story paralleled her life and then introduced suspense as an added feature. Thus, the real situation was more than adequately represented by the metaphor, which "laid it all on the line" by its parallelism to all important elements in her current problem. It also provided both symbolic and dramatic distance from her immediate limitations and concerns. It accomplished this unconsciously by making a story similar to hers a story of suspense.

The concept of an undependable bathroom scale was equivalent to the unsettling turns in her life. The scale itself is associated with self-care and self-upkeep and that was the framework implied by Florence in explaining her motivation. It symbolized the same priorities as those personally valued by Florence. The scale was modern and computerized and this was not dissimilar to her own experience—trying to improve herself in today's modern society.

Terms used in the story, such as "balance" and "wrench," directly reflected Florence's very words. But the metaphoric comparison offered her options not previously realized. That the scale intended to be precise, but was not, clarified the idea that her life was indeed out of balance. The imprecision of a precise tool of measurement symbolized that it was not just her imagination that something was wrong—something really was out of kilter.

*Paradox→ To Resource Retrieval

Transitions were then made to tangential themes and other anecdotes. We refer to these as resource metaphors and we have dedicated an entire chapter to discussing resources and trance phenomena. In order to convey the general therapeutic pattern, we refer you to the chart at the end of this chapter, particularly the portion designated by the box "C1." At this phase we employ the first tangents away from the parallel matching metaphor to begin retrieving resources. In this case it begins with a paradox that presupposes the experience of balance; several anecdotes to reinforce the point are then used to retrieve various resources.

The abrupt departure from the beginning metaphor is a well calculated strategy to help prepare the client to operate from a new framework. Erickson typically retrieved trance phenomena and other experiential resources after removing attention from the original theme by several frameworks. In this context, the client is more willing to entertain novel and important resources that could not be experienced and used in the original framework brought to therapy. We call that phase simply "retrieval of resources." Although the theme of balance continued in some fashion in every metaphor, the story of the scale was temporarily but abruptly suspended. And again, retrieval of resources began with the paradox which relabeled Florence's ability to notice imbalance as prerequisite to her achieving and having balance:

C: Now proper balance is very important. I don't need to tell *you* that! And when I mention *balance*, a particular set of associations comes to mind because balance is a concept you've thought about in a very personal way. You know what balance is by your ability to *notice imbalance*. (Pause.) And even your hands have achieved a balance of position, though slightly asymmetrical. Your left hand has fallen to your side with your palm down, fingers touching your thigh, while your right hand has fallen to your other side with its palm up. And similarly, a tear first came from your left eye but was followed soon afterward by another tear from your right eye, thus creating a balance even of your tears on your cheeks.

And I know, too, that you've been reviewing your history very recently. And I imagine that you can *recall that sheet* that was important as you created it, as you remembered those various experiences and the wealth of associations. I don't need to mention what those particular experiences were because you've very recently gone to the effort of writing those experiences down, thinking about each one as you did so. And I couldn't help but notice as you showed me your sheet the interesting balance with the pleasant experiences listed on one side of the page and those fearful experiences listed on the other side. And yet even though one group of experiences was listed as *having been fearful then*, I would expect that in remembering those experiences, *certain strengths come to mind*, certain valuable lessons that were learned in the process of living through and surviving even those fearful experiences.

Of course, I could mention some of the specifics. I could mention simply a word like *"adventuresome"* and I don't know exactly what comes to mind but perhaps it is one of those romps through the wildflowers . . . (Florence displays an instantaneous broad smile.) and that's a pleasant experience! So just take a moment to *memorize that feeling*, soaking it up. . . . That's right. And I could mention *"confidence"* and another whole group of experiences are likely to come to mind.

It's not important for *me* to know just what those experiences are though I would certainly find it enjoyable to chat with you about them sometime. But for now, just revel in *your* memory of those experiences, noticing how you can *really learn* in the face of unexpected challenges and unforeseen circumstances. And enjoy that confidence and flexibility which is yours by virtue of so many countless learnings. And there are a lot more qualities that your unconscious mind values and uses automatically to regulate your responses in hundreds of transactions every day. Perhaps you don't even know what to call them consciously, but they are collected feelings. So *really enjoy all of your feelings*—they are yours and you're entitled to them.

The first paragraph in this section began with a direct mention of the client's own metaphor "balance." In order to open a window to new associations and a change that is, by its very nature, unexpected, a paradox was offered. "You know what balance is by your ability to notice imbalance." Having used such a paradox the therapy took on a certain positive bind: If Florence thought about imbalance, it was a sign that she could think about balance, and if she thought about balance instead, so much the better. A new framework had been given in which the client could not deny her ability to know the feeling of balance. This opened the door to her use of new experiences which she might learn how to initiate. The unconscious mechanisms she needed to creatively adapt to her challenging life changes were within her personal history and those mechanisms could be retrieved via this entrance.

The metaphoric context throughout the next section concerned a client who had taken a personality test. The real client, Florence, had also just taken a personality test in addition to the aforementioned "balance sheet" she had drawn up, so this introduction was expected to especially engage her conscious and unconscious attention. The other client is only mentioned intermittently as the backdrop and ostensible reason for all the tangents taken.

Speaking first about Florence's "balance sheet" was likely to pull many positive unconscious resources into the foreground. Florence had been observed completing this list and it seemed to provide her a pleasant experience. The experiences that she organized included smiles, posture changes, and a constellation of proprioceptive, respiratory, biochemical, perceptual, and cognitive associations. It was a complex experience she had no means of adequately expressing verbally.

It is not likely that all the complex associations could ever be consciously known. Casually mentioning the list, however, and later the metaphorical personality test allowed her to recall and reexperience those feelings and the associated learnings in a framework that she didn't need to integrate, explain, or fear. This entire matter of resources and confidence only appeared as a tangent to help explain something about a bathroom scale. So, there was little or no apparent threat to Florence in experiencing the confidence and "adventuresome" frame of mind. It was just a convenient way to help her unconsciously use her resources.

The actual line used was, "I would expect that in remembering those experiences, certain strengths come to mind, . . . " Labels were used to provide future reference to these "strengths" and complex and meaningful nouns and adjectives like "confidence" and "adventuresome" were purposefully chosen since they seem specific but offer a broad metaphoric base for associating personal meanings.

Florence continually provided feedback in the form of ideomotor behavior. For example, at one point a broad smile came across her face. Thus, it was known that her associations to the images used were pleasant and that they were producing muscular and bodily phenomena. Such feedback is not only convincing for the therapist but is essential for the Ericksonian approach. Attentiveness to the ideomotor details creates an opportunity to respond by continuing, modifying or stopping a set of images, thus taking care to treat each client as an individual. Here, the feedback was used as a cue to reinforce and crystalize the heightened awareness Florence had of her pleasant experience.

At that point in the session one tangent had been completed and several experiential resources had been retrieved. Once those readily available resources had been retrieved, additional tangents were taken to align more subtle resources. It is at this point that the other client who had taken the personality test was introduced.

Metaphor to Retrieve Firmness

C: I had a client recently who filled out a personality inventory at the beginning of her therapy. Looking at the results she was surprised to discover there was almost a complete lack of willingness or identification with responses which indicated either assertiveness or obedience. She didn't want to tell people "no" but she didn't want to obey them either. I thought that sounded like quite a fix and imagined that dilemma was a large part of what brought her to therapy. So, in the course of working with her, I told her a story about a humanistic psychologist who went on a sailing adventure with some other psychologists in the Bahamas on vacation.

I told her about how two boats set out simultaneously heading for a nearby island. The trip was progressing enjoyably as everyone had hoped until the boat that *he* was in began to veer dangerously close to some rocks as we approached the island. I was in the other boat with a more advanced sailor and I was glad of it because the course didn't look very easy to me. As his boat veered closer and closer to those rocks, the advanced sailor on my boat shouted out to him rather urgently: "Throw me the rope!"

Well, instead of throwing the rope he turned and with his hands stubbornly on his hips said, "Not until you ask me nice!" She couldn't believe he was concerned with how she asked him to throw the rope when he was in danger of crashing into the rocks. So she repeated her command with a bit more urgency and conviction: "Hurry up and throw me the damned rope!!!" He still insisted on her asking him nicely, however. He really didn't have to worry about that much longer though because shortly thereafter he crashed into the rocks and had a whole new set of things to worry about!

Now, that is the story I mentioned to her . . . and I wasn't quite sure what learning she would have consciously. I expected it would have to do with her ability to *be firm when necessary* and *do not worry about being told what to do* but, rather, to realize the logic and wisdom of responding obediently when circumstances require.

Concerned with issues of balance (in the context of a bathroom scale metaphor), Florence had been sequentially lead through various metaphoric frameworks. The previous four paragraphs told of a client who was similar to Florence according to her own definition and who, as a result of taking a test, was told a true story of an overly nice psychologist who proved to be a fool because he did not deal with the obvious moment. It was a short metaphor to shape attitude. The consequence of the psychologist's attitude made having it undesirable.

The final paragraph illustrated several special benefits of relating facts metaphorically. First was the emphasis on the conscious and unconscious learning conveyed in the statement, "I wasn't quite sure what learning she would have consciously." And second was the purposeful alteration of pronouns to make direct instructions addressed to the literal unconscious mind. The last sentence illustrated that with *"be firm when necessary"* and *"do not worry about being told what to do."* The preceding sentence had insured that her conscious mind would not object to the learning (after all, it is admittedly difficult to understand). The "direct," albeit metaphorical, instruction then suggested an unconscious learning that could become individually tailored and suited to her own unique world of circumstances. It can be totally out of awareness or partially conscious. Furthermore, the conscious part can be framed in any number of ways useful to the client.

The first metaphoric experiences shifted her emotional experience from frustration to balance. Now attitudinal changes were suggested. She could be expected to shift her perceptions and attitude to help explain her previous emotional shift. Subsequent metaphors detailing behavior changes would, then, be especially attractive to Florence and that is exactly what she was to hear next.

*Metaphor to Retrieve Sexual Associations

C: I also mentioned in response to a sexual problem *she* had discussed another story, again about sailing: how a sailboat swooshes through the loving wetness, carrying precious cargo that will be unloaded at the end of the journey; but how the journey itself is so enjoyable: the sailor at the sensitive tiller, the vessel subtly responding to the moves of the sailor and the rhythm of the sea. . . . And I went on expecting that she would create a pleasurable association to sexual learnings.

I was really quite surprised when, at the end of her trance, as she discussed her associations, she said, "Every time you told a story about boats, the boat in my mind's eye would tip over and I'd find myself in the water. It wasn't traumatic because I found that I was able, each time, to get back in the boat somehow. But it is interesting that I keep finding myself in the water. What do you make of that?" I wasn't quite sure what to make of it except that the *process* of *righting* the boat and getting back in it seemed to be symbolic of one of the less developed aspects of her relationship. And I assumed balance was a central issue in need of further direction.

The use of dramatic surprise was designed to enter some doubt about how her life fit the storyline. Up to this point the stories seemed to be easily related to her life, but sexual ramifications were not on her mind. Any associations elicited by the sexual reference would be used to reinforce the common experience of aggressive "energy." And since the sexual difficulty was happening to someone else, it allowed Florence to cease the direct application of the metaphors to her own life. Thus, consciousness was off guard and less defensive about learnings conveyed in the story.

Dream Metaphor → Elicit Confidence and Flexibility

C: So in her next trance I told her another story about a boat. I told her about a dream that another client had in trance, . . . a dream following a very disruptive personal experience, an experience that left her feeling insecure, inadequate, and doubting her self-worth. She had been abandoned by her lover and she couldn't understand how it was he could prefer another woman when she loved him so much. She was certain that she would never find joy in this life again. She only wanted to avoid everyone. She didn't smile. She didn't whistle. And she didn't know if there would ever be an end to that depression *until* the night of that dream.

In the dream she imagined that she was going on a canoe adventure. The canoe had been transported to the water on top of a van. At the mouth of the river into which the canoe was to be inserted, she climbed up on top of the van and sat in the canoe in order to steady it as it was lowered into the water. She made sure in preparation for her adventure to have with her certain items, her car keys so she could leave in her car when the adventure was over, her wallet and all the security involved in a wallet—identification and power—and finally a small golden cross which reflected the radiance of sunlight in such a way that it lent a special charm over her experiences so that she could *discover* and *really experience the spiritual joy and beauty of everything* around her. These three things were very precious to her, each for its own reason. She carefully secured them in the bottom of the boat as it was lowered.

But, it was certainly worrisome when she noticed the angle at which the canoe was approaching the water. She was quite concerned that the nose of the canoe would dip into the stream in such a way that the canoe would fill with water and sink. And there she would be, floundering about. She didn't have time to worry about that very long because, indeed, the nose of the boat did dip into the stream and the boat did take on *some* water, not so much as had been feared—because about that time the back of the boat finally cleared the top of the van and came crashing down into the water with such weight that the front of the canoe was suddenly lifted out of the water. Now this was a relief in some measure but provided a new host of problems to grapple with—

the boat was wobbly, and the woman, to stabilize it, had to *concentrate all her energies* in bringing it to balance.

Finally, she accomplished that and her mind turned to her three precious belongings. Where were they? As she feared, they had washed overboard. She had only a brief sensation of panic before she looked over the edge of the boat and in the very clear, shallow water saw, unharmed and within reach, her wallet, keys and the golden cross. It was such a pleasure and relief to just *reach over* and *bring back* to possession *those things so precious.*

When she woke up from that dream feeling very good, somehow she knew her depression was over. Her conscious mind did not yet know the specifics of how her life would proceed but *your unconscious mind can reassure you in subtle ways allowing your conscious mind to take comfort from symbolic images.* Even though the boat had been in danger of sinking, it didn't sink. She had retrieved her balance and security, mobility, identity and ability to enjoy life's extraordinary pleasures.

The symbols of the keys, wallet, and golden cross were chosen to correspond to the concerns she raised about being a good mother and wife (practical symbol of wallet), student and teacher (growing opportunity symbol of keys), and spiritual and religious practices (symbol of golden cross). The series of metaphors involved details of actual behavioral changes. They illustrated preparation for a trip, securing the things she valued, concentrating her energies, and relying upon her unconscious resources (which had already been retrieved).

Now that she had thus "prepared for a trip" and retrieved resources she valued, another metaphor was begun that emphasized exactly the same thing as the last one, with the exception that the world was less kind and the protagonist had to "exercise" or direct her sense of control. But again, behaviors were detailed by metaphoric comparison. When adversity struck in the following metaphor, the protagonists found a way to handle it. With attention engaged in following the story, the client can be expected to organize some degree of understanding about how one goes about finding a way to handle adversity. Note how the story begins with a mystery and moves into suspense. This story constitutes phase "D" or direct work.

Boat Metaphor → Direct Her Sense of Control

C: And I told her that story because I expected that it would match her experience of having boats being unstable but being able to *create a balance*. Then I went on to tell her about another boat adventure that hap-

pened in real life on a small sunfish boat. My neighbor, his friend and
sister set out for an adventure on what appeared to be a very calm day.
In the beginning they joked among themselves, "Well, let's go" and
"When do we start," because the wind was blowing so slightly it seemed
ridiculous to think they were going anywhere powered by *that* wind.
But as unexpected circumstances do go, suddenly out of the absolutely
clear blue sunshiny sky came the most ferocious wind, which instantly
transformed their lazy little boat into a wild horse to be carefully controlled. They did a good job of controlling things (pause) for about five
minutes.

That's right. You continue to make various adjustments to insure
your comfort. We all make adjustments to insure our comfort. They
had taken lots of gear: diving equipment, towels, refreshments, sun-
glasses and tanning oil to insure their comfort. The *first* time the boat
tipped over it surprised them considerably when they found themselves
thrashing about in the water. The rudder had come loose, the center
board had popped out, and all that stuff was floating in several different
directions. One swam for the rudder, my neighbor went for the diving
gear and I don't know what John did but I'm sure it was survival oriented. There was plenty to do! Because after retrieving the pieces they
had to right the boat, load it again, climb aboard, set sail and regain
control of all those ropes and levers.

Now as I speak about this boat to you, I said to her, I expect that you
can listen with your conscious mind and notice that boat in your mind's
eye while your unconscious mind can *recall a situation in your life
which requires balance.* And as I continue, I expect that your conscious
mind will be particularly interested in *how* your boat *is* righted while
your unconscious mind can simply *enjoy* your ability to right the boat
or perhaps *your conscious* mind will *enjoy* your ability to *create balance* while your unconscious mind notices *how* you do it.

I don't really know but I do know that none of them particularly enjoyed getting dumped in the water that day and yet looking back on
that experience provides a completely different perspective than looking at could ever provide. And it's nice to allow your conscious mind to
enjoy your unconscious and automatic flexibility that is revealed as you
deal with unexpected obstacles.

They weren't back in the boat five minutes before another wave and
wind combination dumped them right back in the water. They had to
go through the entire process again: Find all the pieces, right the boat,
put it all back together again and bring the boat to balance. Take a moment now to just *enjoy the balance,* enjoying it without knowing how
long it will last. But be secure and confident in the knowledge that you
needn't strain to hang on to and try desperately to *keep* balanced because you can *recreate that balance* again and again. And so let that
boat tip over another time and even enjoy the change of scenery and

sensation involved as you just relax a moment in the water, floating easily. That's the way they felt the third and fourth time they found themselves back in the water again. That circumstance had long ceased to surprise or worry them and they soon found ways to enjoy it since it seemed to be an inevitable part of that day's adventure.

And one way to create an interpersonal and psychological balance is through the relief mechanism of tears. So have your tears, feel them flowing over your cheeks, and as they do, appreciate them as your psychic regulating device, balancing and equalizing your emotional experience. Now back in the boat again, take another moment to *enjoy the balance*, the breeze, the warmth of the sun, but most of all enjoy the calm and *confidence* of knowing *your conscious mind can retrieve and recreate balance* in a variety of ways again and again.

Now I had this client in question go through that procedure at least 15 times. I bet she thought I would never stop dumping that boat over. (Florence smiles.) You'll be glad to know that I'm not going to dump over this boat any further. I don't think it's necessary because the intensity of your response communicates to me a very important message about your learning and the intensity of those learnings.

This metaphor poses the question, "What is going to happen?" and therefore again appeals to the client's sense of suspense. The suspense of the boat metaphor reframed the entire adventure from one of adversity to one in which unexpected pleasure was gained because the protagonists found a way to act with power and control via interacting with the inevitability of the elements.

Having framed an alteration of the symptom in symbolic ways in phase "D," the therapy moved to the linking phase ("C-2") to link the retrieved resources and new learnings to upcoming situations in the client's life. In this case a form of self-image thinking called "emanated image" was designed. She was asked to imagine herself successfully in the desired future and then look back to see how that "went." Thus the process "shaped" her perception so that if and when she encountered such situations in real life, they would not be perceived as obstacles but instead as useful steps toward the desired goal. She will have presupposed success and will have a rehearsed "map" to follow that depicts her using her resources in a way she values as she pursues her goals.

Link Resources With Self-image Thinking

C: Instead, I'll ask you to remember again that list you've drawn up. That list I saw heavily emphasized your accomplishments and fears of the very remote to the very recent past. And I know another part of your experience was to think about the desired accomplishments and anticipated fears of the future.

I know from talking to you that you have many well defined goals for the future and I expect that you have others which are not nearly so well defined but are only intuitive—in fact, you couldn't put them into words but you *have a sense of how you'd like your future to be*. One thing I'd like you to do first is to see yourself again as you were in that parade, seeing yourself wearing your favorite clothing, validated, confident, balanced, with a sense of self-worth and delight. Seeing yourself with those qualities, I'd like for you to imagine one of those future goals, maybe your graduation day holding that Ph.D. diploma so proudly—so tightly! Imagine that vividly and soak up those feelings of accomplishment—well deserved.

Because there's really no sense to wait until then to enjoy some of that accomplishment even now at the outset. Enjoy that accomplishment and in that situation of the future, imagined as if real *now*, I'd like you to just fall into a daydream and *look back* over the many steps you took to arrive at that destination. Looking back, you'll see those experiences that seemed like insurmountable obstacles at the time they were encountered. Side by side you'll see and perhaps allow your conscious mind to have an awareness that the valuable learnings your unconscious mind has stored from encountering those obstacles makes having encountered them so worthwhile that you wouldn't trade it now for anything, even though at the time you may not have liked the idea of living through them. So notice all of your experiences on the way to that goal. Notice how you righted your boat time and time again. And *watch yourself* with that validation and balance and confidence. Find even those situations you imagined would be most difficult, looking at them from the vantage point of the future *now* with the advantage of hindsight. Of course, the graduation goal was only the overt goal. Looking back on the experiences leading to that larger goal you notice many other smaller but nonetheless important goals which were each meaningful for different reasons. Perhaps one of those is simply to not keep your balance on the way but retrieve and recreate it almost effortlessly at those moments you notice its absence. Be thankful for your conscious mind's ability to *notice imbalance and thereby alert your unconscious mechanisms to automatically realign your personal balance*, possibly through a brief time of tears, or in a dream, or in a myriad of other, yet unknown ways that you can be pleased to discover as they are revealed to your conscious mind.

And I would suggest that you continue this daydream in a dream at night, imagining yourself in those situations you most desire and fear. Be a bystander and an observer of that dream as well as the star. Notice how *she* lives through those situations, even ones which she fears may be difficult, only to find that with grace, charm and confidence she maintains balance because she knows how to recreate it.

Here again, the paradox was used to open a "logical" way to explain to Florence that she has some reason (albeit paradoxically expressed) to find the balance she seeks in her current cognitive framework and map of experience. The paradox is useful when no elements of suspense, mystery, or other drama are involved to fixate attention. The matching metaphor ("B-2") was now ended.

*Complete the Matching Metaphor

C: My friend finally had it with that infuriating scale. She had just stood on that darn thing five times in a row and gotten five different weights ranging within ten pounds. She knew that she couldn't fit into her favorite bluejeans anymore and that the scale had not adequately reflected the gain in her weight. What was the point of standing on it everyday if it didn't tell you anything accurate? She was sick and tired of its being so undependable and went right out and bought a new one. Now I don't know if she did so indiscriminately, impulsively, if it reflected her being hard-headed, or if it was just the logical thing to do, but at any rate, she knew she had to have a scale that balanced just like the one at the doctor's office. It had to slide so that it displayed the exact weight within a quarter of a pound.

She was really quite surprised *what a difference such a small change can make in your life.* It was so pleasing to know that the weight reflected there was exactly correct. You couldn't really say that because she had that bathroom scale she had balance in her life and yet, somehow, in some psychological way, the symbol of balance it provides *allows your unconscious mind to retrieve a real sense of balance* that can *radiate* throughout all your experiences, especially those that have nothing to do with weight.

The minor suspense of the introductory metaphor ("Now about six months ago . . . she expected. . . . But no sooner . . .") is ended in this final segment. The client is implicitly reminded that such suspense has existed throughout this set of metaphors and, somehow, they now represent closure for the original story. Since this original story was parallel in its structural elements to Florence's unbalanced life, the closure of suspense in the story provides an unconscious ending to the suspense of her life. But the closure is not an illusory closure. The closure is based on the actual retrieval and use of perceptions, emotions, attitudes, behaviors, and unconscious associations of several successfully learned experiences. The use of drama as an unconscious device to hold together the entire treatment process has only served to fixate her attention and unconscious search.

Throughout the entire transcript is an abundance of indirect suggestions and binds. These appear and are used as "glue" to hold the experiences together during the work and to help the client link the resources to situations outside of therapy. The topic of indirect suggestion is detailed in the next chapter. Here, we have emphasized the logic of formulating dramatic theme metaphors that detail various therapeutic outcomes. Now that the metaphors were concluded the preliminary learning was over. After the trance she would have to use the learnings successfully in her daily life.

Reorient to Waking State

C: Now you have used trance today to learn something relevant about yourself, to make a variety of new associations which can *jell* in a particular mold your conscious mind desires and *your unconscious mind designs* in your best interest or perhaps *your unconscious desires* that mold and your conscious mind can participate in creating the design. Just like Erickson said when he reoriented a man from his first trance: Your learnings are not fully set immediately after a trance—it's a lot like plaster of paris; learnings have to set. So be patient with your learnings.

I think it would be an excellent idea if your unconscious mind will deliver to you as a sign that you have unconscious learnings available a particularly delightful experience, perhaps it could be as simple as especially enjoying the taste of your dinner this evening or the softness of your bed or your emotional feeling response to seeing your loved ones' faces or perhaps all of those things. Allow those delightful surprises to be evidence that your unconscious mind will *give you pleasurable experiences* and is indeed a constant and powerful wellspring of inner strength, peace, wisdom and balance.

And I wonder whether or not you can *follow that parade-feeling back* out of trance in the same way you used it to go into trance. You'll likely remember those especially delightful cheers at the end of that parade which escalated into thunderous applause bringing you to happy laughter at the time you heard it, imagining yourself the star of that attention. So *have that sense of self-worth* and enjoy it fully as I count back to 20. It's really not necessary to count in order to end trance but I could count by 5's, reorienting you much more rapidly than when you developed trance because your learnings can continue past this official state of trance.

It's all right for you to take as much time as you like to return to full awareness of the room, your participation in this group. You might begin by noticing the sounds of the traffic, 5, 10, the feeling of your body against the chair, 15, perhaps the need to stretch, 16. So enjoy coming back, 17, even though trance can be so comfortable, 18, you're interested in reality. But do take another moment to thank your unconscious mind for making this relationship possible, both the relationship with yourself and the relationship with me, because it's a pleasure to do good work with good material, 19, 20! And you can open your eyes even through all that moisture and find this kleenex very enjoyable!

Florence left the office soon after this session and the treatment was not discussed. One month later Florence called to report with pleasure and satisfaction that "Every time I began to feel out of balance I could somehow quickly get balanced again. It was just like that boat or whatever it was!" This statement of her achievement attests to the reassociation of experiences that was accomplished in these altered fameworks. Calmness and enjoyment had become associated to the first signs of her anxiety. The embedded structure seen here accounts for the partial amnesia Florence experienced and reported. The embedded structure allowed the work with her on self-image thinking to proceed with little or no resistance.

The embedded structure was used by Erickson when he wished to achieve the same outcome: amnesia and dissociative protection within the session. The following example, transcribed from personal communication (August, 1977), demonstrates Erickson's own version of embedded metaphors containing elements of drama and other aspects of metaphor similar to those just described.

TRANSCRIPT OF ERICKSON'S EMBEDDED METAPHOR

The following set of metaphors was delivered by Erickson during a training seminar. Although spoken in response to a question from an anthropologist, it was directed to a meek young man in the process of divorcing. The anthropologist's question was about the use of and dependence on the unconscious as a mechanism for change. Erickson's response seemed to be a circuitous answer at best. The metaphors were possibly offered to indirectly answer her question but primarily addressed the concerns of the participant just mentioned, a psychologist from Michigan in his late thirties. He had expressed, in the immediately previous introduction, concerns regarding his upcoming divorce.

In responding to both participants as he did, Erickson created a situation that taxed the conscious understanding of each. Presented out of context in this manner, the meaning would not be immediately grasped as the stories were related. They were not immediately grasped by the conscious mind but, of course, the experiences which were elicited were linked unconsciously. Thus, the meaning of the intervention was determined at the psychological level. We present the structure of the intervention as an example, albeit brief, of multiple embedded metaphor.

The session opened with a summary of each person's reason for coming. At this point the meek psychology professor we will call George explained that he came to learn how Erickson did inductions. He mentioned that he wanted to learn how to do inductions and continued to explain:

Also, if there is time, I would like to have some private time with you. I, uh, would like to, uh, well, I'm in the process of a divorce after 12 years together, and I'm not certain if it's the right thing. I mean, I would like to be certain that I don't make another mistake.

Erickson watched him for a few moments, assessing his sincerity, nodded his head and said nothing. The other trainees introduced themselves; none of them requested therapy this day. After the introductions, Erickson called for questions, as he frequently did, to initiate the teaching seminar. All were silent. Finally, the anthropologist (A), who had become a frequent visitor to the training sessions, spoke again, continuing the question she raised before the others arrived. Erickson answered that all of her training had "been to justify outward signs." Ignoring the complexity and the personal nature of that response, she briefly continued to question. Erickson then began telling a set of stories at length, during which he looked at George. George became motionless, fixated, relaxed, and eventually began producing ideomotor responses to Erickson's stories.

A: It's a viewpoint that's totally . . . It's too difficult to accept.
E: I know. All of your training has been to justify outward signs.
A: It's that you have to put yourself in a special state so that your unconscious will work.
E: The lithograph in my bedroom . . . do you remember it?
A: The what?
E: The lithograph in my bedroom . . . "The Beachcomber."
A: I don't remember it. I would remember seeing that one.
E: Now when the artist wanted to do an oil landscape he got in his car and drove at random around Michigan and suddenly found himself at the edge of a marsh. It smelled bad and looked unlovely. He saw a small stick in the mud about 20 feet away. He knew that wasn't the landscape he wanted. He hadn't found one. So the next day he went and drove in the opposite direction, turning at random, finally wound up at the same marsh and saw that same stick. Again without finding the landscape.
    The third day he went out, taking care not to wind up at that marsh, and turning right and left at random. He suddenly found himself at the edge of the marsh looking at the same little stick. After that happened 12 times he said, "My unconscious is trying to tell me something." He waded through the mud and got the stick. Took it back to his studio. Washed it and dried it and then balanced it in various positions. I walked in the studio, saw it. So I started playing with it, and balancing it. He said, "Do you like him?" I said, "Looks interesting, whatcha going to do with it?" He said, "I don't know." Then one day he walks in my office and says, "Here's a lithograph of that stick standing on two of its branch-

es striding along like a man. A weird man." He labeled it "The Beachcomber." And it took him 12 trips.

Here we have the basis for the matching metaphor that parallels George's
12-year marriage. The client had expressed the problem of not knowing what
to do about the divorce. This was a man who consciously didn't know what
he wanted. The metaphor of a man searching and unsure of what he is looking for was a direct parallel match to George's inability to be happy after 12
years of marriage. We speculated the use of the phrase "stick in the mud" was
a purposeful selection of an idiom for a man "stuck" in the way that George
seemed to be stuck in his marriage.

> He won the international prize for an oil painting one year. Amil had
> his own way of doing things. He would plan a picture and use old en-
> velopes carried in his pocket and he'd draw long horizontal lines, short
> horizontal lines, upright long, upright short, and oblique lines working
> out the composition of the picture.
> And one day in September he told me, 'I've examined my teaching
> program at U. of M. and I'm going to paint that circus picture I've been
> wanting to paint for 10 years. I've got my envelopes in my pocket and
> I've figured out so many hours beginning December 20th. It will take
> me about 70 hours to do it." And for some unknown reason he decided
> to alter his usual practice. On the 20th of December he went into his
> studio and nailed the canvas to the frame!—something he had never
> done before a painting had been completed. When he went into the stu-
> dio at noon he took with him a sandwich. He fastened the canvas to the
> frame while chewing his first bite and he reached down to take a second
> bite of his sandwich. And to his amazement it was dry and hard. He was
> very puzzled by that. Until he saw the clock. The clock said, "Six
> o'clock." And in dismay he leaned back where he was standing and
> looked around and he went upstairs to where he lived, looked at the
> clocks there. They also said, "Six o'clock," and he called me up and
> said, "I've got something to show you, something I don't understand."

Erickson began what seemed to be a tangent with the story of the international award, which was presented as a mystery. Somehow, the international award was going to help explain the original question. Attention was
thereby fixed. Erickson appealed to mystery with such phrases as "for some
unknown reason" and "I've got something to show you."
The reference to "teaching programs" was a curious statement. George
was a teacher but this was the first mention about the artist being a teacher.
The use of such references to the client's real life elicits rapport (this is like
me), confusion (is this about me?), and unconscious search (what's the con-

nection?). The reference to the sandwich being dry and hard sounded to us like an allusion to sexual symbolism. Thus, the entire story began to take sexual overtones. Since "dry and hard" is not nearly as sexual as "wet and hard," we understood that there was a sexual connection troubled in nature. George smirked and audibly exhaled so as to nearly chuckle when Erickson said, "dry and hard." With attention held and unconscious search insured, Erickson continued.

> He told me the story: He'd been tacking the canvas to the frame; the next time he looked here was the picture, even signed with his name!—something which he never did until the picture was finished. He told about the sandwich, then you said, "You know I've got the envelopes in my pocket. I haven't completed my composition." I looked at the picture and said, "Amil, if I'm correct tell me so.
>
> "Is the shade of blue on the coat jacket being worn by the clown the same shade of blue on the ribbon on the horse's tail and the same shade of blue for the merry-go-round?" He said: "Yes, they're the same shade. Something's wrong there. They're the same shade but I feel they aren't the same blue colors. But it's the same shade."
>
> So I put him in trance and said: "Are those shades of blue the same?" He said, "Yes, but I had hard work finding different pigments for each blue shade and getting them just right." So I said: "Do you want to know about that shade of blue?" He said, "No, it's out of my system now." So I awakened him. He was still puzzled at painting a picture, . . . an oil painting in between noon and six o'clock, . . . completing it. And it was perfect in his estimation. So I didn't tell him the meaning of the picture.

The element of mystery was intensified with the story being told by Amil to Erickson. George appeared entranced and confused by the use of the color component and what it might represent. He was deeply thoughtful about the apparent meaning of the color. He appeared to be trying to figure it out like a dutiful new student who thought there must be a meaning and he did not "get" it.

The color was found on the horse's rear end, the clown, and the merry-go-round. In the framework of a circus these are all perfectly acceptable. The client was not likely to consider the symbolic connection in any derogatory or self-deprecatory manner. The matter of suspense further distracted George from any ramifications of these symbols.

The use of voice tone shift on lines such as "If I'm correct tell me so" was a request for ideomotor response from George. The answer, in the form of ideomotor behavior from the unconscious, was insured by the multiple embedding of stories. George nodded his head and smiled in response. This tangential embedding presented an overload to the conscious mind. The appeal to the element of drama fixated the client's attention and the combined effect left the listener able to present uncensored signals of identification back to Erickson. He therefore requested feedback from the client's unconscious experience regarding the "clinical picture" he was about to paint.

E: It was a beautiful picture of a circus. There was a horse, a girl riding the horse, a dog, and everything you would expect to see at a circus. The clown was standing beside the horse but the blond girl was sitting on the horse wearing a blue jacket. The blue ribbon on the horse's tail was appropriate . . . in different pigments, same shade as the merry-go-round in the background . . . same shade of blue. Amil had been my patient and his first wife had kept him and treated him like the south end of a northbound horse, had made a clown out of him and kept him on a merry-go-round never knowing if he was going up or down. I don't believe yet that he knows what that picture means. It's out of his system.

The previous request, "If I'm correct, tell me so," prepared George to present ideomotor information back to Erickson. George had complied with a head nod and smile, thus indicating that those would be the "yes" signals. This presentation of the symbols in the picture were obviously symbolic representations of a possible interpersonal relationship George and his wife had. Erickson, it seemed, wanted to assess the possibility that this scenario applied to the marriage of the client in question.

The client, at this point, was nodding his head "yes" and smiling with regular responses to each image in the picture. By contrast, no one else in the office was nodding, although a few smiled when they heard Erickson's catchy manner of speaking. The anthropologist, by the way, was not nodding her head, as she sat motionless, exhibiting all of the signs of search phenomena previously outlined and discussed.

Since George had indicated the scenario did apply, we can use the additional diagnostic information to elaborate six parameters of the diagnostic framework. The client had the social and intellectual skill to become a psychologist and interact appropriately. He was sensitive and perhaps oversensitive to the feelings of others. His age of developmental fixation seemed to be that of a seven-year-old, judging by his "shrinking" to authority, his meekness in behavior with peers, and his hesitant and discounting manner as he requested what he wanted from Erickson. His stage of family development was uncertain depending upon his divorce decision. He and his wife had no children. As in many families, the adjustment to having children or not (when, how many, for what reasons, etc.) is often a crucial point in the survival of the marriage.

Erickson obtained an important piece of information about George that could help put several elements into place. If the transactions between George and his wife were of the nature depicted in the picture, then his meekness and shyness were actually the symptom and a key piece to his successful personal development. Whether he stayed married or not, his lack of comfort with his own aggressive impulses was a therapeutic issue. His conscious request for help had been accompanied by that meek behavior unconsciously. One might say that it constituted the unconscious contract for therapy. We summarized this session as follows:

* *Matching metaphor → Confusion of levels*
* *Confusion of levels → Diagnostic picture*
* *Confusion of levels → Aggression resource*
* *Aggression resource → Social network ties*
* *Social network ties → Matching metaphor*

Erickson had learned that George experienced himself in a submissive role in the marriage. The interpersonal and unconscious information showed George as a man needing to be comfortable with aggression. Whatever resource of aggression Erickson might elicit in this session would be useful only if related to George's map of social interaction. It would not be enough to have George able to experience comfort with aggressive impulses in the office. The real "cure" would be in his ability to have thoughts of his wife and the experience of aggressiveness in proximity of her. To facilitate that arrangement by linking resources, the therapy moved back to the earlier discussion of the international award.

E: And that got the international award for oil paintings. It was shown in Brazil, displayed all over the world. "The Circus" is the title. And I, and I alone, and Amil's unconscious *know the meaning of that picture*. And he hadn't completed his composition on the old envelopes. There were straight lines, vertical and horizontal, long and short. If it won the international award it had to be a good painting. It's been displayed all over Europe, South America, U.S., in Asia.

And Amil's second marriage is very happy. And I had Amil's wife do all those nasty things she wanted to do that drove Amil so far up the wall that he divorced her. After the divorce she wrote him acrimonious letters intended to hurt his feelings. He showed me the letters and they were very nastily worded. So I had him underline phrases here and there and put under them in fine writing some other words. And she stopped writing. She couldn't stand seeing her writing with those additional words added.

And it's like a trick I use or a maneuver or a manipulation or a trait, one term for it that I've employed. At Elouise I had to discharge some old timers who weren't doing their work. And one of them got angry enough to come into my office and say: "You're a dirty bastard." I said: "You're quite mistaken. I'm a dirty, bloody bastard of a . . ." "No," he said, "you're a dirty son-of-a-bitch." "I'm a dirty, bloody son-of-a-bitch of a bastard." And he couldn't think of any way to improve that. So subsequently new attendants were encouraged to come to my office and insult me. So I always improved their insults.

And he didn't know how to improve on that stick. He didn't know that the branches of that stick looked like a man striding along on the beach. It took 12 trips to discover it. But his unconscious knew, must have known. And that "Beachcomber" lithograph is hanging in the bedroom.

Erickson obtained the needed information regarding the client's unconscious assessment of his marriage and returned to the development of the overall story and next stage of intervention. Returning to the earlier tangent regarding the international award marked the end of the most embedded intervention. In so doing he began to remind the listener's conscious mind about the overall theme of the presentation.

His next intervention was aimed at eliciting resources of aggressiveness and assisting the man in becoming comfortable with his own aggressive impulses and with critical input from others. This was done with purposeful verbal vulgarisms which Erickson repeated under the pretense of getting the story perfectly correct. These aggressive thoughts, "modeled" by Erickson, were then linked to thoughts of communications from the first wife.

Thus he was helped to find and accept the aggressive aspect of himself and he could not help but associate to aggressiveness when thinking about communications from his wife. But the thoughts would be framed in the metaphor offered by Erickson. George would have psychological defenses other than denial to protect his conscious mind from the impulse. The metaphoric framework allowed experiences to be entertained that would have been outside of his normal framework.

Finally, Erickson mentioned the second marriage. Although this was a brief mention of the future it indicated that the man in the story did not continue to meekly put up with the conduct of his wife. The man in the story stood up to the wife (in the context of letter writing) and eventually divorced her. The actual connection between the central theme of these stories and the tangent about the color chosen by the artist is not clear and, subsequently, not important to the conscious understanding of the overall theme. In the end Erickson came full circle and mentioned the original trip to the mud and the lithograph over his bed. He thus ended just as he had begun.

The general flow of this multiple embedded metaphor is typical except for the diagnosis phase in the central position. Otherwise, the form is consistent. We have shown this basic pattern in a chart at the conclusion of this chapter (Figure 1). Chapter 7 elaborates several cases in which this pattern was used with minor variations. Many aspects are the same as shown on the chart. In this case the diagnosis in the central section is a major departure. But since it occurs in the middle it is concealed from conscious censorship. The most embedded material is likely to remain out of awareness. Amnesia is, in fact, a common outcome in such treatment work. The story completed, the anthropologist responded.

A: Well I can accept the, you know, example you give me in terms of artistic inspiration . . . that you can somehow receive this inspiration . . . but for most people who want to increase their potential or their creativity or solve problems to say to just kinda leave it to your unconscious. I mean I see it as depending on your conscious effort and your experience. I just have no relation to this kind of statement.

Some other factors of interest in this case include the use of a picture of the marriage framed as a circus. It took the form of a "punchline" and also symbolized the client's concern over his marital relationship of the past. By painting a picture, Erickson transformed the problem from feeling information to visual information. Something may feel very bad as feeling data, but when it is transformed to the visual realm it becomes, at worst, an unsightly picture. As such, it does not provide unnecessary discomfort. A problem which may seem unbearable when taken as a mass of feelings becomes more manageable and more easily comprehended when seen in a new framework by the client's conscious mind.

Leading up to this direct work, Erickson suggested the trance phenomena of time distortion. This began with the phrase "One day in September. . . ." As he built this section, the drama was developed around mystery to hold the client's attention. This came to the first unresolved ending with the apparently purposeful pronoun alteration: "And then *you* said, 'You know I've got the envelopes in my pocket. I haven't completed my composition'." This intentional violation of grammar served the purpose of adding to the general overload of George's conscious mind and unconscious search.

The symbol of "blue" and its appearance on the horse's rear end, the clown, and the merry-go-round was an impressive stroke of creativity. This sort of creativity may be difficult for others to recreate. However, the embedded structure can be recreated by others who wish to diagnose and intervene in this manner and yield similar results. Erickson's style is available to all therapists and not merely to those who consider themselves especially creative.

In this example Erickson conformed to a schedule of associations that began and ended with references to the matching metaphor. He then embedded a metaphor or set of metaphors for the purpose of eliciting experiential resources, including trance phenomena, and he further embedded any treatment work literally or symbolically related to the symptom. He began with the story of a man who made repeated attempts to get what he wanted from a swamp. It ended, following the story of new doctors being sent to Erickson to be insulted, with a final brief reference to the stick in the swamp.

Embedded within this lithograph story were several stories with several purposes: the story of Amil's international award for achievement, suggestions for time distortion, associations to Amil's second marriage, the end of his first marriage with the resource of assertiveness, and finally, in the middle of the metaphors was a symbolic painting of a circus used to elicit diagnostic information from the client about his marital role. If we add an induction and reorientation to either side of the set of metaphors the entire pattern now becomes:

A1. Induction.
    B1. Begin (matching) metaphor.
        C1. Resource and trance phenomena metaphors.
            D. Direct work addressed at symptom.
        C2. Link resources to social network.
    B.2. End matching metaphor.
A2. Reorient to waking state.

We will briefly summarize these steps and relate them to the previous transcript.

A1. Induction

Of course, no formal induction existed in this transcript. The induction step is included here only for completeness as we offer this first glimpse into the structure of the multiple embedded metaphor modality. The use of paradox and metaphor fixated attention and tended to elicit trance phenomena even when none were suggested.

Suggestions for trance may be very subtle indeed. "This is the essence of the utilization approach to indirect communication; talking about food can make us actually hungry; a discussion of the dynamics of hypnosis with interesting case histories can evoke an actual experience of hypnosis in the listener" (Erickson & Rossi, 1981, p. 259).

B1. Matching Metaphor

Again, we define the matching metaphor as that metaphor which is placed in the primary position and which offers a dramatic theme parallel to the presenting problem. The purpose of the initial metaphor is to engage attention and capture conscious and unconscious perception. It is frequently one of the six metaphors developed from assessing the client's possible comprehensive changes.

This metaphor is begun but not resolved. The elements of suspense and mystery are manufactured to hold and fixate attention and tangents are begun which leave the drama unfinished and the client "on the edge of settlement." In this example Erickson presented the story of the man driving repeatedly for 12 trips to the marsh to find the landscape he wanted for an oil painting.

C1. Retrieve Resources

In this phase various desired resources are retrieved with tangential metaphors designed to stimulate and elicit them. These resources might be called automated patterns of feeling, perceiving, and behaving. Sometimes the resources exist in fact and frequently they must be "created" by bundling together associated bits and pieces of experience.

Erickson digressed for any length of time necessary to create the resource. The embedded metaphor framework becomes increasingly odd to the conscious mind of the client but continues to be relevant for learning needed by the unconscious mind to deal with the problem.

Trance phenomena are developed as vehicles by which one passes into experiences disallowed by the original frame of reference. Trance phenomena might be said to be tools for investigating experiential resources. They are the microscopes, telescopes, time machines, and x-ray machines that facilitate clients' attempts to expand and use subtle and fleeting mental mechanisms for therapeutic gain.

A variety of characters, anecdotes and embedded commands can be used at "C1" and they need not be related either to one another or to the original story. Metaphors designed to address attitude restructuring or emotional role goals are often useful devices at this stage of the embedded structure. In this example Erickson used the story of Amil and his mysterious time disorientation and demarked the arrival and departure at this phase by the repeated use of the line about the international award Amil won.

D. Direct Work

In the direct work phase interventions are customarily aimed at the "heart of the neurosis," as Erickson would say. The interventions in the direct phase often do not address the concerns expressed by the client's conscious mind. Rather, the direct work phase is aimed at the "real" or most serious difficulty. This is the phase where the therapy works to resolve unconscious emotional conflicts and, metaphorically speaking, to free bound energy that needs to be directed more constructively in the client's life.

One may, as Erickson did, communicate most directly with the client, even request speech from the client, and give literal instruction at this phase. In this case Erickson painted a symbolic picture and requested ideomotor feedback for diagnostic purposes, thus accomplishing investigative work. Verbal investigation at this phase is occasionally directed at gaining the client's help in determining the function of the symptom and leaving the client with amnesia by suggestions to that effect on both sides of the embedded investigation.

Some direct work patterns that we repeatedly find useful have been referred to with separate titles to distinguish the type of treatment each offers. These include building self-image thinking, reciprocal inhibition for ideas and feelings, and simple "punchlines" of instruction. The complete list discussed in Chapter 8 includes:

1) Directives or "punchlines."
2) Scramble.
3) Reframing.
4) Dissociative reviewing.
5) Reciprocal inhibition.
6) Redecision.
7) Life mazes.
8) Creating social interface.

In Erickson's example, he used metaphoric punchlines to further diagnose his client. He requested, "Amil, if I'm correct tell me so." He then continued with the details of the picture: "She treated him like the south end of a northbound horse, had made a clown out of him," etc. Although this is a graphic example of Erickson's poignant humor, one need not use humor at this or any other stage of the multiple embedded metaphor. Working literally to direct experiential changes in the symptom at this midpoint in the multiple embedded metaphor structure maximizes the dissociation of the conscious mind. Therefore, the client is most protected from disturbing images introduced in the therapy at this juncture.

C2. Link Resources to the Social Network

It is desirable to order and link resources to images that will serve as cues for association to the resources in the client's immediate social world. If this is done correctly, the client will have gained a map of conduct that can direct him or her to necessary and desirable experiences when they are needed in actual social situations in the future. Cues in those social situations will stimulate associations to unconscious learnings from the therapy session with as much ease as possible. This is what Erickson suggested when he detailed how George was to assertively and effectively talk back to his first wife.

This linking can be done within the context of the embedded metaphors while resolving tangential metaphors that were begun in "C1." Building in images of future situations serves to associate the client to desired resources during real future incidents. Such map-building operates in much the same way as posthypnotic suggestion stimulates behaviors which are to be enacted subsequent to the session. The associations also, therefore, preshape perceptions that the client will have at future growth choice-points. Resources are linked to current and anticipated developmental tasks to insure relevance to the client's actual life circumstances. Since the client will make the best choice possible, it is necessary to help the client build associations to resources that operate as efficiently, easily, and rewardingly as less adaptive experiences have operated.

B2. End Matching Metaphor

The end of the original metaphor brings meaningful resolution to the multiple tangents that were taken in the session and provides closure for the conscious mind regarding the original story that has been suspended for so long. These "endings" are often designed to model desirable outcomes, taking into account the client's overall expected adjustment. The time frame may be immediate or long-range and the outcome need not always be positive. It may be surprising or humorous. The design of the outcome is less important than the reassociations of experience that were accomplished at an unconscious level during the entire multiple embedded sequence. That is, the outcome in Erickson's story with George was a less important influence on his behavior than the actual elicitation of time distortion, aggressive behavior, and "standing up and talking back" to his wife. The transition from the previous metaphor may have no logic. Amnesia is enhanced by the lack of associative links from one stage of the structure to the next.

If associations between relevant resources and the client's next logical developmental task or upcoming stage of family development were not built in the previous phase ("C-2"), then such associations would need to be created within the context of ending the matching metaphor. The previous stage will have linked resources to the immediate social situation and this stage will propel the associations further, into the next logical phase of development. In that way the client's immediate changes are incorporated into a map which is mindful of and conducive to the client's future change and growth. The client will not have resolved a problem in the immediate future that is incompatible with the broader cycle of life and ongoing development. In other words, immediate changes create the foundation and associative mechanism which facilitate and actually generate further changes. We refer to this phenomenon as "generative change."

A2. Orient to Waking State

When induction has been used the overall effect of the metaphors is heightened because the client is able to invest increased attention in the session. The hypnotist, upon arousing the client, may reinforce final statements and suggestions about learnings or tasks with paradoxical binds, suggestions for phenomena such as amnesia, conscious and unconscious specialization in the therapy tasks, learning styles, posthypnotic suggestion, and so on. Affirmations and paradoxical suggestions are useful here, as well as references to the here-and-now context. Also, any utilization begun in the initial stages of induction might need to be "recapped" as the client exits from the altered state.

IDEOMOTOR RESPONSE AND CLIENT FEEDBACK

The client's ideomotor feedback in the direct work portion of the Erickson example was specifically requested ideomotor behavior. You will recall that Erickson asked for the response with the line: "Amil, if I'm correct tell me so." Ideomotor feedback from the client during metaphor is continuous even when it is not requested directly. Erickson preferred to:

> . . . utilize a patient's own natural means of ideomotor signaling whenever possible. Whatever natural and automatic movements a patient makes in ordinary conversation can be studied for their metacommunicative value. Besides the more obvious head and hand movements, eye-

blinking (slow or rapid), body-shifting, leg movements, arm position (e.g., crossed over one another as a "defense"), lip-wetting, swallowing, and facial cues, such as frowning and tensions around the mouth and jaw, can be studied for their commentary on what is being said verbally (Erickson & Rossi, 1981, p. 122).

It is accepted that the original scientific explanation given by Chevreul in 1854 still applies to ideomotor behavior. He suggested that ideomotor movements are minute muscle responses set in motion by the unrecognized thoughts of the subject. Similarly, Bernheim explained all of hypnosis as a matter of ideomotor behavior which he considered "the aptitude for transforming the idea received into an act" (Erickson & Rossi, 1981, p. 114). Although the idea of using ideomotor behavior for tracking inclinations of thought did not seem to occur in the clinical field until the early work of Erickson and LeCron, using it in metaphoric treatment is a constant requirement. Erickson believed that all behavior was ideomotor behavior.

It is not surprising that the importance of this psychological level communication is best known to hypnotherapists. Hypnotic effects of "normal" (not officially considered hypnotic) communication are so prevalent that therapists are often less aware than hypnotists of the ongoing nonverbal communication revealed in a session. In addition to the difficulty of sensing ideomotor behavior during verbal therapies is the problem of what to do in response to nonverbal information once it is observed. By far the most well-known and frequently used response to ideomotor behavior in nonhypnotic therapies is to comment on its occurrence. This type of commenting about a communication or "metacommenting" is usually posed as a therapeutic confrontation or investigation. Unfortunately, requesting insight and information from a client's conscious mind about the meaning of unconscious and unnoticed behavior is rather like asking the black box to explain itself.

In hypnotherapy, however, such subtle responses from the client are seemingly amplified by their juxtaposition with the client's verbal silence. Erickson tended to conduct therapy differently from insight-oriented therapists in regard to metacommenting and thus developed a number of more creative responses to ideomotor behavior. He utilized the response to metaphor, both when it was spontaneously produced by the client as in normal conversation and when it was explicitly requested as in the above case. According to Erickson, "All forms of body language can be understood as systems of ideomotor signaling" (Erickson & Rossi, 1981, p. 119). The operator need only learn to distinguish ideomotor signaling from the behavioral indicators of the unconscious search, which consist of a loss of tonicity in cheek muscles, pupil dilation, eye scanning, slowed blink and swallow reflexes, increased skin pallor, muscle lassitude, and general loss of movement in the gross muscle groups.

Generally, the use of ideomotor behavior with metaphor is like the use of a clue in a treasure hunt. The very fact that a clue was found indicates that hunting is a valid pursuit to continue. Although the clue does not indicate any particular "answer" with certainty, it does delimit the range of searching one does after finding it.

The movement of an eyebrow during a metaphor does not necessarily indicate a "yes" or a "no" or a "I had that experience" communication. It does indicate, however, that the topic under discussion and the turns the topic has taken are relevant and worth pursuing. It indicates that the client has a map of experience that makes a distinction of difference at that point. It is like that which Bateson called "the difference which makes a difference" (Bateson, 1972, p. 381). Further pursuit of such differences by means of metaphoric details allows a therapist to track which angle of the story was the most relevant and essentially diagnose aspects of the client's understanding, memory, disposition, and affect.

In a training workshop, a psychologist began tearing as she listened to a psychiatrist produce a metaphor about a special pumpkin growing in a pumpkin patch. The psychiatrist had actually anticipated the opposite response to his metaphor about a special and highly desired growth process. Noticing the tearing he began investigating the client's changes in ideomotor response.

By varying elements in his story it was possible to ascertain that the client had cried remembering performance pressure she felt as a child. Introduced into the story was the farmer who was intent on this being the prize pumpkin at the state fair. The "client's" affective involvement was intensified when the farmer's various activities designed to enhance the growth of his prize pumpkin were described. This intensification seemed to be the result of her related associations to chronic expectations of superiority she felt from her father. When the psychiatrist added that, despite the farmer's best intentions, the little pumpkin must have felt very sad sometimes, she emphatically nodded her understanding.

This flexibility in responding is characteristic of the Ericksonian approach, which is typified by utilization of the client's natural ideomotor behavior to guide the therapy. Reliance on feedback such as this relates the Ericksonian approach to schools of client-centered therapy and depth psychology.

SYMBOLS AND CONCEPTS IN THE DRAMAS

Speaking of depth psychology, one final mention of the use of symbols in these metaphors is now necessary. Mental engagement depends on the search phenomena initiated by the word-images offered to a client. To the extent

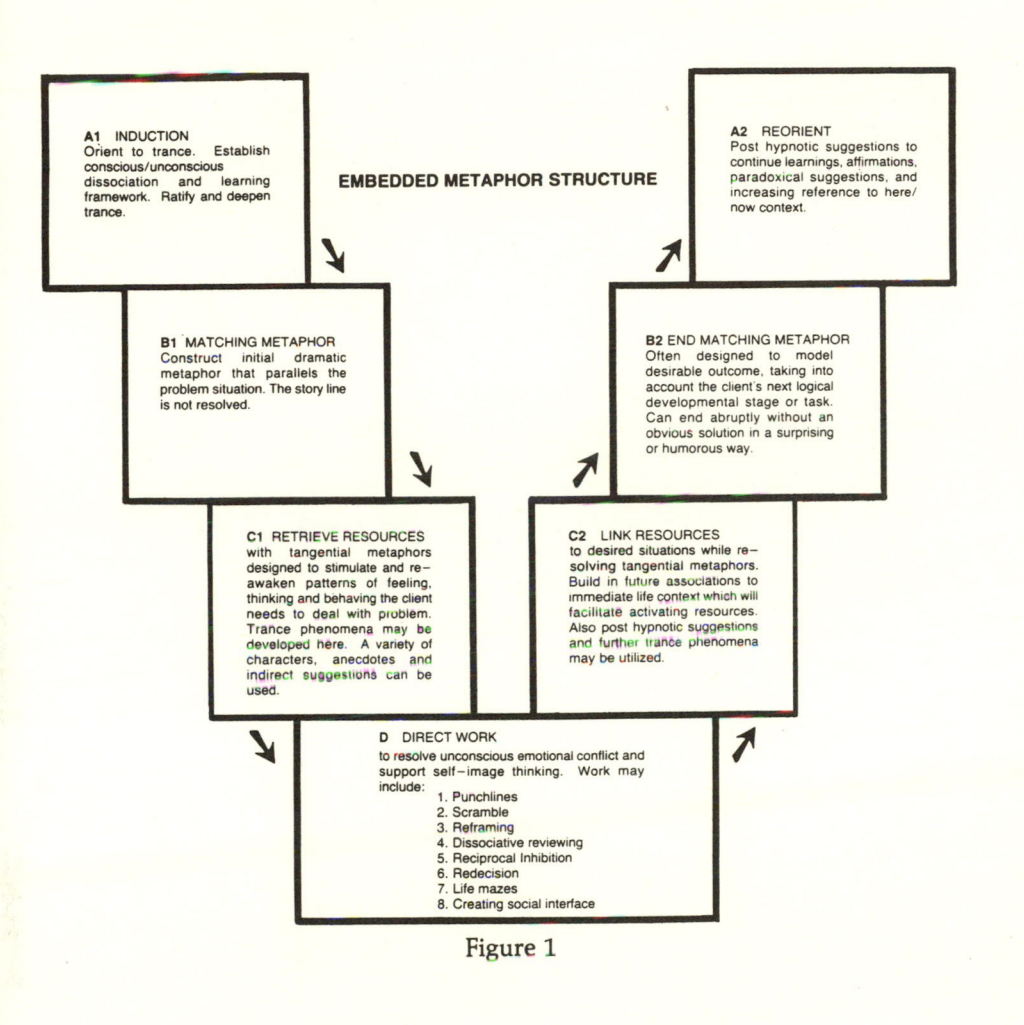

EMBEDDED METAPHOR STRUCTURE

A1 INDUCTION
Orient to trance. Establish conscious/unconscious dissociation and learning framework. Ratify and deepen trance.

A2 REORIENT
Post hypnotic suggestions to continue learnings, affirmations, paradoxical suggestions, and increasing reference to here/now context.

B1 MATCHING METAPHOR
Construct initial dramatic metaphor that parallels the problem situation. The story line is not resolved.

B2 END MATCHING METAPHOR
Often designed to model desirable outcome, taking into account the client's next logical developmental stage or task. Can end abruptly without an obvious solution in a surprising or humorous way.

C1 RETRIEVE RESOURCES
with tangential metaphors designed to stimulate and re-awaken patterns of feeling, thinking and behaving the client needs to deal with problem. Trance phenomena may be developed here. A variety of characters, anecdotes and indirect suggestions can be used.

C2 LINK RESOURCES
to desired situations while re-solving tangential metaphors. Build in future associations to immediate life context which will facilitate activating resources. Also post hypnotic suggestions and further trance phenomena may be utilized.

D DIRECT WORK
to resolve unconscious emotional conflict and support self-image thinking. Work may include:
1. Punchlines
2. Scramble
3. Reframing
4. Dissociative reviewing
5. Reciprocal Inhibition
6. Redecision
7. Life mazes
8. Creating social interface

Figure 1

that the imagery is consistent with something in the client's history, it will engage deep unconscious search. Symbolic imagery such as that illustrated by Jung (1959, 1964) is perhaps the most captivating. Natural and cyclical imagery, meditative objects from all traditions, religious and spiritually moving symbols, and some abstract symbols make appropriate content for metaphors or serve meaningfully as components within metaphors. For example, in the Florence transcript, one of the "precious possessions" that washed overboard in the unbalanced canoe was a "small golden cross," which was included to symbolize those spiritual developments which were important to her. Other symbols of identity and mobility were also included.

It might be argued that "higher" symbolism appeals to a higher principle in the human psyche and is of intrinsic value for that reason alone. While this is an optimistic and refreshing thought, there was little encouragement from Erickson for pursuing this aspect of symbols. The apparent value in using symbols is far less arcane. The commonality of experience expressed by symbols simply guarantees that a client will have some personal meaning to attach to the imagery. The universality of the symbol multiplies the number of probable associations the client is likely to make.

Having examined the components of diagnosis, paradox, dramatic metaphor, multiple embedded arrangements, ideomotor behavior, and symbolism, we now turn to considerations about conscious/unconscious dissociation induction and indirect suggestion.

Part Two
INDUCTION
AND RESOURCES

5 INDUCTION AND INDIRECTION: THE INTERPERSONAL FRAMEWORK

Let's begin by dispelling the myth that some people cannot be hypnotized. Erickson has said, "Hypnotism and hypnosis are the terms applied to a unique, complex form of unusual but normal behavior which can probably be induced in every normal person under suitable conditions and also in persons suffering from many types of abnormality" (*CP* III, p. 21). Again he wrote, "One hundred percent of normal people are hypnotizable . . . A mentally ill patient can be hypnotized, but it is difficult. The feebleminded person can be hypnotized, but it is difficult. Various types of neurotics can be hypnotized, but again, some of them are difficult subjects" (*CP* III, p. 29). Since hypnosis is merely a modality in which people communicate ideas and understandings and intensify concentrated internal awareness, we like to say that anyone who can be socialized can be hypnotized.

As we have stated, Erickson believed that hypnosis was a special form of relationship. He also believed that a person's cooperation was necessary for trance to be developed, although he added: ". . . but sometimes this cooperativeness is well concealed behind a superficial attitude of unwillingness, with a consequent distortion of the true situation" (*CP* III, p. 25). For that reason he believed that people could not be hypnotized against their will.

Erickson's typical approach to induction represented a departure from the historical use of devices and direct suggestion. Erickson captured a person's attention with paradox or metaphor, or by utilizing the presenting behavior. Fixation of attention is itself a minimal alteration in consciousness and produces signs of light trance. But Erickson was quick to appeal to a client's ability to dissociate patterns of thinking. By establishing a polarity in the client's thinking called the "conscious and the unconscious," Erickson helped his clients produce a uniquely personal hypnotic trance.

Trance is by its nature interpersonal. Subsequent autohypnotic experiences might still be considered interpersonal since they are elaborations of the initial interpersonal framework. "It is construction of such interlocking networks of associations that gives 'body' or substance to trance as an altered state of consciousness with its own guideposts, rules, and 'reality'" (Erickson & Rossi, *CP* I, p. 464). Original communications that teach trance to the client, memory of these communications, and the various affects and mental mechanisms that are elicited by the communications may be seen as a package of associations that comprise discrete altered states of consciousness. Each learned state will be rule-governed when the trance is repeated in private, just as it was originally rule-governed when it was constructed in an interpersonal framework. Conversely, discrete ego states or altered states of consciousness may be traced to their particular etiologic beginnings: interpersonal communications.

SAFEGUARDS AND ILL EFFECTS

Erickson dismissed questions about harmful effects of hypnosis. "Concerning harmful effects, no well-experienced hypnotist has ever reported any," he stated (*CP* III, p. 25). However, he was well aware that a hypnotist's personality problems could stimulate hysterical behavior in the clients with whom he or she worked. In these cases ill effects were traceable to the personality of the hypnotist and not the hypnosis.

Erickson's ethical attitude toward his clients and trainees, while reflected in humane principles of treatment, was polished by practical considerations which grew from studied observation. He wrote, "Any attempt to force upon hypnotic subjects, however deep the trance, suggestions unacceptable to their total personalities leads either to a rejection of the suggestions or to a transformation of them so that they can then be satisfied by pretense behavior. . . . The need to appreciate the subject as a person possessing individuality which must be respected cannot be overemphasized" (*CP* I, p. 146).

Elsewhere, he stated that "the patient must be protected at all times" (*CP* IV, p. 459). Even when paradox and other shocking psychological interventions are used, safety is produced because the "patient and therapist are bound together in therapeutic encounter by powerful psychological forces" (*CP* IV, p. 458). Erickson believed the forces of a relationship created a sort of shield. Within the protection of the interpersonal framework, various experiences could be safely entertained and therapeutically used. Erickson's decisions to use the mild shock of surprise or paradox were studied decisions. Similar interventions by Ericksonian practitioners should be carefully designed and considered in light of the total treatment.

Since he believed that "the personal relationship established between the operator and the subject is of great importance" (*CP* III, p. 29), his establishment of that relationship was different with each client and was influenced by the client's motivation for seeking treatment and his or her special circumstances. Erickson's genuine intent to establish a strong relationship was continually manifested by his willingness to enter into the perceptual and experiential world of the client. His unusual interventions were manufactured in the framework of that relationship, based on assessment of the unique individual.

Safety was further insured by the practical aspects of associations he helped clients make. No less important than his sincere intent was his degree of understanding about aspects of practical living. Knowledge and understanding were provided by his personal experience and observation. Ericksonian hypnotists will have difficulty matching Erickson's range of personal experience accumulated over nearly eight decades. They can, however, enter into relationships with clients and reflect a sincere interest in each unique individual. Everyone can relate to "down to earth" wisdom, practical aspects of living, and simple operations of conduct such as those Erickson shared. Thinking meaningfully about the seemingly mundane imparts a certain security and peace of mind. But even more importantly, the sense of being understood is imparted within or by such a therapeutic relationship. In turn, a client can be expected to make practical and meaningful interpretations of the suggestions and ideas presented in the therapy session.

Also, a veil of protection can be extended around those relationships based on complete respect for each special client. The device of metaphoric frame protection was one of the most notable elements of relationships with Erickson. Respect for and protection of the client are part of the package of metaphor. Like metaphoric frame protections, hypnotic induction can also provide a protective frame as a safeguard when conducted as an explicit dissociation between conscious and unconscious activity.

ATTITUDE AND CONFIDENCE

The Ericksonian hypnotherapist must have a personal manner that gives credibility and potency to his or her interventions. It can be called congruity, sincerity, or confidence. Erickson stated, "A good therapist should be utterly confident" and he held the attitude: "You are going to accomplish your purpose, your goal. And I am very confident. I look confident. I act confident. I speak in a confident way . . ." (Zeig, 1980, p. 61). He observed that his degree of confidence and congruity facilitated the therapy and led him to succeed where others did not. Clients sensed it and were likely to rely upon his suggestions. Haley explains this interpersonal dimension of trance as a relationship typified by Erickson's holding the special right to define the context or meaning of the interaction (Haley, 1963). This was a special right that he would never relinquish and would rarely allow others to doubt or question.

SOCIAL FOUNDATIONS OF HYPNOTIC LANGUAGE

Hypnosis depends upon communicating and ultimately on the cultural system of language. The development of the individual and the "self" is intimately connected with the development of the language and social interaction. "Out of language emerges the field of the mind," wrote Mead (1965, p. 195). It is altogether fitting that we find in Erickson's hypnosis an interpersonal framework:

> In brief, hypnosis is a cooperative experience depending upon a communication of ideas by whatever means available, and verbalized, ritualistic, traditional rote-memory techniques for the induction of hypnosis are no more than one means of beginning to learn how to communicate ideas and understandings in a joint task in which one person voluntarily seeks aid or understandings from another (*CP* I, p. 336).

Within this interpersonal framework one can examine the communications he used for his artful inductions. The use of indirect suggestions and binds was his trademark. Even the beginning Ericksonian hypnotist will discover that the way suggestions are expressed is a very important clinical skill. The difference between using indirect suggestion and using direct suggestion to produce a trance was the critical difference in Erickson's work that frequently produced results where none were likely. We would like to expand on the types of indirect suggestion so that we might demonstrate the applicability of such language to induction, to therapeutic communication in general, and to metaphor specifically.

Erickson's use of indirect suggestion may seem similar to building the foundation of a house with toothpicks. The apparently "feeble" little sentences were transactions far removed from forceful behavior. The seeming paradox was expressed when Erickson underscored that "hypnosis is a cooperative experience." The obscure relationship between everyday social suggestions and behavior is clarified, however, when the hypnotic and influential results of everyday communication upon experience are considered.

The thoughtful use of common and everyday language has always provided the foundation for systems of education, debate, negotiation, and philosophy. It is logical, therefore, to understand Erickson's use of language in hypnosis by examining common, everyday language. We find in colloquial language the precursors of hypnotic language and hypnotic response. That is, natural language makes possible a range of implied commands and definitions of reality and these make it the powerful socializing tool about which Mead wrote.

This category of "normal everyday induction language" contains certain leading words and words which link, presuppose, or imply commands in a special way. For example, if we say, "You can read faster," we have suggested the command "read faster," but have not alerted your conscious mind to resist. This is a curious command because it seems the use of the word "can" alerts listeners to question their ability to perform the activity that it qualifies.

These socially acceptable channels for induction and transpersonal influence (Laing, 1967) seem to provide a broad basis for understanding and creating hypnotic responses in everyday "normal communication." We believe that they contribute, as do other concepts in this book, to the demystification of communication in general, and hypnosis in particular, by advancing empirical and logical understanding of the dynamics of micro and macro patterns of communication and experiential response.

The simplicity of these "commands" would make them easily transparent except that they are used with such frequency that most people are desensitized to their occurrence. In normal communication there is a range of frequency of use of these indirect directives that varies from family to family. Transactional experts agree that there is a normal range and that excessive use beyond that range in everyday family communication is pathological (Hart, 1976). The scope of this "normal range" is difficult to say. It has been estimated that 25 to 50 percent of the sentences spoken in an average family contain some element of implied command, redefinition or other alteration that challenges perception. It has been speculated that use above the frequency of 75 percent is increasingly pathological.

A hypnotherapist's abundant use of implied directives would run the risk of drawing attention to the manipulative influence of this normal mechanism. This would create resistance and allow the conscious mind of the subject to attack the hypnotist's suggestions, be on guard, or detract from the rapport. Perhaps this is why people have grown hypersensitive and suspicious of the Madison Avenue sales pitch.

We teach the following categories, however, to increase awareness of everyday trance-eliciting speech and promote therapists' skill in noticing the influence they have on their clients during even the least sophisticated verbal exchanges. The social mechanisms of influence are built into the language and are as pervasive and powerful in normal conversation as they are in the therapy session. Heightened awareness of the effect of such speech on others often creates a temporary artificiality or self-consciousness when speaking. The therapist is, however, far more aware of the psychological effect of the words and phrases than the listener is. The apparent problems of redundancy and repetition in using these culturally allowed patterns can easily be remedied with metaphoric drama and indirect suggestions and binds.

Implied Directives

Implied directives (Erickson, Rossi, & Rossi, 1976, p. 188) include all sentence forms containing auxiliary words such as "can," "will," "might," "should," "must," etc. In contrast, consider three examples of directives:

1) "Sit there quietly and close your eyes."
2) "Concentrate on your relaxation and listen to my voice."
3) "Don't move."

Although there is nothing incorrect about these sentences, they do invite a certain resistance, doubt, or skepticism from all but the most compliant client. They are so direct that they alert the listener to the needs of the hypnotist and they seem to ignore the immediate needs of the client. More than any other form of speech, direct commands define the psychological relationship between the parties as metacomplementary (Haley, 1963) or one that ulteriorly resembles authoritative leadership and compliant follower. Redundancy or overuse of this type of directive eventually invokes the various transference responses clients have in regard to authorities.

But using implied directive induction language, the previous directives become:

1) "Can you sit there quietly and close your eyes?"
2) "Will you concentrate upon relaxation or will you listen to my voice?"
3) "You may find that if you need to move you will do so very slowly."

In these examples a certain permission seems to be offered by the therapist and, as with any permission, a command is being given at the psychological level in a conversational and nonchallenging manner (Lankton, Lankton, & Brown, 1981). The result of this "packaging," if done well, is a reduction in the client's resistance, doubt, and skepticism. The judicious use of this simple alteration of speech provides clients with the maximum opportunity for individual, creative, or unique responses. These responses, however, will be explained as occurring for some "other" reason at the conscious level, due to the unspoken cultural rules that prohibit exposing the implied directive.

Implied directives which use words about consciousness such as "wonder," "surprise," "curious," "know," "doubt," and "hope," for example, will affect clients in still another noticeable manner (Erickson & Rossi, *CP* I, p. 435). Erickson asked a client: "Aren't you surprised you can't stand up" (Erickson & Rossi, 1979, p. 127) and in so doing focused the client's awareness not only on her inability to stand up but also on her awareness of her state of consciousness (surprise). (The reader might consider household examples from the same species, such as: "Aren't you ashamed of yourself?") In the first example, Erickson suggested that the client would be unable to stand up but he had done it by simultaneously shifting her awareness of her consciousness and not simply her awareness of her muscles.

Contrast this indirect approach to its direct-command counterpart: "You can't stand up," which certainly may invite resistance and testing from a client. This direct command may be a clever ambiguity which tends to blur the line between observation (the person is relaxed and cataleptic) and the desired outcome ("don't stand up"), but it is likely that the experience will be limiting and unnecessarily challenging to the conscious mind of the client. Later in this chapter we discuss the selection and use of indirect suggestions and binds for particular outcomes; for now, however, we will simply state as a "rule of thumb" that it is best to choose the most indirect suggestion at every juncture.

Psychological Implications

Adding an understanding of "normal, everyday" presuppositions can transform implied directives into more dynamically artful suggestions. Presuppositions are speech patterns that "take for granted" some unspoken information or experience which must be accepted in part or in full if the listener is to be understood. Particularly enticing are psychological implications that presume an entire group of experiences by the use of words like "certain," "one," and "just." These are presuppositions of existence, number, and occurrence. Erickson used various presuppositions to create psychological implications (Erickson & Rossi, 1976, p. 59). The socialization and hypnotic influence in normal communication can be attributed to the combination of psychological implication and implied directives.

Example one, before alteration, was: "Sit there quietly and close your eyes." As an implied directive, it became: "Can you sit there quietly and close your eyes?" or "You can sit there quietly and close your eyes." Embellishing it further with psychological implication, it becomes: "Can you just sit there and only begin to close your eyes?"

Example two, before alteration, was: "Concentrate on your relaxation and listen to my voice." Altered to imply a command, it read: "Will you concentrate upon relaxation or will you listen to my voice?" Embellished with psychological implication it reads: "Will you begin to concentrate upon a certain relaxation or will you only listen to my voice?"

Example three was: "Don't move." The implied directive transformed it to: "You may find that if you need to move you will do so very slowly." This

sentence, with psychological implication, becomes: "The first thing you may
find is if you need to move you will begin very slowly." In each example the
same command is implied within the sentence. The client may notice the command, but will only notice it unconsciously. At the conscious level the communication is only a polite and response-inviting communication. At the
psychological level the client not only responds without the interference of
conscious resistance but also engages a certain amount of self-motivation due
to the involvement of the unconscious search elicited in the hypnosis of ·
everyday communication. When the client's mentations are thus stimulated
s/he assists the therapist with the hidden inner activity of a personal search
for meaning.

Meaning-full Words

This type of natural induction language consists of complex nouns such as
"hopes," "dreams," "resources," "talents," "sensations," "thoughts," "unconscious," "beliefs," "memories," and "learnings," and abstract or vague words
such as "brilliant," "courageous," "adventuresome," "loving," "genuine,"
"stubborn," "head-strong," and "individualistic." These words, in everyday
use, pack more meaning per syllable than any speaker could really hope to
convey to the listener. Yet, these meaning-full words are frequently part of
"normal" communication. Indeed, they impart to "normal communication"
a pretense of "real" understanding being conveyed between people exchanging words. Hence, they comprise an important part of the social hypnosis of
our culture. Erickson used them purposefully to the client's advantage in
treatment sessions.

In daily communication people share an illusion that they have communicated, that is, that they have shared experiences and caused one another to
think of the same images each had in mind as speaker. This illusion is imparted by the vagueness of words which seemingly are full of meaning. If a
specific meaning is thought to be requested, people respond to these words
with the same search phenomena mentioned earlier: flattened cheeks, dilated
pupils, muscle lassitude, etc. By contrast, many people respond to such
meaning-packed words with instantaneous head nods and ideomotor behavior. The words have so much meaning attached in colloquial experience that
a listener is bound to identify one or another of the meanings (unless it is implied that a particular meaning is intended).

The hypnotist or therapist creates unconscious search by fixating conscious attention. Fixation occurs if the therapist implies that the meaning-full
words actually convey a precise meaning. Search phenomena are the result of

attempting to eliminate the large number of optional meanings and find the particular implied meaning. This is exactly the effect that Erickson capitalized upon during almost every moment of his sessions.

The effect of meaning-full words is found in their semantic impact. A noun, as you know, is a person, place, or thing . . . unless it is an imaginary or abstract "thing." In the latter case the word (a noun) conveys to the listener (and perhaps the user) that the abstracted idea is indeed a "thing." A simple noun conveys the impression of a relatively stable and unchanging experience. When you think about a "book" it is something that is, in your mind, a less transient experience than kissing. Kissing, a verb, conveys in its meaning an ongoing change of a particular type. A book, by contrast, conveys an idea of permanence.

Let's suppose a client says he is "hurting." He has conveyed an idea of some experience that changes over time. If another client says she has "hurt," she has conveyed the notion of a persistent and unchanging situation. The same is true when a therapist tells a client that s/he has "learnings." That purposeful use of the noun form conveys a persistent "thing" to the client. Using the word "learnings" presupposes a positive and unchanging quality of something learned. The client would have to be a master at linguistics in order to undo the attributions of positive qualities that Erickson would mention in a typical induction. He also offered supportive facts that seemed to back up the positive attributions he made: "Your unconscious contains a vast repository of experiences forged with integrity. . . . Do I have to prove it to you? . . ." Then might follow several anecdotes. His stories about learning the alphabet, learning to drive, turn, to stop an automobile, etc. usually proved sufficient to convince a client. But the natural role of conversational hypnosis will lull a listener into believing that there is a great deal of meaning, a priori, in the "meaning-full" words: "unconscious," "experiences," "repository," and "integrity."

Erickson was careful to select words that framed experiences in positive terms and emphasized the intelligence of each individual. He did not offend a client's sensibilities with his language except in those rare cases when such offensiveness was the aim of a thoughtful diagnosis and was intended as a therapeutic intervention. His approach was "to ask patients primarily to give their attention to one particular idea, . . . to center their attention on their own experiential learning, . . . to direct their attention to processes which are taking place within them, . . . directing patients' attention to processes, to memories, to ideas, to concepts that belong to them" (CP III, p. 29). The bulk of his verbiage contained examples of those meaning-packed ambiguous words: "ideas," "processes," "concepts," "memories," and "experiential learnings." A client's hypnotic response to these communications is guaranteed by the everyday social experience of hypnosis intrinsic to native speakers of a language.

We would like therapists to eliminate the use of complex nouns and adjectives which attribute undesirable or negative qualities to clients. We believe that, in the process of assisting clients with personal change, it is unnecessary to induce them to have conceptions of "resistances," "blocks," "impasses," and so on. Focusing awareness on these negative understandings is iatrogenically dangerous. It creates disorders stimulated by the therapist's suggestions. Normal communication has prepared people to become entranced by the use of such words. Such words should be used purposefully in accordance with Ericksonian principles, rather than prescribed by the dictates of tradition, theory, or ignorance about the interpersonal framework in which we all hypnotize one another.

The therapist's manner of delivery and presentation of any idea is especially important, since the impact these words (and their nonverbal counterparts) have on the client is all that will be available to make difficult reassociations of experience. Research at the University of Utah has demonstrated that the semantic labels used by the therapist will influence the course of therapy and will affect the client's reporting of experience. Patton, Fuhriman and Bieber (1977) used computer analysis to compare the verbs used by the client and the therapist over time. The verb categories used were called: experiencer, stative, benefactive, and agentive. They found that the frequency and usage of the verbs they categorized changed over the course of therapy and that the frequency of usage for both the clients and the therapists changed in unison. Therapists should expect, then, that word selection is of utmost importance, regardless of specific content, be it sharing theoretical constructs with clients, offering explanations to them, or framing their experience. This is true in all therapies and perhaps more so in hypnosis, where the therapist typically does the majority of the talking.

Based upon these language forms, hypnotic communication can be easily recognized in everyday social communication. Hypnotic communication is a part of every social context. The idea that simple grammar plays a part in hypnosis can serve to emphasize that all verbal and written communication has hypnotic properties. We will examine hypnotic influences in "nonhypnotic" therapies in Chapter 6, but for now our goal is to stress the fixation of conscious attention that results from such communication, as we detail more elaborate and formal methods of inducing trance. The dissociation between conscious and unconscious functioning alters experience more profoundly than the everyday communicational influences we have examined. These patterns do, however, provide the foundation for such dissociation.

CONSCIOUS/UNCONSCIOUS DISSOCIATION

Erickson's conscious/unconscious dissociations distinguished the trances he induced. His method facilitated an experiential distinction between the recognizable operations of conscious and unconscious functioning. The functioning of autonomous mental (and bodily) mechanisms and the operations of synthetic and autonomous ego mechanisms constitute the bulk of that which is referred to as the unconscious. Consciousness, by comparison, operates linearly, and often with qualities that might be called doubt, ambition, pride, confusion, and so on. Consciousness is aware of results of ego defense mechanisms and conceptualizes experience with linguistic and verbal functions.

Erickson's inductions often involved methodical delineations between the different functions of the conscious and unconscious minds. Creating trances that will be productively used requires careful attention to the same details. Erickson's conception of the unconscious mind, in contrast to the conscious mind, was the same as the difference between right and left hemispheres of brain functioning. Erickson and Rossi wrote: " . . . it is clear that a neuropsychological model utilizing the differences between right and left hemispheric functioning is also implicit in Erickson's work" (Erickson, Rossi, & Rossi, 1976, p. 277). The difference in hemispheric functioning might best be characterized by a chart that Erickson himself authored (Erickson, Rossi, & Rossi, 1976, p. 277).

Left Hemisphere (Awake)	Right Hemisphere (Trance)
Linguistic	Pantomime, kinesthetic, musical
Logical-grammatical	Visuospatial
Rational	Intuitive
Abstract	Perceptual-synthetic
Directed	Spontaneous
Focal	Diffuse
Effort	Comfort

Erickson offered anecdotes and suggestions as a means of educating and sensitizing clients to move away from their habitual left hemispheric patterns of thinking. He elaborated the labored learning of the conscious mind and the relatively relaxed learning of the unconscious. The conscious mind struggles to learn the shapes of letters of the alphabet, while the unconscious, unnoticed by the conscious mind, learns to make visual images. The unconscious frequently does the lion's share of learning and allows the conscious mind to attend to merely a portion of what is occurring. When a child is learning to walk, the unconscious learns to regulate breathing and muscle coordination, while the conscious mind keeps busy thinking about which toy will be picked up or what the parents are thinking.

Erickson considered the conscious mind to be the weaker, less intelligent, least reliable, and most easily fooled. But the valuing of the unconscious mind is not confined to Erickson's approach; it is common lore. Alfred Adler commented: "Man knows more than he understands" (1938, p. 258). Likewise, Erickson commented that "you know more than you think you know." These differences in functioning can easily be discussed with clients as a means of helping them learn trance. This dissociation frequently became the focus of Erickson's conversations. He insisted on using time during training and therapy sessions to educate individuals about the potentials of trance based on differences between their conscious and unconscious functioning. Following in his tradition, we find the naturalness of such observations makes clients feel that the topic is perfectly relevant and helpful.

THE FLOW OF INDUCTION

The following is a protocol for a complete conscious/unconscious dissociation induction. Although it is expressed as seven distinct steps, an overlapping of the steps is expected in any actual case. Steps one through four represent the induction itself. Steps five and six refer to treatment done in the trance—multiple embedded metaphors, for instance. Step seven refers to terminating the trance, final reorientation, and structuring the normal waking state.

1) Orient to trance (including physical, attitudinal and psychological orientation).
2) Fixate attention and rapport.
3) Create conscious/unconscious dissociation.
4) Ratify and deepen the trance state.
5) Establish a learning frame or learning set.
6) Utilize trance state and hypnotic phenomena for clinical goals.
7) Reorient to normal waking state.

Orienting the Client to Trance

Clients often need to be psychologically as well as intellectually oriented to trance. Psychological orientation often only involves asking clients if they have experienced trance before and how they experienced it. The discussion will focus them on previous trance experiences and foster the creation of a present trance. In the process of remembering any previous trance, psychological mechanisms used in it will be revivified. The focused client will revitalize and display a number of behaviors and feelings that operated in previous trances. The hypnotist may see muscle lassitude, slowed blink reflex, and even levitative movement of one arm, any of which can be "magnified" and used to encourage the current trance work. Even if clients have not been in "official" trance before, we ask them to imagine what they expect to experience. We might remind them of "common everyday" experiences of trance as a way of helping them retrieve trance abilities with which they are already familiar.

It is appropriate to begin each trance with a discussion of the client's beliefs about hypnosis. The discussion will also alert the hypnotist to any myths and negative biases that may be inhibiting the client. Many people are misinformed about trance and clinical hypnosis. Their misinformation creates anxiety, discomfort, and occasionally threatens the therapeutic relationship. It is not uncommon for clients to express a desire to avoid the use of hypnosis. When questioned about their preconceptions, they may reveal subscribing to one or several of these negative prejudices, biases, and myths about trance:

1) Hypnosis is a stuporous state in which they may lose their control.
2) They will be exceptionally vulnerable and may do something they do not wish to do.
3) They may not awaken after the trance.
4) If the trance is successful, they must be oblivious to what is said and done.
5) Hypnosis is the work of Satan.

We take these typical misunderstandings to be the logical result of both historical aspects of hypnosis and the current image of hypnosis portrayed by media. We remind clients that they are in a professional and clinical setting and that hypnosis will not be used to accomplish the results obtained by entertainers and stage performers. We give thoughtful and truthful answers to each concern. The fourth concern is not to be passed over quickly. Often clients who believe that they must be oblivious to events during trance in order to have been successfully "hypnotized" actually do develop an adequate trance but spend much of their time in trance doubting the effects. They doubt the validity of the trance because they have accomplished a heightened awareness and concentration and can hear everything said to them. These clients have a more personally rewarding experience when they first understand that trance is defined as a state of increased concentration and heightened awareness—not oblivion. The fifth myth is rarely voiced, even in the so-called "Bible belt" states. When it is a concern, however, it is the most irrational one and perhaps the most difficult to dispel, so we share here one of our customary responses.

When a prospective client fears hypnosis on the basis of believing it to be evil or the work of the devil, we take special care to speak the client's language. For example, we often refer to the King James Bible and the book of Acts. In Acts 10:10, the word "trance" is used. Simon Peter is placed into a trance by the Holy Spirit and prepared for the visitation of two others sent by the Spirit. Simon Peter receives visions and symbols in the trance that somehow prepare him for this upcoming encounter, though he has no conscious idea what the trance was about when he emerges from it.

We respectfully explain our understandings to clients. "It is important to give them the opportunity of discovering they can trust you" (Erickson & Rossi, 1981, p. 5). We consequently are as honest and objective as possible. We do intend, however, to be in the controlling position about which treatment approach we use with each client. Sometimes a client who is reluctant to experience trance labeled as "hypnosis" has no difficulty proceeding with eye closure, relaxation, focused inner concentration, and revivification of memories, traits, and personal resources.

In the induction example following this discussion of induction steps are several short but important statements which illustrate Erickson physically orienting the client (S.L.) to trance: "Would you turn your chair slightly and lean back in your chair with your hand on your thighs and look in this general direction. Don't move. Don't talk" (Erickson, personal communication, August 1977).

Fixating Attention and Rapport

The second step, rapid engagement and fixation of attention, is an aspect of rapport between individuals. "Now in hypnotizing the psychiatric patient I think one of the important things to do first is to establish a good conscious rapport" (Erickson & Rossi, 1981, p. 5). Erickson's manner of establishing rapport frequently involved three approaches:

1) He would customarily "speak the client's language," literally repeating the key words the client had used.
2) He used metaphors as an additional matching device.
3) He would match the facial expression, body posture, voice, tonal patterns, and the breathing of the client as a way to guide the speed of his verbal delivery. In so doing, unconscious as well as conscious rapport was established quickly.

Erickson speculated that one reason his approach created effective results in brief therapy settings was that he created rapport quickly and got the client's full attention. The Ericksonian style accelerates transference phenomena and transference responses from clients. It therefore facilitates investigating the client's most personal map of limitations and subtle resources within the shortest possible time period. He concluded from a review of research and clinical results: ". . . in the hypnotic interpersonal relationship, full-blown transference phenomena may develop rapidly, at times within hours or even minutes" (Erickson & Rosen, *CP* IV, p. 108). Consequently, many ideas can be communicated and much can be learned in a short period of time.

In order to further engage fixated attention, Erickson needed only to begin a mysterious, surprising, or suspenseful metaphor, or a surprising observation, revelation, or lesson. With attention thus captured and engaged, as previously explained, the client is prepared to entertain a novel framework that can be used in problem-solving. The relationship, thus established, serves as the basis or foundation for creating the mild confusion or learning embodied in the conscious/unconscious dissociation.

Erickson, for example, followed the orientation sentences described above with: "And I'm gonna talk about something that occurred in your childhood." Needless to say, the idea that he was going to discuss something about my childhood (of which he knew nothing) startled me. This was a surprise which captured attention! He continued: "And had to write the letters of the alphabet. It seemed like a terribly difficult task, all those letters, all those different shapes. Do you dot the 'e,' . . . 't' and cross the 'i'? And where do you put the loop on the 'b' and the 'd' and the 'p'?"

So, it was true that he spoke of something that had occurred in childhood. And soon the original mystery was replaced with curiosity, which was the experiential result of recalling mental mechanisms used to learn and remember the loops and dots of which he spoke. Fixation of attention in the relationship occurred due to nothing more than rapport and the normal "hypnosis" of everyday communication.

Fixation of attention tends to develop certain alterations of light trance previously described as search phenomena. Fixation on a stimulus initially presents the mind with a situation that calls for a novel or unconditioned response. The client's normal train of conscious associations is broken when the fixation is begun. As a result, reorganization may be stimulated. The primary device used by Erickson to create this reorganization was the conscious and unconscious dissociation.

Creating Conscious/Unconscious Dissociation

The dichotomy of mental functioning and presumable brain hemisphere lateralization gave rise to a frequent pattern in Erickson's "formal" inductions, as we have described. This same experience-building interaction was found in his anecdotal, metaphoric, and naturalistic inductions, but it was far more apparent in its pure linguistic form.

To simulate the polarity of thinking that is embodied in the conscious/unconscious dissociation induction, we present the following simple verbal exercise. An important prerequisite for actually conducting this type of induction is familiarity with the language used to convey the experience. We have frequently used this exercise to build that verbal fluency. It can be rehearsed privately, although we suggest that it be practiced as an interaction. Typically, one therapist creates and then delivers to a partner a sentence which contains one phrase about the conscious mind (from the first column), one causal link (from the middle column), followed by one phrase about the unconscious mind (from the third column). The partner only listens and experiences the effect of hearing it. Then, using that experience as a guide, the partner creates and shares a similar sentence. Likewise, the first therapist examines his or her subjective reaction to the dissociation sentence being offered and proceeds to deliver another example of conscious/unconscious dissociation statements back to the partner. It does not matter if the sentences begin with the unconscious statement and then proceed to the conscious statements. Indeed, variety adds interest.

Referring to the chart, the first therapist may say, "Your conscious mind is listening to and hearing my words and your unconscious mind is interested in what's most relevant." The second therapist, after evaluating the experience of receiving such a communication, may respond with "Your conscious mind is interested in learning one thing and your unconscious mind has its own ideas about what your needs are." In this way, therapists can create a wide variety of sentences by "mixing and matching" the items on each side and embellishing the arbitrary phrases given.

Therapists who wish to gain a substantial ability in being relevant for their clients and at the same time want to be sincere with the use of such special terminology have practiced the exercise methodically, adding other levels of complexity. The final level of complexity is achieved when therapists can comfortably generate a continuous series of dissociation sentences and direct them to the client's actual experience in the here and now. For instance, the first therapist of the hypothetical practice team might say, "Your conscious mind is thinking about what you just said while your unconscious mind allows you to continue experiencing the effect of my words." An advanced response from the second therapist might be, "The pride of your conscious mind is made possible by the broader knowledge of your unconscious." Another embellishment involves using synonyms for either the conscious or unconscious mind, such as "one part of you," "another part of you," or "your unconscious mind knows more than you do," in which case "you" is synonymous with the conscious mind.

Exercise 1
Conscious/Unconscious Dissociation Language Exercise

Your conscious mind:	Causal link:	Your unconscious mind:
—is listening to and hearing my words	and	—is doing something else
—may be interested in learning one thing	and	—is interested in what's relevant
—may have that doubt	and	—is developing a line of thought
—is possibly curious	and	—isn't even interested
—operates linearly	and	—thinks globally
—won't do much that's very interesting	as	—is really doing a lot for you
—is interested in one depth of trance	while	—has its own idea of what you need
—can focus on one spot	while	—is learning a great deal
—doesn't know how things will culminate	since	—makes things happen in your best interest
—is sorting, categorizing, and pidgeonholing	just as	—understands the context
—may be easily distracted	because	—can let your conscious mind discover later
—may be wondering about certain things	because	—holds a vast storehouse of learnings, dreams, and potentials
—is oriented to situations of the moment	at the same time	—acts in your own behalf

Our ongoing example of Erickson and the author (S. L.) reveals the artfulness, skill, and poignancy with which he used such dissociation statements to create a polarity of experience:

> Your unconscious mind knows much more than you do. Your conscious mind has an awareness and it's oriented to the situation of the moment. And so you're aware of desks and bookcase, wall hangings, telephone, which have nothing to do with your purpose in coming. But your unconscious mind can disregard all of those irrelevant facts and pay attention to my words, and pay attention to its own reactions. And much of the thinking we do in our unconscious mind occurs without our knowledge.

This example is only a step removed from the activity practiced in the previous exercise. Occasionally, his dissociation suggestions were more "straightforward," as in the exercise, but often they were even more subtly concealed within numerous anecdotes.

In most cases, this dissociation need not be developed with rigid adherence to one or another approach; rather a combination of approaches can be utilized. Erickson frequently used indirect suggestions to build the dichotomy of consciousness; then, at some point in the trance prior to clinical utilization, he would deliver numerous, specific conscious/unconscious language statements, especially if the client was first learning trance. Subsequently, the polarity was mentioned intermittently in the form of conscious and unconscious double binds, as shown later in this chapter. The high frequency of such language appeared to be a training of the client's perception shaped by the continuous reinforcement created by frequent use of the words. Subsequent reference to the dissociated functioning was interspersed in a manner typical of intermittent reinforcement. Perhaps due to this reinforcement paradigm, the learning of trance behavior is not prone to extinction while the relationship between the hypnotist and subject is maintained.

Any example of everyday unconscious operations could be utilized for Erickson's artful splitting of the conscious and unconscious: forgotten names, automatic driving, special concentration, learning to drive or read, and so on. In the transcript begun above he reinforced this polarity with several anecdotes, including the following:

> The speed of thought is the speed of electricity. And there are billions of brain cells, and they are constantly in action. And you had time enough to become aware of only a few of the thought processes that go on in your brain. And one simple stimulus can extract from your unconscious mind a great many thoughts that are apparently unrelated.

Ratifying and Deepening Trance

Communications calling the subject's attention to alterations which have resulted from fixated attention and dissociation of mental processes are referred to as "ratifying." Communications which intensify the potentials for trance phenomena are referred to as "deepening." Focusing a client's awareness on those alterations which have developed provides him or her a measure of conviction that tends to verify that an unusual set of events has indeed occurred.

Typical ratifying communications are evident in the induction we have been examining:

> And while I've been talking to you your respiration has changed. Your blood pressure has changed. Your muscle tone has changed. And your muscle reflexes have changed. Close your eyes now and feel the comfort. And the more comfort you feel the deeper into trance you'll go.

In another induction the same style can be recognized. Note, especially, the concentrated use of conscious/unconscious dissociation statements at the time of ratifying.

> Your unconscious can try anything it wishes but your conscious mind isn't going to do anything of importance. You'll notice that your conscious mind is somewhat concerned since it keeps fluttering your eyelids. But you altered your rate of breathing. You altered your pulse. You altered your blood pressure and without knowing it you're demonstrating the immobility that a hypnotic subject can show. There is nothing really important except the activity of your unconscious mind. And that can be whatever your unconscious mind desires (Erickson in Erickson, Rossi, & Rossi, 1976, pp. 9–11).

Establishing a Learning Set

Erickson encouraged learning regardless of the modality in which he worked. In hypnotic trances, however, a special emphasis was frequently delivered as an overall guiding plan for portions of the therapy. In the trance being traced he continued:

> And in the trance state you can let your unconscious mind survey that vast store of learnings that you achieved, that you have achieved during your lifetime. There are many learnings that you have made without knowing it. And many of the learnings that were important to you consciously have slipped into your unconscious mind.

While it is clear that this language continues the dissociation between the conscious and the unconscious, it also emphasizes a particular review of the client's memories: "learnings that you have achieved." The learning framework of this trance is one of increasing the client's awareness of "achievement" and competence derived from such achievement.

While each client or each therapy session calls for a different learning set appropriate to the tasks at hand, one thing remains constant: The unconscious is offered a framework in which to entertain the entire set of learnings in the session. Erickson's use of a learning framework applied to every level of the therapy. In contrast to a framework of "working through," "dealing with," or "self-actualizing," he stressed the generic term "learning." He applied the term to the global task of adjusting to life as a result of therapy, as well as the minute task of focusing on subtle unconscious movement in the therapy session. A learning framework permeated the interpersonal bond he formed with both his clients and students and it is therefore an essential part of an Ericksonian approach to treatment.

Utilizing the Trance for Change

Utilizing the trance for clinical goals requires considering the personality as a whole. We strongly discourage simply offering direct suggestions for symptom relief or removal. We hope this point has been made apparent from earlier discussions of history and diagnosis. It bears repeating, however, when one recalls the vast number of works on hypnosis that amount to nothing more than a formula that is one hundred years old: Relax the patient and inhibit the symptom with direct suggestions for health. Operating in that manner will secure the same difficulties to which Freud objected when he denounced hypnosis. Direct suggestion will bring only temporary relief, will intensify the transference relationship toward authority, and will increase repression of the conflict that led to the symptomatology.

A uniformly startling revelation to many therapists who have learned to induce and stabilize hypnotic trances is that they do not have an understanding of how to best make treatment interventions in the trance once it has been established. Once the idea of using direct suggestion has been surrendered, what then? There are three major categories or approaches that Erickson used to retrieve therapeutic experience for his clinical work in trance:

1) Using indirect suggestions to elicit experience and design the change.
2) Using metaphors and short anecdotes within the metaphoric framework to stimulate experiential resources and illustrate the change.
3) Providing literal explanation, fantasy rehearsal, and therapeutic prescriptions for using resources.

In his later years Erickson rarely resorted to telling a client what to do directly. For example, instead of telling a client to "think about your reason for coming here," he would be more inclined to say, "And so you're aware of desks and bookcases, wall hangings, telephone, which have nothing to do with your purpose in coming." This fine example of indirect suggestion illustrates one of the foundations on which his hypnotherapy treatment was grounded. Although the purpose of the suggestions was to build and associate therapeutic experience, the delivery of each topic was thoughtfully cloaked in indirect suggestion.

The use of metaphor and short anecdote was illustrated in the embedded metaphor story of George (see p. 118):

> And one of them got angry enough to come into my office and say: "You're a dirty bastard." I said: "You're quite mistaken. I'm a dirty, bloody bastard of a . . ." "No," he said, "you're a dirty son-of-a-bitch." "I'm a dirty, bloody son-of-a-bitch of a bastard."

Erickson did not directly command the client by saying, for instance, "Now you are going to become aware of unpleasant vulgar thoughts!" Instead, the anecdote begs an experiential participation from the client. It thus allowed but did not force the client to organize an appropriate response. That response was dictated by the client's personal history and the degree to which he could find the experiences useful in his frame of reference.

Erickson included personal experiences elicited by metaphor in the same category as the common trance phenomena. These consist of operations such as amnesia, age regression, time distortion, positive and negative hallucinations, and posthypnotic conduct. Indirect suggestions intermittently referring to the conscious/unconscious dissociation previously established help the client continue the framework in which new experiences are elicited. The conscious mind, which could be troubled by the inclusion of these previously excluded experiences, is reminded by the suggestions that it need not apply conventional reasoning to the new experiences. The outcome, therefore, is the client's willingness and ability to develop trance phenomena, examine novel experiences, and change operating frameworks.

Erickson seldom gave literal directives unless accompanied by experiential rehearsals. Sometimes these rehearsals took place outside of the office (considered "strategic" interventions in contrast to hypnotic interventions). Other cases, such as the well-known case of Monde (see p. 68), reveal Erickson being quite literal at certain points in the treatment. Novice hypnotherapists and those who persist in conducting hypnotherapy as it was a century ago must be reminded that Erickson's use of literal instructions in the case of Monde followed a lengthy series of indirect suggestions and anecdotes. The experiences elicited by the literal instructions were periodically shaped into therapeutic directives with indirect suggestions. An example follows:

> And you're going to go through a learning experience, and see just me. And that's all. You hear my voice. And now will come to your mind some very nice, happy experience out of your childhood. And I want you to describe it. (Description follows.) . . .
>
> And was two-year-old Monde having a very good time? And memorize all those good feelings, because there's a lot of them. It's a learning. Just as learning an alphabet and learning to recognize letters and numbers is the basis for an entire future of reading, writing, enumerating, so are the good feelings of splashing with total abandonment in water—something that you learn and will stay with you in later life to be used in a directed fashion (Lustig, 1975).

Here are very literal instructions for an age-regressed memory. However, these literal instructions did not occur until the ideas for the same phenomenon had been seeded and indirectly suggested several times: "Go deeply into trance, so that your unconscious can deal with that vast store of memories that you have." "And perhaps something very nice that you could recall that you haven't thought about for years." "And I think it'd be most interesting if you would find some childhood, infantile memory that you haven't thought of for years." "And sooner or later, I don't know just when, you will be wondering about something that you would like to see." And finally, "I talked with a young woman the other night and she's known what that good feeling was. She was holding her dog, and that was before she went to school."

These indirect suggestions for the phenomenon he eventually spoke of literally were intermittently woven into the previous 15 to 20 minutes of Monde's trance. It should be entirely obvious, then, that Erickson's apparent literal instructions, when used, came after a great deal of preparation with indirect suggestion.

Finally, the literal instructions were delivered when Monde had achieved deep trance. Literal instructions in deep trance are important tools because of the literal response to suggestions and images that the unconscious may make (Erickson & Rossi, CP III, pp. 100–101). We will further discuss literal instructions under the title of "punchlines" in the section on direct work patterns in Chapter 8. The majority of this text, however, deals with the more difficult and aesthetic aspects of the Ericksonian approach embodied in the first two of the above three major categories of his trance utilization: using indirect suggestions and using metaphors and short anecdotes. The multiple embedded metaphor structure is seen as the vehicle in which all three of the approaches to treatment may be used.

Reorienting to Waking State

Reorienting the client to normal waking state is not difficult. Erickson wrote, "There is the age-old question about the possibility of not being able to arouse the hypnotic subject from the trance state. This actually cannot occur" (CP III, p. 29). Occasionally a manipulating client may insist upon staying in the trance, but utilizations such as symptom prescription can be implemented to soon correct such interview management matters brought about by improper diagnostic assessment and procedure.

The reorientation stage is a time for the therapist to place final touches on any dissociation instructions, such as those for amnesia, posthypnotic behavior, and progressive integration of the trance learnings. Any special considerations used in the induction should be respected and used in the reorientation. If the client was challenging, a challenge may have been given during the induction: "Your conscious mind may not be able to notice that your unconscious can alter your experience." Likewise, during reorientation any theme begun in the induction should be recapped: "Your conscious mind may or may not have learned a great deal from your unconscious; I wonder if it can learn to refamiliarize you with your surroundings here in the office?" If the client was induced by curiosity, as in, "Your conscious mind will sooner or later wonder what kind of trance your unconscious will manufacture," the reorientation ought to include a similar exit: "Your unconscious will soon develop your conscious curiosity about awakening from the trance."

DELIVERY

At every stage the hypnotherapy session emphasizes an interest in the particular client's individual needs. One must consider clients' needs to save face; their need to use themselves more constructively in their own behalf; their need to find relief for their problems; their needs, as whole people, to respond creatively to their social circumstances and their particular station along life's journey. The alteration of consciousness takes place in an interpersonal framework that protects a client's sensibilities and establishes the therapist as a potent source of ideas and stimulation. Throughout the trance the focus is increasingly turned toward the client and the client's attention is increasingly turned toward the self.

The cognitive and experiential frameworks offered by metaphor and the strategic use of trance phenomena become the stage for new discoveries. But refinements in the delivery of the suggestions and metaphors increase the therapist's gentle influence. The use of voice tone shifting and indirect suggestion increases the unconscious participation within the interpersonal and cognitive frameworks offered by the hypnotist.

Erickson remarked that he read the entire unabridged dictionary before he completed third grade and that it gave him a great understanding of the meaning of words (Zeig, 1980, p. 309). This was certainly demonstrated in his writing and speaking. His nonverbal delivery was also remarkable for its subtlety. He, in fact, wrote about entire inductions done in pantomime (Erickson, "Pantomime Techniques in Hypnosis and the Implications," CP I). In this writing we confine our emphasis to voice tone shifting and indirect suggestion. Our goal is to demystify and convey a logical understanding of these important components of delivery.

Voice Tone Shifting

Voice tone is a feature of interaction that few pay attention to in daily activity. Unfortunately, there is a paucity of semantic labels and vocabulary available to discuss tonal qualities in a colloquial manner. One term that is well-known is "soft voice." In an article entitled, "Two-Level Communication and the Microdynamics of Trance and Suggestion," Erickson described his purposeful use of tonal capacity: "Yes, the phrase to the unconscious is spoken softly. I use one tone of voice to speak to the conscious mind and another to speak to the unconscious" (Erickson & Rossi, *CP* I, p. 438). This is a direct statement from Erickson about his use of systematic nonverbal, as well as systematic verbal, communication.

We urge therapists working to develop abilities as Ericksonian hypnotherapists to learn to conduct the conscious/unconscious dissociation with voice tone shifting toward soft tones when the unconscious experiences are mentioned. Such a procedure focuses the client's awareness on the previously unnoticed automatic behavior of the unconscious.

Once the conscious/unconscious dissociation language has become familiar to the therapist, client responsiveness can be increased with the advanced technique of tonal shifting. The reason for this shifting is the psychological level meaning conveyed in the delivery. A sentence that contains a tonally shifted subportion stimulates the conscious mind to consider it with rules of logic and judgment but alerts the unconscious that something more is being implied than that which is being said. Hence, an unconscious search is initiated and that search fosters a readiness to accept alterations in variance with the person's usual conscious framework.

Tonally shifted portions of the verbal communication need not be confined to eliciting a singular phenomenon such as conscious/unconscious dissociation. Rather, a useful therapeutic strategy is to employ tonal shifts for eliciting phenomena that the client has not yet demonstrated. Once a client has begun the suggested phenomenon, the tonal shift can be replaced with the "normal" voice tone. The shifted vocal tones can then be placed on suggestions regarding the next trance phenomenon or experiential resource that is to be used in the trance. In that way a dynamic movement of the voice tone interspersal can be accomplished to reinforce the dissociation of the client's thinking and to help the client form a creative leading edge to his or her unconscious thought. If this is effectively done, the unconscious rapport is enhanced because the therapist's communications become, at the psychological level, an aid in the client's own unconscious problem-solving.

The following practice exercise involves two people. One plays the role of client and the other takes the role of therapist. The client "fakes" an arm levitation to initiate this exercise. By voluntarily raising an arm slowly in short jerky motions which simulate the actual unconscious jerky motion of a genuine arm levitation, the "shill" in this exercise sets up a context in which the therapist can practice tonal shifting. The therapist comments on only two features of the client's behavior: the arm levitation and the depth of trance achieved by the "client."

This exercise on arm levitation represents the forward movement of tonal shifting. The first use of the shifted voice would occur for fixation; as fixation is achieved tonal shifting would then emphasize the conscious and unconscious dissociation. Following the dissociation, marked by the ratifying of the altered state, tonal shifting might then occur for suggestions to develop arm levitation. The following exercise simulates the next logical shift in such a sequence, in which arm levitation has already begun and voice tone alteration shifts to trance deepening. The exercise can be used as a way to gain comfort with tonal shifts during the course of therapy, regardless of which phenomenon is chosen to be elicited by its use.

Exercise 2
Tone Shift Practice

Normal Voice	Altered Voice
Your hand is beginning to move . . . ➜	And as I count from 20 to 1 ◄
. . . those small jerky movements . . . ➜	you can just relax, 19, 18, 17 . . . ◄
. . . just a quarter inch at a time . . . ➜	and wonder what you'll really learn, 16, 15, 14 . . . ◄
. . . up toward your face ➜	and still relaxing more . . . ◄
. . . higher and higher ➜	as you develop that depth of trance, . . . ◄
. . . sometimes just floating there ➜	13, 12 . . . ◄
. . . until it reaches your face. ➜	you think you want . . . ◄
. . . And you really don't know when it will touch. ➜	11 . . . ◄
. . . It's as if it has a mind ➜	or may want . . . ◄
. . . of it's own. ➜	10, 9, 8, 7 . . . ◄

(continued)

Exercise 2 (*continued*)

Normal Voice		Altered Voice
. . . still higher,	→	to deal with that store of learnings and memories.
		←
. . . and another quarter inch,	→	6, 5, 4 . . . and breathing comfortably,
		←
. . . sometimes faster, sometimes slower . . .	→	going deeper and deeper . . .
		←
. . . until it comes to rest,	→	3, 2 . . .
		←
. . . and when it reaches your face . . .	→	and at 1, with that satisfaction and readiness for change.

THE COMPLETE INDUCTION

We now present the entire induction transcript that has been analyzed in parts. Notice how Erickson overlapped the steps of induction and the sophisticated manner in which he used common anecdotes to convey an understanding that the conscious and unconscious work independently and hence built the conscious/unconscious dissociation. These anecdotes include a smooth blend from the fixation first elicited in discussing learning the alphabet to the difference in conscious and unconscious functioning elicited in continued discussion about learning the alphabet, learning to walk, and learning to drive.

E: And What do you mean by a formal induction?
S: Where somebody tells you that he is going to hypnotize you. That's a pretty loose definition (laught) . . . as opposed to the common kinds of trances that we go into as people talk to us.
E: Would you turn your chair slightly? There. Lean back in your chair with your hands on your thighs. And look in this general direction. *Don't move.* Don't talk. And I'm going to talk about something that occurred in your childhood and *first* went to school. And had to *learn to write* the letters of the alphabet. It seemed like a terribly difficult task. *All those letters.* All those different shapes. Do you dot the "e," . . . "t" and cross the "i"? And where do you put the loop on the "b" and the "d" and the "p"? And how many humps on the letter "m"? *Gradually* you

formed a mental image of each letter, *many mental images* because let-ters are in script and in print, various shapes and sizes. And finally *you had mental images* located somewhere in your brain and you added mental images of *persons* and words and numbers and objects *and even ideas. Not knowing* at the time you were forming mental images.

While I've been talking to you your respiration has changed, your blood pressure has changed. Your muscle tone has changed. And your muscle reflexes have changed. *Close your eyes now* and *feel* the sense of comfort. And the more comfortable you *feel* the deeper into *trance you'll go.*

And in the trance state you can let your unconscious mind (pause) *survey* that vast array of learnings that *you achieve,* that *you have achieved* during your lifetime. There are many learnings that you've made without knowing it. *And many of the learnings* that were very important to you consciously have slipped into your unconscious mind and have become *automatically useful to you.* And they are used only at the right time, in the *right situation.*

Learning to walk was a very difficult task *but you achieved it.* And now you don't *know* just exactly how you *walk down the street,* how you *move your feet* and *your legs,* your arm, move *your head,* how far from the curb you *slow down,* what buildings you *veer toward* and what buildings you veer away from. You don't know which way you first *move your head* when you first reach an intersection. But you will look to the right and to the left *and ahead.* You'll *make a lot of move-ments.* You'll make a lot of movements even if there is no traffic of any kind.

And when you first learned to *drive a car* that was a very big task to put on the brakes and stop at the intersection when you are traveling 10 miles an hour. But as you became an expert driver you could *see a stop sign in the distance* and it didn't make a bit of difference whether you were traveling 70, 60, 50, 40, 30 miles an hour. *At the right time,* at the *right distance,* with the *right degree of force* you applied the brake and rolled to *a gentle stop.* And you don't even *know* how you measured that distance. You *don't know* what sense of body movement entered into it; what your peripheral vision told you. And *now* I could sit in the back seat of the car *you are driving* and I would *know* at least a half a block in advance when *you were going* to *turn right* or left by your body language. I might know it even before *you realize,* "Oh, here's the street I turn on."

Your unconscious mind knows much more than you do. Your con-scious mind has an awareness and it's oriented to *the situation of the moment* and so you're aware of desks and bookcases, wall hangings, telephone, which have nothing to do with *your purpose in coming.* But your unconscious mind can *disregard all those irrelevant facts and pay attention to my words,* and pay attention to its own reactions.

And much of the thinking we do in our unconscious mind occurs *without our knowledge*. The speed of thought is the speed of electricity. And there are billions of brain cells. And they are *constantly in action* and you had time enough to become aware of *only a few* of the thought processes that go on *all the time* in your brain. And *one simple stimulus* can extract from your unconscious mind a great many thoughts that are apparently unrelated. . . .

We present, by contrast, another of Erickson's inductions. The client was a man named Nick (Lustig, 1975). In this example Erickson again follows the typical outline given, beginning with his first question and statement, which orient Nick to previous trance experiences he has had. The short paragraph about arm levitation is a confusion and fixation technique that capitalizes on the previous trance Nick just had while watching Monde.

The second-to-last paragraph contains both the suggestions for fixation (which had already occurred) and conscious/unconscious dissociation. In this case Erickson did not belabor the dissociation with anecdotes prior to the use of the dissociation language. He did in subsequent statements, not shown here, educate Nick about the difference in functioning between the two modes of thinking. As stated, this is a most common means of trance training used by Erickson. Here we see the variety possible while still following the outline because the dissociation language occurs without the embellishment of supporting anecdotes.

In the final paragraph Erickson ratifies the trance. And again the manner of ratification is a straightforward focusing of attention on the alterations which display search phenomena.

E: Did you know that you went into a trance while I was working with Monde?

N: No. I thought I did. I wasn't sure.

E: And this is the first time you've had any experience with hypnosis.

N: Yes.

E: So you're going to find a lot of new things out about yourself. Only you really won't know what you're going to find out until after you have found it out.

All your life you've known that you could lift your hand and lower it. But there's something you learned long ago, and that was that you couldn't lift your hand; that you didn't know it was your hand. You were an infant, and your hands were just objects.

And one of the first things that a person does when he goes into a trance; he looks at some one spot. He doesn't need to move, he doesn't need to talk, he doesn't need to do anything except let his unconscious mind take over and do everything. And the conscious mind doesn't have to do anything. It's usually not even interested.

And while I've been talking to you, you've altered your respiration, your heart rate is altered. I know from past experience that your blood pressure is changed, your pulse is changed, and your eyelid reflex is changed. And you really don't need to keep your eyes open, but you can close them now. That little flutter is learning to get acquainted with yourself at another level of being.

Unfortunately, the elements of personal confidence and shifting of voice tone are not easily conveyed on the written page. Erickson's actual deliveries of the above inductions did, in fact, employ these elements.

VARIETIES OF INDIRECT SUGGESTION

The final skill one must confront to understand Erickson's masterful delivery of hypnotic interventions is indirect suggestion. In an article entitled, "The Indirect Forms of Suggestion" (CP I), Erickson and Rossi discussed 13 forms of indirect suggestion and included a category called "other" listing 10 more. Many of those categories are discussed and illustrated with examples below. A useful way to understand the concept of indirect suggestion initially is to contrast it with direct suggestion. As we mentioned in Chapter 1, direct suggestion was practiced by Bernheim and Charcot about a century ago (Bernheim, 1895). Direct suggestion includes such specific, stereotypical statements as, "You will now go into a very deep trance." Indirect suggestion, by contrast, is much more ambiguous and allows greater latitude of personal interpretation: "Sooner or later you'll be wondering about going into a very deep trance. And you may do that suddenly or gradually." As the client fills in the gaps created by psychological implication, there is an opportunity for a unique personal response.

Direct suggestion can facilitate rapid change when a client knows exactly what change is desired, is congruent about wanting that outcome, and has the necessary resources available and aligned so as to produce that outcome. Obviously, this is a hypothetical situation which rarely occurs in a therapy session. The use of indirect suggestion as a device to help create self-motivation in clients is, therefore, paramount.

We hold the premise that personal limitations are learned. The use of indirect forms of suggestion bypasses the client's biases, learned limitations, and expected conscious sets. "Indirect suggestion tends to bypass conscious criticism and because of this can be more effective than direct suggestion (Erickson & Rossi, CP I, p. 455). Indirect suggestion is frequently more effective for these reasons:

1) The client is permitted to display unique responses and potential.

2) The therapist draws upon the previous psychodynamics of the client's learning: the ability to associate, compare, contrast, examine congruity, etc.
3) The suggestions tend to bypass conscious criticism.

We encourage a careful study of the forms of indirect suggestion presented here. We believe these are the minimum categories for organizing indirect suggestion. A therapist who is able to construct these in any type of therapeutic setting has enormous advantage. These can be used in settings with or without trance, although we believe they are trance-inducing for reasons explained. Using these approaches helps fixate attention, concentrate the client inward, and initiate unconscious and autonomous processes.

Embellishing either induction or metaphoric treatment with indirect suggestion greatly increases the degree of client involvement. However, while increasing the involvement of the client, the therapist does not increase the degree of client resistance. Indirect suggestion is the real art or "secret" of fine Ericksonian communication and therapy.

Despite the permissiveness and respect for the client inherent in an indirect suggestion approach, it has often been the object of distrust and criticism. The fear is that indirect suggestion is manipulative, that it "makes" someone do something of which the conscious mind is unaware. The word "make" seems to be central to this misunderstanding. A therapist utilizing indirect suggestion does not make anyone do anything; rather s/he offers words and nonverbal stimuli to a client, who, in turn, creates a unique personal meaning.

To the extent that therapy proceeds in this fashion, the client operates more and more from this personal meaning while depending less and less on instructions and direction from the therapist. In this regard, indirect suggestion seems to be far less manipulative than a direct approach, since it offers a wide range of options to the client. Consider this statement to a client: "I wonder if you can just close your eyes and go into a trance." The client can, of course, follow this suggestion but also has the option of refusing. If the choice is to not develop trance, developing rapport has not been fractured and the client is not labeled "resistant." S/he has only accepted one of the two options offered and has communicated to the therapist something about the relevance of the suggestion to current needs.

An important component of indirect suggestion is relevancy. A client will not follow an indirect command which is irrelevant. In Erickson's early research of indirect suggestion, specifically double binds, he found that suggestions irrelevant to the best interest of the other were ineffective. For example, if he asked whether someone wanted to give him one dollar or five dollars,

the result was interpersonal alienation and no dollars were given. Conversely, when both parts of the bind are in the best interest of the client, a "win-
win" situation is created for the client. For example, the therapist could say to
a client who values and wants to experience tenderness: "Would you like to
begin to feel that sense of tenderness Thursday or Friday night?" In this way,
an illusion of choice is offered and the client can proceed without a sense of
giving up control to the therapist. Such therapeutic binds in the best interest
of the client are, as mentioned in Chapter 3 on diagnosis, like mirror images
of the no-win binds described by Bateson as typical in schizophrenogenic
families.

The congruency and expectancy of the therapist also influence the effectiveness of indirect suggestion. If the therapist expects that the client will not
want to follow the suggestion being given, then that expectancy will be conveyed far more significantly at the psychological level than whatever the
words imply at the social level. Delivering suggestions in a congruent way
tends to increase the client's sense of trust that the therapist knows what to
do. We encourage therapists to thoughtfully design indirect suggestions likely to be relevant to a particular client and then to offer them congruently with
the courage of conviction.

We present here 11 different forms of indirect suggestion with examples of
each. It is possible and often useful to select a desired response and
"package" suggestions for its occurrence in a wide variety of forms. Asking
for a response one time and in one way may not produce it, whereas asking
for that response from several different "angles" will increase the likelihood
of the client's achieving it. This subtle repetition will not be perceived as offensively redundant, but will provide the client with several opportunities to
create unique personal meaning and respond in accordance with it. In all of
these forms there is a common element of presupposition, as well as a particular style of embellishment.

1) Open-ended Suggestions

This category, as the name implies, includes suggestions which are vague
and subject to the widest range of interpretation. They are often useful to introduce a more specific suggestion for a particular response. For example, if
the desired response is sitting, the subject could be broached with an open-
ended suggestion, such as: "There are certain postures that a person can take
to be more comfortable." Having thus "warmed up" the client to begin thinking about those postures and comfort, a suggestion more specifically naming
the desired outcome "sitting" could be given.

With any of the suggestions and binds the therapist needs to be aware of the current goal in the session and formulate suggestions to help the client reach that goal. Expressed and implied goals will continue to change throughout treatment. Goals will be different for each client and in each session. However, the form of the indirect suggestions and binds remains identifiably similar.

Some frequently identified goals include: sitting comfortably, talking about a situation, sharing history, selecting a problem, setting a goal, going into trance, raising a cataleptic arm, deepening trance, age regressing, having amnesia, finding useful experience, linking to social network, reorienting to waking state, using only the useful suggestions given, etc. We have selected several of these common goals and given examples for them through all of these eleven categories. First, typical open-ended suggestions for:

Beginning orientation: "You can learn in many ways."
Developing trance: "Hypnosis is a way of learning about yourself at a different level of being."
Arm levitation: "A person can show a wide variety of movement and posture."
Age regression: "Your personal history can be experienced and the learnings can be used."
Learning from experience: "You can develop a line of thought for your own use."
Using learning after trance: "And keep your learnings and memorize them and use them in the days and years to come."

2) Implication

This category involves the use of presupposition in a featured way, especially simple presuppositions of time and number (before, when, as, after, one, the proper amount, etc.). For example: "Before you tell me the important information about your purpose in coming here, I would like for you to take just a moment to feel comfortable in my office." An example from Erickson's work is about a psychologist who explained why she would probably fail to become hypnotized. Erickson's first response was, "You haven't failed this time since we haven't started yet" (Erickson & Rossi, *CP* III, p. 74). Examples of implication suggestions for typical therapeutic goals are:

Beginning orientation: "Since you began when you arrived in my office . . ."
Developing trance: "The first thing people do when they go into trance . . ."
Arm levitation: "Before you find out if your arm raises all the way to your face . . ."

Age regression: "You may find the most influential experience of your childhood."

Learning from experience: "Which lesson do you imagine you will learn first?"

Using learning after trance: "The more you find ways to use the learnings now, the more you're likely to use them each year."

3) Questions or Statements That Focus or Reinforce Awareness

Questions that focus awareness operate on two different levels. Consider this example: "I wonder whether you can begin to relax as you listen to my words." On one level, this is just a question designed to get some information; perhaps it is a rhetorical question. At another level, it is necessary for the client to focus awareness on relaxation in order to answer the question. "There are a lot of ways to relax." This statement would reinforce the focus on relaxation that has already begun as a result of the preceding question. Other questions or statements to focus or reinforce awareness include:

Beginning orientation: "I wonder if you experience yourself ready to begin."

Developing trance: "Have you been in trance before?

Arm levitation: "Can you feel your arm getting lighter?"

Age regression: "One might wonder what five-year-old experience will be remembered."

Learning from experience: "What can a person learn from an experience?"

Using learning after trance: "Have you decided when you'll use this learning?"

4) Truisms

Truisms are statements about human or cultural conditions which are practically undeniable. They are particularly useful in eliciting an attitude of agreement before suggesting therapeutic possibilities which the client may regard with less certainty. For example, everyone who walks into a therapy office has obviously learned to walk. Therefore, it is a truism to say to such a client: "You've learned to walk." The client, agreeing with that, is more likely to also agree with subsequent therapeutic statements, even if they purport "truths" that are less undeniable. To subsequent statements which are also indirect suggestions, such as, "So you can learn a lot of other things," resistance is hardly possible.

Truisms can also be used to remind clients of "universal" skills, thus increasing the likelihood of their occurrence in the context of therapy. For example, the statement, "Everybody knows how to nod a head or signal nonverbally," will invite ideomotor feedback.

It is often useful to introduce a particular topic with an abstract and general truism which serves the purpose of bringing potentially problematic thoughts into the foreground in a nonthreatening way. For example: "In every culture there are people who will have more status than other people." This truism can open an indirect discussion of relationships between parents and children, social status, or other related concerns which may be relevant to a particular client. Once again the comparative examples are provided.

Beginning orientation: "Chairs are intended to be comfortable and serve a function."

Developing trance: "Each person goes into trance in a unique manner."

Arm levitation: "Sooner or later you will want to raise an arm up in the air."

Age regression: "Everybody knows what the world was like at five."

Learning from experience: "Experience is a great teacher."

Using learning after trance: "Everyone knows the importance of doing some homework."

5) Suggestions Which Cover All Possible Alternatives

Suggestions covering all possible alternatives will certainly focus awareness on the response being discussed, but the primary benefit here is that a "fail-safe" situation is created for both therapist and client. When all alternatives of a response, including not responding, are offered and endorsed by the therapist, then any response that develops is at the direction of the therapist and can be considered evidence of continuing cooperation and rapport.

Similarly, the client is relieved of any performance pressure to respond "correctly," since even no response is acceptable. Consider the following suggestions regarding hand levitation: "Your left hand may rise up toward your face; it may stay right where it is; it may get heavier; it may only float halfway up. I don't really know what's going to happen. Let's just wait and see." It is possible to increase the likelihood of a particular response with vocal tone shifts which are softened on the desired response. If, for example, the hand levitation is to be an important learning or is to be used to ratify trance, then a soft voice tone on the phrases "rise up toward your face" and "float up" will facilitate the occurrence of one of those responses by "stacking the deck" a bit in their favor. Also, the images evoked by the many possible alternatives will increase the likelihood of at least some response. So, even though no response is a possible alternative, it is only mentioned once, while several other gradations of desired responses are mentioned in the overall presentation of options. Again, compare examples of all possible alternative suggestions to several possible goals:

Beginning orientation: "You might be able to sit there with your arms on your lap or folded, or your hands apart or together, with your feet flat on the floor or crossed, with your eyes open or closed."

Developing trance: "You can go into trance slowly, gradually, suddenly, with your eyes open or closed, or not at all."

Arm levitation: "Your arm may rise up to your face, it may stay right there, it may float up halfway to your face, it may raise only slightly, it may get heavier and drop, or it may find its own unique location."

Age regression: "A time may be selected, or it may be prescribed; it may come into your mind or only intuitively occur to you; you may not know at all what age you'll select."

Learning from experience: "You may learn some or all of the material, and you may know what you learn or not know what you learn, and you might learn nothing at all."

Using learning after trance: "You may not use this or you might use this learning; you might modify it when you use it; and you can use all of it or only part of it; or you might mix the distinction between what you learn and what you invent."

6) Apposition of Opposites

Suggestions to create an apposition of opposites involve a juxtaposition of two behaviors which are changing in opposite directions. With such suggestions, it is useful to begin at a somatic level in order to establish credibility before suggesting more complex psychological changes. For example, "The heavier your body feels as you develop trance, the lighter your arms can feel," or, "The more tense you are at the outset, the more deeply you can relax in the trance." Having created a somatic experience to parallel the desired psychological one, additional suggestions can be given, such as, "And in the same way, the heavier your problems seemed as you walked in, the lighter those solutions can be; and the longer you wait to pick up those solutions, the shorter the time can seem."

Here are other examples of apposition of opposites suggestions:

Beginning orientation: "It's fine to take a long time beginning, as we may get to the solution with less waste."

Developing trance: "The less you notice the tension, the more you have a capacity to concentrate on relaxation."

Arm levitation: "The lighter the left arm becomes, the heavier the right arm may feel."

Age regression: "The older you feel, the younger your thoughts may often be."

Learning from experience: "The more you have been in the dark, the more enlightening a learning may be."

Using learning after trance: "Since you waited so long for relief from the problem, you are entitled to use it throughout your vast future."

7) Binds of Comparable Alternatives

Erickson and Rossi have described this category of binds as "free choice of comparable alternatives on a primary level with the acceptance of one of the alternatives determined on a metalevel" (*CP* I, p. 422). Since clients come to therapy of their own free will and wanting to change, there is an increased likelihood that they will accept at least one of the therapeutic alternatives offered without challenging the metalevel. Binds of comparable alternatives can be offered as statements: "I don't know whether it's your right hand or your left hand that will rise up toward your face," or as simple questions: "Would you like to go into trance now or later?"

Selecting sets of alternatives most relevant and reinforcing for a particular client will, of course, facilitate therapeutic response. It is often helpful for the therapist to supply a "reason" for the client to choose one of the alternatives. For example, to a client who has been offered the bind of either the right or left hand rising up to the face: ". . . because your unconscious may prefer to know you can do these easy tasks before you engage yourself in the more complex learnings in trance." The suggested reason often precedes the bind. We provide the following comparative list without any accompanying "reasons." The relative complexity of the binds can be seen in the suggestions:

Beginning orientation: "Would you prefer to have me begin talking or would you prefer to begin talking?"

Developing trance: "You may develop trance immediately or gradually."

Arm levitation: "Perhaps your left arm or maybe it's your right arm will rise up toward your face."

Age regression: "I don't know if you will recall something during your fifth year or something during your sixth."

Learning from experience: "You may learn from the experience or merely use the experience."

Using learning after trance: "You can select the way you will use this after trance or discover the way you will use this after trance."

8) Conscious/Unconscious Double Binds

In this category of double bind, the comparable alternatives offered specifically facilitate an education about the unconscious and a therapeutic interaction between the conscious and unconscious. Erickson and Rossi indicated that "the double bind request at the primary conscious level appears to effect a change at the unconscious or metalevel" (*CPI*, p. 424). They cite the following example: "If your unconscious wants you to enter trance, your right hand will lift. Otherwise your left will lift."

Prior to offering a double bind from this category, it is often useful to establish a duality of thinking by using conscious/unconscious dissociation language to educate the client about how these two "parts" operate. The use of binds phrased in this manner will intermittently reinforce the dissociation established during the induction. As a result, the altered state of the interpersonal framework is less likely to be extinguished during the session. Examine this brief example of such educational language: "You came to therapy and I doubt if your conscious mind really knows what your true purpose is, but perhaps your unconscious knows more and does know why because your unconscious mind operates globally. Your conscious mind thinks linearly, while your unconscious is interested in what's relevant. Your conscious mind has those doubts but your unconscious mind proceeds on your behalf automatically."

Transition to a conscious/unconscious double bind can follow such language quite logically. For example, include this possibility as the last sentence of the preceding series: "So you can allow your conscious mind to enjoy your unconscious mind enjoying itself." In this double bind, "enjoyment" is the one variable that is inherent. The illusion of choice deals with whether the conscious mind is able or not to enjoy the unconscious enjoyment. The series of goals worded as conscious/unconscious binds may sound familiar:

Beginning orientation: "The conscious mind may not notice when the unconscious mind is beginning to work toward a solution."

Developing trance: "Your conscious mind may think you desire or need one level of trance, while your unconscious mind develops the proper depth of trance."

Arm levitation: "Your conscious mind may not notice how your unconscious will raise your arm up to your face."

Age regression: "Your conscious mind can recall some important early experience while your unconscious mind develops a reliving of it."

Learning from experience: "An unconscious learning from the experience may be developed in the conscious mind as well."

Using learning after trance: "Your conscious mind might already have some ideas of where you will use this while your unconscious handles the job of doing it correctly."

9) Double Dissociative Conscious/Unconscious Double Binds

This category is an extension of the single version conscious/unconscious double bind just discussed. Let's take a typical conscious/unconscious double bind and convert it to the double dissociative version. Assuming the client wants or needs to experience interest and excitement about his family, and assuming therapy has prepared the client to experientially understand these ideas, we could first offer this conscious/unconscious double bind: "Your conscious mind can find ways to show interest in your family, while your unconscious mind has the excitement . . . "

Converting this to a double dissociative can be accomplished by making a compound sentence and reversing the "assignment" given to both conscious and unconscious minds in the first part of the sentence: ". . . or perhaps your conscious mind would prefer to think about that excitement while your unconscious mind automatically deals with how to show interest." This procedure can be represented with a formula: "Your conscious mind can X, while your unconscious does Y, *or* your unconscious can X, while your conscious does Y." When both X and Y are therapeutic alternatives, this bind assumes that both will be "chosen" and the illusion of choice here only refers to which will be done consciously and which unconsciously. We can thus extend the previous list to become double dissociative binds:

Beginning orientation: "Your conscious mind may have begun with the aid of your unconscious or perhaps your unconscious is ready to begin with any aid you can offer consciously."

Developing trance: "Would you prefer to let your conscious mind lead your unconscious into trance or your unconscious to lead your conscious mind into trance?"

Arm levitation: "Your conscious mind didn't know that your unconscious would choose your right or left arm to raise up, but the conscious mind could wonder which arm the unconscious chose."

Age regression: "Your unconscious may let your conscious mind know how you lived in the past or your conscious mind may already know what your unconscious can relive."

Learning from experience: "Your conscious mind can be interested in what you learn from the experience and your unconscious mind can take care of really learning from it, or perhaps your unconscious mind only allows you to develop interest as your conscious mind develops a learning."

Using learning after trance: "And one might let the conscious mind select the site for using the learning while the unconscious is trusted to carry it out, or one may allow the conscious mind to carry out a learning and let the unconscious select the location, and time."

10) Reverse Conscious/Unconscious Double Binds

This category of binds is primarily used only with clients who are offering a challenge or behaving in a routinely oppositional manner. Erickson described several instances in which he used this approach, including his first intentional use of it in his early boyhood. He was watching his father's futile attempt to pull a calf into the barn. When young Erickson laughed at the spectacle, he was encouraged by the father to do a better job if he thought he could.

> Recognizing the situation as one of unreasoning stubborn resistance on the part of the calf, I decided to let the calf have full opportunity to resist, since that was what it apparently wished to do. Accordingly I presented the calf with a double bind by seizing it by the tail and pulling it away from the barn, while my father continued to pull it inward. The calf promptly chose to resist the weaker of the two forces and dragged me into the barn (*CP* I, p. 412).

Before using the reverse conscious/unconscious double bind with a client who demonstrates "unreasoning stubborn resistance," it is useful to engage the client in a relationship which is defined at one level as a fight. This can be accomplished with a simple metacomment like: "As your therapist it is in my power to make you do a lot of things and I intend to do just that because it is my job." This antagonizing summary statement about what is to follow would likely crystalize the client's intention to resist and thus bind his or her consciousness at the social level of awareness with the relationship and resisting. The therapist would then be in a position to give instructions at the psychological level, thereby inviting the client to exercise the reverse response at the psychological level. For instance: "It's very important that you not learn anything from strangers and you certainly don't need to sit down while you're here. I insist that you listen carefully to my words so don't relax and allow your mind to wander as I speak."

Continuing a similar line of "instructions," the client could be induced to trance and therapeutic associations by enjoining him or her not to do so. As with all forms of indirect suggestion, however, the reverse set outcomes must be relevant to the client's goals or the suggestions will not elicit cooperative response. The client must cooperate at some level to co-create outcomes with the therapist, but, as Erickson has stated, the cooperation is not always overt or easily recognized (Erickson & Kubie, *CP* III, pp. 125–126).

We present the following examples, based on the assumption that, in each case, the first step of verbally engaging the conscious mind in a struggle has already been accomplished before the specific suggestion is given. Such engagement would, of course, be designed to be relevant for the particular individual. For example, one might begin to hold the challenging client with a series of statements such as: "I'm not going to tell you anything you don't already know. I don't know why you are here. What could I, a total stranger, know that is helpful to you? You may not even have any choice in the matter of staying here and listening to me. You probably couldn't listen comfortably and really learn something useful for yourself. . . ." Following such summary statements to elicit therapeutic "opposition," the following suggestions might be given:

Beginning orientation: "Because it is really too soon to get started with your treatment."

Developing trance: "You ought not go into a trance any time soon."

Arm levitation: "It would be most useful if you left your arms right where they are."

Age regression: "Most important, you are not to feel like the child you once were when you reexamine that earlier memory."

Learning from experience: "You probably won't know how to generalize from and use your knowledge and your unconscious experience. And you certainly would not be expected to apply any such nonsense to your real life."

Using learning after trance: "You wouldn't want to let the thought stay with you when you leave the office."

11) Non Sequitur Double Bind

With this type of double bind, one part of the suggestion tends to indirectly imply the desired response, while another part requests the desired response more directly. Or, as Erickson and Rossi stated: "In the non sequitur double bind there is a similarity in the *content* of the alternatives offered even though there is *no logical* connection. . . . [Thus] one cannot figure it out, one cannot refute it, so one tends to go along with it" (*CP* I, p. 426). They give this "going to bed" example: "Do you wish to take a bath before going to bed, or would you rather put your pajamas on in the bathroom?"

The formula we use to make this form of suggestion most easily understandable is: direct request + implied alternative = non sequitur double bind. In the case of the above bind "take a bath before going to bed" is directly stated as a choice and "put your pajamas on in the bathroom" is another choice that relates to the former only by implication. It implies that the child will be doing something in the bathroom with clothes off! The most obvious variable in all binds is still present: the client has a sense of choice and both choices are in the client's best interest. So, finally, contrast these non sequitur bind alternatives to the previously stated goals:

Beginning orientation: "Let's begin now or use the time constructively."

Developing trance: "You will be able to either go into trance as we speak or you will alter your consciousness and experience."

Arm levitation: "Your unconscious will either raise the hand off your lap or your conscious mind will notice it halfway to your face."

Age regression: "The memory may be from the age of five or about the time you entered grammar school."

Learning from experience: "You can either learn from this experience or teach it to your children."

Using learning after trance: "Will you use these learnings after trance or change your maladaptive behavior?"

These 11 forms of indirect suggestion can be advantageously used in various combinations to effectively elicit desired responses and retrieve desired resources while diminishing resistance. Having listed and briefly discussed each one, we now offer a hypothetical example and an actual induction transcript to illustrate possible combinations designed to elicit particular trance phenomena or therapeutic tasks. The specific type of indirect suggestion used will appear in parentheses. Italicized portions within the transcript denote phrases spoken with a softer voice tone.

In eliciting the trance phenomenon of age regression we might proceed as follows:

You've known all along what it's like to be a child (*truism*). Everybody has been a child at some point in his life (*truism*). In every culture we start out as children and grow older (*truism*). The first thing I'd like to have you do before I ask you to think back on your past vividly is to just relax (*implication*). We all know that our personal history contains a lot of information and I'd like you to be able to *find* that personal information in your history (*open-ended*). I wonder if you know which times during your life you have been age regressed (*question to focus awareness*). As you experience hypnosis I don't know whether you'll find yourself age regressing to a time you were five years old, or perhaps six years old, maybe a time before five, maybe a time after six, or possibly a time right in between (*all possible alternatives*).

Once you've found that you can think about times in your life when you've felt older, you'll know that you can reexperience times in your life when you were younger (*apposition of opposites*). While your conscious mind is concerned with the here-and-now demands of what I'm saying, your unconscious can think about a time when you were younger (*conscious/unconscious double bind*). Your conscious mind may be wondering just what happened to you when you were six years old and your unconscious can allow you to reexperience that or perhaps it's your unconscious that's having you think about the time you were six and your conscious mind will be able to participate as you relive that experience (*double dissociative conscious/unconscious double bind*).

The following transcript is presented to illustrate how these forms of suggestion and binds (in parenthesis) can be utilized throughout induction, treatment, and reorientation. The "treatment" portion of this transcript is very brief, since the "client" volunteered primarily to experience trance as part of a demonstration of indirect suggestion during induction.

INDIRECT SUGGESTION TRANSCRIPT

Induction

S: Is there something particular you're learning or changing that I can address to be personally relevant to you (questions that focus awareness) during this demonstration (*implication*)?

H: I'd like to learn to be tidier in the things that I do. I'm tidy at work but my personal life isn't as organized as my work.

S: Hypnosis is a way for you to *become familiar with yourself* at another level of being (*open-ended*) and you've known all along that you can *learn* while you're *relaxed* (*truism*). I just wonder if you know your conscious mind focusing on some spot and anticipating going into a trance might not have time to catch up with your unconscious mind which has already *gone into a trance* (*conscious/unconscious double bind*). So you can go ahead and *close your eyes* all the way and perhaps you'll find that you quickly dropped into a trance or maybe you'll find that you slowly go into a trance as I talk (*bind of comparable alternatives*), but I do know that everyone finds their *own speed* to *go into a trance* (*truism*). So you use my words, suggestions and ideas as a stimulus for you to *do your own thinking* (*open-ended*).

Arm Levitation

Now, I don't have to talk all the time (*truism*). (Pause.) I could suggest that your right hand or your left hand will *rise up toward* your face, maybe one of them will (*bind of comparable alternatives*). Your conscious mind has allowed you to *think about your problem* in a certain way (*focus awareness*). I don't know whether or not you *know* what the full meaning of your problem is (*implication*), but I do know that your conscious mind can be aware that your unconscious is *raising your right hand* off of your lap (*conscious/unconscious double bind*).

Everyone as a child knows the experience of having an arm *move up* to the face in order to *bring a rattle* to your mouth (*truism*). And it's a *pleasant thought when you remembered that* (*focus awareness*). Everyone has a personal history that they can draw from (*open-ended*) and it's good to know that your personal history can be organized (*implication*). And just waiting . . . (*open-ended*).

Conscious/Unconscious Dissociation Establishing a Learning Frame

I wouldn't have to say that *you can think* about anything you want at the conscious level while your unconscious *listens to my voice* (*conscious/unconscious double bind*). I know that your conscious mind can listen to me while your unconscious learns a great deal and sometimes your conscious mind even *learns a great deal while you listen* (*double dissociative conscious/unconscious double bind*). Everyone knows how to concentrate to such an extent that you *don't notice* other stimuli around you (*truism*) and if I talk so rapidly that you don't notice what I say, you're still going to be able to *develop an organized* line of thought for your own betterment (*open-ended*). Now your hand is halfway toward your face (*focus awareness*) and I wonder if your ideas about how to solve your problems are halfway out of your unconscious (*implication and focusing awareness*). It's moving up toward your face (*truism*) and as it does it would be useful for you to realize (*compound suggestion used to link to next part*) your conscious mind doesn't need to *participate in order* for *you* to have a learning (*conscious/unconscious double bind*).

You've known all along that you can dream at night and wake up in the morning with a solution to a problem (*truism*). I'm sure that you're aware, as many people are, that the feeling of having a fly land on your finger causes an automatic stimulus *and need* to move your hand *ever so slightly up* toward your face (*truism*). And I'm sure that you're aware that in dreams at night the benzine ring was formed in the mind of the dreamer and that's *a tidy way* for a person to represent a very complex set of experiences (*open-ended*). A straight line is another way for a person to connect the shortest distance between two points (*truism*) so you might wonder about the benzine ring which was formed in the dreamer's mind as a way to *organize a complex set of data* (*focus awareness and open-ended*).

Now your life and your personal life is a complex subject (*truism*). I wouldn't expect to represent that I *understand it* in any way . . . and perhaps that person's conscious mind had no idea of the simplicity with which his unconscious could organize that benzine ring (*conscious/unconscious double bind*) . . . and in the same way I wonder if your conscious mind is going to be able to understand how your unconscious can *organize* something as complicated as *your own life* or whether or not your unconscious mind can even understand it . . . but I do know your conscious mind can *appreciate the organization that you provide for yourself* (*double dissociative conscious/unconscious double bind*).

Now I doubt that you really understand how your hand raises up to your face (*focus awareness*). You've known all along that it does (*truism*) and so you can't deny that your unconscious mind knows how to formulate ideas in a dream that you don't understand (*implication*).

Metaphoric Frame Matched

Now this matter of being tidy . . . (*focus awareness*). A client came to see me one time who was a compulsive character (*implication*). I asked him what his difficulty was or whether or not he could *just reach in his pocket* and hand me a set of notes he had written to represent his problem (*focus awareness*). He had *a great sense of rapport with me because of that*. He reached in his pocket and he said: "I don't have a set of notes for you but I do have this ball of yarn and it's all intertwined in knots and tied up in a bundle and it's been this way *for years*" (*focus awareness*). Now I didn't know whether or not to tell him your problem has been tied up in knots for months or *for years* or whether it had only been tied up that way in a bundle in disarray for a few minutes prior to the therapy but I did know that it certainly was *a difficulty* (all possible alternatives).

Direct Work with Sexual Symbolism Punchlines

I said, "Since you've presented your problem to me in a symbolic fashion I'm going to have to present my answer to you in a symbolic way" (*open-ended*). I asked him to *fall into a sleep* (pause) and "just enter into that ball of yarn as if you were *a small flea*, moving your feet in tiny little ways to walk right inside the string. Because you know, just as if it seems like a difficult problem to raise your right hand off your lap when your left hand feels so heavy, trying to untangle that ball of yarn so small and so interwoven seems like a big job to somebody as large as you (*apposition of opposites*). So if you can dream yourself to be so small that the problem that seemed enormous is even bigger, then you can just *walk right* in to the heart of the matter *and see it from the inside out* (*apposition of opposites*). And when your conscious mind can see it from the inside out, your unconscious may find that *it's a delightful learning*" (*conscious/unconscious double bind*).

Many children have had dreams about being in their erector set box all night long to find out how those pieces get along with one another when they fall asleep at night (*truism*). They wake up in the morning being able to *screw the pieces* in different ways than they ever knew possible because they *feel at one* with the nuts and bolts and the girders (*implication*). It's an eye-opening thought to be in the center of a ball of yarn looking out and the ball of yarn which could be so perplexing to the compulsive character became *a warm, furry cocoon to support and soothe* him while he looked out from inside (*apposition of opposites*).

Now I know your unconscious mind thinks about a lot of things as I speak (*truism*). I wonder if your conscious mind can appreciate how that man realized his original problem, being preoccupied with that ball of yarn, led to that sense of security and comfort that he had when he *imagined* being *right at the heart of the matter* (*focus awareness*).

Linking Resources to Immediate Social Concerns

And just looking around inside the ball of yarn, I asked him to find a place where one of the strings came to an end (*focus awareness*). "I *know that you'd like to tie up loose ends*," I said, "and it gives everyone a great sense of personal satisfaction to *tie up loose ends* (*open-ended*). When you learn to tie a knot you really couldn't just say how the knot is tied, but your conscious mind being unable to say how you tie the knot doesn't stop your unconscious mind from tying it *again and again* (*conscious/unconscious dissociation*). And so your conscious mind can concentrate upon the awesome experience of being in *the center of that universe* of string and looking up at the strands as if they're stars sparkling in the night, while you let your unconscious mind begin to *tie some of those loose ends together* (*conscious/unconscious double bind*).

"And before you're done, you're going to find that you can get out of that ball of yarn just as if somebody had taken a deep journey into a cave but tied one end of the string to their belt and left another end of the string outside of the cave (*open-ended*). And hopelessly lost in the caverns of the cave was no problem for the conscious mind because your unconscious knows in the back of your mind you can just *follow that string* back to the daylight whenever you'd like (*conscious/unconscious bind and implication*).

"And knowing that means you can look around and explore that cave at will (*open-ended*). And I don't *know what you're going to find* inside that cave but I do know that there are a lot of things and you may have to look very closely because the life that grows on the walls of the cave can be something that a conscious mind doesn't *fully appreciate at a distance* (*focus awareness*) and it's good that you've made yourself tiny and crawled into that ball of yarn, and maybe you've tied together another string and another loose end (*implication*). I don't *really know* (*implication*).

"I do know that I've spoken a lot and your conscious mind has been listening and your unconscious mind has been doing a lot of thinking on your own (*conscious/unconscious double bind*). You may have a lot more thinking *to do* about *a lot of things* (*open-ended*) and it's thinking that you can do at night when you leave my office and go home, or thinking that you can do when you're alone some place by yourself; and it doesn't matter whether you do the thinking in small pieces or all at once or whether you postpone it or *do it right away* (*all possible alternatives*). All that matters is that you know that, even though your conscious mind has listened to my words and there may have been more to think about than you were able to, your unconscious mind is going to be able to organize your thoughts in such a fashion that you can find your own satisfaction" (*conscious/unconscious double bind*).

Ending Original Framework and Reorienting to Waking State

And the man, still thinking he was a small flea, crawled from the inside of the ball of yarn to the outside following one of those strings, going around and around and around and over and sometimes through it, emerging from the outside, leaped off the ball of string and suddenly became the person he was when he started (*implication via the metaphor frame*). And he opened his eyes and looked at me and he said, "By the way, what was it you asked me before the hypnosis started?" Which is only a way of implying that you *open your eyes and come back to the room* (*implication*). Hi (*focus awareness*) (Lankton, video, 1981).

Even though the preceding transcript was not intended as a total treatment for this client's problem it so happened that, as a result of this brief intervention, the client was able to frame his problem differently. Several months later he reported that it had been so meaningful to him that he played the recording of the session repeatedly.

With the Ericksonian approach a primary goal is to allow the client's fixation on something to be a vehicle through which the frame of reference being used to consider the problem is changed. Changing that frame of reference allows new associations which can be stimulated by the therapist's use of indirect suggestion. These suggestions should be compelling, interesting and relevant enough to engage the client in creating new solutions which may have been unavailable within the old framework. Once this process begins, it is as if a car engine has started. It is much easier to get a car to move once its own engine is started. We suppose some therapy approaches might be more like pushing a car away and hoping the engine will start once the clutch is released.

6 THE RESOURCES AND TRANCE PHENOMENA FRAMEWORK

We assume that clients come to us with a vast array of learnings, resource experiences and useful patterns of thinking acquired and developed in the course of their lives thus far and stored in their memory. Erickson was well known for his typical statement to clients that "your unconscious contains a vast storehouse of learnings and resources." He would usually elaborate about a representative few of these learnings, mentioning in detail such undeniable basics as learning to walk, learning the alphabet, etc. In the course of his discussion the client would typically begin to feel capable, confident, etc. regarding abilities and learnings which had simply been "forgotten" and taken for granted. Having thus "retrieved" or pulled into the foreground those resource experiences, the client was optimally "fortified" and ready to tackle a variety of therapeutic tasks. These "therapeutic tasks" often involved the reassociation of experiential life we have mentioned already. Erickson believed that "clients are clients because the conscious mind does not know how to initiate desired psychological experiences and behavior changes to the degree that one would like" (Erickson & Rossi, 1979, p. 18). In other words, we're not dealing with a shortage of desired psychological processes but with a shortage of associative links to initiate psychological processes in specific situations.

When people attempt to cope, adapt, create, and enjoy an environment, they will associate to the most useful experiential resources they have available. Experiential resources include motoric flexion or extension, perceptual readiness, cognitive apprehension and comprehension, emotional appropriateness, and the knowledge of role demands. This tendency to adapt in a total gestalt of resource may be best explained by social researchers (Cartwright & Zander, 1968, pp. 139–151). To the extent that a person is able to self-stimulate or co-create experiences effectively, maximum benefit and growth from exchanges with the environment will result. To the extent that a person is unable to associate to needed resources, there will be increased stress on the available resource mechanisms. The result may be temporary discomfort and anxiety or may be as extreme as traumatic shock and fixation of further growth and learning. In either case the stress response alerts the person to use measures of defense. The person will attempt to associate to necessary resource mechanisms to creatively cope; however, when an inability to locate and organize the needed resources occurs, irrational, superstitious, and psychopathological symptoms are developed instead.

A 29-year-old single nurse came to us for therapy presenting the problem of bulimia (cyclical gorge eating and vomiting). She had been unable to break that pattern for 16 years. She was literally disgusted with herself as a person and very sure that anyone else would judge her similarly. She conceptualized her problem as having no "self-control." It was true that in circumstances regarding food she demonstrated little self-control. She spent $250 per week at the grocery store and shoplifted additional items. She generalized from these situations and convinced herself that she was entirely deficient with regard to self-control and all its related behaviors. This was the total presenting problem as far as her conscious mind associations went.

Although she was concerned about her eating, her regressive behavior was becoming more apparent as she grew older. The social pressures she faced were becoming increasingly beyond her ability to handle. That is, she couldn't handle social pressures and expectations with the same skill as others her age.

Understanding her case may be facilitated by recalling one of the principles described earlier: She was making the best choice of behavioral adjustment that she knew how to make. Her social withdrawal was an adaptation but the choice was not desired; it was merely "easy." This is not to say that she was taking the easy way out; indeed, her lifestyle must have been extremely difficult and stress-producing. It was easy only in the sense that she understood the roles, thoughts, emotions, perceptions, and behaviors used in that set of choices. She did not understand the components of other choices with the necessary degree of integration to habitually create more appropriate adjustment. Furthermore, her conscious thinking did not compel her to even try in a more effective manner.

Fenichel (1945) explained from the psychoanalytic framework that failure by the unconscious to find necessary coping mechanisms results in damage to preexisting personality organization and regression of age-appropriate functioning:

> Thus, actually, regression is a means of defense. What must be admitted, however, is that the part played by the ego in regression is different from the part it plays in all other defense mechanisms. . . . Regression happens to the ego; in general, regression seems to be set in motion by the instincts which, blocked from direct satisfaction, seek a substi-

tute. The precondition for the use of regression as a mechanism of defense is, therefore, a peculiar weakness of the ego organization (p. 160).

We presume that this "weakness" is the lack of learned ability to initiate the associative links and experiential resources a client needs for his or her adaptation, growth, creativity, and enjoyment. Our client had apparently developed bulimia at a time in her life when she could not, in that context, find a better way to deal with the stress she faced. The acquisition of bulimia was thus a way to adjust which prevented subsequent maturation and learnings. Her resulting regression left her markedly unable to cope with the social demands made by her peers and her community.

In the situation of adult life demands she was increasingly unable to cope and increasingly regressive. She was suicidal. Since she believed she had no "self-control," we decided that creating with her a sense of self-control would be our first therapeutic task. Now even though the concept of self-control can be easily stated as a noun phrase, in actual experience "it" is a complicated arrangement of attitudes, perception, memory, and motoric behavior. The actual psychological mechanisms involved in any easily worded resource are actually complex and beyond conscious understanding. They defy articulation.

However, resources are colloquially understood and so we know that with proper measures of communication we can increase any client's personal understanding and experience of the needed resources. These communication devices include dramatic themes in metaphor, indirect suggestion, anecdotal examples, strategic use of trance phenomena, and binds. Much of therapy is concerned with the task of eliciting resources, bundling resources, and associating resources to desired contexts.

After a brief interview with this client, we entered the treatment phase with the immediate therapeutic task of building a sense of self-control. Keeping in mind our understanding of her situation along the broader dimensions of the diagnostic framework, we questioned which additional resources she would need to retrieve and develop in order to go beyond mere symptom removal. We will examine these questions and answers briefly so as to convey the master plan that existed by the time we first asked her to go into trance.

First, what did she need to deal with her current family and social network? Next, what was needed to make a transition into the upcoming stage of family development? What was her psychological age and did she need to accomplish any individual developmental tasks? This question was particularly relevant since her developmental "age" would determine the type of experiences she could understand and which psychological and social "tasks" required attention. It would also influence her availability of resources.

This woman, although 29 years of age, looked, sounded, and acted much like a 13-year-old girl. Perhaps she was much the same as she was at 13 when she first developed the bulimia symptoms. As we went about the task of metaphorically retrieving various resources, we spoke to her much the same way one would speak to a chronologically normal 13-year-old person. The resources needed for her adaptive adjustment to social and network demands included a sense of self-worth, enthusiasm, accomplishment, improved comfortable awareness of her body and enhancement of her body image, and an acceptable framework in which to collect knowledge and curiosity about her sexual and age-appropriate social development.

We considered these resources prerequisites to her development and adjustment in her present world. She had undoubtedly found life's pressures difficult, since acquisition of age-appropriate skills and behaviors had been thwarted at age 13 when she attempted to develop them naturally in her family of origin. As a 29-year-old woman, she was timidly avoiding people, operating on her belief that they were just too demanding to deal with and that she was too disgusting to interest them. She had experienced 16 years of proof that she did not "have what it takes."

Regarding attitude restructuring, she needed to believe her needs were important enough to express. In response to needs and demands from others, people do not always comply; she needed to be able to willingly accept that about others. She needed to know, too, that she could voluntarily choose to limit or comply with "demands" from others according to her own values and priorities. Regarding social roles, changes in the above areas would require an ability to comfortably comply when it would be desirable for her to do so and gracefully refuse requests and/or demands at other times.

Regarding her transition to the next stage of family development, she needed considerable information about dating, secondary sexual characteristics, and general social skill involved in anticipating, expecting, planning, deciding, and co-developing plans. She needed to learn how a couple becomes romantically involved by enhancing and enriching each other's personal world of perception and experience. At 29 she had very limited social experience and felt in no way prepared to court, select a mate, and begin a family, or to decide among other lifestyle options.

Thus our initial therapeutic assessment was formed. We conducted a conscious/unconscious dissociation induction utilizing her conscious mind concerns as the vehicle to achieve fixation. She was concerned with being disgusting and worthless in interpersonal situations, so we informed her that the use of hypnotic trance was an interpersonal situation and that she might consciously investigate her ability to "do her part." She might either, for example, consciously consider that her involvement was not satisfactory or she might consciously consider that her ability to judge (the quality of her involvement) was not satisfactory. In either case we assured her that her *unconscious* would be capable. In that paradoxical manner, then, we prescribed her "resistance" and utilized her existing frame of reference for the induction.

The metaphoric framework was established with a series of anecdotes revolving around the theme of working with a client who was not well-known to us. We reminded her that people make sense of communications offered to them by relating the words to their own experience. We therefore established a way to help her elicit memories and experiences from her past that she might find useful in solving her problem.

Particular experiential resources were those perceptions, proprioceptions, and behaviors associated to "self-control" and to "being loved." In order to enhance her experiential involvement with these personal resources in a nondefensive and nonthreatening manner, we talked to her of other clients we had. By speaking about reminding other clients of their experiences, we indirectly focused her awareness on her own understandings of related experiences.

We detailed the experiences that all midwestern college students have had: getting up on a cold morning to attend class when, with nearly every ounce of their being, they would prefer to stay snugly in bed. And all persons have known the necessity of waiting when they've gotten to the bathroom with an urgent need only to find someone else there ahead of them. In such frameworks she soon remembered an entire winter during her nursing training when she had not only gotten up very early each morning but also driven across icy backroads to care for an invalid woman in her charge. As she remembered this experience in trance she provided "loud" ideomotor feedback: She held her shoulders back, smiled, and seemed to thoroughly enjoy the unexpected sensations of "self-control" retrieved from her very own history. She later expressed surprise that her experience with self-control actually "counted" therapeutically, since it didn't involve food. She was willing, in the trance and metaphoric frameworks, to co-create a variety of automatic associations to her sensation of self-control in those situations where she most needed it involving food. Thus, our first therapeutic goal was accomplished, but treatment was far from complete.

In a manner very similar to Erickson's "February Man" (Haley, 1973), we had our client age regress in trance to early adolescence and "meet" a special friend who was interested in her talents and learnings. Using age regression mechanisms, she was able to strengthen her sense of self-worth. We allowed her to explore that map of relationships she had not learned enough about. She gained an ability to expect people (at least some of them) to be encouraging to her during life's successes and challenges, and to pleasantly anticipate that others could give logical and appropriately permissive advice regarding dating, sexual development, etc. The metaphors, indirect suggestions, and binds we used elicited experiences and taught her that more choices existed in her world. These were resources she had not overtly requested but were experiences and understandings that she needed in order to live her life meaningfully once she no longer structured all her time and energy around her symptom. Consequently, her unconscious interest and appreciation of the therapy allowed it to continue.

Finally, this first trance was concluded and her age regression reversed. She communicated that she knew, albeit unconsciously, how to follow the suggestions and binds to alleviate her presenting problem. We can summarize these learnings here with an example of the binds we suggested: She could hold a sense of being loved and cared for in the back of her mind while she consciously experienced the joy of self-control or she could consciously experience the pride of being loved while her unconscious kept the ability of self-control in the back of her mind. The words used in the bind referred, after all, to the experiences that had been elicited in the metaphor.

She immediately discontinued her bulimic behavior after this first trance. She contacted us by phone during the evening following her first session to inform us that she had passed through a grocery store and purchased no "junk" food even though she had intended to do so as she entered the store. Since her changes had occurred in the metaphoric framework, and thereby bypassed conscious resistance, she demonstrated how the unconscious thinking processes benefit from the reassociation of resources. Her changes at the unconscious level came into her awareness that evening and subsequently allowed her to realize that she had much to learn from herself.

Her sense of hopefulness was greatly improved. Subsequent sessions continued learnings elicited in age regressed fashion. Rules and conduct of social encounters of various types were related by means of meetings with the imaginary friend and stories of how such imaginary meetings were successfully used by the other clients. Our purpose here is not so much to detail the treatment scheme used with this particular client as to share several aspects of producing therapeutically useful experiences with any client.

Certainly the retrieval of needed resources or psychological processes is not always easily accomplished. Every therapist has encountered those clients who seem so impoverished, so lacking in positive experiences, that they seem to have nothing "going for them." We maintain that even these clients have the psychological mechanisms and resources needed for change and growth, although retrieving those resources may require piecemeal work conducted over several sessions. Almost every client has learned to walk, ride a bicycle, use the alphabet, and has experienced excitement at tying a shoe the first time or buttoning a button, etc. Even when one or more of these experiences is biased by trauma, others exist intact. All clients know something about surviving, coping, and changing, although they may not know it or communicate it consciously.

The resources needed by clients lie within their own personal history. The client we have discussed here serves to exemplify this principle in two different ways. The experience of "self-control" was one she had actually experienced. "It" was elicited easily and relatively quickly, despite her original conviction that she had no self-control available. The metaphoric framework alteration was the factor that made it easy. That is one type of resource.

However, experiences related to the behavior, comfort, understandings, and perceptions of social encounters, friendships, having "girlfriends" and "boyfriends," dating, sexual experimentation, commitment, and loving were not directly available in her history. These learnings were co-created and developed via her resources of age regression, imagination, imagery rehearsal, and so on. In other words, the mechanisms she needed in order to learn other therapeutic resources were themselves resources. In this regard, all clients have the resources needed available in their unique repertoire of learnings.

When resource retrieval is inhibited by the impoverished personal history of the client, trance phenomena may be employed to maximize favorable potentials. The process is similar to fanning a hot coal until it eventually flames and ignites a larger fire. Trance phenomena can be used as a special framework through which the client can examine hidden, forgotten, minute, and obscure personal experiences and find them valuable for the changes they need. We have compared trance phenomena to other tools such as magnifying glasses, telescopes, time machines, and amplifiers. They are tools of investigation that make previously unavailable worlds of unperceived experience perceivable.

Erickson believed that the potential for every resource is inherent in the person by virtue of being alive; in Ericksonian therapy our role is to help clients maximize their own resources in order to accomplish desired changes. In that regard the strategic use of trance phenomena facilitates a special relationship in which the therapist helps clients find within themselves both the tools and the raw materials for change.

CASE TRANSCRIPT AND ANALYSIS

Having thus introduced the basic principles of retrieval and reassociation of experiential resources, we will now examine typical resource retrieval and reassociation in the context of an entire treatment session. This session deals with helping a woman overcome a chronic headache. Because the etiology of this problem was far in the client's past, her social situation had largely recovered from the shocks that created the problem. This simplified her overall diagnostic picture. Therapy was directed less toward helping her adjust to her current social network pressures and more toward her psychological adjustment.

The transcript provides a preponderance of examples of specific interventions related to eliciting a new constellation of resources and trance phenomena to be used for relief from her headache. Some resources involved cognitive framing and were created with dramatic metaphor; others were attitudinal resources (such as those psychological mechanisms referred to as "hopefulness"); some were perceptual (utilizing such trance phenomena as dissociation and negative hallucination); and finally, some were resources intended to predispose her behavior and social priorities about using time. In every case the resources used provided her with verifiable experiences. She could use the experiences to validate the perceptual and cognitive frameworks elicited by the use of metaphor.

Before the actual transcript, a brief review of initial impressions, background information, overview of the therapy, and the outcome of the session will be helpful. "Tracy" was a woman in her late fifties. She sought therapy for severe, chronic headaches which she experienced "48 hours a day." The headaches began ten years earlier, several years after her 22-year-old son's violent death.

Our specific contract with Tracy was to help her find relief from the persistent stress and pain of the headaches. Our overall goal, as with many clients, was to allow her the discovery and use of her naturally occurring trance phenomena to achieve a "regression in the service of the ego." First, we briefly assessed the psychological and social ramifications of her problem along the six parameters of the diagnostic framework.

We primarily used experiences of dissociation, time distortion, age regression, and positive hallucination to help Tracy find the method she needed to get beyond her pain. We also used uniquely personal experiences, which included what we might refer to as "hopefulness" and her general ability to organize perceptual predispositions to behavioral and social cues.

The outcome of the session was dramatic. She began with a headache and achieved desired relief in this single hour-long session. Upon reorientation from trance she reported time distortion and partial amnesia for approximately half the experience. Leaving the session, she reported the headache gone. She added that she had "hope for the first time," and said she felt "as if a load had been lifted." Follow-up several months after the session produced the same reports.

Physically, we had helped her broaden her map of her bodily abilities to include the use of dissociation. Her final comment that a load had been lifted was especially relevant to her achieving the psychological goal. That conscious understanding was her only way of referring to her intuitive sense that her unconscious resources alleviated the covert dynamics that gave rise to the pain. Far from finding a superficial or remedial solution for her problem, she stopped the dynamics that produced the symptom. And socially, she has far more of "life" available, since she does not spend energy recoiling from the stress she has felt.

In the transcript, "T" represents the client, Tracy, and "S" and "C" indicate Steve and Carol.

History

T: This is my first experience with this.

S: You were saying you hadn't been hypnotized before?

T: No. This is a whole new experience.

S: What's the difficulty that you were referred for?

T: I've had severe headaches for 10 years and they have now reached the point where they are not controlled by drugs or any kind of medication and I need help.

S: For 10 years?

T: Yes.

C: Do you have one now?

T: Yes, I have one most of the time.

C: How do you experience it?

T: There are two kinds. . . . One feels like there is a band around my head that's being screwed tightly and the other feels like it's exploding top and sides.

S: Do you know anything about the origin of it?

T: Yes, particularly since teenage years I've had many situations that were beyond my control and these have created frustration and anger that's unexpressed and then in 1968 my 22-year-old son was killed attempting to rob a liquor store and I added guilt to these feelings and about three years later these headaches began. On the conscious level I've accepted his death and know that if I had it to do over again I'd do it the same way but on the unconscious level I wonder, "How could I turn his life around so it would always stay a good life?"

S: Are there times when the headaches are gone?

T: Not really. I go to bed with headaches and I wake up with headaches and I have them all the daylight hours.

S: Well hypnosis may be one thing you can use.

T: That's why I came. Hypnosis is the one thing I have not tried.

S: And, if for some reason we fail to be helpful . . .

C: It doesn't mean that you've experimented fully and that there is no relief possible.

S: You are really only studying the Lanktons here.

T: I realize that.

C: And you are only training your hypnotic response. Depending upon the depth you are able to achieve quickly, you may be able to get all the change you want immediately and you may also want to continue to develop your own ability at trance so you can develop your resources more in the time to come.

T: I'd be interested in that.

C: Have you developed trance-like states in the audience here?

T: I really related to Patty—I was sitting in that other chair while she was here.

As stated earlier, our original contract was treatment for chronic headaches, but our plan was totally contingent on interaction with the client. Any part of the plan could have been changed to accommodate new or revealing information about her unique peersonal needs and social network. After initial assessment we were, however, satisfied that her problem was not significantly a result of her current social network transactions.

She had a loving husband and apparently had a good relationship with him and her other children. Communication with her was no problem and we expected our session could have profound effects on her experience of pain. A modified embedded metaphor modality was selected as the vehicle to organize the therapy for her headache and the general changes which success about the headache would bring to other facets of her life.

The psychological aspect of her pain seemed to be a matter of her learned use of her body and the unconscious meaning of inner criticism created by cognitive dissonance. Headaches did not seem to be occurring contingent upon secondary social gains, roles, or stimulus conditioning. We formulated the following treatment plan in view of our assessment of her as a woman with many resources, including emotional and role flexibility and sensitivity to others. We modified and completed this plan by selecting anecdotes, metaphors, and a delivery style appropriate to her particular view of the world.

We formed metaphors that might be easily understood by a seven- to 11-year-old child, due to the regressive nature of her interpersonal actions. Upham (1973) has written:

> Stress, particularly stress that affects areas of vulnerability or unresolved conflict or stress that is traumatic in nature, tends to produce regression to earlier development levels. This regression must be distinguished from regression in the service of the ego, a useful defense that

allows the ego to retreat and pause in its endeavors to rally its forces (p. 119).

Although Erickson, as we mentioned, formulated no unified theory of personality, this concept is consistent with his remarks about regression and stress, e.g., "She had no resources with which to struggle against her anxiety and depression, but at any signal she collapsed deeper into illness" (CP III, p. 132). This woman's "collapse into illness" involved daily bouts with pain. The diagnosis of her age of development was a way of conceptualizing her regression resulting from the stress of the problem. Our assessment of Tracy's state of regression was further based on her compliance, willingness, naiveté, and language. We speculated her functioning as that of a child during latency years.

During this session, we occasionally spoke simultaneously, particularly when we wished to deepen the trance by confusion and overload. This was, of course, primarily during induction and facilitated the establishment of a conscious/unconscious dissociation. At other times we spoke intermittently and often about the same experience, interspersing indirect suggestions with short anecdotes.

During the entire trance we depended on Tracy's ideomotor behavior for feedback that our suggestions had produced the desired experience at each choice-point in the treatment. Such ideomotor behavior is often the only indicator that experiences have been sufficiently developed for transition to the next stage of therapy. Respecting these ideomotor signals insured a smooth experience for Tracy, as well as a positive sense of our credibility and potency.

The therapy can be divided into four phases: history-taking and beginning of induction; elicitation of trance phenomena and training of the patient to use these phenomena to alleviate the physical aspects of pain; use of metaphor to reorganize the psychological aspects created by the problem; and creating a generative orientation to her future. The following outline expands these phases.

History and Induction
*History → Fixation and induction
*Induction → Relaxation
*Relaxation → Dissociation from pain

Trance Phenomena for Pain
*Dissociation → Time distortion from pain
*Dissociation → Negative hallucination

Psychological Work with Metaphors
*Suspense metaphor → Orient to future
*Mystery metaphor → Orient to future
*Dissociation + future → Self-image thinking

Reorientation to Waking State
*Posthypnotic association → Use learnings daily
*Self-image thinking → Social network

Fixation and History → Induction

C: You've heard our explanations to others about what hypnosis is—you know that you needn't be oblivious to what we're saying, that you can hear and listen and understand in a heightened awareness sort of way, as you just relax and learn from yourself at another level simultaneously. So, if you're ready, you can begin to develop that depth of trance that you already know how to, just by getting comfortable and finding some one spot to look at and focus your attention on. And of course, that's only your visual attention because your conscious mind is full of wondering about what's really going to happen. You're aware of this fairly unusual circumstance. S: Close your eyes, down they go. C: I hope you're aware of your courage. S: So that you can find that depth of trance that you think you want, or may want in order to solve a psychological difficulty with physical ramifications.

Induction → Relaxation

S: Now you know that you've sat and been very relaxed in your past. You've been so relaxed, in fact, C: that you've been able to fall asleep sitting up, not that you're going to fall asleep today because you're interested, S: And float right out of your body . . . C: in what's happening and in what you can really learn . . . S: Your conscious mind is interested in what we're saying, what you'll learn and your unconscious mind is regulating your breathing. Your conscious mind is showing that anxiety and trepidation while your unconscious mind is relaxed and waiting . . . C: And you've already learned more than you know about. S: Your conscious mind thinks you might want to hold on for dear life and your unconscious mind knows it's all right for you to explore things in a relaxed fashion. C: Certainly you've explored things in a relaxed fashion somewhere in your history, perhaps as a little girl exploring the different patches of shade underneath the trees in your yard—those little hideaways . . . S: And our voices can turn into your own voice . . . C: that you could just relax in . . . S: the voice of strangers, friends from the past . . . C: as if in a world of your own . . . S: even the voice of the wind and the rain. *C:* You could hear your mother's voice calling you from that imaginary, private world of your own. And you had a choice, whether to stay or return. You always have that choice.

*Relaxation → Dissociation From Pain

S: Now this matter of floating away from your body. You've done it when you were a child lying on the freshly mowed lawn. It's something that you've learned and may have not used for a long period of time, Tracy's ability to just float up out of her body like a breath of fresh air, leaving the body behind. *C:* feeling lighter and lighter. *S:* You've read about people who have that experience at the time of death, floating around the hospital bed. *C:* And you know that your body's perfectly safe, that it waits for you to return to it when the time is right. *S:* You're aware of the doctors, things that are said . . . *C:* and you're also aware of the freedom. *S:* And of course, they return back to their bodies before they awaken, but for a moment they thought that they weren't going to re-awaken, and in that moment they floated up out of their body—so it's a common experience. As a small child you can lie in bed safe between the sheets and you know you're not having a dream because you're much too alert and you can feel yourself float up out of the top of your head . . . *C:* and enjoy the curiosity of watching yourself. *S:* And float around the room exploring places with such vividness that it would seem as if you weren't really asleep. *C:* It would seem as if you're both here and there and floating somewhere still beyond.

S: Now you bring a lot of difficulties with you. You don't really need those difficulties. Leave them in the chair as you float above your body. I just want to talk to your unconscious mind about letting those difficulties have some rest. *C:* And why not allow them some rest. You've carried them around diligently, heavily. Just experience the sensation of taking them off, the same way you would take off a coat that you leave hanging over the back of the chair, and taking off the hat which you leave beside the chair, and just floating free, unencumbered. And perhaps will come to mind the sense of floating that *you* experienced earlier as we spoke to Patty as she floated and you floated, deeper and deeper imagining yourself in the context of water, breathing comfortably, wearing heavy equipment that somehow renders you weightless. *S:* When you're in a trance, you know the words spoken to you are a stimulus for your own thinking, that if you should choose to, you could answer a telephone or attend to a crying child, move out of the way of a falling object. But there's no need to move, no desire to move. *C:* You can thank your unconscious mind for making all those arrangements that make it possible for you to be here and just listen and respond with undivided attention.

In the first paragraph we helped her learn to dissociate with the use of an anecdote about death. At the same time this provided further information about her unconscious associations to death to add to the information she had given verbally. She showed signs of deepening her relaxation and dissociation and did not show signs of mental or physical distress as we spoke about death. This response strengthened our hypothesis that she had completed most or all of her grieving for her son. Also, we had expected that she was likely to be familiar with the topic of dissociative experiences at times of near death, since she had been preoccupied with the subject of death for so long.

Suggestions were interspersed in the anecdotes by means of "soft" voice tone shifts. These included: "float up out of her body like a breath of fresh air," "your . . . body perfectly safe," "float up," "much too alert," "you're both here and there." By interspersing these suggestions within the anecdote, commands such as "float up" could be repeated without sounding offensively redundant.

Beginning with the second paragraph we initiated discussion of her "difficulties," but only after we had received ideomotor feedback that she had achieved dissociation from feelings. She thus became aware of our intention to be relevant to her concern and her treatment contract. The embedded command "have some rest" was of particular importance. Since it was spoken in the context of relaxation and dissociation, it was a direct instruction for her unconscious, literal mind to make a new association. Her difficulties were being spoken about in an abstracted and removed manner, thus increasing her dissociation for the duration of the session.

The metaphor of taking her difficulties off as one would "take off a coat" simplified the understanding to an age-appropriate level of conceptualizing and made maximal use of her understanding of how she might use her new experiences to remove the pain. The latency-aged description gave an apparent logic to the new frame of reference—dissociation experiences provided still further validation of the logic of the framework provided by the metaphors.

As resources were elicited and her experience became increasingly novel, it was useful to provide reassurance about the power and control available to her. Such reassurance was indirectly stated in reminders, such as, "If you should choose you could answer a telephone or attend to a crying child." Both of these actions were likely to be of especially high priority to a woman like Tracy. Rapport was furthered by implying that we, too, were aware of these important things. This type of reassurance is consistent with Erickson's style of always turning control over to the client and letting the client's concentration become increasingly turned inward to discover a unique and personal power.

The final sentence is a conscious/unconscious double bind. It was designed to further the dissociation in two ways. First, it informed her that her unconscious was learning and doing something she was not quite able to consciously comprehend. Second, the bind heightened her awareness of being absorbed in listening to us, even while seated in front of dozens of observers.

S: You may be interested in finding out if your unconscious will raise your left or your right hand up toward your face as a way of helping educate you about what trance can be like . . . C: and what you can do in trance without even trying to. S: First you feel small muscle alterations that signal that hand getting lighter. Then you feel a jerky movement of the index finger which is an indication to you that you weren't consciously thinking about it. C: It gets lighter and wants to rise up off the handle of the chair. And while you're thinking about doing that, finding out whether it's the right or the left hand that's going to float up toward your face, . . .

S: I'm going to speak about some other things. C: And just continue to develop that trance more deeply. S: We don't know why things happen. Perhaps it's enough to know that God only knows. The information's unavailable to the average person. But enough bad luck can come one's way. You know you don't need to add to it. You'll always have a good supply of that. But you do need to add to the good luck and the good things that come your way. C: Some people think they have to wait for good luck, that they have no choice in the matter of being lucky, but that's because they're not really thinking of luck as choice, as that unique moment when preparation meets opportunity.

S: I'm going to ask you to find some time in your childhood that will begin to come to your mind and you may want to think about it sooner or later, some scene from your childhood that was pleasant and delightful, or maybe it was from your teens. I don't know. Some period of your life that you forgot to speak to us about because it was pleasant for you then. C: And you didn't really think you needed to mention those pleasant times. You could just take those for granted. And they are granted in a way and yet you can reach in and bring one of them forward. There may be so many that you can't decide which one to bring forward and it's a pleasant task to sort among charming childhood experiences, letting the image of first one and then another flit to mind.

S: And while your unconscious is doing that, Tracy, your conscious mind may be interested in how your left hand is going to stay put in the air in a cataleptic fashion. And I'll just help you and show you what I mean (Steve takes her wrist, lifts it and releases it in sporadic, random fashion.) C: and waiting, perfectly willing to cooperate with an unexpected assistance, and notice how easy it is for you to just leave that hand floating . . . *S:* because your unconscious can change the way your body tends to work. You can change the way you digest food. Everyone knows that tensions and agitations of the mind will change the way your digestive system works. It makes the Rolaids people very happy. *C:* And it's certainly no fun to eat a meal when you're tense. You don't enjoy the food at all. And that's your unconscious mind making alterations in your experience. *S:* And your hand is as light as it could be, it seems to have no weight. *C:* It's so light it could continue to float upward now that the initial momentum of rising has already been accomplished.

In the first paragraph of this section we presented her with a bind of comparable alternatives regarding arm levitation. We intended to use the arm levitation as a means of proof to her conscious mind that her unconscious really could alter her body in unexplainable and yet controllable ways. "Soft" shifts in voice tone occurred on key suggestions such as "raise your left or your right hand up," "feel small muscle alterations," and "lighter." Those interspersed suggestions were presented within indirect suggestions, as contrasted to an interspersal within anecdotes. We made the alteration for variety's sake and to allow her maximum latitude in her own thought development.

The second paragraph introduced the relevant theme of her misfortunes. This was done in the framework of conscious/unconscious double binds to help her remain comfortably dissociated as we discussed it. Intermittent reference to the polarity of mental functioning reinforced the trance, as well as the understanding that new experiences and new frameworks were temporarily in effect. As discussed previously, we encouraged paradoxical confusion when we defined the occurrence of her misfortune as "bad luck," which only means she has "choice." It was implied that she should go ahead and notice her bad luck because it was an indicator of a "unique moment when preparation meets opportunity."

On the same wave of confusion and overload, we immediately associated her to the therapeutic regression in the third block of instructions and commands. We used a variety of indirect suggestions to help her find these resources:

- *Open-ended suggestion:* "I'm going to ask you to find some time in your childhood . . ."
- *Truism:* "You may want to think about it sooner or later . . ."
- *Implication:* "Some period of life you forgot to speak to us about because it was pleasant for you . . ."
- *Embedded command:* "You could *just take those for granted.*"

Finally, that paragraph ends with several comments designed to match her unspoken experience and continue rapport: "letting the image of first one thing and then another flit to mind." At this Tracy nodded her head with what appeared to be an involuntary jerk.

Arm levitation was achieved in the last paragraph when we reached and manually lifted her arm. It is uncommon but not altogether rare that we will help elevate an arm. We assumed that she had so completely dissociated from her cataleptic arm that she could not initiate levitation without assistance. The levitation was again framed in the conscious/unconscious double bind. The next several statements provided a context for suggestions (interspersed via voice tone shifts) that it remain levitated.

Finally, the point of all our work was to establish a learning frame for the session and to lead her to an understanding that change is possible. The levitation and anecdotes were used to convince her that " . . . your unconscious can change the way your body tends to work." Our tone shifting on the final phrase added to the growing number of learnings directed at her unconscious. The induction and establishment of the learning frame were then complete and we turned our attention to the matter of reducing her pain.

S: Now sometimes an animal doesn't know how its role in the world is to unfold. A butterfly is born from a cocoon and I just wonder if that caterpillar weaving that cocoon around itself must think that it's closing itself in in a way that it'll never escape from. It must wrap those little filaments tightly around the neck, the head till it secures itself and it knows it won't fall. And then it secures its feet and legs, one at a time, until finally an entire cocoon.

S: Things must look very black to that caterpillar at that time. And I wonder whether or not the caterpillar really knows that you have a future that's bright and interesting . . . C. and colorful and free. And change begins to happen within that cocoon.

C: You don't know whether or not the psychological processes that you've been living with, Tracy, are nearly completed with the learning but you do know that you've lived in that cocoon long enough, that things have looked black and they couldn't look any blacker. And the changes are so gradual that they're almost imperceptible. S: But change does happen. You can't deny that your hand is rising up toward your face automatically only because your unconscious has relinquished control for a moment and allowed a new relationship to happen, one that your hand will find with your face when it reaches your face.

C: And you don't really have to do anything to become that butterfly, you can't help but let that metamorphosis take place and change everything. S: It's an easy matter to tell you to memorize the feeling that your unconscious is giving your conscious mind about that hand. It's an easy

matter to recognize that your right hand is sitting there. Maybe it's thinking about rising up or maybe it's thinking about staying right where it is. But your left hand knows how to make an alteration in your body and you can memorize the feeling because you know it; it's your feeling and you learned it long ago when you were an infant and the hand didn't seem to be attached to your body, you hadn't discovered it.
S: And similarly you can move that feeling of detachment in your left arm and let it be the basis and the seed for growing a feeling of detachment in your shoulder, C: knowing that detachment is a feeling you can experience safely trusting other parts of yourself to hold on to that which is necessary to hold on to. And now making the alteration in your neck. So nice for your neck to belong to the other person. And your head is tilting slightly to meet your hand and you don't really know when they'll touch, but you're interested. S: Let that feeling of detachment move from your neck into your jaw and maybe just into the left side of your face. C: And you can just wait comfortably while we say other things while you feel that detachment of the arm moving into the neck and left side of your face and your hand continues to move toward your face where it will stay.

The first three paragraphs presented the initial matching metaphor by use of analogy to the darkness and loneliness inside a cocoon. This was enhanced by the use of "soft" voice shifts on such phrases as "must wrap those . . . tightly around the neck, the head," "things must look very black." This metaphor was temporarily ended with an embedded command created with tone shift and pronoun change: "you have a future that's bright and interesting."

Paragraph four presented a surprise that change is inevitable due to metamorphosis. If Tracy had identified with the caterpillar and its problems, she had to accept that change must happen eventually. Her arm levitation was cited as further proof that her unconscious was in fact already changing things: "You can't deny that your hand is rising up toward your face automatically."

Finally, dissociation was moved further toward her face. A learning set had been established, was reinforced by her experience, and at the same time gave an explanation as to how she could use the resource of dissociation. Then she could not deny that change happened, even to her. The implication was created by association. Her unconscious skill in dissociation was gradually moving to her headache area.

S: I had a client one time who was suffering great pain in her shoulders. She thought psychologically it had some roots in her past. So I asked her to have a dream and in that dream she was going to find out something symbolic about the meaning of that pain. She dreamed about a small piece of grass between two slabs of sidewalk. She didn't know what the dream meant consciously . . . *C:* but she had a very vivid image of that sidewalk with the bit of grass growing between the slabs.

S: And when your hand reaches your face just let that same feeling from your hand flow into your cheek and flow up the left side of your face and be memorized by the muscles of your scalp because it's pleasant to know that that's something you know how to do.

C: She had a second dream, this time we instructed her to dream less symbolically but only to the extent that she could remain comfortable. The symbols changed. This time she said, "Somebody's trying to pull that weed from between the pieces of sidewalk and it's a tense situation—the grass doesn't want to come out, the pulling force is relentless." She awoke from the dream and her conscious mind didn't understand the meaning but her unconscious knew . . .

S: So let that feeling which is flowing from your left hand into your cheek, face and left part of your skull also move into the right part of your skull, including the very top of your head and down the back of your neck to join that same feeling at the bottom of your neck, and around to the right side of your neck. So that in a circular fashion that feeling of detachment and being able to float light . . . *C:* just goes around and around. You've gone around and around a lot. *S:* I wonder whether or not you can let that same feeling of dissociation of your muscles go round and round as often as you've gone round and round with *that.* And the third dream she had, even less symbolic than the first ones, revealed to her that her mother always used to pull her hair and that was the meaning of the weed between the slabs. *C:* But you can let that same feeling of detachment go right into your hair as well. And that's what she was able to do too because in the trance she could discover a new comfort.

S: You need to really look at the things in your past and learn from watching them. You can make a picture of yourself right now comfortably sitting in the chair, and I'll describe it. Your left hand is against your cheek. Your index finger and ring finger nearly touch the corner of your mouth. *C:* The muscles of your face are very smooth and there is a relaxation over your eyes and the lines of your mouth. The lines of your neck are relaxed and you are breathing quite rhythmically . . . *S:* which is evident from watching your neck and upper chest. There is a pink cast to your skin and perhaps you can notice there is occasionally rapid eye movement because Tracy is picturing something, *C:* something known only to her, stimulated by our words. *S:* And it's a picture of yourself sitting there comfortably. You need to look at a lot of things from your past and understand them as clearly as possible so that you can feel comfortable.

Paragraphs one and three involved a dream while paragraphs two and four kept returning to her gradually developing dissociation from the pain.

This arrangement insured us of several things. Primarily, the polarity between conscious and unconscious minds had been utilized and reinforced. Within the framework of a dream she would come to understand that her conscious mind could ignore her mental workings. As a result, amnesia could be expected. The dream content itself referred to self-criticism from internal parental figures. Symbolically, she was invited to call to mind her difficulties. From her own experience she had a way to disguise her thoughts symbolically to prevent distress that might be encountered consciously if such unconscious material came to awareness rapidly. Each client can be assisted in locating and using resources in symbolic form within altered frameworks that make new possibilities manifest but which remain several steps removed from consciousness.

We considered this maneuver as it related to two aspects of her physical and psychological functioning. The first was the diagnostic assessment of the relationship between the client and her internalized mother or, one might say, her superego influences. Her ideomotor response did not give us cause for further concern about that source of self-criticism by Tracy. The second aspect involved the dissociation created by the three switches between the symbolic dreams and the focusing of attention on the feelings of detachment and floating.

Therapy is useful when it helps the client create a reassociation of experiential resources. One such associative link was established nicely with the line: "I wonder whether or not you can let that same feeling of dissociation of your muscles go round and round as often as you've gone round and round with *that*." Relating dissociation to ideas about "going round and round" gave Tracy a direct associative link. Readers might be aware of the usefulness of the simple but meaningful noun, *"that."* As previously mentioned, deletion of reality referents to nouns like *"that"* facilitates the client's motivation because the client must think of what it is we mean from all the possible associations we might mean. We asked her, therefore, to find her own images of some experiences with which she had gone "round and round."

In the final paragraph we used another element of the dissociation phenomenon from which she might profit. Her ability to look at her situation rather than feel her way through was yet another important resource, since her feeling associations related to her son's death were so painful.

*Dissociation → Time Distortion From Pain

S: One of the things you need to look at is your ability to have that feeling of detachment in your left arm last for hours and hours. Now the woman with the pain in her shoulders only had that problem intermittently. We asked her to find out that you can change the way you experience time. You've known how driving in your car it seems as if you're at your exit too soon. You've driven past plenty of exits unknown to your conscious mind . . . C: because there was no need to attend to those exits. They didn't concern you at all. S: And although you had been driving for what must have been 45 minutes or an hour . . .

C: Your mind had been full of your own thoughts . . . S: and it seemed as if only five or ten minutes had passed. C: You couldn't even remember what you had been thinking about necessarily but you know you enjoyed it. S: That's a learning, Tracy, that your unconscious mind can change your subjective experience of time. You have that ability. You know you've had it on the highway. You may also realize you've had it while you were absorbed in a television show or listening to a lecture. In other words, you can make time go fast or slow.

S: And we explained that to the client and told her to make those moments of pain very, very short, subjectively, C: and the moments of comfort seem to last forever. And just letting the feeling of detachment go round and round. S: Everyone goes into trance sometimes and they don't always listen to our words. It's amusing to recapitulate the responses which other people have and wonder if we can have them ourselves. And one of the clients that we worked with found out that she could make the feeling of pain last only a moment, C: and the clock time didn't matter at all because she applied that learning that your unconscious knows about.

S: And the way you can do that very mechanically, for the practical minded, is to remember that time in the car you've driven for such a long period of time and it all seemed like five minutes. Have it handy. Keep it handy. At the first sign of pain in the morning, you reach into that memory of driving and the next thing you know, you're not thinking about the pain at all. C: You're thinking about whatever those thoughts were that brought you so much pleasure then. You try to remember, following that feeling of pleasure.

In these four paragraphs anecdotes were used to retrieve the phenomenon of time distortion from the alterations already created with dissociation, and to then link that resource to the existing frame, and eventually, to the mechanisms for reducing the headache pain. We emphasize that even though this was accomplished in only four paragraphs with Tracy, with another client it might have taken two or 20 paragraphs. With some clients anecdotes of time distortion in automobiles might have been completely inappropriate because of their personal history with automobiles. So, again, therapy is guided by the ideomotor feedback from the client.

The metaphors we used were not arcane or difficult. They were developed according to Erickson's method of utilizing common everyday trance experiences to create colloquial understandings of trance phenomena. The conscious mind may recognize, recall, or retrieve an experiential memory of a trance phenomenon; as that happens, the unconscious mechanisms involved in the phenomenon will also be operating. That phenomenon can then be strategically associated to other mechanisms by further elaborating the metaphoric framework that produced the anecdote.

Indirect suggestions were continually used to reinforce experiences elicited by the anecdotes. They are tools that aid in linking experiences and frameworks together, as well as in linking experiences with other experiences. They provide the glue that holds a framework together with living experiences. In the first sentence of the first paragraph a softened voice tone emphasizes the suggestion "have that feeling of detachment in your left arm last for hours and hours." As an unconscious search was instigated, several indirect suggestions were formed:

- *Truism:* "You know how driving in your car . . ." and "Everyone goes into a trance sometimes . . ."
- *Implication:* "It seems . . . you're at your exit too soon. . . ." "You may also realize you've had it while. . . ." We further implied that she might want to do the same for herself with: "the way you can do that . . ."
- *Open-ended:* "They didn't concern you at all," and "You have that ability," and "Have it handy. Keep it handy."
- *Focusing Awareness:* "You were thinking about whatever those thoughts were that brought you so much pleasure then," and "You try to remember following that feeling of pleasure."

The use of anecdotes here allowed her to change her frame of reference, which in turn facilitated her ability to make new associations to her experiences that might be applicable to solving the problem of her pain. There were several short anecdotes in this piece about driving, television, and other clients: ". . . you must have been driving . . . 45 minutes," "absorbed in a television show," "the responses which other people have," and "And one of the clients we've worked with found. . . ." These anecdotes were simultaneously embedded in the metaphoric context of the earlier story of the woman with the dream about her mother: "Now the woman with the pain in her shoulders. . . ." Although this represents one version of the multiple embedded metaphor, this transcript is presented here to illustrate the use of anecdotes and indirect suggestions for resources and trance phenomena.

Another reason for using these anecdotes was to facilitate an understanding in Tracy's map of the world that would be consistent with time distortion. As stated before, Erickson considered metaphor and indirect suggestion to be the basis for changing frames of reference and exchanging ideas. Tracy's case provides a practical application of such change and exchange.

Trance depth was maintained by rapport we had originally established, but one specific rapport maintenance suggestion was the direct reference to her mechanical use of time distortion for her presenting problem: "At the first sign of pain in the morning. . . ." A casual mention of the presenting problem seems to produce more rapport and motivation from the client. The change we were helping Tracy organize can be described as therapy by reciprocal inhibition. We will discuss that in Chapter 8. As far as Tracy was concerned, she knew that everything said had been for the purpose of solving her problem and she must do some thinking of her own to use the ideas she'd been having. The trance was additionally maintained by conveying our observations of her ongoing state of experience.

Because some of our sentences seemed both to relate to her present state and to elaborate on the topics being discussed, she likely experienced a confusion of contexts: "Your mind had been full of your own thoughts," and "it seemed as if only five of ten minutes had passed," and "don't always listen to our words," and "You couldn't remember what you had been thinking about. . . ." That set of suggestions gave her direct instructions for using the understandings and experiences she had been entertaining. This directness of suggestion about reassociation occurred only after the retrieval and linking had already been explained many times metaphorically and with psychological implication.

*Dissociation → Negative Hallucination

S: Now that arm on your righthand side may seem to you to have stayed down, but upon careful examination you can probably recognize that there were lingering feelings of your hand being down. But it's interesting to notice that you can have those alterations in your experience. It's very difficult to determine the exact location of a hand. C: You know when you've been asleep, you don't really know the position of your body. The train going by outside the window at night doesn't even bother you. But you don't know where you slept when that train went by and you can wake up in the morning and find that you've turned around in bed entirely. S: Your head's down where your feet were supposed to be, your feet are on the pillow. The train passed and you don't even know why you changed your position, but it did change. And while you were asleep it didn't seem as if you had moved at all.

C: That must be what happened to that right hand. It must have floated up while you were paying attention elsewhere. You can dream that you are standing up when all the while you are lying comfortably, surprised to wake up and discover yourself as you really are lying in the bed. S: It's interesting to realize the kind of alterations your unconscious can make. C: There are a lot of them. It's easy to do.

S: So you can, as another client of ours did, not notice a stimulus that happens in your body somewhere. You've known how to go for a long period of time without noticing your hunger as you are a mother and all mothers have to put their feelings of hunger aside sometimes to take care of other business. C: And not just their hunger but all of their urges sometimes go on hold.

C: Also, you've realized while driving in a car that you couldn't stop to go to the bathroom, and, so, you didn't even notice your bladder. S: But as soon as that car came to a halt you knew that there was something that you needed to do. And you went directly to the bathroom because your unconscious can keep track for you . . . C: without your conscious mind having to keep it in mind at all. In other words, you can use that same learning to forget about whether or not you're having a headache. S: So you can speed up the moments of pain so that they seem to last a very short period of time and then forget about them entirely.

Suggestions regarding the resource phenomenon of negative hallucination seeded earlier were elaborated in this section with four anecdotes: not noticing the passing of a train at night while asleep; dreaming and changing position in bed; ignoring hunger experiences; and ignoring bladder experiences. These were linked to the overall framework with several indirect suggestions:

- *Focusing Awareness:* "Recognize that there were lingering feelings." "It's interesting to notice that you can have those alterations." "It's interesting to notice the kind of alterations your unconscious can make." Voice tone was shifted with each of these on "recognize," "notice," and "notice."
- *Truism:* "It's difficult to determine the exact location of a hand." "You've known how to go a long period of time. . . ." "You don't know where you've slept. . . ." "You can dream. . . ."
- *Implication:* "That must be what happened to that right hand" (something happened).
- *Open-ended:* "You can use that same learning to forget. . . ."

The straightforward explanation of the mechanics of using negative hallucination for her pain control again served to reinforce rapport. Although she didn't know how to doubt her pain, she did know how to doubt other bodily phenomena. We presented the implication that her distraction in the trance was also a learning (known to the unconscious) and she could apply that learning to the awareness of pain. Thus we expanded her map of experience to include associations away from her sensitivity and preoccupation with her pain. Her conscious mind would not be able to articulate just what those learnings were, but they were real by virtue of being lived rather than spoken about.

We could then turn to the psychological problems. We had developed a wide range of trance phenomena with anecdotes and suggestion. These resources were organized in order to direct her energy that had been bound in psychological tension. We addressed her future life situation and the psychological implications of becoming free of the headache. Thus, we further suggested success in relieving the pain by discussing matters that presupposed relief.

We were aware of her ability to use suggestions. Her ideomotor behavior had continually indicated her "staying with us" and/or our "staying with" her. Her trance was deepened only because of the extensive alteration she experienced in her conventional frame of reference. Since the indirect suggestions she followed seemed to be having a cumulative impact, we knew our reference to her future would not have to be lengthy in order to be profoundly experienced.

*Suspense Metaphor→ Orient Her to Future

S: And you're going to have to think about something, aren't you? And what can you think about? You've thought, planned and dreamed a long time in your life. I had a friend who built a boat in his garage, a large cabin cruiser. He worked on it and polished it and ordered parts for it for years. C: Day and night, every moment of spare time was poured diligently into the polishing and finishing of that boat. S: By the time I met him, the boat looked to me to be seaworthy, but he said there was a lot of work to do; the boat was not yet ready to go off on its own. And he worked on it. He made plans for sailing it around the world.
C: He ordered charts; he was very precise; he bought cameras. And, of course, before it was time to set it on its way and let it go, he was left floating with some ideas about how he was going to have to change part of the mast, the cabin, the rudder, and he would tear it apart and work on it even longer. S: Now I really hoped that the day would come when I would see that boat in the water and I would get to ride on that boat. C: Because he had planned on the sailing of that boat for so long, and working on that and polishing it and shaping it and dreaming about it and hoping for its future for so long.
S: He looked forward to the day when he could rest on its deck and it would take care of him. It seemed like a good investment. And I know that he didn't have anything else to think about except how he was going to finish that boat and launch it and look forward to the days when he could be taken care of on its deck, by its sturdiness. C: And it's true that the preparation for a journey should be equally enjoyable as the

journey itself and the journeying to the destination should be equally enjoyable as arriving at the destination.

S: And one day I heard from my parents that the man had died and the boat never made it out of the garage. They had to tear down the garage to salvage what they could and sell the rest. C: We hoped he had enjoyed the preparation because he wasn't going to enjoy a final journey on that boat. But I know that the preparation was all that there was at the time for him.

C: And now the wife has a lot of things to think about. She doesn't want anything to do with that boat. She had watched, frustrated, for a long time, wishing he wouldn't spend so much of his time on that boat in the first place. She certainly didn't want to spend any more time thinking about it now. S: She wanted to make her hopes and dreams about other things for years and now was her big opportunity. But she had some goodbyes and some grieving to do and she did it. And time passed. It seemed as if she was ramming her head against the wall for a while and getting nowhere. Every time she started to think about something in the future that damn boat would come to mind—and then other complications came to mind.

In the first few paragraphs of this section a metaphor was told about a man building a boat that he would never get to use. The boat-in-the-garage symbol captured her attention unconsciously due to its parallel with the situation regarding her son's life and death. Meanwhile, her conscious mind may have fixated on the mystery: "What is happening to this man that it merits an explanation?" Tracy's despairing at the death of her son is similar to the time of desperation for the wife in the story.

As the drama unfolded, Tracy was gently pointed , by modeling, toward future projects, as the wife in the story discovered and created options. The next section presents going back to school, choosing a career, teaching, and nursing as possible options. At that point in the trance, however, Tracy did not know how the story would end. She only knew that the sudden change in life plans was similar to her own. Clients do not usually think of their lives as they think of history or dramatic movement. We convey to the client an understanding that is present in all dramatic themes: Change happens! This is another resource, that, although not directly present in Tracy's functioning, could be retrieved because of the ease of communication in the hypnotic trance.

Implication and other indirect suggestions in the metaphor produced elements of mystery and suspense. The implication that something other than the boat had to be the object of thought was conveyed with: "We hoped he had enjoyed the preparation because he wasn't going to enjoy a final journey on the boat," and with, "She doesn't want anything to do with that boat."

The symbol of the boat or ship is frequently used as a symbol for the self in the form of the human body (Cirlot, 1962, p. 29). Cirlot illustrates that the symbols of ships are "symbols of the human body and of all physical bodies or vehicles" (1962, p. 281). He also indicates that the ship symbol is associated with transcending existence and therefore with the existence of the soul. Thus, the boat related to her son on conscious and unconscious levels, as well as on the archetypal level. In the context of the metaphoric framework, even a simple word like "boat" becomes a "meaning-full" utterance.

The image of the man and the boat involved something that one of us had heard from our parents. The introduction of the preceding generation was not merely true, but also deliberately left in the story for the implications of credibility that it may have provided by virtue of modeling. That is, it was a lesson about life that we had learned and it might serve as a lesson to her without being so labeled. Within that framework the entire story further served the purpose of reassuring her about her trance learnings.

"But she had some goodbyes and some grieving to do and she did it," referred to the grieving that Tracy had already done. If there was more grieving to do still, as there might well have been, she was directed to do this with her husband. It was mentioned earlier that this relationship was supportive and comfortable.

Finally, the last line mentioned that, whenever the boat came to mind, "other complications came to mind." The word "complications" is another example of the deliberate use of a "meaning-full" word to create a search for the unchanging elements of Tracy's dilemma. We led Tracy to consider her frame of reference as the logical and inevitable springboard to the future and, therefore, an end to the framework of the past. New and unexplored ideas were possible and she was asked to question them: "And you're going to have to think about something, aren't you? And what can you think about?"

We briefly mentioned trance maintenance suggestions that confused the context with "organ language" or sentences ambiguously worded to refer to situations both in the physical-biological sense (judged by the positioning of her body) and at the same time in the psychological sense. Phrases like "left floating," "rest," and "didn't want to spend any more time thinking about it now" spoke to that issue.

*Mystery Metaphor→Orient to Future

S: Finally, emerging from a cocoon the butterfly somehow manages to flap its wings in the air for the first time, C: to work its way completely free from the cocoon. Holding its wing in the air, drying it in the sunlight and getting a new feeling of being light, airy, on its own feet, able to float, so mobile for the first time. *S:* And from a heightened perspective, the butterfly can use eyes to look down and see a lot of things that were unknown to that same brain while it was trapped in that cocoon. *C:* And there were a lot of things that she had planned on dreaming about someday. Now seemed to be a perfect opportunity. Someday had arrived. Now was a good someday. *S:* What kind of hopes and dreams do you suppose she had? It didn't have anything to do with boats but she had been nursing some dreams in the back of her mind and those were a fine thing for her to be thinking about. Now you may not believe this, but she went back to college. She studied nursing. She found out that she had a fine mind, that she could read, could remember and could put ideas together. *C:* She could put ideas together in a way such that others could benefit. It was especially delightful to her to read to children, teaching them from her vast wealth of experience. She studied teaching and began to be absorbed in teaching. She thought she might go for a masters degree in nursing and teach nursing. When friends would mention to her that she was really too old to be considering such things, she was undaunted by their ill advice and limiting beliefs.

Returning to the butterfly metaphor created the effect typical of the multiple embedded metaphor structure. She again realized that the entire story-web was connected. Since the cocoon was originally presented as a heavy, oppressive, and dark wrapping, she could have identified with it as a symbol of her gloomy life. But the cocoon took a metamorphic twist. Carefully chosen words encouraged Tracy to apply the metamorphosis to herself. One such line was: "the butterfly can use eyes to look down and see a lot of things that were unknown to that same brain while it was trapped in that cocoon." Embedded questions and open-ended suggestions, such as, "What kinds of hopes and dreams do you suppose she had?" and statements that "she had a fine mind" and "put ideas together," were references to her intellectual future. She could look at things differently. These were open-ended suggestions about her future thinking, parallel to the idea from the metaphor that the butterfly will think of things not known to the same brain before metamorphosis.

The careers of teaching and nursing were mentioned, not as ideas about her most likely career choices, but rather as indicators that the woman in the metaphor concluded her study with decisive action. Tracy, therefore, was given several options, including returning to school, studying, entering a career, as well as the myriad of other associations that she might make independently. The opportunity to begin something new was a resource to be linked to a specific time period, that is "someday." In fact, "Now seemed to be a perfect opportunity," "someday had arrived," and "now was a good someday." These open-ended suggestions linked to the butterfly emerging from the cocoon were designed to help Tracy break from the past and look to the future.

*Dissociation + Future → Self-image Thinking

C: Now you've been floating, floating above your body; your hand float-ed up to your face. S: The tension in your head floated I know not where, and from that angle you can imagine looking down and seeing yourself on stage just like a butterfly can look around and see where it once was sitting on a limb. C: And see where it wants to be sitting on another limb. Just look around and see where you'd like to go, knowing you can go anywhere. And you have a long time ahead of you so look far. And when they told Milton Erickson in 1947 that he was living on borrowed time, he responded that he couldn't think of a better time to live on. S: And he looked long into the future. C: Many full years.

S: And now you can be alone with your memories and look at them from on high, get a new view and a new understanding. And, just as you could look at Tracy feeling comfortable and detached, so too can you stay comfortably detached while you look at Tracy over there with that headache in her head over there, many feet away.

S: And you could look at that headache in her head and gain a new under-standing of your ability to stay at a distance, detached. Look at it every which way and maybe that headache will look like a helmet of some kind. C: A hard substance attached to her head and just watch so that the color and substance of that headache you see out there matches every ugly dimension of the pain you once felt. And if at any time you feel any bit of that pain, translate it immediately into the picture, watching the color, shape and texture change accordingly. S: And now I want you to watch that deplorable, ugly, hideous headache in your mind's eye change to a different color, maybe a different shape.

C: Watch it pulsate with a new rhythm, finally changing into a balloon.

S: A helium filled balloon C: that can float away. S: And once you see that balloon filled with that once ugly shape just let go of it and let it float . . . C: further and further away, higher and higher until it becomes only a small pinpoint of a dot. And try as hard as you will to continue watch-ing it, it goes out of sight very quickly. S: And a balloon that you let go of can never come back. And then, too, watch yourself take that helmet off, the remains of that helmet which had been the pain. Just take it right off like a cap and leave it over there.

C: And then sit back in this chair in front of us. And just like people return to their bodies from floating before they wake up . . . S: We've been in-structing a lot of parts of your unconscious mind to make alterations in Tracy's experience. We've asked that you remember to look far into the future because you're going to be around for a long time and you need to examine the goals and dreams. Now I don't know whether or not your conscious mind has a sense of needing to cry. I don't know what you expected from hypnosis but I do know that the process of change is started just like your hand has stayed glued to your face.

Referring to her floating above her body was facilitated by using her arm levitation as a tool for conveying to her the reality of such alterations. This section ended with a reference to her arm: "I do know that the process of change is started just like your hand has stayed glued to your face." While the logic was actually a convoluted modus tollens* paradigm of reasoning, the ratification of the cataleptic arm was an indisputable indication to her that some kind of change process had happened. This example again underscores the use made of all messages from the client. Arm levitation usually serves no greater purpose than that. Why not a change in her life as well as in her body?

The first paragraph ended with the compound suggestion that just as she could "look at Tracy feeling comfortable and detached, so too can you stay comfortably detached while you look at Tracy. . . ." That statement was structured as a bit of a bind. Before she might challenge the detachment she was experiencing, she was asked to reinforce her ability to look at herself in visual imagery with that detachment. This was the final association of her experiential resource of dissociation with her previous experience of pain. The use of visual imagery was a mediating device calculated to provide still another route or mental avenue for her continued ease. We then began self-image thinking and a translation of her physical pain into a visual symbol.

Utilizing the visual image of her headache involved still another frame change. Her dissociation was reinforced by the visual imagery of a helmet which she could see herself remove. This was still another metaphor understandable to a child in the latency period. By presenting her such a visual, conscious mind analogy, we gave her a method that might congeal the kinesthetic learnings of detachment, time distortion, and negative hallucination presented in anecdotal form. Behavioral research by Bandura (1969, p. 133) has indicated that learnings represented in two imagery representational systems endure longer than those mapped in but one system.

Suggesting that she look into the future ("remember to look far into the future because you're going to be around for a long time") was an open-ended suggestion to bridge her awareness toward the establishment of goals men-

---

*Modus tollens is the logical principle which licenses the following sort of inference: If α then β. It is not the case that β. Therefore, it is not the case that α. ("α" and "β" are linguistic variables for which any sentence may be substituted.)

tioned in the previous section ("and you need to examine the goals and dreams"). Finally, we offered a "disclaimer": "I don't know whether your conscious mind has a sense of needing to cry." This suggestion to focus awareness on any residual grief, as mentioned above, was being referred to gently and gradually. In the next section it was linked to emotional expressions she could choose to share with her loved ones.

*Posthypnotic Association → Use Learnings Daily

C: I do know you developed a very nice trance and you'll be able to use the same process of change in the next few days to make further alterations. And you have the ability to create trance for yourself anytime. We've mentioned six ways for you to change your headache but doubt very much whether you could consciously say what they are. S: But I do know that your unconscious learns very quickly and is holding on to those ways and will use them. And I don't know if Sunday is too soon for you to have total relief. C: Wednesday is a very good day. S: I've enjoyed Wednesdays most of my life. C: Or Tuesday afternoon. S: I hope that you'll enjoy Wednesday as much as I wish . . . C: and you'll probably enjoy it more than we can know. S: One time we had a client who didn't want to get rid of her problem and we suggested she get rid of it on Wednesday but just to show us she could get rid of it her own way, she got rid of it on Tuesday instead.

*Self-image Thinking → Social Network

C: And it's important to do things your own way, so go right ahead and get rid of your pain when the time is right for you. S: And let that feeling of detachment you've had in your arm be something that you memorize again. Let it travel into your bloodstream and to anywhere in your body, such as your heart, and relax your heart. C: You've already relaxed your mind and you can relax that tear that wants to come. You've relaxed your breathing and just enjoy that swirling relaxation traveling to all parts, down to your feet. S: And that tear is about to embark on a journey down your cheek. C: And enjoy its journey, saying goodbye to that sadness that it represents. . . .

Reorientation from trance was begun here by giving her a compliment on her "very nice trance." For a client less eager to please others, this statement might not appeal. The open-ended suggestion that she would use the same process to change in the next few days was followed with a conscious/unconscious bind that she couldn't (consciously) say what the six ways were but her unconscious was holding on to them. And finally, these were followed with suggestions for changing on particular days of the week.

We insisted that she change in her own way and in her own time in order to place the real success for her change within herself. Using the symbols of her heart and bloodstream was a "down-to-earth" reminder of her state of detachment and relaxation. Concurrently, the symbol of the heart associated her relaxation and closure with the cardiovascular system. At that point her relaxation and circulation indicated her success at relaxing the tension in her head. The capillary relaxation was an indirect way of referring to her lack of headache without using the word "headache." Colloquially, the "heartache" which developed from losing a son by death could be countered with the association carried in the poetic phrase "relax your heart." That associative link was especially powerful since it was offered at the conclusion of her successful dissociation trance.

The tear that had formed in her eye was a message about her responsiveness to our suggestions about such matters. We commented on it and reframed it with the suggestion that she enjoy its journey. It was a touching message from Tracy that our suggestion to "relax your heart" was important to her.

The tear came at a time of conclusion rather than earlier when we had mentioned possible residual grief. Had it come earlier we would have taken a different direction and asked her to continue that grieving in trance. At the time this tear occurred, nearly an hour had passed. The session was almost over and we were impressed with this tear not so much as an indicator of uncompleted sobbing, but rather as an appreciative expression of completion.

S: And a seventh way, that I'll continue to speak about while you explore that tear, is to let the residual pain in your headache area travel down your cheek in the vicinity of your tears, C: over your mouth, into your fingers and into your little finger. S: And if it's necessary to have tension somewhere, your little finger is a very good place. C: Others spill over onto your blouse, rolling gently away or absorbed easily there. S: One of our clients was very pleased to know that her little finger could serve such a valuable purpose in her life. The little finger was very happy to have the tension that had once been in the back of her neck move to her little finger. Sometimes it tried to move into the palm but it always stayed just in the little finger behind the knuckle, C: Because the knuckle of the little finger so adequately represented a barrier to prevent its traveling any place else. And now we'll soon ask you to reorient abruptly, 1, 3, 5.

S: 7 C: 8, 9 S: Sometimes, we've had clients who, having certain emotional experience, realize that a continuance of that emotional experience would relinquish various tensions that they've kept with them. You're going to have to find the appropriate time to continue the emotional experience that you're having because you would like to share them with

your loved ones. And I know that you have before and you will again. It's a great honor to be able to have someone like you share that experience. And so, your conscious mind may not really understand fully what we're speaking about but I do hope you remember to tell that man how fortunate he is that you will share that experience with him.
S: And now we need to temporarily reawaken you. C: and instruct you to go back at the appropriate time to finish the work your unconscious is doing. Sunday is a very good day, as is Wednesday. 10, 11, 12, that's right, beginning to be aware of the situation in which you are. S: And I'm going to ask you to awaken rather rapidly so that you can experience yourself back in the room here on the stage, keeping all the changes tied in at the unconscious level. C: 14, 18, 20.

Since the tear appeared when we discussed a heart relaxing, we provided her a final, paradoxical way to change: Continue the tension if she must, but continue it in her little finger. In the second paragraph we offered her the opportunity to continue tearing as a tension release with her loved ones. The suggestion was purposefully open-ended so that she might choose the most appropriate person in her social network: "It's a great honor to be able to have someone like you share that experience," and "Tell that man how fortunate he is that you will share that experience with him" were implications to her about her personal value and importance and non sequiturs to bind her into her social network with that grief. We framed her emotional sharing as something wonderful and therefore reframed any of her thoughts to the contrary. The fact that we had just spent our time with her in such a way attested to our seriousness about that!

As we reoriented her by counting backwards from one to 20 we interspersed conscious/unconscious dissociation suggestions. The use of counting was simply a device that suggested such minor increments of change that she would be unable to deny that a slight reorientation was happening with each count. The work she had accomplished did not need to be verbalized. The retrieval of trance phenomena resources and the reassociation of other experiential resources to the previous headache stimuli had taken place without providing her much conscious awareness. Just what her experiences had been was a matter for unconscious linking. Her conscious mind could concern itself with her enjoyment of the changes and her future plans, as suggested in the last sentence: "you can experience yourself back in the room here on the stage (consciously), keeping all the changes tied in at the unconscious level." Each conscious/unconscious dissociation suggestion implied a conscious/unconscious bind. The bind was secured in the reality that she would either be consciously aware of her changes and able to speak about them or she would not be consciously aware. If she could say how she had changed, then she would know she had; if she could not say how she had changed, she would be aware of herself on the stage as per the last suggestion. And, if she was following that part of the suggestion, she couldn't disclaim that she was keeping her changes unconscious. Regardless of her conscious disposition, then, changes could be presupposed and she would have many ideas for organizing subsequent changes after the session.

When Tracy was reoriented, she stated that she did not have a headache and had a sense of hope for the first time. As of this writing her headaches have been gone for one full year. In summary, she was helped to find relief from severe headaches by the strategic use of trance phenomena as tools to develop and use common personal experiences as resources. We initially elicited dissociation and proceeded to help Tracy create other related phenomena, including time distortion and negative hallucination. Much of this elicitation was accomplished with anecdotes about common human experience in everyday life.

STRATEGIC USE OF TRANCE PHENOMENA

The strategic use of trance phenomena is a topic infrequently addressed in the clinical use of hypnosis. Many therapists have expressed to us that they are not knowledgeable about the basic logic involved; instead, they seem to have the impression that the use of trance phenomena is reserved for the special use of experimental hypnosis (and, unfortunately, entertainment demonstrations by nonclinical stage hypnotists).

The experience of age regression is a well-known trance phenomenon, which, although regularly used, is seldom discussed in the explicit context of eliciting it for therapeutic use. "Psychiatrically, regression may be defined as the tendency on the part of the personality to revert to some method or form of expression belonging to an earlier phase of personality development" (CP III, p. 104). Hartmann, advancing ego psychology, addressed the idea of useful, therapeutic regression:

> Though fantasy is always rooted in the past, it can by connecting past and future, become the basis for realistic goals. There are the symbolic images familiar in productive scientific thinking; and there are poetry and all the other forms of artistic activity and experience. . . . Kris (1934) spoke of these in terms of a "regression in the service of the ego" (Hartmann, 1958, p. 34).

Laughter is an age regression experience frequently considered beneficial. Imagine, if you will, a situation in which someone in a group begins laughing.

There may be a joke or not; the other people begin laughing at their own thoughts or at laughter of others. The age regression is unconsciously contagious. Partial recall of such a situation is often enough to bring the laughter back. Even a snicker is contagious at times. A snicker developed in the process of remembering can become part of a sense of reliving the original event. The unconscious amplification of memory into reliving is a naturally healthy unconscious program. The experience of partial or total recall from such a memory brings with it muscular, somatic, attitudinal, and perceptual changes. We find that even highly linguistic and cerebrally oriented material (such as punchlines) produces positive physiological changes that are easily verifiable by personal experience. It is this mental pattern that is therapeutically used in hypnotic regression—the recall and amplification of a memory from initial cerebral involvement to eventual total body involvement.

Age regression experiences are frequently useful in all therapeutic work, including clinical hypnosis and nonhypnotic therapies such as Gestalt therapy, Transactional Analysis, psychoanalytically oriented psychotherapy, or behavior modification. Consider the use of memory, fantasy, and physiological relaxation in systematic desensitization, for example.

Evoking an experience such as laughter and its associated bodily and perceptual phenomena is, then, part of the potential "regression in the service of the ego." Although this notion of serviceable regression is controversial, we consider this an essentially valid conceptualization.

Analyzing Erickson's work reveals four primary ways of developing trance phenomena which are adaptable to any clinical setting:

1) Direct suggestions to have the phenomena.
2) Indirect suggestions, especially those framed as conscious and unconscious dissociations and binds.
3) Anecdotes or metaphors which call to mind common everyday occurrence of the trance phenomena.
4) Structured methods which elicit the trance phenomena.

Table 1 summarizes typical anecdotes and common clinical uses of each phenomenon.

Dissociation

Tracy's case illustrated the use of dissociation for pain control; yet there are many other psychologically related uses. Self-image thinking, which we have referred to in several cases, is a derivative of dissociation. Erickson used the ability to dissociate when he worked with "Monde" (Lustig, 1975). He helped Monde learn something about herself and her ability to enjoy life by

Table 1
A Clinical Use of Trance Phenomena

Trance Phenomena	Anecdotes	Clinical Use
Dissociation	Watching movie/car window reflection/view from plane/mirror	Pain/rehearsing new learnings/describing past
Age Regression	Laughter/ballgames/ABC's/walking/learning sets	Relive trauma/resource retrieval/investigate facts
Pseudo Orientation in Time	déjà vu/time zones/wake up lost/get up on weekend thinking it's Monday	Go into future, get feelings to bring back/leave eyes young when they worked/plan "backwards"
Amnesia	Tip of tongue/forgotten names/song you can't recall/erase blackboard/change TV channel	Trauma protection/critical instruction/protect in memory/posthypnotic suggestion
Time Distortion	Difference between second hand and time/driving/movies and lectures	Pain control/in and out of trance/sensation delay
Automatic Writing	Doodling/automatic behavior/dealing cards/talking in dreams	Deepen trance/recover information
Positive Hallucination	Zeigarnik illusion/watching fires/crystal balls/clouds/heat mirage	Intensify resource/dealing with depression/or pain
Negative Hallucination	Concentration/reading in car/miss phone or child while reading/overlook work in library	Oversensitive to social cues and somatic cues—pain
Hypermnesia	Recalling all of song/suddenly aware of new road features	Married couples—recalls courtship behavior/test preparation/recall rapist

viewing age regressed experiences from a dissociated position. The technique he used in her case was eliciting dissociation by a series of indirect suggestions separated by discussions of several other matters, including deepening, learning, arm levitation, amnesia, and opening her eyes in trance:

. . . it is as if you're traveling a highway, passing this scene, that scene, in your life. And perhaps something very nice that you could recall that you haven't thought about for years. And I think it'd be most interesting if you would find some childhood, infantile memory that you haven't thought about for years. . . .

. . . I would like to have you single out some one thing that you could talk to me about, that you could talk to strangers about, that you could share. Something very pleasing, very charming. . . .

. . . Now somewhere out of the past you'll come upon a happy scene. And I want you to visualize it. A happy scene. And just reach in and take it and bring it forth. You don't have to have everything, just the happiness. . . .

. . . And sooner or later, I don't know just when, you will be wondering about something that you would like to see. . . .

. . . And I want your attention just on me, while you sense and see that scene from the past . . . and you're going to go through a learning experience. . . .

Erickson's approach with Monde can be contrasted with that used with Tracy. It exemplifies the difference between using only indirect suggestion and using both anecdotes and indirect suggestion. The phenomenon may be approached with either set of communications. The personality of the client provides a clue in selecting the proper approach. Monde was comparatively intellectual and had previous trance experiences with Erickson to build upon. Tracy, on the other hand, had no previous experience with us or trance and was not so intellectually inclined. Anecdotes used with Tracy included a personalized mention of out-of-the-body death experiences, floating experiences many children have on lazy summer days, watching a lengthy movie, and taking off a jacket. Finally, her arm catalepsy and eventual levitation were also used as convincing references to her dissociation ability.

Other useful metaphors for eliciting the dissociation phenomenon convey the experience of observing one's reflection. This may be as common as looking in a bathroom mirror, or may involve a more romantic imagination of seeing one's face in a crystal reflecting pool. We frequently use the transfixing experience of watching one's reflection in an automobile window. Other familiar experiences of dissociation can be elicited and organized by relating anecdotes of time when an inside map light of a car is on after dark, when a vehicle with an illuminated interior enters a tunnel, or when an airplane window reflects a passenger seated beside it on a night flight.

These examples of dissociation lend themselves nicely to tangents within a metaphoric framework encouraging a client to view novel rehearsals of current or probable future behavior. The client can also build a readiness and predisposition to behave in ways that have been comfortably examined in a dissociated, objective, and thoughtful manner. That is, in fact, the purpose of dissociation in fantasy rehearsal and self-image thinking. Dissociation can be used, then, for both simple symptomatic relief (such as pain) and for personality change (behavioral rehearsals and training).

Age Regression and Pseudo Orientation in Time

Anecdotes which suggest common situations involving regression mechanisms include: laughter, ballgames, parties, learning the alphabet, learning to walk, and indeed, any early learning, such as holding a pen, learning to set a table, learning to pet a dog, learning to use a hammer, etc. These examples are offered as an aid to the clinical induction of age regression. Erickson expected, as a general rule, to allow 20 minutes of trance time to establish induction and a regression (CP III, p. 106). Any of the anecdotes actually delivered to a client should be thoughtfully worded and fortified with indirect suggestions, as demonstrated in the preceding transcript.

An anecdote about laughter has already been shared. Likewise, several anecdotes for dissociation, negative hallucination, and time distortion appeared in the Tracy transcript. We will not detail examples of anecdotes for all the phrases listed on the chart; rather, these references are offered as "seeds" which can be elaborated when actually used in therapy.

It is important to remember the client's role when using anecdotes and indirect suggestion to elicit responses as profound as trance phenomena. Ideomotor feedback is always important. The responses that validate a trance phenomenon are subtle and do not readily lend themselves to verbal description and distinction. The responses that represent the occurrence of age regression or other phenomena for a particular individual can, however, be learned. We suggest that practicing clinicians experiment with colleagues who agree to be subjects for studying the elicitation of trance phenomena. Erickson studied many trance phenomena with careful experiments, noting, for example, that age regressed subjects usually reported the identification of their experience accurately, including the day of the event. But he found from careful observations that the way the day of the event was remembered changed according to the age of the regression: sometimes as "tasks" (test day), sometimes weekdays, and sometimes actual dates of the month. The method used for regressed-state-identification varied predictably according to the age regressed to in the trance (CP III, p. 114).

Erickson's procedure was to use anecdotes or suggestions to first retrieve a cognitive part of an earlier experience and then add the other components of that experience. Sometimes a subject's particular talent for age regression would suggest initial retrieval of a part other than cognitive, but this was the exception. The regression would always be oriented to some time just before the period actually desired. Finally, the client would be age progressed to the specific desired age, often in a literal and precise manner. The decision regarding year and point of orientation to which the subject was regressed could often remain the subject's responsibility. Erickson would assist with such seemingly definitive descriptions as, "And now it will soon be your 16th birthday," or, "You are now 13 years old and school will soon begin again" (*CP* III, p. 113). In that way the control could be placed with the client, consistent with Erickson's manner.

In addition to this manner of utilizing common everyday anecdotes to elicit age regression, Erickson pioneered and reported a method of structuring the phenomenon (*CP* III, p. 107). He helped the client proceed through a nine-step sequence which involved eliciting with indirect suggestion and optional anecdotes the following experiences:

1) General emotional indifference.
2) General confusion.
3) Slowness, uncertainty (especially for the current day).
4) Confusion (re: person, place, time).
5) Amnesia for events of the current day, week, month.
6) Amnesia for the past year and even for its existence.
7) Feeling and believing to be a specific age.
8) Realizing a pleasant experience at a specified age will soon be enjoyed.
9) Knowing that age is being experienced.

When a person is regressed, mental operations of hearing, comprehending, performing, etc. can be expected to operate at a level similar to that possessed at the earlier age. Age regression, then, creates an intensification of certain experiences and, as such, is frequently useful in these three areas: reliving traumatic experiences, resource retrieval, and investigative work of various kinds.

Erickson occasionally used age regression to have a client relive a trauma. He reported that repeatedly reliving a particular trauma resulted in the loss of a subject's previously phobic avoidance behavior caused by the trauma. He concluded that "Hypnosis can be employed to produce significant personality-situation changes, as evidenced by the definite psychic and somatic effects produced by the reorientation to, and the reliving of, a past experience as a current process" (*CP* III, p. 52). Reviving skills and experiences that are currently lost and forgotten to the client also becomes possible. "Regression in a hypnotic state to an earlier period of life is possible, with the reestablishment of its corresponding patterns of behavior uninfluenced by subsequently acquired skills" (*CP* III, p. 49).

When regression is used for these purposes, the skills and resources retrieved in the experience are best organized in the out-of-awareness, unconscious mind. Conscious mind associations are likely to interfere with biases and prejudices about the efficacy of earlier resources. After all, clients coming to therapy will have exhausted all available resources as far as they know. We once again use Monde to illustrate. When Erickson reoriented Monde from her trance, he instructed her to grow up so she could meet him and he reminded her that the "duck chasing Monde," the "water splashing Monde," and the "window breaking Monde" of the past would not know him. These parts of her past had been used to elicit resources and she had been reminded with indirect suggestions that she could link the learnings from these parts to situations in her current world where she needed them. Finally, she was expected to have amnesia for the regressed therapy.

Another example concerned the young woman mentioned earlier who had vomited on her date and considered herself filthy. Erickson investigated her map of early parental instructions by using age regression and concluded with amnesia (Haley, 1973, p. 78). Likewise, his famous case known as the "February Man" involved repeated use of age regression in conjunction with amnesia. These two are commonly used in conjunction for the client's protection.

Erickson was a firm disbeliever of the notion that age regression could be encouraged to the extent that a person might identify a pre-birth experience. He stated, " . . . to request information preceding their birth would have been a falsification of the emotional content inherent in the hypnotic state" (*CP* III, p. 116). He considered such notions on the part of the hypnotist to be a sign of professional inexperience.

Orientation into the future, rather than the past, may be considered pseudo orientation in time. Common anecdotes for helping clients create their own personal experience with it include moments of déjà vu. Déjà vu, while not well understood, is a common, real world experience known to many persons. The phenomenon of déjà vu may, in fact, be nothing more than a sudden experience of the trance phenomenon of pseudo orientation in time (backward or forward) to a similar context. Many persons have the experience of waking on a weekend and momentarily believing the day of the week is Monday. Others are familiar with time zone changes and the confusion brought about in an effort to properly adjust a wristwatch. These anedotes in conjunction with indirect suggestions may be therapeutically used to elicit the response. As with the other phenomena, pseudo orientation facilitates an altered framework through which a client can create experiences in a novel or uncommon way and examine therapeutic uses of previously unknowable experiences.

Amnesia

Related to regression in clinical work is the phenomenon of amnesia. Often the two will be used in conjunction so that the reliving of an earlier trauma, if necessary, is not threatening to the conscious mind of the subject. Traumatic relivings in trance allow a "revival of the experience with its associated responses [which is] permitted as if it were in the course of actual development" (*CP* III, p. 50). Erickson's respect for messages sent by the client included respecting the conscious mind's right to not know something which the unconscious mind considered too inappropriate or painful. He expressed this permission to Monde by saying: "Your unconscious mind can keep from you anything it doesn't want you to know; that way you can lessen the pain" (Lusting, 1975). We stress again that hypnosis is a way to communicate ideas and understandings so that a subject can concentrate on experiences that may become useful when reassociated in certain novel ways. Having a client relive a trauma without the protection of amnesia and/or without the fortification of subsequently learned experiential resources (or defenses) would be cruel by any definition. The use of both reassociated resources and amnesia, by contrast, provides a framework through which a client may reexamine and gain from even the unpleasant experiences of the past.

Clinical amnesia for various portions of trance work often develops spontaneously. We typically do not discuss work just completed unless initiated by the client when the session comes to a close. We expect that by not referring to what we've done we provide an amnesia option, allowing new associations, like newly planted seeds, to take root and develop undisturbed by conscious mind interference and analysis.

Amnesia, like the other trance phenomena, can be elicited with anecdotes and indirect suggestion. It can also be produced with a structured method originally pioneered by Erickson. The multiple embedded metaphor format is compatible with eliciting amnesia via this structured method.

Structured amnesia is accomplished by making something which is to be forgotten occur in the midst of other material which has been suddenly interrupted. Strategically, a story or poem may be started and suddenly suspended without completion. In the middle of this otherwise "whole" unit, instructions, metaphors, and other therapeutic material can be inserted. When this inserted material is completed, amnesia is facilitated by a sudden returning to and completion of the story or poem that was left suspended. Transition between the original story and the material placed in the middle is of no importance. Making no associative links to the portion sandwiched in the middle facilitates amnesia. Since this structure is inherent in the multiple embedded metaphor, spontaneous amnesia for much of a session can be expected from a large percentage of clients receiving such treatment.

Time Distortion

The preceding transcript illustrated one use of time distortion to alter the constancy of headache pain. Tracy was sensitized to her own understandings of time distortion as we related anecdotes of driving in a car, watching television, and experiences of other clients. Indirect suggestions to stimulate her involvement in developing the resources were interspersed throughout the anecdotes.

A structured manner of eliciting time distortion was also used by intermittently referring to such experiences while oscillating back and forth between other thematic metaphors. We spoke about time distortion, then about a client having a series of symbolic dreams, then again about time distortion. We shifted between time distortion and the dreams several times, so that Tracy was led to experience time distorting in the process of hearing about time distortion.

Erickson's own physical difficulties motivated him to use a form of dissociation from pain that he called "protective dreams." He commented about the use of most common trance phenomena in controlling pain and concluded: "Hypnotic dissociation can be employed for pain control, and the usual, most effective methods are those of time and body disorientation" (*CP* IV, p. 242). With Linn Cooper, Erickson investigated the phenomenon of time disorientation and wrote:

> While the hands of a clock move from one position to another, an infinite number of other changes take place in the cosmos. And wherever that phenomenon which we call awareness exists, there is probably a sense of the passage of time, and a sense of sequence . . . Time seems to be of us, and inseparable from our very existence. Furthermore one is tempted to think of subjective time as extending from future to past in a direction at right angles, so to speak, to other experiences (*CP* II, p. 232).

Many common anecdotes exist for colloquial experiences of time distortion, since it is a socially acceptable human experience. These include the subjective sense of slowing down that one has when observing the movement of second hands on a clock, waiting for a kettle to boil, waiting for a line of people to move, watching a movie or listening to a lecture, and dreaming of fall-ing off a bed—all of which, while taking only seconds, seem to take much longer. Time may be subjectively shortened or lengthened, as in the ex-perience of a narrow escape or in moments when much imagery is received. Moments of pain can seem very short and moments of pleasure may seem to last forever for clients who learn to use this experience.

The case of "Sandra W." (CP IV, p. 70) cryptically illustrated the strategic use of a client's ability to subjectively distort time. Sandra was a woman who suffered from frequent catatonic withdrawals for "a day or two, sometimes even a week." In the course of the first therapy session Erickson reduced the occurrence of these episodes and the deleterious effects they had on her life.

He did not ask her to surrender the personally rewarding activity of hallucinating and withdrawing into daydreams; rather, by helping Sandra use her natural sense of time distortion, he taught her to reduce the moments of catatonia to a mere two or three minutes of clock time. She was pleased that, by utilizing the mechanisms of time distortion, she could continue to en-joy the activity that brought her so much pleasure while eliminating the ag-gravation of losing jobs and alienating those in her social network as she had done in the past when "gone" for long periods of clock time.

This use of time distortion was not the whole of therapy with "Sandra W," but the case demonstrates a strategic use to alter sensations. Since the sensa-tions of hallucination are uncommon, this example is somewhat arcane as a result. Erickson used time distortion to assist several clients with symp-tomatic relief while continuing to treat their various personality problems.

One man had obsessive concerns about a troublesome habit of frequent urination. He would often soil his suit pants and took several pairs with him each day. Therapy began when Erickson confused the man about his orienta-tion in time. Subsequent interventions taught him to appreciate how time might seem subjectively slower or faster. The result of the session was im-mediate. The man who had insisted on urinating every 20 minutes "lasted" at least six hours from the time he visited the therapy office. Time distortion can facilitate removing a symptom so that broader therapy might proceed more efficaciously. However, even a symptom with the magnitude of a psychotic episode can be contained. The case of the psychotic client helps convey con-fidence that other, more clinically common, symptoms can be treated with therapeutic uses of time distortion.

Automatic Writing

Writing is an automated behavior that operates comfortably if not scruti-nized by the conscious mind. Erickson frequently used this phenomenon in conjunction with amnesia. On one occasion he helped a woman retrieve forgotten information as he engaged both her conscious and unconscious minds with induction and then suggested that ". . . a third level of consciousness in a response to hypnotic suggestion would 'emerge from the depths of her mind' and would express itself by guiding her hand in automatic writing, of which she would be aware neither consciously nor subconsciously" (*CP* III, p. 40).

In another case utilizing automatic writing reported by Erickson the client was requested to underline letters from a printed page. The words created by the underlining were to reveal the cause of her symptomatology. Eventually, at the proper time, she came to read what she had underlined unconsciously (*CP* IV, p. 165). At other times he used automatic writing to deepen trance by asking the client to write some important information that had been withheld from the interview. When the writing was completed the client was instructed to put the paper out of sight. Erickson would not look at the paper and thereby imparted a sense of control to the client. The result was often a deepening of rapport and trance.

In another case the ability to automatically write and draw was used to relieve a state of acute obsessional depression (*CP* III, p. 164). As Erickson demonstrated, there are many uses for automatic writing in the broad area between investigation and personality restructuring. The only limit to the use of automatic writing in clinical treatment may be the possible limits of the therapist's creativity.

Common everyday experiences of automatic expression which can become the basis for anecdotes to retrieve automatic writing include doodling, automatic behaviors of the hands such as dealing cards, transcribing dictation, simplistic manual behavior such as playing tiddlewinks, and even automatic behavioral expressions such as talking in one's dreams and shouting out if one's foot has been stepped on. Each client will learn the actual behavior in his or her own unique time and manner. This phenomenon is often associated with deep trance experiences. Although it is not difficult to organize clients' resources to help them create automatic writing, some clients have special needs to express their problems and solutions in other ways. When a client has sufficient reason to do so or is operating within a framework which makes automatic writing efficacious, then that client will manifest the phenomenon.

Positive and Negative Hallucination

Negative hallucination, simply stated, refers to the action of not noticing something that is actually present. Many clients bringing problems and questions about growth and change to therapy seem to require more contact with reality. They need enhanced awareness of reality as a prerequisite for their being improved or cured. It may seem ironic that an encouraged hallucination might somehow be therapeutically enhancing. Not noticing certain sensations or stimuli, however, can facilitate more intense awareness of other details.

Perhaps the most rewarding use of negative hallucination is pain control. In the preceding transcript, anecdotes about ignoring the bladder, pain, and even the entire body position while dreaming were used to help Tracy learn to ignore some of the stimuli in her "map" of headaches. The location of her "right" arm also became the subject for indirect suggestions which were precariously balanced in the ambiguous zone existing between "description" and "command." Earlier we spoke of common everyday language rules that allow for common everyday inductions of hypnotic states. Ambiguity, such as that found between accurate descriptions and psychological implications of everyday hypnotic language, served as a vehicle to therapeutically confuse Tracy. She was suspended in the moment between confusion and understanding. That very suspension was a convincing experience which we used to reinforce her ability to notice that she could "not notice sensations" in her body. In this way we created an experiential or structured way to help Tracy establish her skill for negative hallucination.

There are structured, indirect and anecdotal methods for eliciting any particular phenomenon, but which one(s) to elicit is always a matter determined by the needs and abilities of each client. Negative hallucination has been helpful in reducing the sensitivity of clients who have been overconcerned about or oversensitive to certain stimuli. In the case of the client with bulimia, her ability to negatively hallucinate "problem" foods in the grocery store allowed her to gain a sense of hope and increased her motivation for therapy. It also served as a mechanism to assist her development of the "self-control" she needed to stop the operation of her major symptom.

The phenomenon of anesthesia is actually negative hallucination used for easing bodily pain. Erickson wrote that:

> Hypnotic anesthesia is a . . . method in treating pain. This is often difficult and may sometimes be accomplished directly, but is more often best accomplished indirectly by the building of psychological and emotional situations that are contradictory to the experience of the pain and which serve to establish an anesthetic reaction to be continued by posthypnotic suggestion (CP IV, p. 241).

Likewise, an experimental induction of color blindness can be created by the special direction of amnesia to all associations regarding color (CP II, p. 20). In other words, several hybrid experiences in everyday life may be understood, at least experimentally, as special uses of resources and trance phenomena.

Suggestions to develop any of these phenomena must be in the service of the therapeutic goal, just as all options in a double bind must be in the client's best interest. "Suggestions must be given only for the purpose that is being served, never for any other purpose" (Erickson, Hershman, & Secter, 1961, p. 84). Erickson did not believe that hypnosis would ever replace the practice of chemical anesthesia, but he did believe that hypnosis had several preoperative and postoperative advantages. Among these advantages may be the reduction of neurogenic shock in difficult surgical procedures, as an aid in the prevention of postoperative atelectasis and pneumonitis, and a reduction in respiratory depression following preoperative chemical anesthesia. For example, he suggested using preoperative hypnosis to relax patients who would be candidates for sedatives, since the reduction in sedatives would reduce any preoperative respiratory depression. Furthermore, advantages to mothers-to-be and newborn babies in the process of delivery are obvious. Each of these procedures constitutes a special case of negative hallucination directed at specific bodily sensations.

Several anecdotes that suggest colloquial occurrence of negative hallucination include moments of intense concentration, mechanisms used when reading in a moving automobile, not hearing the sound of a ringing telephone, and the frequent experience of not noticing that which is "right in front of one's eyes." Again, the client is the final guide as to the appropriateness of any particular anecdote. For the blue-collar client an anecdote of missing that which is right before one's eyes might be most appropriate and for the college graduate anecdotes of studying in a library and ignoring the opposite sex might be more relevant. The client's developmental age of psychological functioning further determines the selection of any particular story. A client operating like teenager, psychologically, might relate to not hearing the call of a parent or a younger sibling. A client operating as a toddler, psychologically, might relate most intensely to tales of concentration such as that of a preoccupied child who soils his or her pants due to exciting social stimulation.

Both positive and negative hallucinations have a place in clinical hypnotherapy. Positive hallucination, the experience of sensing something that is not there, is most rewarding when it facilitates a client's amplifying his or her experience of a needed resource. It can serve as a means to pretest for new learnings. A client can "try on" a trance learning and essentially sense a reality about that experience. The ability to do this spontaneously is known to anyone who has dreamed about being awake and engaging in some task or adventure while actually being in bed asleep. In a similar way a client can reduce the unfamiliarity with new frameworks and learnings and become better prepared to utilize the new learnings in the world outside the therapy office.

Since involvement with a hallucination precludes involvement with reality to some extent, positive hallucination can provide a way for extremely depressed clients to enhance positive experiences in less familiar areas of life. We once encouraged a depressed client to do just that by having her develop, in trance, an intense memory of watching a cow lie down. She found the sight extremely pleasant and subsequently used the memory of the pleasure (but not of the cow) to sensitize her perceptions to other pleasant events. She then found she could actually notice delightful components in previously stress-producing situations which had engendered depression.

Hypermnesia

In a word, hypermnesia is remembering. In two words, it is detailed remembering. Detailed recall is an important skill for many clients. Recall of early courtship behaviors, for instance, can allow married couples to recapture some of the enchantment and good will they once had for each other. A client preparing for an oral exam learned to quickly drop into trance (time distortion) and have vivid recall of test related material she had studied. She quickly reoriented to the test taking situation, and although she forgot some material in the rapid transit between the two states, she created an increased ability to elaborate her answers accurately and creatively. Many others have been successful using hypermnesia for recall involving legal matters, such as remembering automobile license plates, establishing and verifying alibis, and remembering physical details of a criminal. In these cases especially, the suggestions must be precisely related to learning to remember. No suggestions should be given which might bias an accurate "reading" of the "facts" held in the client's memory.

Anecdotes useful for eliciting hypermnesia include all types of recall, such as recalling all of a partially forgotten song. The use of songs can be especially powerful if one of the songs used is from a time in the client's life when the requested material was learned or experienced. Anecdotes about suddenly becoming aware of construction features along a frequently traveled highway are cogent since the observer must overcome the usual effects of familiarization that tend to create satiation and lack of awareness related to everyday surroundings.

TRANCE PHENOMENA IN NONHYPNOTIC THERAPIES

Clients' hypnotic responses are the major focus of this chapter. Readers are encouraged to expand this hypnotherapeutic framework, apply it to other therapeutic situations, and notice similar phenomena occurring in various nontherapeutic situations. Trance phenomena have been noticed to occur in several "nonhypnotic" therapies. Albert Scheflen, for instance, studied therapy films of Carl Whitaker and Tom Malone, noting manifestations of "dissociation" which he detailed with behavioral descriptions for a four-and-one-half-minute portion of the interview (Scheflen, 1973, p. 146). As shown below, therapy excerpts of other practitioners reveal a wide variety of such trance phenomena.

The following transcripts provide only brief glimpses, bits, and pieces of total therapy sessions. While they certainly illustrate the theoretical proposition that hypnotic communication is present and operating in all therapeutic approaches, these portions are still only isolated parts of the interpersonal framework developed by the therapist at the time of the therapy. In describing their communication as hypnotic we do not intend to diminish the other (unmentioned) aspects of interpersonal influence these therapists create in their working styles. While analyzing their work for unconscious attention given to indirect suggestion and trance phenomena, we do not wish to minimize other elements which give rise to rapport, congruence, honesty, believability, and effectiveness. The therapists have already examined and described many of these elements in their own explanations or theories. We do not intend to subtract from those previous explanations by adding our own.

We do hope to extend the historical trend which presently makes the role of communication and interpersonal factors of influence the focus of scientific investigation. We find that increasing an understanding about the influence of communication adds to a demystification regarding the active role played by therapists. This active role can be noticed by examining the suggestions made by any therapist and by observing the influence of those suggestions in the client's responses. We are interested in indirect suggestions and psychological level communication, in contrast to direct suggestions, because most therapists are already cognizant of their use of direct suggestions. Erickson's agreement with Berne's "rule" that outcomes are determined at the psychological level encouraged us to dissect the "hidden" structure of communicational influence. Using the previously described varieties of indirect suggestion, we will look at each example of trance phenomenon and analyze the psychological level of communication in the nonhypnotic therapy that produced it.

We have selected examples from foremost therapists who, while respecting Erickson's work, do not in any way claim to emulate the Ericksonian types of indirect suggestion. Our intent is not to link them with Erickson to any extent greater than they wish to be linked to him; rather, we wish to illustrate the successful use of indirect suggestion as it "naturally" occurs in the work of noted experts. Furthermore, noting the workings of naturalistic suggestions present in nonhypnotic therapy removes still more of the proverbial "black box" effect of the therapy session. The presence and order of indirect suggestion and trance phenomena in nonhypnotic therapy trace the link between therapists' internal beliefs (map of the world, presuppositions about people and problems) and the options they make known to the clients they treat.

Although only small portions of several transcripts appear, it is evident that any similar, albeit short, segment of therapy will reveal similar results when analyzed for the presence of hypnotic elements. Let us begin with this excerpt from a session with James Framo:

Framo: When you have issues how do you deal with them?
Florence: (Looks at him, pushes her chin forward, her face muscles are immobile, and her cheeks flatten. Several seconds pass. Here Florence has the signs of search phenomena that we illustrated earlier. We speculate that she is in the process of attempting to identify some portion of her map of the world that could be relevant to Framo's question.)
Framo: Do you ever have fights? (More information is being offered to Florence. It is the same type communication we have typified as [unspecified] "search language." We would expect the client to now demonstrate further internal search and demonstrate how she uses members of her family to facilitate finding resources or maps to follow.)
Florence: (Continues above behavior briefly and then suddenly purses lips, smiles, shakes her head twice, and turns toward her husband. It seems that she has briefly continued an internal search and then terminated it with a head nod of identification. Then she orients herself toward her husband as if getting further stimuli from him is now her best choice.)

Even in this short transcript there are many elements of hypnotic communication. The therapist's use of unspecified search language could be purposeful or accidental/automatic. If used purposefully, the therapist's goal at that point could be diagnostic, investigatory, or inductive. Since Framo did not accelerate the internal search that Florence began, but rather let the search continue to its conclusion with her final attention to her husband's response, we conclude that he used these transactions diagnostically.

Despite the brief time involved, Florence displayed three distinct behaviors: search behavior, ideomotor identification, and social network contact. We suggest an interconnectedness among these three. In the normal course of events the cycle is:

1) Social-perceptual cues produce (induce) inner search.

2) Internal search may or may not develop trance phenomena to aid in resource retrieval.
3) Ideomotor identification signals recognition of some aspect of the induced resource (or the absence of it).
4) Social contact, frequently verbal, is initiated to provide more information or co-creation of the outcome.

Search Phenomena

The following transcript between Carl Rogers and a client named "Gloria" illustrates the simple occurrence of search phenomena in the counseling session and actual hypnotic interplay of indirect suggestion and response.

R: And so it is quite clear that [it isn't only her problems or the relationship with her] it's in you as well.
G: In my guilt. I feel guilty so often.
R: What can I accept myself as doing?
G: (Shakes head "yes.")
R: And you realize that instead of sort of subterfuges . . .
G: (Eye blink slows to one in ten seconds, cheeks flatten, head tilts to the right, and breathing slows.)
R: . . . so as to make sure that you're not caught or something, you realize that you are acting from guilt.
G: (Shakes head.)
R: Is that it?
G: (Still shaking head) Yes, and I don't like the . . . I would like to feel comfortable with whatever I do.

There are essentially five sentences from Rogers. The first is a suggestion that focuses awareness ("It's quite clear that it's in you as well") and the second is a question that focuses awareness ("What can I accept myself as doing?"). The first sentence accelerated the rapport by offering a summary statement regarding visual imagery in her map of the world. The next suggestion began therapy by changing the frame of reference with a subtle split. The split played on the idea that within Gloria was guilt (for doing what she doesn't want) and this also implied the "other side of the coin" (what she might find acceptable in her behavior). Rogers reframed the self-critical stance she was taking by asking or suggesting that she question, "What is acceptable behavior?"

We especially like Rogers' interesting use of the word "subterfuges" in the third line. This seemed to be a deliberate choice of a complex noun, which would bring to mind many ramifications of Gloria's problem. Yet, it was like-

ly to bring them to mind within the new therapeutic framework just established, thus reinforcing the new framework. While the unanswered question,
"What is acceptable behavior?", remained cogent, the use of "subterfuges" implied hiding a part of herself. Thus, she accepted the presupposition that she
had acceptable behaviors. This split, then, was accentuated by her interaction with Rogers and his use of indirect suggestion.

Gloria's response was typical of experiences commonly developed in therapy sessions. Contrasting her responses after the second and third lines reveals what Erickson referred to as a momentary "common everyday" trance.
Her initial attitude was reflected with an immediate head nod, high degree of
muscle tonicity and responsiveness after hearing Rogers' first and second
comment. After his third statement (about "subterfuges") Gloria demonstrated classic signs of search phenomena (flattened cheeks, slowed blink,
and slowed breathing).

In the last two lines Gloria shows ideomotor signs of recognition (head
shaking) followed by verbal output. This pattern of search, unconscious recognition, ideomotor response, and finally speech or sound is, as mentioned,
a common chain of experiences. Gloria's actual verbal response is interesting
since it indicates that Rogers' "frame change" was successful. This is something rarely examined in observations of client-centered approaches.

Note that she began speaking about what she didn't like and concluded
with what she would like. Is this not the same point contained in Rogers' therapeutic interventions? He began by meeting her map of the world (the problem is "in you, as well") and offering indirect suggestion (focusing awareness)
with a rhetorical question: "What can I accept myself as doing?" In her final
line she began stating what she didn't like about herself and interrupted herself to state that she did want to be comfortable. This is a concise example of a
client altering her initial framework in response to indirect suggestions at the
psychological level of communication in client-centered therapy.

In this typical example of therapeutic process we find the fundamental elements of hypnosis as practiced by Erickson: indirect suggestion and the occurrence and use of hypnotic response. Some observers, following the line of
reasoning developed by Haley, speculate that interventions made by
Erickson fall in one of two categories: hypnotic or strategic. We concur with
this in general but add that, in a broader sense of the word, "hypnotic" applies to all communication, especially that done in the name of therapy; any
"strategic" rearrangement or social manipulation of the client's life is only a
social counterpart of the same principles. In the examples given, it is apparent
that influential elements of hypnosis occur in much of the talking done in
nonhypnotic therapy. These same elements of hypnosis extend into any
social interaction and are, in fact, the glue of social networks. With this

broader speculation in mind, let's look at the three-person therapy group in the next transcribed segment.

Search Phenomena and Ideomotor Behavior

In examining the following therapy episode, again with Framo, we focus on the search phenomena and ideomotor response phenomena. The wife is the subject of this investigation; however, her husband—not the therapist—is the "hypnotist," by accident of nonawareness and his inadvertent use of indirect suggestion. The transcript begins with the husband speaking about the history of the relationship. As a result, the wife began searching to discover her own version of their history. As we enter this session, the husband's suggestions about relaxing seem to be taking his wife right into trance.

H: Then after that it was more or less being able to feel comfortable with her . . .
W: (Limbs are cataleptic, head tilts left, cheeks flatten, breathing slows, blink rate slows, pupils dilate, and mouth is closed and relaxed.)
H: . . . being able to talk, able to relax.
W: (Swings head rapidly to the left now and looks at Framo.)
F: Being able to relax?
W: (Nods head "yes" and smiles.)

We especially liked the dual induction effect in this session when the therapist used an indirect form of suggestion (question to focus awareness) as an empathic comment to the husband. But since the wife had oriented to the therapist it was apparent that she was ready for input from a source other than her husband. It so happened that source became a "co-hypnotist" with her husband; together they facilitated her relaxing and having a pleasant feeling. The ramifications of this simple example are important.

This effect is often accomplished in family therapy and, for that matter, in families not in therapy! Discourse among family members affects the experience of anyone who is attending consciously or unconsciously. Communication helps people alter frameworks. When communication contains indirect suggestions or elicits trance phenomena (as in professional therapeutic relationships), frameworks can be altered such that listeners who have sufficient skill for developing the phenomena do so and thereby expand their experiences. An elaboration on this theme could explain socialization and enculturation as hypnosis; however, at this point we will return to common uses of these phenomena.

Therapists frequently wish to set a mood in therapy prior to presenting an idea and want their words to be considered in the most appropriate or favorable context. Trance phenomena are vehicles through which frames of reference can be established. When preparing a client's mood for receiving certain information or interventions, the therapist should assess and utilize any currently operating trance phenomena. Recognizing the mutual inductive effect that discourse among family members has on each member, family therapists can consider themselves to be co-hypnotists—co-hypnotists, that is, with the family members. Consciously observing the indicators of search and ideomotor communication provides an advantage to the therapist over others in the family, who operate oblivious to this psychological level (Whitaker, 1982).

Returning to Framo's work, we can display a logical "flip-flop" of the same effect. The following conversation between therapist and wife reveals the same phenomena illustrated above in reverse. This time the wife is spoken to and her husband shows the search and ideomotor response.

F: You know, Pat, I heard a woman once say: "I can give milk to my child to the extent to which my husband gives me love." Does that make sense to you?

H: (Watching and listening, shakes head three times "yes," raises brow, and tilts head to left so as to watch his wife.)

W: (As Framo speaks she stops moving, stops smoking, and looks at him. When Framo stops talking and as Gary [the husband] shakes his head, she remains perfectly still, looking at Gary, and then tilts her head to the right, tenses her brow slightly and holds this perplexed look, shaking her head and looking back at Framo to verbalize with lowered voice.) Yeah, I think what I'm asking from Gary is that I just don't want to be stuck with all the bad things, too.

The therapist's short anecdote elicited the predicted search phenomena. Apparently, that search process stimulated the wife to view her husband (she oriented her head to him and then back to the therapist) and frame her experience vis-à-vis the therapist's metaphor, that is, what does she want from her husband? This is a nice example of the family therapist using short metaphors, rich in symbols, to reinforce and fixate rapport. Since a new cognitive framework was being offered, the metaphoric probe was useful both to uncover diagnostic information and to simultaneously focus awareness in a new framework. That moment of confusion the client spent in "getting the hang" of this new framework provides another example of "common everyday trance," and it follows that the communication of the therapist constituted a form of naturalistic induction.

The next vignette with Framo and another couple reveals the same phenomena but a different outcome. In the previous cases we saw clients congruently responding when they identified maps of experience induced by the therapist's indirect suggestions. In the following interaction the client responds incongruently and her response is diagnostically important to the therapist.

F: How would you characterize your parents' marriage?
C: (Moves her eyes up and to the right, tips head towards right, cheeks flatten, places hand on lap and remains motionless.) Uh . . . (Thrusts chin out and stares into space.) I think they both love each other very much but (moves both hands to display palms) I think (moves head back) and I think (moves eyes down and left) um . . . (tenses brow such that vertical creases form, stares into space, moves head right to left, and then stops in vertical position) and I think they could still (looks at Framo) work on some problems (cheeks flatten, pushes chin forward, moves eyes to right, horizontal) um, and relate (moves eyes straight up, then up and right) possibly (moves eyes down and left) more, um . . . (moves fingers in space, tilts head to left and slowly closes eyes) but . . . (sticks tongue out through lips slightly and pushes lower lip down with tongue).
F: You mean they are not very demonstrative?
C: Yes, if they could talk without getting emotional.

The therapist asked for a metacomment (Haley, 1963) from the client, although he had not first retrieved from her a mood or mechanism of summarizing or metacommenting. Apparently she was a bit "taken back" by the unexpected task. It was not a choice that was easily possible in her existing framework. We would not interpret her hesitance or incongruence as resistance to answering the question honestly but rather as an indication that her unconscious response was quick to cooperate. She immediately began search phenomena (eye movement, head set, flattened cheeks, staring, motionlessness). After her search phenomena began she identified an understanding which she attempted to verbalize. The words that actually came out were, essentially, "they love each other, but . . ." The client interposed common signs of incongruence after the "but" and throughout the entire spoken portions ("um," "I think," and various seemingly random nonverbal movements). She subsequently added that they are too frequently emotional as they "talk."

It appears, then, that the therapist's question set this client on a project of summarizing or metacommenting on the character of the marriage and, poorly prepared for a metacomment, she communicated, through her own incongruent behavior, the incongruent experience associated with this part of her family map of the world. In other words, her parents' relationship might best be typified as incongruent. When the client relives it, she also reports incongruently.

We wonder what questioning would have revealed about her parents' marriage if the therapist had first indirectly suggested that she recall her ability to stand back and observe and to then summarize or metacomment globally from the detached position. If we assume that her response represents her best attempt to summarize "cold," so to speak, we become aware of the difficulty she had (or has) becoming detached and appropriately uninvolved in her parents' fighting. To assume something else, such as that she is "invested" in the parents' difficulty, would be an unfortunate attribution to make about this client. Perhaps, more than anything else, this incongruent response informs us that this client needs help using her normal ability of dissociation and conceptualization. In particular, she needs this help in situations paralleling her parents' relationship.

Catalepsy, Dissociation, Identification

The transcript below with family therapist Frederick Duhl is longer than those previously discussed. The statements are numbered for reference in the subsequent discussion. This transcript illustrates, in addition to the search phenomena and ideomotor behavior, more subtle and profound hypnotic responses from the client: catalepsy, dissociation, and possible deep trance identification with the therapist. In this session Duhl spoke about a client with whom he had not had rapport. This client, who was the daughter of the current client, Peter (P), had recently committed suicide. Duhl (D) opened by remarking that she had looked at the world differently from the way he looked at at it.

1. (Peter's nonverbal behavior is noticeably nonexpressive.)
2. *D:* I can come back from that (closes finger, crosses legs, forms hands into bowl) and recognize we're in two different frames of reference. She was looking at the world (moves palms away from body) differently than I could look at it.
P: (Clears throat, crosses ankles and looks straight ahead, away from Dr. Duhl, with his right hand on left wrist.)
3. *D:* Somehow I couldn't (spreads fingers and "fans" hands) get myself to look at it the way she was looking at it.
P: (Smiles and nods "yes.")
4. *D:* So, I could only argue with her sometimes or confront rather than feel into it (moves left hand with right hand and makes a "dipping into" motion, moves eyes up and left, places hands into "web" pattern and turns palms toward self).

P: (Turns head slightly toward Dr. Duhl in a jerky fashion. Cheek muscles jerk. Smiles slightly. Slowly begins to unfold arms, right is in lap, moves left to side.)

5. *D:* The piece I feel really concerned about is I didn't say that.

P: (Remains very motionless.)

6. *D:* I didn't own the difference of saying: "I am unable to reach you or I cannot understand where you're at," or "I do not feel that I know how to move in a way with you" (moves arms and hands out and in alternately).

P: (Cataleptic, slow blink, smiles, otherwise doesn't move, appears dissociated from body.)

7. *D:* So, what else is there to do?

P: (Bites lower lip with upper teeth and keeps this posture.)

We notice, by the therapist's own account, that he is not neutral. He is, in fact, a model. In the beginning, Peter is extremely nonexpressive. We consider this lack of mobility a sign that he is very possibly already in trance and cataleptic. In line two the therapist began open-ended suggestions and directed his listeners to entertain a visual fantasy ("was looking at the world"). The open-ended suggestions were phrased as self-reports but this made them no less effective as indirect suggestions in lines two and three. In line four he used suggestions covering all possible alternatives to presuppose or imply his belief that some other responses must have also been possible.

In response to both of these suggestions Peter listened and nodded his head in identification, apparently bringing a "map" forward (induced by the therapist's indirect suggestions and his own fixated attention) which included these same suppositions. In line four Peter even responded by changing his posture in near unison with changes made by the therapist. Unconscious identification had begun and is noticeable from this point forward. It is as if his arm movement was impelled by Duhl's visual suggestions.

In line five the therapist offered an indirect suggestion ("the piece I feel really concerned about . . .") focusing awareness. He stated it in the previously established first person pattern (which Peter had been following with both map distinctions and ideomotor behavior). It was not surprising that Peter would then bring his own sense of concern into the foreground. Whether or not he felt this "concern" as a conscious response would be influenced by the intensity of the experience and the focus of his fixated attention. Biting his lip, however, did seem to indicate identification, though in the trance state Peter demonstrated, it was quite likely that he would develop spontaneous amnesia for what was spoken there and have no conscious memory of details about it. In response to that focusing, Peter became even more motionless. He demonstrated a search experience in his own map. His motionlessness was indicative of his going more deeply into trance.

While Peter "went away" more deeply in the search process, the therapist continued in line six to offer indirect suggestions. He interspersed embedded commands "do not feel" and do not "move" in a metaphoric expression of his own unfulfilled attempts to gain rapport with the daughter. Peter listened to the therapist's report as a metaphor for his own experience and, no doubt, got lost in its subtlety. He responded literally and (at line six) became totally cataleptic and dissociated, as one would in somnambulistic trance. If the therapist had planned to dissociate and make this client motionless, he succeeded completely. If he wanted to elicit hope and perhaps inner strength of some kind from this man, he did not succeed. Perhaps his unspoken goal was to provide a model and a map for the client at a time when he may not have had one. It would appear so. He concluded with a question to focus awareness when he asked, "So, what else is there to do?" As expected, Peter changed his behavior (biting lip) as an ideomotor indicator that his map had again changed in response to the therapist.

Deep Trance Identification

In the following example, Virginia Satir and her client engage in the co-creation of several deep trance phenomena, including deep trance identification. By line five, the client speaks "as if" she is her husband. This identification is so intense that she reports thoughts, feelings, conclusions, and memories her husband had (as far as she knows) over a decade prior to this therapy. These statements are observable manifestations of this somnambulistic trance phenomenon. The previous transcript, by comparison, did not contain such utterances by the client, primarily because the therapist did not request such feedback at that time. This comparison can serve as a reminder to notice responses the client exhibits and use them when appropriate, as in this case.

Another striking phenomenon elicited in this session is age regression or pseudo orientation in time. This transcript illustrates both the occurrence and use of deep trance phenomena in nonhypnotic therapy and also how trance phenomena are similar to one another. We categorize this enactment as deep trance identification rather than age regression because of her actual "role playing" the husband. Since she never was her husband, it would be inaccurate to label this phenomenon age regression. That deep trance identity was enhanced by hallucination, of course, but we do not have evidence that her hallucination was more than a "not noticing" of the current surroundings. This form of negative hallucination is present to some extent in all age regression, pseudo orientation in time, and dissociation. It appeared, however, that this particular client displayed a strategy for achieving the identification by initially developing age regression, "going through" it, and then using it as a doorway to the next phenomenon. This is a common occurrence in clinical hypnosis, as well as in common everyday hypnosis. In the transcript, Satir is "S," the wife is "L" and the husband is "P."

1. *L:* (Legs are crossed, crying as she speaks.) I feel as though we were two waifs when we got married, two adolescent kids.
   P: (Remarkably still and looking down at feet.)
2. *S:* Will you be in touch with the fact that that's where you are right now? Be inside you . . .
   P: (Moves head backward with two unconscious jerks.)
3. *L:* We are setting up housekeeping like two little kids (speaking with monotonous voice tone, dropping the end of each phrase in sing-song fashion).
4. *L:* Yeh, Peter's so responsible. He went to my father, asked my father for my hand.
   P: (Shakes head "no" and touches nose with right hand as if to wipe after crying. He quickly moves his eyes horizontally to the right, then up right and return to original position. He then elongates his neck and stares straight ahead.)
5. *L:* (Speaking as if she is husband.) I've got $300 in the bank—maybe not that—but I feel like I can support Lizzie. I'll support her okay. I can earn a living.
   P: (Cheeks flatten and his forehead reveals three creases going completely across and several other smaller creases. His mouth is closed, body is cataleptic, eye blink and respiration are very slow.)
6. *S:* (Moves eyes up-left and up-right alternately, shaking head up and down.) And that which was just a little waif now looks to be even more grown-up . . .
   L: Uh huh (closes mouth).
   S: . . . than one might expect.
   L: (Sniffs and smiles.)
7. *L:* Which one, Peter or me?
   S: Both of you (nods head up and down).
   L: Yeah, that's for sure (laughs).
8. *S:* Just want you to stay in touch with it.
   L: (Shakes head "no.") Oh, I've felt that for the last six months.
   S: And how do you feel?
   L: Very adult! (Smacks lips and puffs her cheeks.)

We mentioned that this phenomenon could be useful in therapy. One might wonder just what purpose might have been identified for this woman to "pretend" being her husband. Several ideas come to mind. Therapeutic gain might result from nothing more than an increased rapport between wife and husband. The actual result in this case was revealed in the final line, as the client reported feeling "very adult" in contrast to her earlier crying. In retrospective analysis, we observe a utilization of the existing (age regressed) behavior of the client, as Satir intensifies and directs it, finally using it to develop a deep trance phenomenon which leads in the end to the client's returning to a more mature state. In brief, Satir used an entirely Ericksonian-like approach to accomplish that end.

Let's take a closer look at the actual indirect suggestions used to create this effect. Line two provides an excellent example of "trance" suggestions often used in "nonhypnotic" therapy. It includes a suggestion to focus and reinforce awareness of the client's spontaneously initiated behavior. "Be inside you . . ." was an open-ended suggestion that met, in a nutshell, the criteria for trance (inward directed, intensified awareness) and utilized this client's behavior. Line three testifies to the fact that it worked! The client displayed and reported a distinct alteration in behavior. In line four she began to partially relive the experience she had previously reported, saying, "Yeh, Peter's so responsible. He went to my father . . ." It was very subtle. That her husband is responsible is a current fact as well as a historical fact. Here she blurred the orientation in time and used that altered framework as a doorway through which to enter the past. In line five she has arrived in the past, so to speak. In retrospect, then, her statement at line four was not a comment about her husband's current responsibility so much as a comment about his responsibility at the time when they were about to marry. This example illustrates beneficial effects trance phenomena can produce when employed to elaborate a client's map of experience.

The husband responded nonverbally at line four with behavior that appeared to be symbolic of tearing even though he was not openly crying. He seemed to be dissociated; perhaps if he had not been he would have actually been crying. He went more deeply into trance in response to the next line (five) when he witnessed his wife "being" him.

In line five the wife delivered a direct quote "as" her husband. It is striking that she included several aspects indicative of a wide range of experience. For example, she spoke of his memories, ("$300 dollars in the bank—maybe not that"), his feelings ("I feel like I can support Lizzie"), his decisions ("I'll support her okay"), and his plans, conjectures, or thoughts of the future ("I can earn a living"). This last comment even represented the husband's self-image, that is, a statement about his range of comfort in using himself. Perhaps the husband intensified his trance in response to that enactment in order to retrieve some of that strength.

In line six Satir called the deep trance phenomenon to an end with the statement, "And that which was just a little waif now looks to be even more grown-up . . ." The wife responded slowly and Satir added, ". . . than one might expect." In line seven the wife expressed confusion as she exited the trance and asked, "Peter or me?" The answer "Both of you" referred to the fact that she is not her husband since he's the other half of "both." The animated "Yeah, that's for sure," followed by laughter, marked an acquisition of the therapist's framework and a departure from the trance phenomenon framework.

Line eight was an open-ended suggestion that the client "stay with it." At the social level one might have asked what "it" was. At the psychological level of communication, however, "it" was an unconscious understanding she brought with her as she emerged from the altered experience. In the last line she displayed final signs of regaining here-and-now body awareness and reoriented from the momentary trance.

Age Regression

We have just examined deep trance phenomena in family therapy and will now compare it to similar phenomena elicited and used in client-centered therapy, an approach often perceived as radically unlike hypnosis. Expecting the therapist's activity to be verbally interactive but not directive in client-centered therapy and "one-sided" as well as overtly influential in hypnosis could create the impression that the two approaches have very little, if anything, in common. Client-centered therapy is generally thought to involve the therapist empathically reflecting the client's experience and demonstrating unconditional positive regard with congruence and genuineness. Perhaps it is under this rubric of "genuineness" that we will find the bulk of those transactions which are indirect hypnotic suggestions. The following transcript from the Carl Rogers film "Gloria," in the set known as "Three Approaches to Therapy," illustrates.

In the session the client displays increasing age regression. In line two Rogers offered an implication that she age regress. We can almost hear Erickson's voice in Rogers' words: "You look to me like a pretty nice daughter."

Although this therapy was probably intended to be nondirective, we suggest that it is directive at the level of psychological communication, as we will show in upcoming analysis. For now, we refer to research findings from a behaviorist perspective: "Sequential analysis of verbal interchanges in cases treated by Rogers revealed that the therapist consistently approved certain behaviors and disapproved others (Murray, 1956; Truax, 1966)" (Bandura, 1969, p. 82). Analysis from a psychological level communication perspective is concerned with therapist and client behavior before, during, and after reinforcement. For that reason we can trace lines of influence in terms of the indirect suggestions which give rise to the client's range of response. Again, these observations are not intended to diminish the importance of genuineness, positive regard, and congruence in therapy, which Rogers himself has already explained elsewhere (Rogers, 1961).

1. *G:* (Voice cracking.) Yes, you know what else I was just thinking? I feel dumb (voice stern, sitting straight, mouth tense and forms smirk) that all of a sudden while I was talking to you I thought (places left hand on cheek, moves hand down to chair) "Gee, how nice I can talk to you and I want you to approve of me and I respect you," (turns head to left and blinks as if flirting) but I miss that my father couldn't talk to me like you are (moves hand back to face). I mean, I'd like to say: "Gee, I'd like you for my father." (Moves other hand up also and smiles, wiggles in chair, moves legs and knees up and back down.) I don't even know why that came to me.

2. *R:* You look to me like a pretty nice daughter. . . . But you really do miss the fact that you couldn't be open with your own dad.

G: (Looks down-right, very still, eyes water, she bites lip and blinks several times.)

3. *G:* Yes, I couldn't be open (moves right hand palm toward her and swings it at wrist) but I want to blame it on him. I think I am more open than he'd allow me. He'd never listen to me talk like you are and not disapprove, not lower me down. I thought of this the other day. Why do I always have to be so perfect? (voice almost whining) I know why (rapid speech, resolved tone). "He always wanted me to be perfect. . . . But do you know what I think I want him to say? "I knew this was you all along, honey (eyes tear, she wipes tears) and I really love you."

4. *R:* You really feel badly that you think there is very little chance he will say that.

G: (Closes eyes.) No, he won't. He doesn't hear. I went back home to him about two years ago (voice cracks) really wanting to let him know I loved him although I have been afraid of him. And he doesn't hear me. He just keeps saying things like (imitating father's voice): "Honey, you know I love you. You know I have always loved you." (Pauses, cries with eyes closed.)

5. *R:* He has never really known you and loved you and this, somehow, is what brings the tears inside.

G: I don't know what it is. You know, when I talk about it, it feels more flip. If I just sit still a minute, it feels like a (voice cracks) great big hurt down there (cries, wipes with tissue, cheeks are distorted in tension). Instead, I feel cheated (cries, mouth opens, cheeks flatten).

6. *R:* It is much easier to be a little flip because then you don't feel that big lump inside of hurt.

G: And again, that's a hopeless situation. I tried working on it, and I feel it's something I have to accept. My father just isn't the type of man I'd dearly like. I'd like somebody more understanding and caring. He cares, but not in the way we can cooperate or communicate (cheeks flatten, eyes become wet, head tilts to right, lower lip out in a pouting of the mouth).

7. R: You feel that, "I am permanently cheated . . ."

G: (Slow blink, eyes up-straight.) That is why I like substitutes. Like I like talking to you and I like men that I can respect. Doctors, and I keep sort of underneath feeling like we are real close, you know, sort of like substitute father.

8. R: I don't feel that's pretending.

G: Well, you are not really my father.

9. R: No. I meant about the real close business.

G: Well, see, I sort of feel that's pretending too because I can't expect you to feel very close to me. You don't know me that well.

10. R: All I can know is what I am feeling and that is I feel close to you in this moment.

G: (Cries, cries, long pause.)

Gloria began an age regression at line one and provided such ample indicators as to make this paragraph an educational classic regarding incipient age regression. Rogers, in line two, implied that Gloria be in the daughter role. This he followed with a suggestion that focused awareness on missing her father. Gloria's response was an intensification of that "painful" part of earlier experience with her father.

In line three she attempted to verbally elaborate her map of the world for Rogers, metacommenting about several aspects of life with her father. Finally, she specified the exact line she would have liked to hear him say. She had age regressed considerably at that point and this is evident in the transcript by her use of present tense: "I want him to say . . ." Rogers (in line four) facilitated an intensification of this experience by his suggestion focusing awareness on the feeling component of this broad regression ("you really feel badly"). Gloria's preceding statement had contained much more material than "feeling" alone. She had reported thinking ("thought of this the other day") and analyzing ("he always wanted me to be perfect") and perhaps more.

Rogers' choosing to focus on the feelings at that moment was selective interaction. It may certainly have been justifiably therapeutic to "help her get in touch with her feelings"; however, our analysis here simply detects those indirect suggestions which shape a subsequent outcome, regardless of the therapeutic aim. The words "very little" in the suggestion that focused aware-

ness ". . . think there is very little chance he will say that" were particularly
interesting. We are reminded of Erickson's interspersal technique as he spoke
to a man suffering great pain. He interspersed phrases about "ease" and
"comfort" into a story about tomatoes and the man's pain went away.
Rogers' selection of these particular words, used in this context, could only
have intensified Gloria's sense of being "very little."

Gloria's response to that transaction was, in fact, intensification. She commented, "He doesn't hear me." As in the preceding case, when the wife used
ambiguous verb tense to swing into the age regression that gave rise to deep
trance identification, Gloria's ambiguous verb tense displayed her intensified
age regressed mood. She shortly experienced voice cracking and then imitated her father's voice, framing it as a child-like role-play which only reported his words. This can be contrasted to the previous case when the wife
framed the enactment of her husband as if she really lived it (thoughts, feelings, memories, planning, self-image statements, etc.).

In lines six and seven Rogers continued suggestions to reinforce and focus
awareness. Gloria had mentioned that she felt cheated and in response to
these suggestions she intensified and elaborated that map. She soon reported
a rationalization that her hurt feeling seemed to justify (in her map): "That's
why I like substitutes." Rogers did not interpret her statement as manipulative; instead, in line eight, he said, "I don't feel that's pretending." In response
she reminded him that he was not her father. She had not understood this
meaning of the word "pretending." Rogers introduced this word. It was from
a framework alien to this client at that time and so she challenged it. This
challenge did not constitute resistance to therapy or insight but was simply a
misunderstanding, created when Rogers introduced a word not associated
with her current age regression framework. In line nine Rogers again reminded her of the alien framework ("No, I meant about the real close business"). Gloria still refused to accept his use of the word "pretending" in that
framework about closeness.

Finally, she age regressed completely at line nine when Rogers expressed
his feeling of closeness to her. By doing so he had escorted her to the outer
limits of her map of experiences and choices. She had redundantly spoken
about her lack of understanding regarding the role of daughter-to-father, especially when that role involved closeness. Rogers had defined the situation
as one in which he could judge (paternalistically?) that she would make a fine
daughter. She externalized her map to reveal that she substituted others in
place of her father and he would do nicely since she respected him. At that
precise juncture Rogers essentially took the very role with which she was
most unfamiliar—a close father. In so doing he gently invited her to learn her
part as a person who could be close as a daughter.

We speculate that Erickson would have metaphorically elaborated a new map of the world for her at that point. By leaving her without any associations to her desired self-image, she only had available for guidance those learnings of the lonely little girl she once was. Metaphoric input to stimulate acquisition of a map to guide more appropriate adult closeness would facilitate a valuable expansion of the floundering little girl framework from which she operated.

Rogers' approach is not Erickson's approach and yet in Rogers' work, as in the work of the other therapists briefly analyzed here, we find a preponderance of hypnotic interaction at the psychological level of communication. We speculate that all effective therapies, hypnotic or otherwise, involve the same elements of indirect suggestion and hypnotic trance phenomena. This psychological level of communication directs the framework of trance phenomena and ultimately the understandings and experiences conveyed. We expect that this situation is true with all or nearly all "normal" communication.

Positive Hallucination

This final transcript illustrates positive hallucination in a family therapy context. It begins as Virginia Satir(S) asks the client, Trina (T), to imagine being her daughter, Lisa, and then to report on that imagined experience. In effect, Satir asks her to report on a hallucination. The discussion opens with Satir asking the client to elucidate upon what she had just said. In previous transcripts the phenomena have been used for intrinsic problem-solving benefits. In this interaction the phenomenon produced a feeling of intense sadness which was subsequently used in the session.

1. *S:* What do the voices say to you (left hand near mouth moves in circular motion) or how are you using them or (head is nodding) what are you getting?

   T: (As if she is someone else and somewhere else) Oh, they are distracting. (Closes eyes, head is down, motions with left hand across body—a "get out of here" motion—but not in reference to anyone in the therapy room.) I hear Trina, Lisa's mom or something . . .

2. *T:* I don't know what they are talking about but I hear us being discussed in there . . . (stops and puts left elbow on left knee, hand on mouth, sighs, eyes remain closed).

   S: Let's just hold for a moment. When you were being aware of being distracted you were in the middle of doing something (motions with left hand), showing something.

3. *T:* It's so hard for me because I was trying to put myself in Lisa's place.

It's very hard (nodding head "yes") for me to do that because I *can* . . .

S: All right, will you . . . (moves hand to mouth).

4. T: What it's like for her when she says: "I'm getting off the bus now!" (Moves left hand above left thigh and suddenly jerks fingers into a grasping position, revealing cataleptic, unconscious jerks. Voice changes and becomes faster. Jerks head back changing posture, makes fist with left hand which still jerks). But I mean (voice returns to normal) at this point it says something very—(touches left finger and thumb to make a "picking up" motion and moves hand back and forth, left to right) it happened suddenly, but all of a sudden it seems (to self) "Lisa, if you're not the center of attention then you get off the bus." It wasn't those words but . . . (palm out and fingers spread).

5. T: And I wonder (touches chest with left hand and changes voice again, raising the tone and continues to play with necklace at midline of chest) how we all want to be the center of attention and how I grow up thinking (whispers) I shouldn't be the center of attention you know. (voice returns, tightens and releases left side of mouth) I'm really part of a whole family—I know I caused a lot of fuss when I was little (moves left hand down to leg)—not only because I was a-a- mistake (lifts hand an inch and drops it). How does one say it better—(eyes are closed, smiles "sarcastically") not plann-nn-nned!! (lifts left hand an inch and touches thumb to finger, palm is up, voice is stressed dramatically on last syllables. She leans forward as she speaks, grits teeth, deliberately moves mouth so that neck and jaw muscles are strained to show blood vessels. Her eyes are still closed and she dips her chin to her chest).

S: Hold it for a minute just right now. Tell me what you're feeling . . .

6. T: Oh—I'm feeling really sad.

S: All right, I'd like you to be in touch with your fantasy.

T: (Tears drip from her eyes. Her head remains down, her cheek muscles strain and she sobs heavily.)

In the first line Satir used questions to focus and reinforce awareness and then implication to intensify the normal occurrence of a trance phenomenon. Trina's first comment in line two had that familiar ambiguity we've mentioned before. "I don't know what they are talking about . . ." could mean she experiences herself as herself or she could possibly be experiencing herself as the daughter. Satir's unspecified search language initiated search and her associations involved mechanisms of hallucination.

At line four Trina was still "on the verge" of a total hallucination. She oscillated between her waking state awareness of herself ("What it's like for her when she says: . . .") and her hallucination, age regression, and deep trance identification ("I'm getting off the bus now"). Staying "firmly" in the role of her daughter would justify calling this yet another example of deep trance identification, but what we have here is not a total identification with another person (feeling, thinking, remembering, conjecturing). Instead, it is a predominance of hallucinations, including the bodily motions described in line four (middle section).

In line five Trina exhibited a mixture of hallucination and identification created via the hallucination. She was not merely perceiving sensory items that were not present but also drawing conclusions ("I know I cause a lot of fuss"). In this section Trina had exceeded the bounds of hallucination and demonstrated again how one phenomenon can create a blend into another. The ability of trance phenomena to blend between frameworks constitutes half their value. The other half involves the opportunity that can be created for exploring previously unused or unavailable experiences. The conclusion of this transcript further illustrates that.

Trina reported her feeling as sadness. Satir asked her to stay "in touch" with the feeling and fantasy. Trina sobbed. Many of the previous transcripts illustrate the occurrence but not the use of trance phenomena in treatment. Here the by-product of the phenomenon was the intensification of a grief reaction for the client. The therapist was alert for an opportunity to use the phenomenon to facilitate eliciting this grief. Satir is exceptional in this regard. Many therapists, mystified by hypnosis, are not yet aware of the hypnotic substratum of communication at the psychological level in therapy.

Responding to our evaluation of the hypnotic phenomena in her work, Satir, in fact, commented that she had first been surprised some time ago when it was suggested that she used trance phenomena. "However, I am quite clear now that I use hypnotic phenomena intuitively as well as more and more consciously (Satir, 1981)." Therapists can become increasingly aware of opportunities available to them by adding to their repertoire an understanding of the Ericksonian approach. Satir is a notable example of the growing awareness of hypnosis in the so-called nonhypnotic therapies.

We have attempted to convey in this chapter the frequent occurrence and use of trance phenomena in therapy, both hypnotic and otherwise. Using clients' normal and natural abilities to alter consciousness is intimately connected with solving problems. Trance phenomena, as we have said, are like tools of scientific investigation; they are the microscope, time machine, amplifier, and log books of experience. With them clients can more efficiently examine those experiences which can be elicited within any metaphoric or suggested framework. This is the reason we find an intuitive and natural use of these elements in the work of foremost clinical and family therapists. Erickson's beliefs about the importance and regular occurrence of the hypnotic aspects of communication led to his articulation of the forms of indirect suggestion, metaphor, and the demystification of common everyday elements of hypnotic phenomena. We turn now to the multiple embedded metaphor modality as a means for planned use of such interventions.

Part Three
MULTIPLE EMBEDDED METAPHOR

7 THE MULTIPLE EMBEDDED METAPHOR FRAMEWORK

We define framework as an association of one or more related metaphors and bundles of experience that results in specific attitudes and influences perception. The rules of recombining experience that a person idiosyncratically follows will be one result of the framework from which s/he operates. When a person is not able to associate (consciously or unconsciously) to mental mechanisms and experiences needed to function properly and enjoyably, psychological problems result. Altering or suspending the personal framework that is limiting a person facilitates the person's ability to entertain novel experiences. Haley, analyzing Erickson, wrote:

> Therefore there must be a framework of helpful assistance, but within that framework there must be an avoidance of a direct demand for more "normal" behavior . . . there must be a framework defining the relationship as one designed to induce change, and within that framework no direct request for a change but an acceptance of the person as he is (Haley, 1973, p. 125).

For example, the child abuser discussed in the diagnosis chapter could not associate to simple muscle sets and thoughts that could be called "tenderness," "competence," "control," or "reasonable," etc. in the context of talking to his daughter about her conduct. Furthermore, his frame of reference was not likely to associate him to those experiences or produce thoughts that were incompatible with striking her. If he could have had such experiences at those times, it might have helped him avoid striking her. In context of thinking about his daughter's behavior, he needed to learn to elicit and use experiences that he was not able to produce in his normal framework. He certainly would not learn that by himself.

In therapy, however, his framework was suspended and a metaphor was begun about a gardener who could not find the necessary time for his plants; his income suffered. The story was ostensibly about how the gardener increased his income and learned to adjust his use of time. Within the midst of that drama were introduced a series of anecdotes about how adults learn from experiences of childhood. Again, ostensibly we were illustrating what was shared with the gardener when we worked with him on the goal of improving his business.

In that second embedded metaphor we spoke at length about the tenderness a boy learns holding a puppy on his lap. We mentioned a hot summer day and a healthy puppy. As we did the client smiled warmly, relaxed, breathed more deeply and generally convinced us that his experience was approximating that about which we spoke. Now, in the framework of the story he was able to experience "tenderness" that he was not able to experience in his own framework when he was with his daughter.

The series of metaphors continued for the remainder of the first session. The same was true for subsequent sessions. The use of the embedded metaphoric frameworks allowed experiences to be examined which were otherwise unallowable to him. The framework of the puppy being held on a hot summer day made the experience of tenderness reasonable, non-threatening, and acceptable so that he could continue to experience ideas, images, and feelings that comprised it. The embedded structure suspended his normal censorship of the experience even when he was subsequently asked to open his eyes in the trance and examine his daughter's face with tenderness (which was then referred to as "the understanding that your unconscious gained"). In short, the experience of looking at his daughter was becoming associated with the experience of tenderness and sensitivity that he had learned, albeit years ago in his childhood.

Within the ambiguity of multiple embeddings of metaphors, other learnings needed to be derived. As mentioned in Chapter 3, this man needed appropriate adjustments in attitude, cognition, perception, family structure and enjoyment of life, as well as role and emotional flexibility changes. These were all touched upon in the multiple embedded framework in the first session and again in subsequent sessions.

Since this highly volatile man could not find an acceptable avenue of association between feelings of tenderness and his perceptions of his daughter, the ambiguity of the multiple embedded metaphors established a learning framework that allowed him to make novel connections (or strengthen the existing weak associations he might have had) to tenderness. It helped him develop an acceptable association between his thoughts about his daughter and the feelings of tenderness from his youth.

The multiple level of embedded metaphor becomes a vehicle for helping clients discover new role behaviors and new emotional flexibility. This is exactly the purpose of the embedded modality. Using it not only facilitates a client's acquisition of therapeutic learnings but does so within the bounds of interventions and principles of ethics established earlier. In summary, clients "save face" as respect is shown for particular personalities; they experience empathic understanding, learn choice, and find the answer within their own personal history. The multiple embedded metaphor provides a framework in which a person can examine, find, or build needed experiences and then reassociate them to situations. Finally, clients can alter original existing frameworks to accept, tolerate, or change the meaning of new experience and behaviors. They can even "not notice" new learnings while nevertheless employing them in daily life.

Later in this chapter we review and examine fundamentals of the multiple embedded structure by presenting and discussing three different cases. The major goal in each case is to alter the client's framework, retrieve necessary resources, and then reassociate them. The reassociation may begin with treatment aimed directly at the presenting problem, directly at the symptom, or directly at the "core issue." The direct work may take many shapes, as detailed in Chapter 8. Then the retrieved resources are linked to the immediate situational or social concerns of the client. Finally, the resources are linked and changes shaped to a broader scope, including the next likely stage of social development. Let's examine the outline again.

INDUCTION

Usually, a multiple embedded metaphor is begun with an induction. If the induction is produced less formally, as the result of the client's fixation on a metaphor, the situation resembles a naturalistic induction. In that case, induction may come as part of the first or second metaphor of the series. Techniques during induction include anecdotes, indirect suggestions, and binds that facilitate the client's producing the unique and personal trance state needed.

We stress only two requirements during induction: the development of the conscious/unconscious dissociation and the paradoxical prescription and splitting of any resistive behavior (whether it be resistive because of subtle or gross factors).

MATCHING METAPHOR

We have defined the matching metaphor as that metaphor which is placed in the primary position and which offers a dramatic theme parallel to the client's presenting problem. The purpose of using a matching metaphor is to fixate the maximal amount of the client's available attention. Hypnosis is a communication modality created by inwardly concentrated attention. Attention is the process of adjusting sense organs so as to preferentially respond to stimuli. So, unconscious attention will be engaged by patterns of stimulation that match concerns being carried on by the unconscious. The matching metaphor must parallel the situation experienced by the client if it is to engage as much available attention as possible.

Modifications, of course, are made within these guidelines to accommodate pragmatics and personal idiosyncrasies of each client. For example, individuals who are prone to analyze and criticize a therapy session might find themselves listening to a metaphor extremely unlike their situation. Their efforts to analyze the relationship between the metaphor and their situation will be entirely frustrated under such conditions. On the other hand, clients who are naive to therapy and skeptical about the rapport and understanding they are likely to receive might be more likely to hear a story that is quite identifiably similar to their situation, thus soothing any suspicions about the hypnotist's lack of understanding or relevance.

In either case, the criteria for success at this stage of treatment are the creation of a successful fixation of attention and the establishment of a new framework. This framework provides the context for the client's learning. It will alter the rules previously applied to limits experienced by the client. People and things in the metaphor will not be required to act as they do in the client's real life. The hypnotist changes the framework and thereby allows new understandings and new experiences to be considered within the framework being established. The opening metaphor generally contains either guidelines for therapy, reference to necessary learning experiences, a positive interpretation of some limiting difficulty, or, at the very least, a dramatic hold that presupposes change in a situation similar to the client's situation.

METAPHORS TO RETRIEVE RESOURCES

Any experience can be considered a resource. Also, any experience can be considered a liability. The difference depends upon the use to which it is put at any particular time in a person's life. Once the client's presenting framework has been altered, s/he must temporarily suspend learned rules that govern recombining experience. Thereby, novel experiences can be elicited and entertained in combinations that were previously unacceptable or impossible for the client. In the continuing context of multiple frameworks, the new arrangements can be judged for usefulness or lack of usefulness by both client and therapist as new associations develop in the session.

Metaphors used at the phase of resource retrieval are best selected with the client's psychological age in mind. It does little good to relate an understanding of trust that is appropriate to an adult when the client is listening with the mind of a child. For example, adult trust and tenderness might be exemplified by an employer who hires a new employee with potential but without actual experience. But, that story might only elicit suspicion and doubt from a client who is operating, as was the case with the child abuser, like a child of three or four years old. The child abuser's psychological age was considered when the story of the puppy was chosen to elicit tenderness and trust.

The primary goal at the retrieval stage is merely to find and develop a readiness for using the bits and pieces of images, experiences, mechanisms, and motor responses related to therapy. Resources may need to be retrieved and organized in small component parts. This phase is analogous to planning a meal. It is useful to find all items in the cupboards and refrigerator before initiating actual preparation. If something is missing the cook will need to find a substitute or some way to secure the missing ingredient so the actual preparation of the meal will not be interrupted.

The client's understanding of any experience is learned. It relates to his or her map of the world and the personal history which has been lived. So the client's psychological age significantly affects the understanding of any resource. Appealing to developmental tasks in the stage of development the client has achieved will provide resources with maximal integrity. Likewise, appealing to developmental stages not yet achieved by the client will provide experiences and understandings which are relatively less solid, less integrated, and less dependable. However, regardless of the client's psychological age, it is possible to organize and bring to the psychological foreground various trance phenomena.

Trance phenomena are useful adjuncts and can be easily elicited at the resource phase to be used independently or to enhance other experiences. As we have already stated, trance phenomena are tools to examine and intensify experiences, while new frameworks provide means for entertaining the experience in the first place. Trance phenomena can help the client better locate and use experiences that were difficult to retrieve in the pre-therapy framework.

DIRECT WORK ON CORE ISSUE

The idea of "direct" work is not contrary to the concept of indirection. An Ericksonian hypnotist strives to be artfully indirect in all suggestions and interventions. The term "direct" refers not to the interventions or suggestions but rather to the target of those interventions. The direct work phase aims at the symptom—the "key piece" of the client's dilemma—or, as Erickson called it, at the "core of the neurosis." This is often significantly different from what the client reports as the presenting problem. For instance, a client may be overweight and consider obesity the presenting problem but the most important "key piece" may be an overcritical attitude held by the client. In such a case the critical attitude may be directly addressed in the vortex of the multiple embedded structure.

If the most important issue or situation is addressed in the center of the embedded structure, it is most protected against biases and limitations of the conscious mind. Clients generally have spontaneous amnesia for material delivered in the direct work phase. The production of amnesia may be similar to the phenomenon described by perception psychologists that predicts maximum memory retention for items presented first or last in a chain of items and minimal retention for those items in the middle of a series. Protection by amnesia is enhanced by several steps of framework alteration preceding introduction of direct work.

The client is often hearing about experiences and guidelines that were discovered by some other client and told to still another client to solve some other problem, etc. The result is that current clients can listen and imagine experiences which may be highly unusual for them or which might normally be entirely too threatening. They not only can examine these experiences and generate applications of them to create resolution of factors that cause symptoms, but can also be expected to do so relatively comfortably, have amnesia for the entire event, and save face.

Targets for the direct work phase of the multiple embedded metaphor are varied. Typically, we reserve the most difficult or most important treatment goals for this spot in the treatment plan. The three clients examined in this chapter represent a variety of goals. In one case the direct work concerns attitudinal restructuring goals to reverse an obese client's cognitions (she took no responsibility for her life situation); in another case, association of the first signal of pain to the childhood feelings of delight in walking was the emphasis of the direct work (relief from acute pelvic pain was most important); and in the third case, enhancing body image and self-image was most important (for acute hysterical anxiety). Accurate diagnostic assessment, combined with clinical acumen gained from experience, will help therapists identify these core issues. To whatever extent possible, the direct work helps the client deal with specific experiences, images, perceptions, and associations, rather than vague and reified theories and abstracted ideas.

Several methods for achieving various goals are discussed in Chapter 8. These include: age regressed reliving of positive or traumatic past experiences (as with Monde); dissociated reexamining of the past (the woman who vomited after her important date); hallucinated fantasies (such as the "February Man" case); talking with the client verbally about the problem or solution (as in the case of "Nick" (Lustig, 1975)); amnesia protected instructions, advice and guidelines. We call this last group "punchlines." Advice given at the direct work phase can be received without interference of conscious beliefs but can still be unconsciously evaluated by the client to facilitate therapeutic gains.

LINKING RESOURCES TO SOCIAL NETWORK

This is a most important part of treatment. The client's unconscious must reassociate to needed experiences in the immediate personal and social arena. Association to resources precedes "coping" that involves using those resources. Work following the direct phase usually deals with map building to associate retrieved resources to current social circumstances. That is, through the metaphoric framework, we work to link desired experiences, skills, perceptions, and attitudes to images and social cues that are or will be present in the client's life.

In the case of the child abuser, perceptions of the daughter and experiences of tenderness were associated in the direct work phase. In the linking phase a framework acceptable to him was constructed in which he could continue to notice his tenderness without being defensive. Briefly summarized, this was done with a paradoxical splitting between his abuse and his need to control. He was told to continue to control his daughter and then we explained how to control—and that, of course, included behaviors built on experiences of tenderness.

In the first case, discussed below, Dorine was offered a way to link feelings of satisfaction (from retrieved resources) and a sense of personal responsibility (from direct work) to her map of the immediate future. In the pelvic pain case, the relief from pain (established in direct work) was linked to images that would help insure a posthypnotic continuance. The woman with anxiety attacks was directed to use self-image thinking "rehearsals" to associate feelings of emotional acceptance (from the resource retrieval stage) to test taking and social encounters.

Verbal posthypnotic suggestions are weak links unless they refer to specific images associated with situational or contextual cues. The cues need to be memories or images from areas in which the resources are expected to operate. The images of a spouse's face, sounds of a voice, memory of a place, or whatever images will be needed are themselves resources which may need to be retrieved prior to the linking phase.

Elaborate sets of images, such as in self-image thinking, require, in comparison to posthypnotic suggestions, the prior retrieval or the client's ability to vividly imagine and do creative mental gymnastics. Self-image thinking scenarios are visual rehearsals useful for creating associative links between desirable behaviors or experiences and specific future settings. These steps are detailed in Chapter 8.

It is not enough that clients solve the problems or symptoms they bring to therapy. We work to help them make subtle shifts in perception and expectation so that change does not take place in a vacuum. Since change always occurs in some social context, that network must also change as symptoms and underlying causes are remedied. Changes in social conduct are frequently dramatic. Often, however, changes in social conduct, attitude and perception are subtle and not something a client can even articulate. In the linking phase the client should create minimal alterations of perception about future social situations so that changes will be reinforced.

Finally, the linking stage brings to closure dramas of the resource metaphors which were initially begun as tangents. Resolution of dramatic themes and outcome of the story are, as we have mentioned, less important than that portion of the metaphor which was detailed with anecdotes and indirect suggestion. With the resolution of these tangents therapy is logically returned to the first framework.

ENDING MATCHING METAPHOR

Desirable outcomes to the original metaphor are usually most therapeutic. Everybody likes a story with a good ending. However, other endings are often extremely useful. These may include: no ending (the story is a cliffhanger), surprise ending (think of Ogden Nash), mysterious ending (let the client imagine), or tragic ending (protagonist fails to take advice or advice alone does not work). The tragic ending might be especially useful with clients who are potentially motivated through realization that "time is running out" and they don't want to put something off that should be done immediately. Generally, stories ended at this phase are more likely to be remembered than those which were more embedded. For that reason the outcome of the story is usually positive and acceptable to the client's belief system.

Distant future social tasks may be referred to here, just as immediate social tasks were referred to in the linking phase. When the next logical phase of social adjustment is addressed here, two things are accomplished. One is an implication of the effects of time on the client's problem. Many clients have not properly considered themselves far into the future. Doing so often conveys a sense of maturity and reality which helps them consciously frame their changes in a broader teleological context. Secondly, generative change is encouraged. It was not enough for Erickson that clients resolve a symptom. If a problem is to be truly resolved, changes in the social network, self-image system, etc. must occur. And if one change can be designed such that it paves the way toward other changes required in the client's next logical set of social demands, then generative change has been facilitated. Generative change is an alteration in the symptom that changes the immediate psychological and social dynamics and also predisposes the client to adaptive changes in developmental social tasks in the future. Clients create immediate changes which prepare them, in ways not yet realized, for adaptations to situations they are most likely to encounter in the course of normal development.

The generative aspects of the therapy work become apparent after initial changes in presenting problems are stabilized. Clients find that the changes initially made have been in step with the new demands being placed upon them. The success of changes first made in therapy generates a momentum that facilitates the adaptation to the next level of growth and development. The child abuser, for instance, did not merely learn to stop his abuse, but was also prepared for the adjustments of being together with his wife after his daughter left the house. Both the husband and wife were also learning something about adapting to the grandchildren they would probably have.

REORIENTING TO WAKING STATE

During this phase the client is reoriented to waking state and to the normal framework that existed before therapy. When the client is noticeably nonresistant, a simple, routine reorientation may be sufficient to support work done in the multiple embedded framework. When the client is resistant in any way (or compliant and overcooperative), it is important to include in the reorientation paradoxical binds similar to those which began the induction.

The importance of termination and what we call "the force of closure" is discussed in detail in Chapter 9. The client will decide, retroactively, on the meaning of the entire session depending on how it ends. This retroactive framing will not diminish the effect of associations and changes created in the session at the unconscious level, but will affect the client's conscious opinion and effort to support the changes. It is helpful, therefore, to leave resistant clients with logic that distracts the analytic efforts of the conscious mind from parasitic sabotage of the gains made in therapy.

CASE EXAMPLES

The first case involves obesity in an immature personality. The client was a 40-year-old woman who was "stuck" in the past. She found herself obsessively rehashing the past and how she had been mistreated, misunderstood, and emotionally deprived. This case has been selected for examination because of the success she experienced as a result of her treatment and also because of the complications the case illustrated. This client presented a complex diagnostic picture; she was out of sync with her self-image, her social network demands, and her family growth and development. We will discuss the various elements of her diagnosis and treatment planning. The session presented, the first, served as a basis for work that she would do both by herself and with further treatment. She was not, however, suited for long-term therapy.

The next patient discussed in this chapter was seen only once, and the transcript as it appears here constituted the total treatment. Of course, many of our clients are seen for more than one session. However, this case, referred for acute pelvic pain caused by an automobile accident, presented a simplified clinical picture so that the treatment was successfully completed in one session.

The third case concerns a woman who had suffered from acute hysterical anxiety. She continued therapy with a therapist in her home state after the session with us.

Induction in the first case began almost simultaneously with beginning the matching metaphor. This was accomplished by our alternately speaking to her. This unusual deviation from the guidelines given earlier is contrasted with the single therapist induction in the next case and the more "standard" dual induction in the third case. The second, diagnostically simpler case of pelvic pain represents a different approach to the multiple embedded metaphor. The session concerns a woman who, due to an automobile accident, suffered the trauma of having both legs driven through her pelvic sockets into her abdomen. The pain was so great that drugs did not seem to help. Her husband, a physician who had exhausted medical options, referred her for treatment. Prior to the accident she was creatively enjoying her marriage and friends. She related well with her parents and had a self-image that was positive and appropriate. Her therapy, therefore, was directed toward helping her achieve relief from her often excruciating pain.

The use of multiple embedded frameworks in the pelvic pain case involved the retrieval and application of trance phenomena to help her not notice the pain while still caring for herself appropriately. The multiple embedded pattern described above was modified somewhat. The matching metaphor was presented in the usual manner but the resources consisted of positively framing the first experience of pain, building safeguards for her physical well-being (despite diminution of the pain), and retrieving experiences of amnesia and age regression. The direct work consisted of the further use of trance phenomena (of age regression) and elicitation of the memory of delight of first walking. The linking phase, while not aimed at her immediate social concerns, was aimed at the immediate situation of pain relief and its posthypnotic continuance. Finally, the end of the original matching metaphor referred her to any necessary changes that might be expressed in her family ties and again reinforced the amnesia suggestions.

While the sequence of therapy was unique, the structure of the multiple embedded metaphor was apparent. The same was true in the third case presented. That case concerns a woman with acute hysterical anxiety episodes. We had an opportunity to observe her during one of her attacks. She had been given an administrative chore that involved her making social contact. Performance of her chore involved too much conspicuous social contact. Achievement pressure, paired with lack of confidence, occupied her conscious mind. She became increasingly anxious to the point of sheer panic and eventually chose to simply avoid the social situation and forfeit completing the task.

She was employed as a bookkeeper, which enabled her to avoid performance anxiety as much as possible. However, she still found herself in anxiety-evoking situations. Her situation was well suited to the use of the multiple embedded structure. Induction stressed the nonperformance aspect of the session. Avoidance of social contact was prescribed as a way to go more into oneself and hence into trance. The matching metaphor proceeded normally, incorporating personal aspects that had been revealed in the diagnosis. The resources metaphor provided the opportunity to build an experience that symbolized an acceptance of her emotional life. It was designed to include arm levitation, dissociation from her body, a personal sense of spiritual meaning, and finally, a central self-image that corresponded to her newly created feelings of acceptance.

The direct work differed from that in the case in which the pelvic pain was the main focus because here, attitude was the focus. She had stopped being ambitious or competitive in the normal and appropriate ways. Her attitude was addressed directly with punchlines and indirectly within a metaphor about a runner. This direct work was similar in process to that done with the obesity case, but exemplifies positive and supportive instructions ("Compete with yourself," and "you're going to outgrow your shell and your shell is only a device to allow you to participate in the real world"). The obese client required challenging and forceful instructions ("Why don't you follow the directives that are good for you, that reduce your difficulty?" and "You're a damn fool for not doing the things that make you feel better!").

The linking phase for the anxious client associated resources to test taking, to talking to others, and to self-expression symbolically represented. The conclusion of the resources metaphor offered a framework in which her mistakes were framed as something positive. Finally, the linking of the resources metaphor ended with a reference to her next social developmental stage.

The matching metaphor ended with a resolution of all the problems mentioned in the original metaphor. We assisted her change in attitude by the detailed resolution (albeit metaphoric) of the problems on which she had fixated her attention in the beginning of the matching metaphor. This case, more than the others, illustrated a person who was frightened and needed to have the interpersonal aspects of her map carefully detailed. She was reoriented with suggestions for amnesia.

It might have been possible, with even more careful planning, to make each of these embedded structures conform perfectly to the pattern presented earlier, but that would be unnecessary. Ericksonian therapy insists, above all, that each individual shapes the treatment. The tools ought to be modified to fit the client situation and not vice versa.

A CASE OF OBESITY AND IMMATURE PERSONALITY

*Information Gathering

This client, "Dorine," was the last client to be treated in a two-day therapy marathon.

C: What did you get a cure for so far? D: I don't know but I've been getting interested in everything, going into trance and listening to everything and hopefully getting as much as possible out of it. C: What were you after? D: (Laughing) Well, I came here to tell you I was overweight, and that I needed a cure for that but that really isn't what I need. I want to deal with some things that happened in my childhood and I found that out by listening to all these things the last couple of days and by being in trance and letting my mind take me back to this. I had a very repressive childhood and parents who said that they loved me but there were no hugs and kisses and cuddles and things like that.

And there was no money to be used for anything. It all had to be saved for college education and so on. And when it came time for college education, I wasn't allowed to go to the college of my choice even when I had done everything I was supposed to do for the goals, and it was a repetitive thing. S: Go to our college and have the money or go to your college without? D: No, it was a thing where I would be given a goal and I'd shoot for it and my reward would be taken away or I just was not allowed to get as much satisfaction out of everything as I wanted and I find that I'm doing this in my own life.

I'm destroying myself by walking around with all this extra weight. My health and my happiness is hurting and, (sigh) . . . S: Have you cried about that hurt? D: Yes, I was in therapy for three years. S: I guess that's synonymous with crying. *D:* Well, isn't it? I worked on a lot of problems and worked out some new goals and made some changes in my life and made a new life for myself and I've almost gotten worse (laughter)! It's like I have a built in "get back at myself" type thing. *S:* What's gotten worse? *D:* I've gained about 50 pounds in the last year since I've moved to a new area. I've set things up so I had a job to take with me to a rural area so I didn't have to live in the city. I live in a beautiful place. I was planning on getting lots of exercise and I have gotten none and my job has not improved. I'm not making more money like I was supposed to. I'm supposed to be up at six o'clock in the morning, on the telephone to call all over the country. I do phone sales. And I'm up and I fool around. I wait until 6:20 or so to pick up the phone and I do fine when I get on but I have to be off at eight o'clock so. . . . I just keep sabotaging myself in everything that I do. *S:* Yes.

C: You live alone? *D:* I live alone, 40 years old. I just went through the whole crisis thing that you go through with that. I have a lousy love life. *S:* I don't go through that crisis. *D:* You didn't, good. *S:* I won't. *D:* That's what I want to get to, that I don't have to go through those things. *S:* You'll have to stop laughing at your misfortunes then. *D:* I'm nervous. I'm not really laughing at them. It's not funny.

S: No, what would you rather deal with instead? *D:* I want to be effective at my job, make a lot of money, lose weight. *S:* You said childhood things come to mind. *D:* I think those are the things that I either need to find out about or just forget about so that I can go on with my life and do the things that I need to do. *S:* Well, I like your attitude about going on with your life regardless of what the right thing is.

You have some idea that finding out about something is important. Maybe if you filled me in I can help make a judgment about what would be useful. *D:* Ummm, well, it's just I don't feel like my parents gave me the things that they promised me or that they said they were going to give me or . . . *C:* Things that you needed? *D:* Yes, that I needed or that . . . I was cheated all the time. Every time I got to the point where I was supposed to . . . I was supposed to make good grades so that I could graduate in the top of my class so I could go to the college of my choice. And out of 1500 students I graduated in the top 300 and then I was told that I couldn't go to that college because it was too far away and cost too much money. I wanted to go away because I wanted to get out of the house 'cause I was tired of going to bed at 8:30 at night every night of my life because that was someone else's rule. I'm still using someone else's rules to rule my own life. I don't have my own control. *S:* You know, Dorine, I understand what you're saying and believe it and all that but I don't understand where I fit in yet. Why don't you just go ahead and follow your own rules? *D:* I don't know how; I don't know how to get out there and do what I need to do. Um, I came here for some magic too. That was the name of your book (laughter from audience).

S: I sometimes ask people to remember something they've had in the back of their minds they'd like to forget entirely. And then they just see what they'd like to forget in my hand, and you can throw little magic sparkles sometimes, until they finally concentrate deeply on what it is they'd like to forget about and then when their mind is responding to that in some appropriate way, I just crumble it up and throw it away. *D:* Sounds like a good idea.

S: You've mentioned a lot of things. You have a lot of bad feelings, and it would be appropriate for you to respond in a way that your parents didn't respond to your feelings every time you have them, that is, to nurture yourself and let those feelings happen. *D:* I still feel very alone and I'm still responsible for my own support and I'm tired. I've put a lot of energy into it. I want to do things. I would like to become a therapist but I don't feel that I can do it until I've gotten myself to the point that I don't have these things holding me back. My father just died in January, left over a half million dollars and that was the person who had never had any money or love to give to me and I have nothing. I'm still struggling. My mother won't loan me any money. She's gonna sit on it and I would just as soon divorce myself from all of that past so that I could go on because I think that's what holding me back.

S: Can you say how you keep yourself hooked into that somehow? *D:* I want it. I think I deserve some of that money because it was promised to me over and over again along with the love and affection and everything that went along with it. It just isn't fair that I was denied all of those things so many times, that I had to go to work at eight years old and buy my own clothes. *S:* You got a bad shake. *D:* Yeah, they made me mad. *S:* Yet, holding on to the thing is something that takes some energy and effort. *D:* Yeah, I think so. Dragging around a lot of dead weight that you don't need. *S:* How do you manage to drag it around with you over and over again so successfully? If we find out how you manage to keep yourself so successfully in mind of the past, the deprivations of the past, maybe you can use that same successful way to proceed in the future differently. *D:* I guess carrying all this extra weight around and having migraine headaches. *S:* Well that's not good enough. I need a better answer. Let me help you shape an answer a little more. When you first start to think about your past, what's the first thing that comes to mind, and, more importantly, does it come to mind as a picture in your mind, or as something you hear or say to yourself or something you feel? *D:* Just a whole vast territory of unhappiness. *S:* That comes to you in what way? *D:* Feeling. *S:* And do you see anything that comes with the feeling? *D:* No, a definite feeling of emptiness, loneliness, unhappiness, and anger.

This woman needed to make many social and personal adjustments in her life. She identified several goals and others were obvious to the professional observer. For example, she stated, "I would just as soon divorce myself from all of that past so that I could go on. . . ." She indicated that "they made me mad" and in response she was ". . . dragging around a lot of dead weight . . . and having migraine headaches."

From the information she gave, a diagnostic assessment was formed according to the six parameters previously discussed (cf. Chapter 3, p. 36). We especially noted her final sentences, in which she spoke about her life as a "vast territory of unhappiness." She avoided people. It would seem that she had no map for understanding her life and social interaction except for her learned set of habitually unpleasant feelings. We structured the treatment with multiple embedded metaphor and set a primary goal of attitudinal change to help her "divorce" the past, as she put it, and learn to socialize. In addition, we hoped to help her perceive, create, and find feelings of satisfaction and develop self-motivation necessary to take responsibility for her own life and use the constructive and self-improving behaviors we knew she had actually learned but was not using.

There were several early transactions in which we established rapport and our authority. Statements such as "you had a bad shake" were delivered as she jiggled in her chair, for instance. Earlier, the sentence, "Maybe if you filled me in I can help make a judgment about what would be useful," was designed to imply that we would judge what form of treatment to use. She had suggested that she needed to "find out" something about her past that would help her overcome her difficulties. While that attitude about treatment might please an insight-oriented analyst, it established Dorine as the expert for her treatment. An approach designed to uncover something in her past would only further involve her with obsessive digging into her past. This woman definitely needed to proceed with her present and future, as she stated later. The need to take control of the direction of therapy was handled by the indirect suggestion that we would make the judgment after she gave further information.

The diagnostic parameters can be summarized as follows:

1) Social network: She lives alone, argumentative.
2) Stage of family development: Age of courtship.
3) Development age: Latency years.
4) Resources: Directly available, good communication.
5) Flexibility and sensitivity:
    Perception—Quick to find faults and shortcomings of others (and self).
    Cognitive associations—Continued concern about how she is being gypped; she is blameless.
    Role behavior—critical, distant, rebellious.

6) Symptom function: Becoming independent through rebellion and ambivalence regarding dependency.

Therapeutic goals for the formation of metaphors include:

1) Attitude restructuring: Put the past behind her.
2) Age-appropriate intimacy: Learn to have "pals" and learn to take social responsibility as a prelude to courtship.
3) Social network changes: Develop friends and stop phobic avoidance of other people; replace the constant obsession with her family.
4) Behavior, emotion, and role demands: Implement the necessary skills to lose weight, "have" her real feelings.
5) Learning enjoyment: Find enjoyment from social encounters, recognize feelings of accomplishment in her own efforts.
6) Self-image enhancement: Improve body image, replace self-criticism with positive self-statements, consider herself worthy of having friendships.

We offer Figure 2 as an overview of the structure that is to follow.

Induction Begins

S: So, let me ask you to close your eyes. It might be interesting for you to realize you can rock back and forth (as she is doing) and become more relaxed with each twist, just finding a nice place to come to balance. You've told me a lot of things about yourself, a lot of things you've told me because you associate ideas in an idiosyncratic way. You've told me, for example, that you can wait, and wait and wait a long time. You waited until the end of this two-day period in order to be our client. C: And you learned something while you waited. S: I notice your eyes are fluttering so I wondered if you were wearing contacts. D: No, it's the light. S: Okay. You waited until the end of two days in order to get your time and how can you be certain that you'll get what you want, so that you don't get gypped again. C: There's no guarantee. S: You don't move, you don't talk, you don't have to do anything except let your unconscious mind take over. But can you really trust the unconscious mind of somebody?

The induction took advantage of the fact that Dorine had waited during two days of the therapy marathon before stepping forward to work. She may have been waiting in a manner that actually undermined her chances of getting what she wanted. However, we interpreted her waiting positively, stating that she was good at waiting. We also began a double meaning "play" on

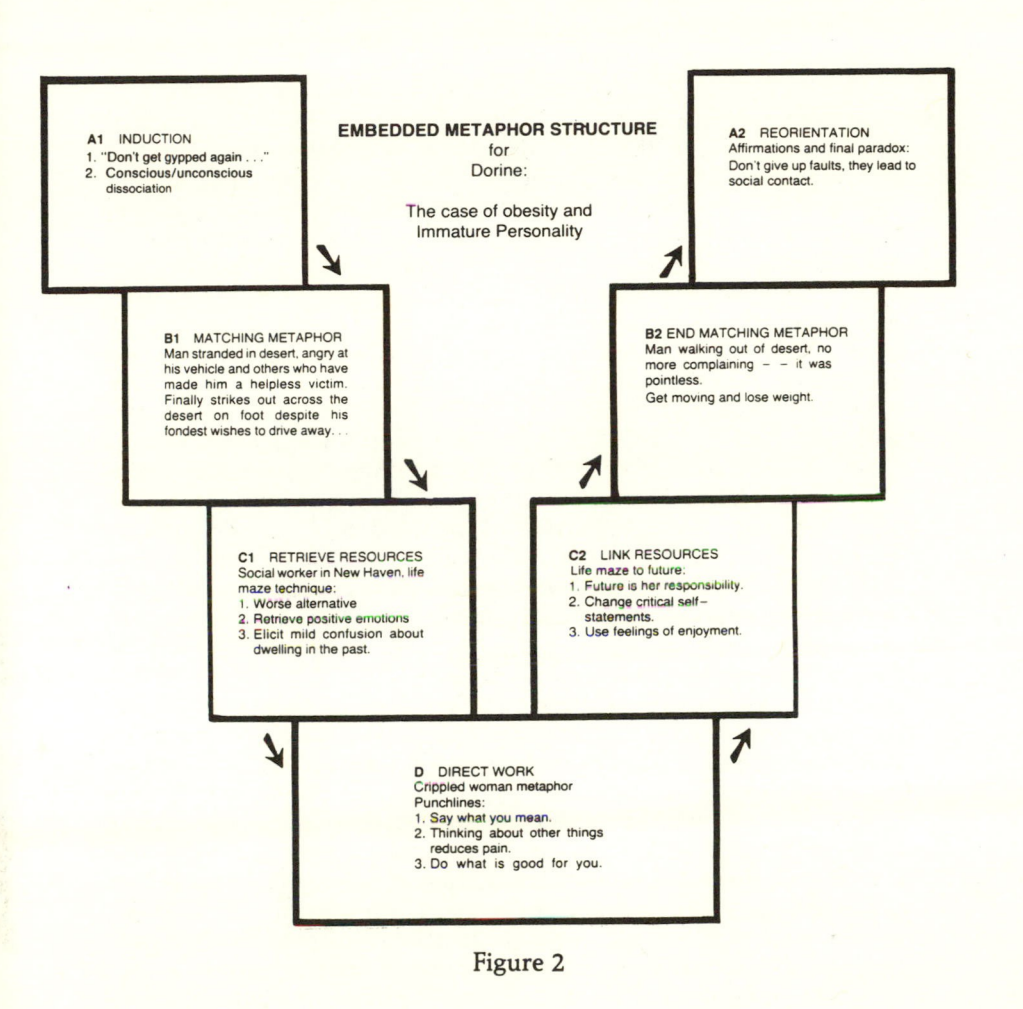

Figure 2

the word, wait (weight), which was continued. In this next section, we began to speak simultaneously to facilitate a rapid deepening of trance as the matching metaphor was begun.

Matching Metaphor Begins

C: It would be nice to return that faulty car, warrantied. S: I had a client who was stranded in the desert. He said the experience was like when you have a dream at night and there's nothing that seems to lay in front of you. It goes on and on like a vast wasteland and you have a sense of isolation and desperation that many people have dreamed about having nightmares of different kinds. I had heard that one before and I knew exactly what he was referring to. Being lost in the desert really was like what your dream predicted.

C: And when he was first lost in the desert, he was quite angry about his misfortune, his innocently finding himself stranded, a victim . . . S: Now your conscious mind listening to Carol's voice . . . C: . . . of his car, without warning, letting him down suddenly, unexpectedly. S: . . . making certain sense of one thing, different sense of another. C: It certainly wasn't fair in any sense of the word. S: . . . and just wondering . . . C: He had every right to be highly agitated. S: . . . wondering what her story leads to and how it can be usefully applied to yourself, in what way. C: He cursed, he stomped, he kicked the car . . . S: . . . while your unconscious mind has been dealing with a lot of things that you're not aware of . . . C: He made threats about what he was going to do to those S.O.B.s when he got that car back to the dealer.

S: And I have a sense of inclination . . . C: And he occupied his thoughts for some time . . . S: . . . that your conscious mind will leave the workshop . . . C: about the unfairness of the situation. S: . . . wondering what's been so fair about your experience here. C: Finally in desperation . . . S: . . . while your unconscious mind . . . C: . . . an inkling of understanding reached his conscious mind . . . S: . . . continues to flounder C: that cursing his misfortune was in no way bringing him closer to his goal . . . S: and wonders in its own way how to let Dorine in on the secret . . . C: . . . that he suddenly realized was all important . . . S: . . . that your unconscious knows and has learned . . . C: . . . the goal of survival . . . S: . . . but which you've overlooked consciously again and again. C: . . . despite whatever lack of fairness had come before. It didn't matter that he was innocently stranded through no fault of his own . . .

S: Your conscious mind thinking some of the things . . . C: . . . he was still stranded. S: . . . that you wish you had said to us so we would have more information . . . C: It certainly would have been nicer . . . S: . . . while at the same time realizing . . . C: . . . to just get back in the car . . . *S:* . . . time was running out. *C:* . . . switch it on . . . *S:* . . . and we had to proceed with such little information . . . *C:* . . . and proceed smoothly down the highway. *S:* . . . about such a big topic. *C:* That was a dream, wasn't gonna come true. He just had to forget that unreasonable dream.

The dual induction continued with Carol speaking to the visual-spatial, nondominant mind and Stephen speaking to the linear-logical, dominant mind. Since Dorine was strongly biased to continue her framework of conscious understanding, the conscious/unconscious dissociation statements from Stephen were designed to set up a polarity of thinking such that she could suspend her normal framework for the duration of the session. Speaking to her intermittently and simultaneously about different topics had the effect of further overriding her normal conscious framework.

The mystery metaphor of a man stranded by his car was begun as a match to her present situation. The man's situation was framed as one in which he was stuck "through no fault of his own" to further rapport and respect her conscious mind belief that she was innocent of any wrongdoings. Actually, she was responsible for her own life, as is everyone, but that message could wait until later in the session, after she was engaged in the process. The conscious and unconscious dissociation was continued throughout the imagery-full metaphor to establish readiness for additional indirect suggestions to come during the resource and linking stage.

Resource Metaphor Begins (C1)
as Matching Metaphor Continues Briefly

S: Now a client in New Haven, Connecticut was a social worker. She had had an abortion. *C:* He struck out across the desert on foot. *S:* She was very unhappy about her situation and very apparently guilty. I don't know about the logic or necessity of her guilt, . . . *C:* He hoped another car would come by. *S:* . . . but she did have it. And she was concerned in a very angry and bitter way that her husband didn't share the same guilt that she had. *C:* No car came by. He trudged on and on, conserving his energy.

S: She explained to me in no uncertain fashion the expectations from her childhood and they certainly didn't include her abortion. *C:* He saw a sign indicating the next city was at least 75 miles down that dusty, desolate highway. *S:* But she had felt guilty about her father's situation throughout her own life, feeling guilty about her father . . . *C:* He thought about a lot of things walking down that road. *S:* . . . trying to change her ways so that her father would be able to make adjustments that he needs to make in life.

In the second paragraph reference was made to this other client's childhood expectations and a special, albeit troublesome, relationship with her father. This metaphoric reference allowed Dorine to have the associated experience but avoid the usual associations and meanings that she might attach to these psychological issues.

S: And you know how a child can misconstrue, how hard they can work to help a parent overcome a difficulty. Out of the kindness of the child's heart, you undertake a path that you think will bring the most peace and harmony to the majority of people. C: It was no wonder that she had grown up and chosen the occupation that she chose.

S: And so I used hypnosis and told her to find the depth of trance that you deem appropriate for a solution that you want and allow yourself to go a bit deeper as I tell direct instructions for the sake of being straightforward. I'd like you to imagine yourself in front of three doors and I don't care where we are. It isn't important. We could be all alone or you could refuse to go into trance because you need to hold on to something. C: You could hold on to that security but curious about how your experience could be altered by following that directive.

In the first of the two preceding paragraphs Dorine was indicated by inference. We stated that any child can be expected to acquire problems in the course of growing up because the child will "misconstrue" and "try hard" to overcome the difficulties of his or her parents. This acquisition of problems by a child, we said, was due to "the kindness of the child's heart." In that way we reframed her interest in the past as something innocent and kind. This framework would contrast the negative one she probably had acquired as a "troublemaker," "problem child," "kid with a chip on her shoulder," and so on. This new framework would put an end to her obsessing about the past in an attempt to figure out that she was blameless for her difficulties. It would suspend her usual defensiveness and "buy us some time" for therapy.

The second paragraph included trance maintenance suggestions, such as "find the depth of trance that you deem appropriate for a solution that you want." Even trance deepening suggestions were metaphorically phrased so that she had an opportunity to follow the directives but not following them could not be construed as resistance. Also, because our wording created a situation in which she could not be considered resistant if she did not deepen the trance, she was in a position that could only increase rapport. That is, if she deepened trance we gained rapport. And, if believing we wanted her to deepen trance, she resisted the suggestion, then she would also have to admit that we hadn't really asked her to deepen *her* trance. We had created an arrangement in which we could not "think badly" about her choice; therefore, rapport was increased. The paradoxical logic in the suggestion to deepen trance came after the reframing mentioned above—that a child is motivated "out of kindness" and the wish to help others.

At that point a set of interventions we call "life mazes" was begun in an attempt to help her do several things to change her attitude: 1) confuse her normal associations to the hardships of the past; 2) provide a worse alternative than the ones she has considered; 3) sensitize her to pleasant emotions she has learned from the past; and 4) prepare her, with a confusion technique, to "divorce" from the past, as she has requested.

S: Holding on to the sound of my voice, refusing to surrender that grip, and your conscious mind can picture the doors in front of you while you follow the directions with unconscious associations to your experience, or your unconscious mind can imagine you in front of the three doors while your conscious mind participates in having the experience as we speak. C: But standing in front of the three doors, one of them represents the past the way it really happened, one represents the past the way you'd like to have had it happen, and one of them represents the past much worse than it ever happened. And take just a moment to glance at those three situations with your conscious mind.

S: Now which one do you suppose she would walk through if she were given a choice? You might think you have an answer consciously. C: You'd certainly think you'd like to go through that door that promises the past as you wish it had happened . . . S: But I'd like to prove to your unconscious something you hadn't thought about so let's first go through the door marked "The Past The Way It Really Happened."

C: So as you walk through that door . . . S: Take one stepping stone at a time, just glancing around, one year for each stepping stone . . . C: Glance to the scenes on the right and on the left and ahead . . . S: Now being a social worker interested in what we were doing as therapists, she readily followed the instructions, temporarily suspending her intense feeling of guilt, stepping on one stepping stone and then another, walking forward into the past . . .

C: Just surveying the way that past unfolded then, noticing all the unpleasant things that she saw around her . . . S: And all the pleasant ones. C: Wondering, marveling how it did look different somehow than when it happened. S: And now without turning around, you've taken enough steps for the time being. Walk backwards into the present, taking a step back . . . S: to the present . . . C: Back out and close the door.

In the previous paragraphs we directed Dorine into her past. As we spoke she exhibited ideomotor behavior which was sufficient to guide our imagery

and speed of delivery. Such suggestions as "notice all the unpleasant things
that she saw" and "and all the pleasant ones" presupposed that she had pleasant experiences even in her real past. The opportunity to help her notice the
unpleasant first and then the pleasant was designed to appeal to her tendency
to notice and complain about her past. We had therefore prepared her to enter into the other doors, all the while following the metaphor of the New
Haven client.

S: Stand in front of the three doors again. Now this time, walk through the
door marked . . . *C:* "Much Worse Than What Really Happened."
Open that door, possibly with trepidation, step on the first stone tentatively and *see* the past much worse than it really happened, worse in
every way. *S:* The worst thing you can imagine and take another step.
She found it so possible to imagine the worst could happen that she
didn't want to take another step but we asked her to take one more step
and then another. *C:* She was surprised to discover that step after step
she could continue to imagine things . . . *S:* . . . and another . . . *C:*
. . . even worse than her own situation had been.
S: . . . and another . . . *C:* . . . a situation she had previously thought
the worst. *S:* Since she was speaking to us in the trance she begged us to
not have her walk any further into that. We had her take another step,
and then another . . . *C:* . . . and imagine how that life would have
felt. *S:* . . . and another and another. And now stepping backwards, to
be certain to step back out of the door marked "Worst Possible Past"
take one step at a time as quickly as possible and walk back to the hallway.

Asking Dorine to walk through a door that represented a past much worse
than what really happened was a maneuver similar to that which Erickson
called giving a worse alternative. That is, if she thought her past was terrible,
it could have been even more so. Suggesting that she imagine how that life
would have felt told her two things by implication: She would not really feel
it being worse, and what she *did* feel was not as bad as it might have been. In
conclusion, her life "was not so bad."

C: Shut that door with relief and turn away from it and toward the doorway marked . . . *S:* "Best Possible Past," *C:* the way you wish it had
been. *S:* And walk in there one step at a time and we're going to force
you to walk down those steps as well, one stepping stone and then another and another . . . *C:* . . . picturing all those details . . . *S:*
. . . learning some of those things Dorine would learn had that past been
the past she lived . . . *C:* . . . experiencing some of that emotional ful-
fillment Dorine would have experienced had that past been real. *S:* I

would even suggest that you temporarily duck off the path and wait until you're met by a large dose of acceptance and love which is lurking somewhere along that path.

C: In fact, it's all over on the path, you could duck off at any given spot. S: Feel the heat in your face that comes from knowing that that dose of acceptance and love is there. You might as well, you've waited a long time to even imagine walking down that path. C: So revel in that path and those sidetrails, that dose of love, acceptance, satisfaction. Experience what it's like. S: Still moving on, step, another step and then another. C: And it's as if even the stars and moon shine upon that past with a special favor, idyllic, fairytale-like setting. And you wish you could stay there forever, grow up there and emerge on the other side of childhood completely equipped in every way. S: And we instructed the social worker to walk backwards one step at a time, back into the present backing out until you face the door once again, closing it.

Directing her to walk through the door representing the best possible past was a way to advantageously follow up on the challenge to her customary framework just established with the use of the worst possible alternative. We asked her to find a sense of satisfaction and elaborate it. She had the fantasy or the map for such satisfaction. In fact, it was represented as everything which she felt had been unfairly withheld. The metaphoric framework provided a means for her to accept good feelings without surrendering her usual conscious bias about her life history. Noticing the change in her skin color allowed us to use the sense of heat in her face as a minor erotic experience. We built upon that minor alteration to help her focus awareness on her body in a pleasant way. Thus, the resources we helped her retrieve immediately fulfilled her explicit desire to find enjoyment.

She needed a better self-image, a much improved body image, and the ability to find satisfaction in social encounters. In order to achieve this she needed a map of social encounters and her own achievements that would allow her to associate to and then notice pleasant feelings. Her desires to find immediate satisfaction would generate an increased sensitivity to pleasant sensations which, later in the therapy, could be directed to enhance her body image and self-image. First, though, she needed to permanently "divorce" herself from the past which she had been compulsively rehashing for too long.

S: And three doors in front of you. You might think three doors and three journeys. And she was wrong. We had her walk one more time into the door furthest on her left . . . C: . . . a fourth door she had previously failed to notice and this door was more special than all the rest.

S: Because with each step on each stepping stone she would shift in a zig-zag fashion between the pasts, so the first stepping stone to help you direct your journey, from the way it really happened, now step to the next stepping stone to advance yourself down the path and . . . C: . . . find yourself right in the middle of the worst imagined past. S: Take another step forward and find yourself in the best possible past . . . C: . . . the one most wished for. And another step again begins the process anew, and a second step . . .

S: . . . into the worst possible past, and now another step in the worst possible past and now a step the way it really happened. C: It's hard to tell which experience will be encountered with each new step. S: And now step the best possible way, another step in the best possible, another step and another year with the worst possible. C: . . . followed immediately by another step the way it really happened that year and another step of the best possible way that year could have happened. Now you're thoroughly lost in the past.

C: And it may be as if all the pasts are whirling around you, a mixture of all the different possibilities blurred with the real; it's hard to tell which is which anymore. S: Now make the world go in the other direction. (Pause.) C: Backing out of that door as well. S: And you do feel relaxed, do you not? You're sitting there comfortably. C: Even reviewing lost in the past . . . S: It's nice to know that, reviewing lost in the past, you can feel comfortable . . . C: . . . connected somehow to the present as you back out of that door . . . S: . . . knowing that you can always feel that comfort of lost in the past in the future.

That final door might have been labeled the "Confusing Past." In the previous paragraph two important points were explicitly mentioned as suggestions for Dorine to confirm. These were both in keeping with her expressed therapeutic goal. The first was ". . . it's hard to tell which is which anymore." In reference to her scrambled journey through the three doors she would most certainly have failed to compartmentalize her feelings as she rapidly switched stepping stones. The result of this failure would be a blending or a blurring of her feelings from the past and the fantasized past. In short, she would find herself with "pleasant" feelings while thinking about the "bad" past.

The second explicit statement concerned the meaning in the sentence "Even reviewing lost in the past . . . it's nice to know that, reviewing lost in past, you can feel comfortable. . . ." That conclusion was highlighted for her so that she could realize pleasant feelings if she should ever find herself lost in the memories of the past again. She wanted to be disengaged from her compulsive thinking about the past but it might happen that she would find herself thinking about the past again. She was well practiced at that. If she

did, she had established associative links to pleasant feelings via the mild confusion offered in those transactions. The therapy now turned to images and
experiences of the future.

C: And when you stand in front of those three doors again with all of them
   closed, this time turn around with your back to them and face your future because your conscious mind may have learned that regardless of
   which past you lived you have to live in the future the way you intend
   to. And it doesn't really matter which past was real, the same options
   are possible. S: While your unconscious knows all of the things you
   learned along the way are going to be of help to you or perhaps your unconscious mind is aware of regardless which past you lived your future
   still lies ahead of you and your conscious mind can be aware instead of
   the many things you learned along life's highway that could be of use to
   you. C: And you can certainly equip yourself with those accom-
   paniments to the journey.

A directive for shaping Dorine's future framework was stated as:
". . . your conscious mind may have learned that regardless of which past
you lived you have to live in the future the way you intend to." That indirect
suggestion would serve to secure and link the newly established framework
that included heightened experiences of comfort, confusion, and memories of
various episodes from the past. She had learned to recognize some feelings of
pleasure, thus satisfying her positive motivation. She also could experience
the pleasure regardless of the type of past memory she might rehash.

The act of rehashing the past would have no true purpose for her if she
could find an acceptable set of positive experiences elsewhere. The sense of
satisfaction was, then, a deterrent or obstacle to the continued pathological
obsession with the past. In addition to the deterrent effect created by satisfying the deficiency-based need, the experience of confusion linked to the
judgmental examining of the past was expected to further assist Dorine in
achieving her goal of putting the past behind her.

The resource metaphor had been completed. One important fact in this
case was that Dorine knew a good deal about proper eating, grooming, exercise, and self-care. She knew enough to survive college and employment, but
she was not using her knowledge. Understandably, she might have been im-
paired with regard to using her self-care and survival skills due to the compulsive and bitter rehashing of the past and the sense of deprivation that she had
experienced both consciously and unconsciously prior to the therapy. Nonetheless, she was learning to have sensitivity to her feelings of pleasure, to separate from the past, and to do so without surrendering her belief that she had

been dealt with unfairly in the past. Part of her motivation was being squandered on complaining, waiting, "weighting." She needed to reinstitute any positive, albeit dormant, motivational mechanisms she had learned and stored away. The direct work metaphorically addressed that issue.

Direct Work

S: I worked with an old woman one time in Jackson, Michigan. All she could do all day long was complain about the pain that she had in that hip. C: It didn't occur to her to think about any of the pleasant associations from her past and why should she? S: She had lost contact with her friends, her husband. C: She was retired from any useful life. S: Even her daughter thought she was malingering. And for some reason or another, I don't know just what, she had come to concentrate only on the miseries of that pain and that hip.

C: Because when she thought about anything else her conscious mind was flooded with an awareness that no one really cared about her. S: She didn't have much money but she asked to see me for a session with hypnosis. I showed up and I told her I'd like her to write a check for $3,000 which would be covering the sessions I'd be seeing her for during the following year. She'd think it over and leave a check for me the next session if that's what she chose to do.

S: And then I asked her to tell me what she wanted to change. She proceeded to tell me about all her misery and pain. "Now you don't want help with the misery and the pain," I said. "You want help with living your life fully and happily." C: "It would certainly behoove you to say what you mean." S: "I can't read your mind. If you don't tell me I won't know." She agreed to tell me what she meant.

"Punchline" instructions to a client are best delivered in the vortex of the multiple embedded metaphor. We created the context with a true story about a suspicious client who developed strong feelings of trust. Lines such as, "You don't want help with the misery and the pain . . . ," and "It would certainly behoove you to say what you mean," were indirect suggestions (implication and open-ended types) to reinforce learnings from the preceding resource metaphor.

S: Then I told her to go inside and talk inside your own head and tell that pain to go away and she did. She said, "The pain is still there." I thanked her for following my instruction and greeted the difficulty she had as an adversary worthy of my time. We sat down, then instructed her to follow the instructions carefully or it would be the last time she would ever see us. *C:* She was to make a graph of her misery on a one to eleven scale and look at that graph each day, each number; one, two, three, four, five, six, seven, eight, nine, ten, eleven—where is the pain today—and mark her misery down.

We told Dorine in metaphor to follow the instructions carefully or it would be the last time she would ever see us. In fact, for Dorine, it would be the last time she would ever see us. So she was presented with a bind: If she followed instructions she would not see us again, and if she did not follow the useful suggestions she would not see us again. Therefore, following or not following instructions could not be the basis for a relationship with us. This bind essentially defused any resistance to helping herself she might have had due to learned noncompliance based on manipulation.

The following interaction was designed to place her symptom in a different framework. The meaning of the client's behavior in the metaphor was similar to Dorine's actual situation, but the rules which dictated how change might happen to that client (a visually graphed description of pain) were different from the rules that would apply to Dorine's complaining and avoiding. Therefore, Dorine could metaphorically imagine a change in her situation and in imagining learn something about her own responsibility for using her life.

C: She was to chart it very accurately with precision. Don't be sloppy. *S:* And the last day that you keep track will be the last day that you ever see us. Now I knew something that you know from listening to me, that she wasn't going to let her misery stay at eleven on an eleven point scale. Anyone in their right mind would at least try to resolve it down to a ten. So I waited to find out how long it would take her to follow instructions given that were in her best interest.

S: I didn't know anything about this client except that during the next session I showed up and she had a check on the table for $3,000. I picked it up and Carol and I immediately launched into a pre-rehearsed role-play. I tore up the check, threw it at her, while Carol said one side of the argument and I said the other. *C:* We took the position that one of us thought she was so stupid and so gullible that she would pay money to a stranger . . . *S:* while the other was surprised that she would do it because they thought she had more sense than that. And we played that drama out in front of her. *C:* She didn't like either option. She didn't like to be considered stupid. *S:* But she could hear that behind our words we had torn up her check and we advised her never to trust somebody that you don't know anything about with $3,000 of your money.

By entering a dramatic surprise into the story, we offered Dorine another paradox. We had been unacceptably rude to the older woman but at the same time deeply honest. Being honest, we had admonished her to "never trust somebody that you don't know." We were, therefore, trustworthy because we did not want her trust. This paradox provided us a rapid means to thoroughly engage this client's attention and gain her trust via contradiction: Trust me when I tell you not to trust anyone. She was thus encouraged to decide for herself whether she could trust us. Leaving that decision to her demonstrated the most respect for her and therefore made us potentially trustworthy.

S: And I watched that graph begin to change over the days we worked with her in hypnosis and the only change it made was the straight line stayed eleven, each day eleven, eleven, eleven. C: Finally on the sixth session she called and said, 'My pain—it's suddenly diminished. I wasn't even aware of it today.'I said, 'That's right, you've been thinking about other things. You haven't been aware of your difficulty."

S: She said she was going to practice the things and the next time we saw her the pain was back to eleven. C: The next time it had fallen to a six and risen back to eleven. This happened three times . . . S: . . . and I knew the reason but I waited until three times of its occurrence and then I asked her straight out, "Why don't you follow the directives that are good for you, that reduce your difficulty?" We let her think about that a long time.

C: She was an honest woman. She didn't have an appropriate answer. S: She said, "Well, when I see you I follow the directives and when you're gone I stop."

S: "Let me get this straight," I said. "When I'm here and tell you things to do and you find them to be helpful you follow them and your pain diminishes. Is that true?" She said it was. C: "But you fail to continue to use that same thing that works in our absence even though you know it will work?" S: "That's right," she said.

In the first paragraph of this series we ratified the notion that Dorine could notice pleasant feelings and continued the conscious/unconscious dichotomy. We implied, by strong presupposition, that she was not using herself to solve her difficulties: "Why don't you follow the directives that are good for you, that reduce your difficulty?" This was asked metaphorically, reducing any possibility that she would be offended by the implication. However, it was clearly conveyed to her that we are aware of such passivity in our clients.

S: Now I didn't know how I was going to tell her so I said to her, "If Milton Erickson was here, he's about the same age as you are, and he'd probably tell you that you're a damn fool for not doing the things that make you feel better." *C:* "Of course we wouldn't tell you that because you're our elder and we respect your age and your status. We'd never say anything like that to you." *S:* "Erickson would tell you how disappointed he was and how growing up on a farm he dealt with plenty of stubborn animals on the farm . . . *C:* ". . . and he might even make a comparison between one of those stubborn farm animals and you."

The first decisive punchline was delivered when we stated: "You're a damn fool for not doing the things that make you feel better." One thing anyone is likely to avoid is acting like a "fool" with knowledge about doing so. By way of that metaphor she could become aware of the possibility of being considered similarly, while still "saving face." We had established ourselves as trustworthy and credible witnesses of a malingering client's behavior. Our opinions about foolish behavior would matter to her at this point because of those experiences which had been previously retrieved. And the punchline had power because it implied the use of those resources and decisive action within the altered metaphoric framework.

S: "I don't know how you're going to get the message because I wouldn't be willing to tell you. I know Erickson would tell you but I wouldn't because I respect my elders and I'm not in a position to mention to you. He's worked with people before who've refused to change after they got what they needed and he's told them they are a disgusting example of the trust that somebody can put in the human race."

C: "Anybody can just complain about everything all of the time. It doesn't take any special talent to do that. I've heard him tell people they were fools straight to their face and I know that he would say something like that to you but I'm not going to. It's not my job and I haven't any right. So I don't know how you'll get the message."

S: Now that's all we did and the next time we saw her the graph was at six, the next time five, the next time four, the next time three and then it got further down to one until finally her pain was gone and at zero. *C:* And she owed that reduction to nobody but herself; the joy of being responsible for your own support is not something to be taken lightly but cultivated.

The next punchline was contained in the folk wisdom that "Anybody can just complain about everything all of the time. It doesn't take any special talent to do that." Dorine was a woman who thought she had special talent. The point was well taken and, in the context of failing at personal improvement, the decision to "do her best" was really in her own hands.

In the paragraph that followed, Dorine was reminded that she would get all the credit for her success. No one would deprive her of the ultimate credit: "And she owed that reduction to nobody but herself." Her dilemma was reframed by the interpretation that being responsible for her own support was a privilege to enjoy (as opposed to her earlier notion that it was an unwelcome burden). Ambiguity in the words "reduction" and "lightly cultivated" in that sentence refer, of course, to her weight problem. The direct work phase was finished with the point of the attitudinal restructuring remaining: She knew how to reduce her weight and adjust her eating habits—to not use her knowledge was foolish.

Linking Resources

S: Now walking into that future was another matter. I asked her to stay on the stool. She was crying some tears that had to do with the feeling she had felt while she was reviewing her past. I told her to imagine a river and she was on a high chair in a river and I had put her there. She was very uncomfortable with her position so I pointed out if you want to be mad at somebody to explain your fate, don't be mad at yourself, don't be mad at your parents, be mad at me. I'm the one who's put you in this predicament right now.

C: And you certainly needn't waste time being mad at the river because it's going to flow regardless of your ranting and raving at it. S: And I'd like you to feel very angry with us, just really stew on that, stuck on that stool in the middle of the river because you can't get off. And then I asked her to go ahead down the pathway through the door of the future, leave her anger behind her outside the door surrounding us like a river . . .

C: But going into the door of the future requires a very special process and you can only back into that door. It would be unwise for a magician to let a person look directly into the future but you can back into the future taking one step at a time and noticing the results of the behavior you're going to do in the future. S: So take a step and look about you and notice what's in your rear view mirror as you proceed into the future. C: Look where you've come from . . . S: . . . noticing whether you like the results of what you're getting, doing, C: noticing how you've gotten there, not really sure where you're going . . . S: . . . and how you've behaved to get those results that you like so well. Because the real learning of backing yourself carefully into the future is not to find out what you accomplished in the future.

C: The future hasn't been created but, as you've anticipated, the real learning is to find out how you're using yourself to accomplish those things, even those things you accomplished by accident that didn't turn out the way you wanted such as falling down. S: You can learn something about that mistake because the way you did it will probably work again. *C:* And why waste time trying to prevent the occurrence of a certain future.

S: And a person who talks about himself all day long with derogatory comments feels bad. So he doesn't need to stop talking about himself. *C:* He can just make pleasant comments instead. The same process that worked so well for him to feel like a dog will work very well to make him feel like a king.

Details of behavioral options were discussed to help Dorine satisfy role demands related to desired therapeutic outcomes. She needed to generate both perceptual and behavioral changes in accordance with her stated goal of separating from the past. First, her attention, within the metaphoric frame, was focused on the interpersonal relationship and her preexisting anger with the paradoxical prescription that she continue her anger and direct it at us.

The three paragraphs which followed then detailed metaphoric prescriptions regarding her taking responsibility for her behavior. Several notable examples are: "It would be unwise for a magician to let a person look directly into the future but you can back into the future taking one step at a time and noticing the results of the behavior you're going to do in the future." "Look where you've come from . . . noticing whether you like the results of what you're getting, doing," ". . . noticing how you've gotten there, not really sure where you're going . . . ," ". . . and how you've behaved to get those results that you like so well."

C: That's certainly what that man discovered as he walked down that road. *S:* And so each step you walk down the path of the past noticing good or bad can be a learning for you to learn not what the future holds but how you're going to use yourself in the future. So take another step and another and be sure to remember that it's appropriate to feel a sense of satisfaction before and during accomplishment of a task. You've accomplished tasks before.

The experience has been created, again in much detail, that she can stop her inner dialogues and negative feelings so that she can feel the pleasantness of life's experiences. The alteration was paradoxical. She was encouraged not to stop the thinking and feeling processes that predictably make her feel bad, but to continue them and make herself feel pleasant with the process instead. The closing remark for this section was another behavioral role detail to help Dorine adjust her social role in her immediate daily social network—to feel satisfaction before completing the task at hand.

End of Matching Metaphor

The previous transition paragraph brought the linking of resources to a relative conclusion. Frame continuance required that earlier stories be finished and related to the framework into which they had been embedded. We shifted from linking the resources to her immediate social situation to the opening story of the man who had been stranded. As we shifted, suggestions to use resources in immediate social situations became open-ended suggestions to focus awareness on accomplishments and responsibility in the distant future.

C: And walking down that dusty desert highway, the man had long since ceased to blame and whine and kick and complain. He had experienced a time of silence during which he let his mind rest, only concentrating on the sight of his feet moving, one in front of the other. S: That was all that made sense. There was no one there to even hear his complaints.

S: First one step and then another. And just like the process of losing weight you lose an ounce first and then a second ounce and then another ounce, one small step at a time. C: And every time you lose an ounce of weight you gain a step of progress . . .

S: And I think it would be an interesting idea for you to lose that weight and with every ounce just know that you've said goodbye to a little bit of hate you've been dragging along with you . . . C: . . . a little bit of bitterness. S: The more weight you lose the more hate you say goodbye to . . . C: . . . until one day you wake up and find no hate left. S: And the best way to hate those people in the past is to lose all the weight, all the burdens that they've made you carry around. C: You might wonder what you'll do with no hate and no burden left to carry.

S: And you can tell by looking at what you'll accomplish as you walk another step into the future, backwards. (Pause.) And then I walked her forward into the past, through the door in the hallway, the river was gone. C: The river is never in the same place twice.

S: She liked what happened in the future. C: She had had a learning about the past and I don't know whether or not her conscious mind paid attention to the past while her unconscious mind took care of her future, S: or whether her conscious mind paid attention to the future while her unconscious mind was interested in her past, but I do know that she came out of trance on that chair, left the office and two weeks later she changed professions.

Reorienting Begins

This section emphasized several matters of general interest: following only useful suggestions, being selective about choosing a hypnotist, the uniqueness of the individual, and protecting oneself from hurt. These aspects were typically emphasized by Erickson and were mentioned here in accordance with the general guidelines of the treatment principles. Giving control to clients and treating them with respect throughout the relationship is crucial to success with Ericksonian techniques because the client is really in control of making it all work.

The success of a session depends upon the client's interpretation of the framework elaborated by the therapist and that interpretation is often significantly influenced by the "wrap-up" and termination of the trance. A positive ending of the session can strengthen a client's willingness to relinquish the rigid bounds of that framework initially brought to therapy.

C: While we've been talking you've been thinking about a lot of things, seeing a lot of things . . . S: And I hope that you'll have a sense that even though you waited until the end the wait was something worth your while. C: The end was the best because of all the things you learned waiting. You know how to wait and I think you've waited long enough for all the things.

S: I want to remind you and everyone that you should only allow yourself to be hypnotized by people you trust. You took good care of yourself checking us out two days and you should only allow yourself to receive suggestions from people when the suggestions are in your best interest, leaving behind all of those which you intuitively understand to be detrimental for your own growth and development. I want to remind you and everyone that no matter what kind of overlay of difficulty or neurosis that they've received in childhood and growing up . . . C: . . . the core of the personality is still intact and is healthy like the center of that sculpture, unable to be harmed by any influence from the outside.

S: And you and others have gone in trance. You should realize that each of you are as unique as your fingerprint. There will never be another one like you in all the world. C: You can never change that, you can never change your fingerprint. S: And of course your fingerprint has a right to be here and you have a right to be here. And I want to remind you and others to take your bad feelings and, as Dr. Erickson said, rush, don't walk . . . C: to the nearest garbage pail and throw them all in. And take care to secure the lid.

S: When he found out how my father had said something to me and had criticized my behavior, he suggested he would have said, 'Don't you think you're underrating how bad I really was?" And you had a slight smile when you thought about that. So I'd like to remind you and others that you use other people for your feelings. You're entitled to all of your feelings but you shouldn't let other people hurt your feelings.

C: You're entitled to all of your faults. You may just need those faults in understanding, accepting the faults of those you interact with . . . S: So don't ever give up any of your faults. You're going to need them to

understand others. The more faults you have . . . C: . . . the more understanding you can be . . . S: . . . or the more others you can know.

The paradoxical bind in the last paragraph exemplifies the role paradox
can play as a final intervention in a therapy session. The bind related to her
interaction with others. She had trained herself to notice the faults of herself
and others, and to use her awareness of them as a way to rationalize avoiding
social contact. The bind prescribed noticing faults! She could notice her faults
as an equalizing quality. If lowered self-worth kept her from social interaction she was instructed that her faults were a way to understand others,
rather than a way to project and blame. If she did increasingly take responsibility for her improvement, use the feelings of pleasure learned in the trance,
orient herself toward the future, and divorce the past, she would notice her
pride and not her faults. In that event she would lose her self-image barrier to
social interaction. In either case she would become more able to socialize and
enter a social network.

Reorientation subsequently continued rapidly and terminated with mutual laughter.

C: We're going to count now back to 20 in twos and threes and fives
. . . S: . . . sevens, nines, elevens . . . C: fifteens and twenty-one. That's
an unexpected number to arrive at. It's good to end on a surprise.
S: It's nice to know that you've ended up further than you intended
to go, isn't it? So just open your eyes and return. It was enjoyable,
Dorine. D: That was a nice trick, I liked that. C: Which trick? D:
21. S: And I think everyone should awaken before they leave. And even
if you only halfway awaken and part of you remains here in the workshop as you leave, do be aware that that's simply a signal to you that
you have different feelings now and you've changed the way you feel.
C: If you felt the same way now as you did when you came in, you
wouldn't have changed the way you felt at all. S: So I hope that you
continue to feel differently all the way home and have a nice evening to-
night, making up your mind what you want to do. C: Just like the river
never stays in the same place. S: Have a refreshing nap and wake up to-
morrow . . .

A CASE OF PELVIC PAIN

This case, as mentioned earlier, is in striking contrast to the previous one
because of the specific, unrelenting pain that was the entire symptom. This
client ("Rose") had a healthy and adequate social network, and had previously had a self-concept which facilitated an easy, and graceful social interaction. Goals were to:

1) Elicit and frame necessary safeguards.
2) Use age regression to amplify her memory of delightful walking as a baby.
3) Associate the first signal of pain (framed as positive) to the feeling of delight in walking.
4) Posthypnotically design the changes to extend indefinitely.

Figure 3 provides an overview and outline of the treatment plan used to achieve these goals.

During the induction phase, Rose was oriented to hypnosis by casual conversations. Fixation and conscious/unconscious dissociation were used. Arm levitation was begun so that possible parallels between the behavior of her

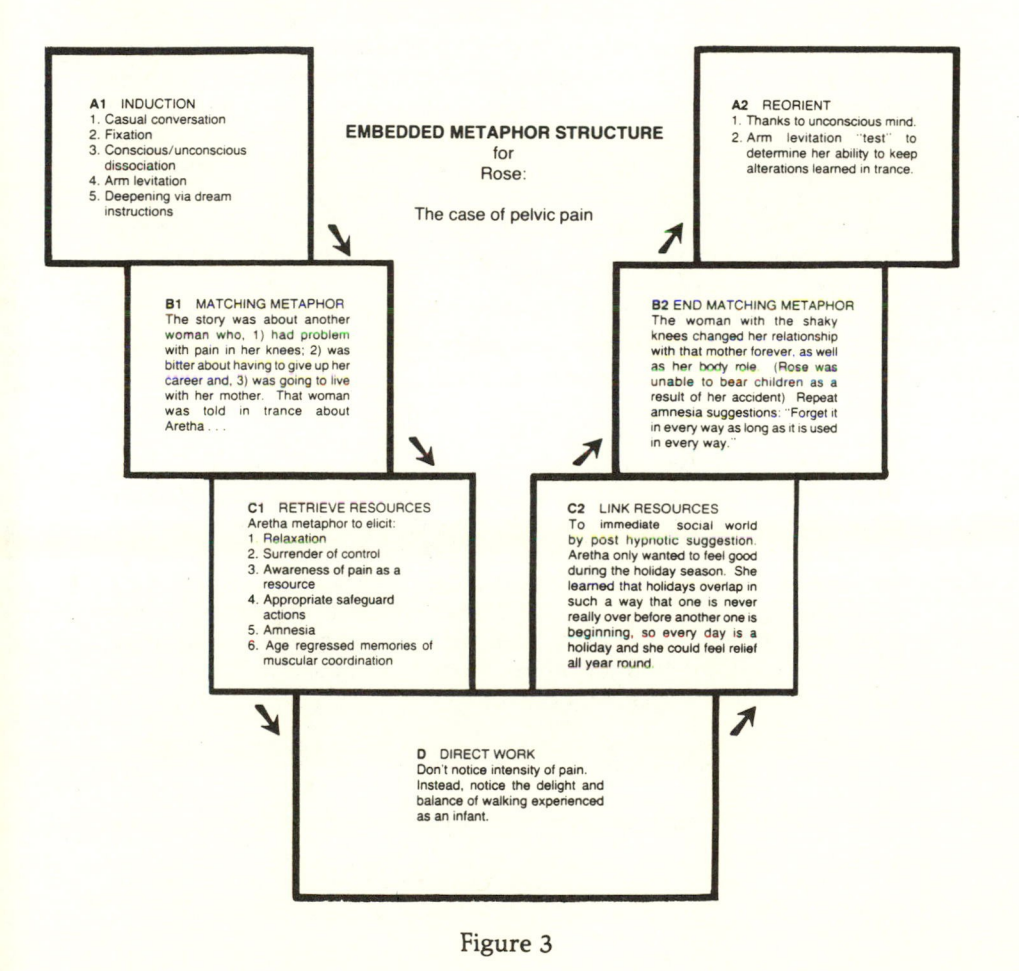

A1 INDUCTION
1. Casual conversation
2. Fixation
3. Conscious/unconscious dissociation
4. Arm levitation
5. Deepening via dream instructions

EMBEDDED METAPHOR STRUCTURE
for
Rose:

The case of pelvic pain

A2 REORIENT
1. Thanks to unconscious mind.
2. Arm levitation "test" to determine her ability to keep alterations learned in trance.

B1 MATCHING METAPHOR
The story was about another woman who, 1) had problem with pain in her knees; 2) was bitter about having to give up her career and, 3) was going to live with her mother. That woman was told in trance about Aretha . . .

B2 END MATCHING METAPHOR
The woman with the shaky knees changed her relationship with that mother forever, as well as her body role. (Rose was unable to bear children as a result of her accident) Repeat amnesia suggestions: "Forget it in every way as long as it is used in every way."

C1 RETRIEVE RESOURCES
Aretha metaphor to elicit:
1. Relaxation
2. Surrender of control
3. Awareness of pain as a resource
4. Appropriate safeguard actions
5. Amnesia
6. Age regressed memories of muscular coordination

C2 LINK RESOURCES
To immediate social world by post hypnotic suggestion. Aretha only wanted to feel good during the holiday season. She learned that holidays overlap in such a way that one is never really over before another one is beginning, so every day is a holiday and she could feel relief all year round.

D DIRECT WORK
Don't notice intensity of pain. Instead, notice the delight and balance of walking experienced as an infant.

Figure 3

arm levitation and her learning the therapeutic goals might later be reinforced.

Finally, deepening was effected with a technique learned from Erickson and slightly modified. The task of dreaming was suggested and anxiety regarding revealing the content of the dream was set up as well. When she had finally completed her dream she was told to forget it until some appropriate time and her task of speaking was dismissed; so, too, was her anxiety about revealing something against her will. The result, as was the case in similar situations with Erickson, was a deepening of trance and increased trust.

Induction

S: Do you go into trance yourself? R: I haven't for a little while. S: Some people go into trance with their eyes open and sometimes with their eyes closed. But you might start by picking some one spot that you stare at and then I want to say just a few general things about hypnosis. I know you already know a great deal about it. The one thing you probably know is that you hypnotize yourself from the suggestions and ideas that I might present. So I'm going to want to present some ideas to you that are relevant to your general concern. You didn't mention what your general concern was. Before you go any further into trance, can you say a few words about that?

R: Umm. Yes, I get . . . I have some referred pain from my hip which I get in my knee quite frequently. It's usually sort of a nagging toothache-kind of pain.

Fixation

S: That's right and just going back to that spot for a moment . . . that's right . . . and just go as deeply into trance as you think you want or may want to go into. . . . The more relaxed you become, the more deeply you go into trance. It's learning to become familiar with yourself at another level of being. . . . Now you're relaxed comfortably in the chair, quite nicely. Your efforts at clearing your mind or concentrating your mind or doing both of those things, one or the other or perhaps neither, is your own personal concern.

Conscious/Unconscious Dissociation

S: Often a client will want to know what to think about and how to think about it. But there is a certain kind of silence that you want. And when I say silence, your conscious mind associates to your own personal understanding, and it's a matter of little consequence that your conscious mind is aware of some of those. So I'd like you to just relax nicely. Go as deeply into trance as you think you want or may want to deal with some small, perhaps deep problem.

Hypnosis should be a way of familiarizing yourself with your own potentials and your own functioning. You may concentrate your conscious mind on a pleasant childhood experience, a lilac bush that you were aware of. I can mention lilac bush and you'll think of some kind of a fragrant flower in your own life. If I mention college, you'd think of the college that was important to you, because my words are just stimuli for your own thinking. And do it in a private way. In fact, my words can turn into the sound of your own voice or a stranger's voice, the voice of a friend. And before we begin fully, I would like to use the opportunity to talk in general about some ways that people use to deepen their trance.

I think it would be quite appropriate if you could have a dream in your own mind. You have dreams at night. Your mind becomes quiet, brain wave activity changes. Eye scan activity changes. And you have a dream at night. Sometimes you don't know about it when you wake up.

Arm Levitation

S: While I've been talking, you've become more restful and your breathing is regular and deep. Your cheeks have flattened out. There is no need to move and there is no need to speak, unless you begin to notice that either your right or left hand is the one that has an impulse to raise up. Now I happen to think it's going to be your left hand., But I want to discuss that dream as your left hand begins to show those small jerky motions from the elbow and the wrist. It's rising up towards your face and will come to rest comfortably somewhere in the air, perhaps halfway, because the unconscious of the other person always meets me halfway, and it shouldn't meet me more than that.

Deepening

S: The dream that you should have by the time I reach the count of ten is a dream you'll be able to organize and have that dream which you can verbalize about your problem, but not until I say so. You'll have a dream beginning by the time I count ten, finished by the time I reach one. And you'll be able to verbalize it appropriately. But don't verbalize it until I tell you. And just going up an inch at a time, showing those nice jerky unconscious movements. And it's floating in the air. Your little finger occasionally feels the texture as it bumps the chair. 20, 19, 18, 17. It's cleared the chair. It's beginning to float. There's no need to mention metaphors about balloons tied to fingers. There's no need to think about air passing underneath your hand and holding it, because your unconscious has learned how to move your hand as if it was the hand of an infant unattached to the rest of your body. 16, 15, 14, 13, 12, 11, 10. And then you'll be able to begin that dream now, and I can speak to anyone I wish. 9, 8, 7.

I can speak to the part of you that really knows how to learn in a relaxed way. You've learned how to relax and raise your hand without your conscious functioning. 6, and that part can learn also how to benefit from past dreams. 5. While I'm speaking to her, she can continue to dream. Time can pass in two speeds. Time of your hand movement means something different from the part of Rose that learns from listening to words. 4. And perhaps you're observing your dream that Rose is having. Maybe you're able to notice a bit of the dream of your own mind. 3. You might be surprised. You are able to . . . have a slow dream instead of a fast dream . . . because you can have a dream at night in five minutes. It seems as if it lasted a lifetime. And more can be learned in the dream than you can possibly bring with you when you awaken. 2, 1. And now you might be in a position to verbalize about that dream but I want you to put it aside and forget about it until the more appropriate time. It's your dream and it's private.

Now I want you just to enjoy the relaxation. It can merge in with the comfort of the chair. You're relaxed, are you not? (Slight head nod.)

Begin Matching Metaphor Frame

A matching metaphor to capture attention begins in the following paragraph. It was a case story of another woman who also had a problem with pain, not quite as painful as Rose's problem but more debilitating. The story associated her to any possible experiences associated to secondary gains that might be occurring for Rose. It served a diagnostic purpose, and there were no indicators that secondary gains were perpetuating Rose's problem.

S: I saw a client in Atlanta, Georgia, who was living with her mother and she was 30 years old. She had been in an auto accident and injured her knees sometime five years prior. And she had also seen her sister killed in her auto accident sometime five years prior. And because of the damage done to her legs then, she had to abort her career being a physical therapist. At least that's what she thought then. Then she held in her mind a memory of those incidents. She went to work as a stenographer each day and she would listen to what the people would say on the dictaphones. As she heard the sounds running through her ears, her body knew appropriately how to do her job. It took very little effort to do that. And with the remaining mental energies she wasn't distracted by anything that happened around her. She concentrated instead on her bitterness and her anger for having to give up that career, and she went home and lived with her mother.

Depotentiate Secondary Gains

S: I used hypnosis to discover the true functioning of that symptom of those jittery legs. And then we watched a playback on the videotape. You could tell precisely the moment when the jittery legs stopped. But her conscious mind didn't understand the connection. She was infantilized by that woman. And that mother had her own reasons for making certain that her daughter wouldn't stand on her own two feet. And so how do you teach a daughter like that to stand up against a mother? Her unconscious knew how to and was leading her on that course quite well prior to the accident.

Begin Resource Development Metaphor:
Create Proper Learning Set—
Positive Frame, Necessary Depth, and Amnesia

Learning sets were established with the second story about a client named Aretha. This insured the resource of relaxation during the trance. The awareness of her pain could be reframed as a positive experience and used as a resource. That became the second goal. The third goal at this resource development stage was to present Rose with necessary safeguards to insure her physical well-being once the pain was removed. Finally, amnesia and age regression memories were developed as additional resources.

S: So in the trance I told her about the secretary that I had hypnotized in Michigan who had a hip pain which caused her to go to a chiropractor daily. A very able woman, very alert woman, very capable woman, who didn't want me to have control over her in hypnosis, very moral woman, a lady. In order to make certain that I had the proper control in hypnosis, I discussed with Aretha in great detail the life of a prostitute who had been my client, a woman who had low moral convictions, a woman who would do anything for money, a woman who would never surrender control to anyone. She wouldn't even let herself listen to something which was not relevant to what she wanted to accomplish for herself.

Change Symptom to Positive Framework

S: And than I told Aretha the prositute wouldn't surrender control to go into trance and Aretha went deeply into trance. And I asked her to find some small signal in the region of her hip, some small indication of the beginning of the pain before it built into an actual pain, and locate that in her mind or imagine it. And then I asked her to let me know about it when it was in her awareness consciously. Her unconscious mind was able to cooperate very readily and I thought she should be very grateful that whatever that pain was doing for her, it had done over all these years so well, although neither of us could speculate on just what that was.

Safeguards for Actions

S: But the pain in her hip was like a toothache. A toothache is something which alerts the owner that something needs to be done, and once you've taken yourself to the dentist you no longer need the toothache pain. So I asked Aretha to warn that feeling in her hip that she had taken action and would continue to take appropriate action. And would the pain be willing to obey and be forgotten about, provided that periodic checks are made, perhaps every three hours or maybe every six hours to be certain that no other course of action needs be taken.

And there was a different angle to that hip pain, something that she could know about from a dream she would have and she would be able to adjust her own balance, given the knowledge of that dream, and we moved ahead, with an understanding that her conscious mind didn't know how to perceive. But her conscious mind knows how to forget a lot of things.

Amnesia and Age Regression as Resources

S: You've forgotten about that sore toe that you had at the time that you stubbed it in the living room as a little girl. And you've forgotten about that thumb that got caught in the car door, or was it the kitchen door. And you can forget about that first indicator of the pain, providing you make a reasonable approach for six hours, or perhaps once a day, to send your awareness to that part of your body and find out if any other need is expressing itself.

You learned how to forget that bitter taste that you had in your mouth when you drank the wrong cup, even when you drank from the right cup and the milk was sour. You were able to forget that taste and you could immediately remember the smell of the lilac bushes. Maybe you've even forgotten about the muscular coordination that felt so wonderful as you were doing a backbend and cartwheel, and how amazed you were to find out that you can ride a bicycle, and that something inside of you knows how to keep your balance. So much so that while your feet move in automatic delightful comfortable fashion your mind is free to pay attention to the passing trees, to smell the fragrance in the air, to hear the sound of your friends calling your name down the road. The same thing is true of roller skating.

Direct Work:
Further Resource Development

For Rose, the direct work was to help her not notice the intensity of the pain. Since it is somewhat uncommon to target the direct work at the symptom or complaint presented by the client, this case stands out. Often, the core of the problem is conceptualized differently by therapist and client but the work at the vortex of the multiple embedding aims at the emotional core. Here, the lack of social complications allowed the client and the therapist to be in agreement about the nature of the difficulty.

The primary work centered around Rose's ability to age regress and recover memories of learning to walk and learning to do it automatically. She also retrieved the experience of delight that she had felt as a child when she realized she could walk at her own willful choosing. When that memory was recovered in the age regression, Rose actually blew a little childish bubble in the corner of her mouth. That ideomotor feedback was a signal to proceed with the confidence that she had, indeed, responded maximally to the stories and was making good use of the suggestions.

S: Your unconscious remembers how you learn to stand up. First, you find that you can support yourself with your hands, but you have to learn how to keep your knees in a particular degree of tension and flexion. Once the baby's mastered this, you fall over from the waist, and you soon learned that another learning is necessary. You use your hands to hold you from falling over at the waist until you learn to balance that chest and shoulders with a certain degree of muscular coordination in the abdomen, stomach. And then first with letting go of one hand and then letting go with another hand, the infant learns that it can move a foot. And what does that infant pay attention to? Only for a moment does it pay attention to that muscle movement. And it's soon automatic and comfortable and delightful to the child because the child can move closer to what it sees with its eyes. It can move closer to the mother or the father or the sister and the grandmother that smiles, saying, "Come here, darling."

And the infant is so delighted about its ability to get where it wants to go, that it can forget entirely about that automatic, smooth operation of the muscular system. Before it knows it, it lets go with both hands and is walking free. First one foot and then another. And then there is something else that the baby notices. The baby notices its shoes and socks and those memories are tied in, tied down, and they're never forgotten.

Link Resource Phase: Posthypnotic Linking
to Immediate Social Context

The five paragraphs of the resource linking phase return to the story of Aretha. The metaphor of establishing posthypnotic continuance for Aretha was used to suggest the same for Rose. The basic logic for posthypnotic continuance was that the client ought not have to suffer on holidays. When Rose accepted that we pointed out that every day could somehow be considered a holiday to somebody by associating her many images.

This type of linking addressed experiences from Rose's immediate concerns. Again, in this case, unlike the other two in this chapter, the client's immediate concerns conformed exactly to the therapy provided due to the straightforward simplicity of the symptom.

S: And Aretha only wanted to feel good during the holiday season. So I pointed out that she could feel no more pain for the remainder of the holiday season. And her chiropractor would forgive me. I promised to send other patients to the chiropractor to make up for losing this one.

But then I pointed out, that no sooner is Christmas over than New Year's celebrations begin. There's no reason to end New Year's so soon when Valentines Day is just around the corner and spring is soon to follow. And she didn't know that March 1st could be a holiday, and March 4th should be a holiday, too. Why not? The name March 4th makes such an interesting sound that every child could appreciate marching forth on March 4th. And March 4th is soon followed by March 21st and then there's Easter and that's a holiday.

And the delightfulness of Easter is really only a symbol that there are things to discover day after day hidden behind every nook and cranny. The child learns to discover the eggs at Easter time. And it's only a metaphor for discovering the cycle of life in every nook and cranny. So summertime hails a new holiday and everybody takes holiday vacations from school in the summer and every child knows that that's a holiday too. And what child doesn't prepare for fall and autumn is another holiday still.

And suspend those learnings even further, on into the holiday of Halloween. Halloween is scarcely over before the holiday of Thanksgiving, then Christmas starts up all over again. And so Aretha really learned a continual holiday in her life would be a very good way to continue that learning for the next year at least, and find out whether or not the following year would have this same dimension and the same holidays.

Sometimes new holidays are added, and as you get older, birthdays for political leaders. And Aretha found it easy to add those to the list.

When she thought about it she realized she could add the sick days from work to the list of holidays too.

End Original Metaphor Frame,
Repeat Amnesia Protection

Returning to the metaphor of the Atlanta client signaled the end of the resource linking phase. Even though there were not outstanding social problems in this case, the changes were linked to the broader social context, as is often done at this phase. It was done, however, only with brief reference to her changing family role—she was now unable to bear children. In the following paragraph, the lines, "It changed her relationship with that mother forever," and "She changed the way her body played a role in life," were references to link the ideas of motherhood and bearing children ("life") to the changes created in the accident and therapy.

Finally, amnesia suggestions were reinforced. The primary reason for amnesia was not so that she could forget the pain but so that her conscious mind would not interfere with the changes by coming to the realization that the delight in observing baby shoes seemed insignificant in contrast to the extraordinary pain she experienced.

S: And the woman in Atlanta, Georgia was a very fast learner. She had delighted in watching those shoes walk across the living room floor, and seeing them on the linoleum. And she had learned something about herself that day. It changed her relationship with that mother forever. And by changing that relationship she changed the way her body played a role in life, and in her life.

She wasn't a woman who was likely to remember what I said. As a matter of fact, I suspected she would be more likely to remember how to forget what I said. It wasn't necessary that she remember it, only that she learned how to use it for herself in her own private way.

I told her she could forget about it entirely as long as she used it in a way that was delightful to herself. Or she could remember to forget it or she could remember a bit of it. She might remember what she thought about it, or that might be what she forgot as well. She could forget it in every way as long as she used it in every way.

She'd forgotten about the sounds around her. You may have forgotten about the sounds around you as I've been speaking to your unconscious mind and there is this squeaking and crackling of a certain sound in the back of the room, and I wonder if you've forgotten about the sounds of the traffic. You might want to pay attention to some of those things.

You might want to pay attention to your arm which has met me halfway. And paying attention to the sound of the wind brings to mind certain fragrances, along with other people inhaling more deeply because they heard that and it brings to mind the fact that we're all in it together.

Reorient to Waking State

She was reoriented from the trance state with thanks for making it possible. This was a way to follow Erickson's advice that the hypnotist always show respect for the client.

A test for the work was then conducted by suggesting that her arm could stay in trance when she came out. Since she succeeded in that she symbolically expressed that the changes in her body could stay with her after trance was over. This single session work for her pain did, in fact, stay with her after the trance. Between the session represented in this transcript and the time of this writing Rose has been without pain for over 18 months. It is, of course, a great compliment to the intelligence of her unconscious that she learned so rapidly to use the resources retrieved in such a short period of time.

S: Now I want to thank your unconscious mind for making this relationship available. And I wonder if you can pay attention to how your hand stays suspended in the air even as I count from one to twenty, and the rest of your body comes out of trance. Just like you can keep your hand in the air when you come out of trance, other things can stay with you, handy, when you come out of trance, can they not?
   1, 2, 3, 4, 5 and breathing more deeply, 6, 7, 8, 9, 10, 12, 18, 20. Hi, how do you feel?
R: Um. I was very nervous when I . . . when I started out. I felt I got really weak like I was going to pass out. As I was looking at my, my, my hip to my foot without the rest of me at all. And, um, it felt, it got really warm and nice and it felt just really, really nice and then I got the pain that I get in my, in my hip and I felt well it's in my hip, in my leg, and I got really tense, very tense, tenser than I think I normally get when I have that. And then it started to go away and I don't have it anymore.
S: Great! How many arms do you have? R: (Laughter) Two. S: Would you like to put that one back down on your lap? Question: Did she have the pain when she came up here? R: No, I didn't. Question: And you don't have it as you leave? R: No. S: Great! Do you have your arm back yet? It's still unattached. It wants to remain with you after this trance doesn't it? Maybe a couple of things. Do you have a sense of having your own control over it now? R: No. S: Close your eyes. Let yourself go back into trance until your arm comes down and this time when you open your eyes and come back out of trance bring it back into balance at your side. You can just take your own time to do that.

S: Do you want to say anything or ask something? *R:* Yes. I've done this before, but I've never really, I felt very um, at one stage I felt very happy and I um just had a very different than I ever had before feeling about, um, and I saw my mother (laughter) just looking at her and feel . . . and responding to her. And just to learn differently. Touching way. It was different and I enjoyed it very much. But once I felt like when I had the pain in my knee, I felt this terrific urge to. . . . I usually straighten it out and it helped tremendously and just my whole side and I just felt myself when I want to straighten that leg out to get it, get rid of it right away. And I couldn't and I, it felt really bad (laughter) much worse than it normally feels. *S:* Oh, you can endure more you know. *R:* Then it just started to go away and it just felt so good. *S:* Great! *R:* But I was a little nervous before but I, after the first little while it, I didn't, I got a big kick out of it going away. What I remember was the wind, when the wind came through the window and I could, I really could hear it and the only thing I can remember is the wind. I remember hearing the wind and I don't hear it now like I did. *S:* And your pain is gone with the wind. *R:* (Laughter) Yes.

A CASE OF ACUTE HYSTERICAL ANXIETY

This case follows the embedded metaphor structure closely and for that reason, as well as the success of the treatment, it was chosen for review. It is the case of a 33-year-old woman ("Katherine"), who suffered extreme anxiety attacks whenever she participated in activities requiring her to "perform" in any way. Her anxiety was so great that it negatively affected her judgment. She reported being afraid to let her emotions "come." We were able to observe her during such an "attack" when she literally fled the business meeting where she was expected to make a financial report. She knew it was not as "scary" as she was making it, but at the same time she felt overwhelming terror. The conflict was a short one. Her terror won.

She described herself as "easily touched"; however, she mentioned that she could occasionally solve a problem such as the business meeting if she pretended she was behind a "curtain" and essentially alone. At all other times she had the problem. Even her career decision had been influenced by the difficulty. She had become a bookkeeper to avoid the likelihood of personal performances.

Katherine was from a southern state and small family. She had one younger sister with whom she was not close. As a child she had been physically abused by her parents at the age of four. She was sexually abused by her father at the age of 11. Her mother had not believed her about the abuse and had not helped her.

She was not able to identify with the role of a woman presented in her family. She described her mother as rigid, uptight, and hypercritical. Her sister was tall, thin, and blonde. Katherine, by contrast, was and always had been short and overweight. Basically, her sense of self-worth was low and experience with expressing herself emotionally was quite limited. As a case in point, she had changed both her first and last names by the time we met her. She called herself Katherine or Kate because the associations and ramifications were far more pleasant than those to the name she had received from her parents. We took this to be yet another example of her low esteem and poor sense of worthy self-expression. She had given up in areas of normal social competition and, of course, performance.

Several things she had shared in the diagnostic interview were incorporated into the session that follows. These include the sense of satisfaction that still came to mind when she thought of her repeated childhood dreams of leaving her body and flying. She had taken comfort in her spiritual nature and gained a knowledge of the essentially esoteric side of spiritual life including, at least intellectually, astral travel and reincarnation. Also related, in the sense that she sought it for comfort, was her extensive collection of panda bears. The collection had become a small hobby for her. Finally, she frequently used the term "caboose it" to mean that the topic under discussion had gone far enough and should come to a close. It was a friendly comment when she used it, but personal and idiosyncratic nonetheless.

We used these features in designing the following therapy session. As mentioned earlier, goals included helping Kate co-create a new sense of emotional acceptance, improved body image and self-image, as well as increased comfort for self expression. This would involve designing, with her assistance, an interpersonal map including desired behaviors and attitudes in both her immediate and upcoming social network. Specific treatment is outlined in Figure 4.

Induction

C: Everyone is settled and you know a lot about going into trance already. And so, Katherine, we'll just ask you to go ahead and start the process of going into trance in the way you're most comfortable with from your own previous experience, whether you place your hands palms up or flat on your thighs. You've already chosen to close your eyes, letting that curtain of darkness fall, and just enjoy the beginning sensations of comfort and privacy that you can have even in this situation. S: And as we speak to you, perhaps you can be with us in limited ways and appreciate your ability to not follow all of our directions . . . C: but to only follow in ways that are particular and unique individualistic ways of your own choosing.

Safety and Protection

S: Your conscious mind may imagine yourself in whatever safe and pro-tected ways you develop, as if perhaps behind a one-way mirror and maybe you can take our voices with you. Maybe you only have to have your own thoughts in response to what you notice about the things we do, the sounds we make. *C:* And so you can choose to look inside only

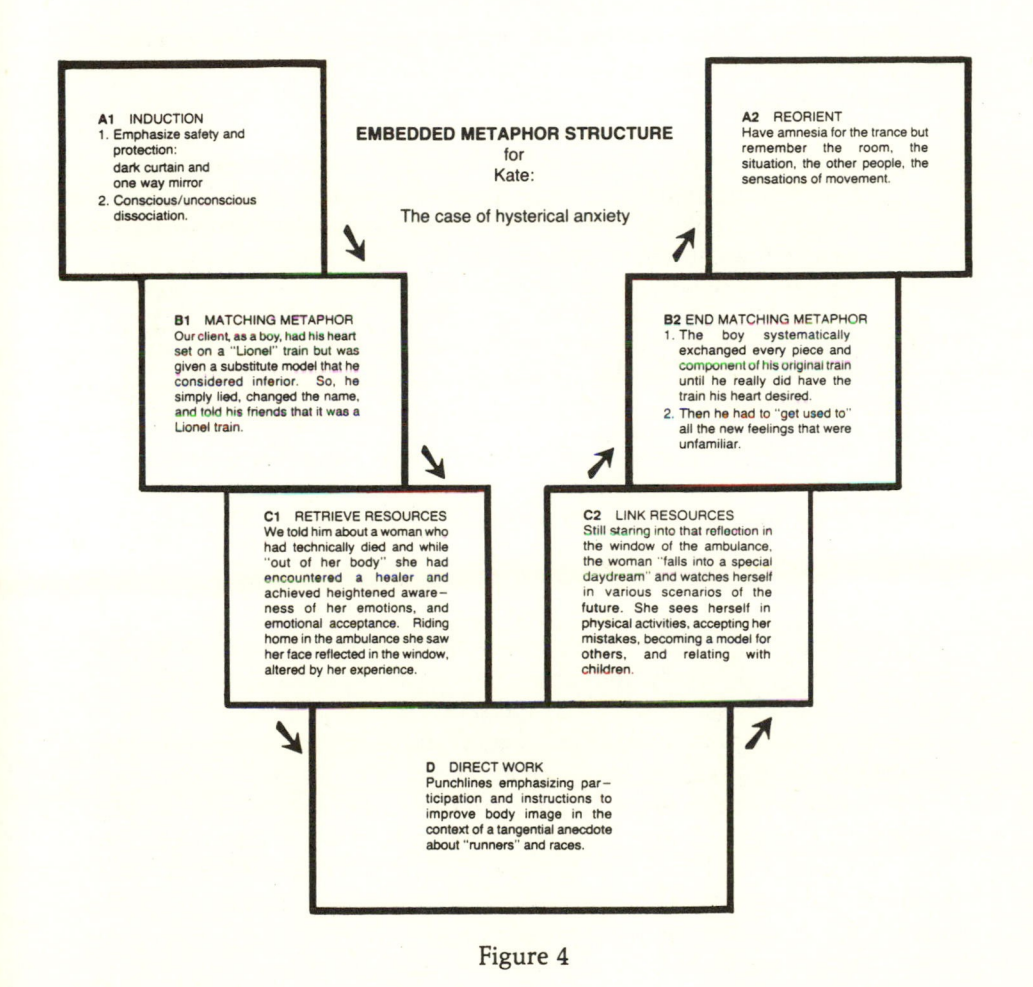

A1 INDUCTION
1. Emphasize safety and protection:
   dark curtain and
   one way mirror
2. Conscious/unconscious dissociation.

EMBEDDED METAPHOR STRUCTURE
for
Kate:

The case of hysterical anxiety

A2 REORIENT
Have amnesia for the trance but remember the room, the situation, the other people, the sensations of movement.

B1 MATCHING METAPHOR
Our client, as a boy, had his heart set on a "Lionel" train but was given a substitute model that he considered inferior. So, he simply lied, changed the name, and told his friends that it was a Lionel train.

B2 END MATCHING METAPHOR
1. The boy systematically exchanged every piece and component of his original train until he really did have the train his heart desired.
2. Then he had to "get used to" all the new feelings that were unfamiliar.

C1 RETRIEVE RESOURCES
We told him about a woman who had technically died and while "out of her body" she had encountered a healer and achieved heightened aware-ness of her emotions, and emotional acceptance. Riding home in the ambulance she saw her face reflected in the window, altered by her experience.

C2 LINK RESOURCES
Still staring into that reflection in the window of the ambulance, the woman "falls into a special daydream" and watches herself in various scenarios of the future. She sees herself in physical activities, accepting her mistakes, becoming a model for others, and relating with children.

D DIRECT WORK
Punchlines emphasizing par-ticipation and instructions to improve body image in the context of a tangential anecdote about "runners" and races.

Figure 4

and at those moments when you're comfortable and curious you can use your unique vantage point to look outside the one-way mirror.

This session was conducted in front of a group of professional therapists. Since the problem revolved around performance anxiety, the circumstances of the treatment presented a special problem for protection and comfort. The paragraphs above, for that reason, focused the client's awareness on the possibility of protection via a curtain of darkness or a one-way mirror. We presupposed the development of "safe and protected ways" and the "one-way mirror" because of the idiosyncratic meaning she gave them. Even though the idea of hiding was inconsistent with the ultimate outcome, our intended use of the protective images during induction presented no difficulty. The remainder of the multiple embedded metaphor would be altering the conscious framework anyway.

S: But your unconscious mind can know and your conscious mind understand the process won't interfere with your unconscious mind getting something that's going to change everything in small ways, just as it allows you to find a proper balance in your life. C: It's something that you can discover gradually or perhaps suddenly in the hours and days, weeks to come. And you're breathing very comfortably . . . S: so I know there's a large range of thoughts that you're having moment by moment, bit by bit, at the conscious level while your unconscious begins to slow down. C: As your face muscles reflect that softness and relaxation . . . S: because your unconscious really knows a lot more than you do. C: because you communicate in ways that you're not aware of. And why should you be? Your conscious mind has many other more interesting things to notice and attend to.

Matching Metaphor

The matching metaphor begins with a story about another client of ours who experienced a "pandemonium of happiness" about an idea he had as a child. This term was used with the expectation that it would bring a smile to Kate since it was a play on the word "panda" and, therefore, a reference to her panda bear collection. She did smile in the trance when that reference was made, which was particularly useful since we were establishing the implication that she would solve her problems. The implication was contained in the line "he had realized how he could solve that problem." We added, "It was a problem that seemed very big" in reference to her weight. So, finding that she could smile at the same time she was being asked to consider solving her emotional and weight problems was an indication of a good prognosis.

As we mentioned, she had changed her name but that didn't change her. So the matching metaphor was constructed about a boy who had been dissillusioned with a toy train given him by his parents. He undertook changing all the parts of the train, beginning with the name. The dramatic twist in this story was that the change of the name was not itself sufficient to bring the boy the happiness he desired. So the story continued, although suspended, until he learned how to make other changes in the toy as well.

C: Your conscious mind may not be particularly interested in our words. S: And neither was the mind of a client of ours who realized while thinking about his childhood that a pandemonium of happiness had broken out in his heart . . . C: when he had realized how he could solve that problem. It was a problem that seemed very big. S: As a child he had received a train and it wasn't the Lionel train he had hoped for. C: He had had his heart set on that Lionel train and he just couldn't bear that he'd have to settle for a lesser model. S: He couldn't share it with his friends. He could hardly stand the thought that he'd received a version of a gift from his parents that wasn't up to standard and wasn't up to par. C: It wasn't what he'd dreamed of. S: It was a very big problem for such a small child.

C: And so the first thing he did was he simply changed the name. S: He told all his friends it was a Lionel train. That brought him a sense of temporary relief but thinking back on it he realized his problem hadn't been solved so easily. C: There were times when he almost believed the fantasy and the lie he had told, S: but he couldn't compete and he wasn't going to be able to keep up. C: He knew his train probably wouldn't compete with those Lionel trains some of his friends had. S: And such were the thoughts that he had in our office as he was in trance and we were speaking about a lot of things.

Resource Retrieval Metaphor

The resources metaphor begins, in the following paragraphs, with the introduction of a client who had technically died. Dissociation was developed in the trance by the metaphoric comparison to out-of-the-body experiences and spiritual interest. The metaphor about a woman who was dead may have further interested Kate since she was emotionally dead in her estimation. From our pre-therapy discussions it was clear to us that she did associate feelings of dissociation with leaving the body. The experience of leaving the body at death was compatible with her conscious mind belief of how people die.

A bind of comparable alternatives for levitation of her arm was interspersed within the "dying" story in order to eventually comment on the feel-

ing of floating, "floating higher," "rising higher," and "higher" and simultaneously to comment on both the position of the arm lifting and the dissociation
increasing.

Trance was ratified with "she couldn't speak, couldn't move" and the levitation comments, "rising higher and higher." The "having no body" comment near the end of the third paragraph that follows was a purposefully
ambiguous reference to her social and physical situation, as well as the transparent "out-of-body" story. Voice tone stress on that comment surely inferred the other meanings while bypassing the conscious mind.

S: Just some of the things that came to his mind as we were speaking about
   another client who technically had died. All of the graphs and all of the
   charts revealed that she was dead. The doctors pronounced her dead.
   C: And, in fact, it's not certain whether during those moments that she
   had died or in those moments preceding the death or perhaps afterwards she experienced that sensation of floating out of her body higher
   and higher and higher.
S: And while you're in trance we can mention a college that we went to
   and you might think of a university that you've attended. You could
   think about how we haven't asked for either your right or left hand to
   do anything and you might wonder whether you'd be surprised to find
   out that your unconscious does something different . . . C: than your
   conscious mind expects or even finds much value in.
S: And so as we spoke to him about the woman floating higher and higher
   out of her body . . . C: how she sensed herself looking back down at the
   bed and the doctors surrounding her, also sensing that tunnel in which
   she found herself. S: She couldn't speak, couldn't move. C: She seemed
   to be propelled through that tunnel by some force. S: It was as if she had
   no body anymore. C: And rising higher and higher she began to sense a
   light at the end of that tunnel. S: And there are so many associations
   that could come to one's conscious mind about having no body. C: She
   didn't think so much about having no body as she did experience a
   growing curiosity about that light at the end of the tunnel. S: Curiosity
   that began to turn into awe as she realized her life was passing before
   her eyes.
S: And our client understood what we meant when we said that you go
   down that tunnel, further and further toward the light, seemingly passing one and then another former person that you've said goodbye to,
   and propelled in some way that you can't understand, moving closer
   and closer to what seems an imminent connection with that light at the
   end. C: You can feel your heartbeat, you can feel the anxiety rise when
   you have no body. But as she came closer to that light, it came into
   sharper and sharper focus revealing the outline of a figure of a being
   that seemed incorporated by that light. S: Everyone knows the exper-

ience of spirituality that rests somewhere deep within, a sense of coming in contact with an external force that puts you in contact with your internal self. And that's what began to happen as we spoke.

True statements, such as "you can feel your heartbeat," and later, "heat comes to your face" and "choking in the throat," served to bring the reality of the drama home to Kate in an emotional sense. Her framework did not allow a way for her to experience emotional acceptance. She had a history so deprived of emotional acceptance that it was unlikely she would find a complete experience of emotional acceptance in her memory. However, in the framework being provided in trance, she could organize whatever her imagination of total emotional acceptance might be. She mentioned that she was easily "touched" by events so the idea of "touching" a truly accepting being after death was more acceptable to her belief framework than the thought of that happening in real life. Thus, without actually dying she could accept the possibility of anxiety and release that might come from being totally accepted.

The experience of emotional acceptance was further reinforced with the sentence about the resource of "spirituality that rests somewhere deep within, a sense of coming in contact with an external force that puts you in contact with your internal self." Such thoughts were part of Kate's belief system. There was "something" deep inside her that was acceptable and worthy, even if this was a non-tangible "spiritual" thing. We attempted to retrieve any kernal of available self-acceptance and belief in her worthiness.

C: And seeing that being come clearer and clearer, you recognize it intuitively as benevolent and wise. S: Heat comes to the face, choking in the throat because of emotions that are beginning to build. C: Kindness radiates forth from that being. S: And then, whether it's an illusion or reality, it's as if that being reaches out a hand and you don't know whether you should raise your hand. C: You anticipate the moment when that hand will actually touch you. S: And there's no way to avoid it. C: It's so gradual though that you have time to really tingle . . . S: as you experience the anxiety which turns into a tingling excitement throughout your body, a mixture of emotions.

S: How interesting it is that a mixture of emotions typifies love. Sometimes it's as if our client remembered moments in her past where there had been an emotional climax after sexual conduct that brought her to crying and laughing and fearing and risking and sadness and joy all at the same moment. She knew that must be the feeling of love back then but now she was having that same experience build up in her chest, moving to her throat, all through her tear ducts, every sphincter in her body.

C: Could she really bear the acceptance of knowing that being, as symbolized by some spiritual experience deep inside, S: was about to touch her in a way that very few individuals have ever been touched and live to tell about?

C: And finally in fact, she was touched and the sensations that flowed through her body we can only guess. S: Tears, if she had any, rolled down her cheeks. The beating of her heart overtook her thinking, if that was something she still had. C: And it's unlikely that her conscious mind fully comprehended exactly the scope of those sensations and that emotion that coursed through her every fiber. S: And she realized that you can really know that love of acceptance for the self that you really are and feel it in the finger, the arm, the shoulders and the chest. C: And it was as if in that moment she was cradled in a warmth of love, bringing a glow . . . S: and feel it in the throat, the neck, the cheeks, the legs, the pelvis, feet emitting that glow. C: And she would have been content to stay there forever. S: And maybe she did.

In the above paragraph the touching between the imagined accepting figure and the woman in the story finally occurred. We had played on Katherine's statement that she was easily "touched" to create an imaginary and metaphoric acceptance of her emotional life. The idea of emotion overtaking her thinking, as was the actual case with Kate's anxiety, was replaced in the metephor as the joy of emotional contact overwhelming her. Several months after this therapy Kate reported that she had cried in the presence of her therapist and several friends for the first time in her life. We can trace that result directly back to these suggestions that she accept her emotional life and share it. But discussing the outcome is looking too far ahead.

We used the positive feelings retrieved in this segment by applying them systematically to an improvement in her body image. This was accomplished by mentioning various parts of her body to simultaneously focus awareness on her body as she experienced the surge of emotional acceptance (whether that was fully conscious or merely a metaphoric avenue for unconscious association).

S: Suddenly though she found herself thinking back on that as she was driving home from the hospital in the ambulance. She wondered if she really had died or if it was only an illusion that people have when they're very ill. Her unconscious, however, knew what your unconscious knows that there's a learning about that deep inside that everyone can find and can memorize and use. C: And she was able to secretly cherish that learning as she sat passively, just watching out the window as the ambulance transported her home. S: She couldn't move. She was overcome by trying to understand the meaning of that experience, and to find out which reality she really was living in.

C: There was no need to move, no need to talk, she just comprehended, apprehended the world passing beside her effortlessly. *S:* And your conscious mind couldn't understand that miracle but your unconscious mind can integrate and use that in a number of ways and so her unconscious mind played tricks on her as she watched her reflection in the windows of the ambulance intermingle with the sights of the trees and the traffic.

C: And when the ambulance apparently entered a tunnel, the shifting reflection was so striking that she saw her own face and body clearly reflected there in that window which had become a mirror. *S:* Her conscious mind watched the reflection of that face, *C:* those shoulders, heart section, *S:* which had been changed and altered in some ways by those emotions that touched her. *C:* The hands, the arms, the legs, all a part of her and yet apart from her in some way she couldn't explain. *S:* Just as your conscious mind couldn't figure out exactly which reality to participate in, your unconscious mind could appreciate the reflection in the window. *C:* And you can memorize seeing that face, that relaxation, changed in some minor ways by the experience of knowing that being touched at that deep central spot was a kind of loving acceptance that your unconscious knows about and your conscious mind couldn't experience. But the face in the window reflected a certain maturity, a wisdom, that was a symbol for the conscious mind to realize what the unconscious knows.

The last paragraph succinctly sums up the work in the preceding short section. Using the metaphoric frame of an ambulance window we took our protagonist, and likewise Kate, through the development of a visual fantasy and a central self-image. We planned to use this resource in the linking phase. But in the resource phase we only needed to help Kate create a framework that could allow her to entertain the concept and the feelings of emotional acceptance and develop a symbolic way of referring to this set of resources. The visual image of her face in the window etched with signs of acceptance was that symbol. We concluded with "the face in the window reflected a certain maturity, a wisdom. . . ." Kate was a responsive subject. She breathed more deeply, slightly erected her posture, smoothed the muscle tone of her cheeks and forehead, and demonstrated rapid eye movement beneath her lids, all of which indicated to us that she was succeeding in the task explicated in the metaphor. We were then ready to begin direct work.

Direct Work

We began this phase with a bind of comparable alternatives: "Unless you win or lose, you really aren't worthwhile at all." This was said to presuppose participation. It does not seem apparently obvious to the listener that one is worthwhile if one loses so the statement may have been a bit surprising. But the experience of being worthwhile could come through participation in whatever manner Kate was able to participate. It certainly would not come as a result of withdrawal. This "punchline" paved the way for the story of the runner which detailed the same learning with anecdote and more punchlines.

S: And while we spoke to our client about the woman . . . C: he understood at the unconscious level exactly what we were speaking about though his conscious mind may have been wondering why we chose to speak about her. Still, he wasn't the least bit surprised when we told him . . . S: unless you win or lose, you really aren't worthwhile at all. C: He seemed to know what we meant. S: His conscious mind was still thinking about seeing his own face reflected, altered slightly by the maturity of knowing that the emotions he had really were something that belonged to him and only him. But his unconscious mind continued to make new associations as we spoke and he thought about something else.

C: We began to speak about runners. Now there are a lot of runners. You see them everywhere you go, day or night. S: Always trying to change the posture in some way as they run, always trying to get ahead. C: And you know very few of those runners ever really win a race. S: But it changes the way you breathe, the way you conduct yourself, the attitude of holding your body in space. And the thing he wanted more than anything was to win one of those races. He diligently tried time after time. C: He trained and he trained. He remembered slogans . . . S: You've got to compete in order to win. C: that said, "no strain, no gain." S: He realized he had to compete with himself and you have to compete with others and the more he competed with others the more he knew you have to compete with yourself. C: Then he would remember other slogans endorsing just the opposite—"Train, don't strain."

C: But he trained and trained . . . S: and every which way he could think to do it he would try because the things you achieve in life are things that are earned, merited. There is no such thing as a free ride. And while he didn't like to think it was true, you have to be tough to survive in a tough world. Other animals find a way to do that. Hermit crabs will take the conch shells they can find and temporarily use them to be protected in a shell against the onslaught of reality. The same is true for other animals who use various forms of protective coloring. C: Now the runner we spoke about never did actually win a race despite his fondest desire to do so. S: But he learned what those hermit crabs know and that is that you can't stay in the shell all of the time. You're going to outgrow your shell and your shell is only a device to allow you to participate in the real world that exists in the ocean in which the crab lives.

Interspersed via voice tone shifting were suggestions including "change the posture" and "get ahead." These were enhanced and supported by the punchlines: "You've got to compete in order to win," "compete with yourself." "things you achieve in life are things that are earned, merited," and "you can't stay in the shell all of the time." Perhaps we should point out that lines such as, "You have to be tough to survive," are not for every client. It does not represent our philosophy of life. Certainly there are many times in civilized living where one has to be tender, flexible, compromising, and even weak in order to survive. For Kate, however, this message was given because she overvalued any experience of anxiety she felt. She used such moments, as people will, to further justify her attitude. She would not, of course, adopt the philosophy we offered to an extreme. It was a maneuver to expand her map of the world in the proper direction to get her involved and to help her become assertive rather than "give up."

The runner metaphor was a logical context in which to mention body image again. The first lines in the next paragraph were about the gains that come through participating. The story was both an anecdote to reinforce previous punchlines and also a means to connect the new competitive awareness with her body parts. Previously we had associated the experience of self-acceptance with her various body parts. Now we associated thoughts of toning her muscles, keeping at the hard work of self-competition and change in the body.

The implication of weight loss as the goal would be obvious to most listeners. Kate, however, was not listening to a story told to her. She was listening to a story told to another client and in turn told to the original client (with the train). She was not likely to apply any usual critical thinking to this or to even recall it after the trance. In fact, our follow-up several weeks after the trance indicated that she was still amnesic for it.

C: And of course, even though he never won a race, it would be inaccurate to say that he didn't win something. S: because in losing those races, your muscle tonus is something that is improved. It's so nice to realize that your digestive system works better. C: Your breathing is deeper. S: You're able to relax more fully. And muscle tonus increased in the cheeks. C: You sleep better at night. S: And you should know how the muscle tonus changes if you're really going to run those races successfully. You should know the good feelings of your cheek muscles and you should know the good feelings of your shoulders . . . C: and the good feelings of your chest. S: He came to know that you can love the way your chest rests upon your rib cage. And having that same sense of learning that he understood about the woman riding in that ambulance, he knew that you can apply that unconscious learning to appreciate your stomach muscles, the way your pelvis feels, C: the way your genitals rest between your legs. S: And come to know the importance of owning a set of legs that carry those genitals from place to place, C: appreciating the strength in the thighs, the flexibility in the calves, S: and the support that he gained in his own back, C: the pride of having both feet support the entire body.

Linking Metaphor

We returned after completing the direct work, with a radical shift, to linking the resources. Linking resources is usually done to accomplish changes in the immediate situations a client faces. In this case we thought Kate needed to extend her sense of emotional acceptance to improve her self-image thinking. That is, we wanted to help her elaborate her map of the world and associate to positive feelings and emotional acceptance in various "performance" related areas.

Visual rehearsal was the vehicle for that and it had already been developed with the self-image visualization she had done in the resource phase of the multiple embedded metaphor. The only remaining task at this stage was to elaborate earlier feelings of worth and confidence and have Kate "transfer" them to scenarios that included elements relevant to her real world functioning. Since the Ericksonian approach strongly emphasizes that cure comes through reassociation of experience and that people use their ability to associate images as a map for their behavior, we lead Kate through a series of visual scenarios to help her create for herself semi-conscious images of her functioning that would symbolically link desired resources to the social situation where they were most needed. These included: test taking, talking assertively to others, self-expression and performance, and more symbolically (we used images of roller skating) enjoying herself with others in aggressive physical activity. All these outcomes seemed to be consistent with the emotional age of the client and the real tasks that she would be likely to encounter.

We began with her arm levitation (already achieved) and stressed the fact that her conscious mind didn't think she really would be able to do what the unconscious mind had done. This general theme is similar to the protagonist's lack of hope in the first two stories of the embedding. What followed was an account of the discoveries made by the woman in the earlier ambulance story. She was discovering new ways to conduct herself because of her unbelievable encounter that ended with the ambulance ride. These revelations in the metaphor were self-image thinking scenarios for Kate.

C: And riding in that ambulance our client experienced a heyday of imagination as her fantasies just seemed to run wild. And your conscious mind can be very pleased to realize that you've been able to achieve an arm catalepsy and levitation that your unconscious mind knew you could do all along and your conscious mind didn't think you were going to. She continued to gaze at her reflection in that window and she found that she not only saw the reflection of her face but the imagination changed to include all of those activities that were of interest to her. S: And she saw herself with that same feeling of surprise and pride and acceptance on her face as she sat taking a test, moving her hand with a pencil, C: automatically. Thinking about the answers to the test, noticing a sense of pride and enjoyment on her face she hadn't realized before. Delighted as she realized she was able to respond to each successive question with competence. S: And just as your unconscious can show your conscious mind that you can learn to do something different with your right hand, she learned that she could write a test with her right and feel that same experience of pride and acceptance.

C: The scene changed and revealed her talking to other people. S: There she was with that same experience of surprise and pride knowing deep inside your unconscious has demonstrated a learning. C: She was standing squarely on both feet, facing the other person head on and seeing that face and posture reflecting those desirable feelings of pride. She would breathe. The other person would breathe. S: It caused an adjustment in her way of experiencing herself to realize that you can stand in front of other people and answer questions and still display that sense of pride and enjoyment, courage and acceptance.

C: She shifted her balance, first stood on her right foot, thinking about one thing, expressing herself one way . . . S: Not thinking about that tunnel that she had walked down but rather finding that you can appreciate the moment. C: . . . and then shifted to the left foot, thinking something else, expressing herself yet another way.

S: I hope you can appreciate the movement of your hand at each moment. Your thumb has moved and it's nice to know that mammals of a higher order have the ability to move their thumb in ways that other animals can't because the human being is a unique creature and you have a whole range of emotions and feelings that belong to you and no other animal can have them. C: And then still speaking to others she would stand back and listen, enjoying that aspect of the conversation where she had to do nothing but hear and notice and appreciate the other person's voice and words.

S: And there was a thumping, a tire going over a crack in the road perhaps that temporarily changed the scene and she saw, as anybody's mind can see, a change in the picture. And then came to mind the same face reflecting that feeling of "I can do it" and "I'm proud of the fact that my feelings have been touched in a certain way."

C: This time the face was on a roller skater, someone on roller skates, herself on roller skates. I don't know whether or not you've been on roller skates but everyone has observed that phase of learning when someone first straps those wheels onto their feet . . . S: Now your hand is halfway and perhaps understandings from your unconscious mind are halfway available to your conscious mind. C: . . . and attempts to find a balance. And she saw that face. And you know you can see yourself doing new activities with that same feeling and just where is the feeling of pride and acceptance located in one's body? It's important to be able to know you're able to appreciate the pride in your legs if you're going to roller skate. And though most of the time it's not particularly pleasant to enjoy falling down you can appreciate the pride in your legs for having the wisdom to stop you and with every fall the knowledge is increased about how to stand up the next time.

In the final paragraph above we focused awareness on pride with "and just where is the feeling of pride and acceptance located in one's body?" The purpose at that point was merely to ratify the existence of the experience that we had spoken about in the linking metaphor scenarios. If we had received an ideomotor response at that time indicating that she did not have any such experience (such as a tensed eyebrow and slight left-to-right head shake) then we would have known that we needed to continue with the anecdotes. Instead, Kate increased her search phenomena response and corrected her posture to indicate that she did feel some such positive feeling.

We concluded the paragraph with a metaphor that made an equation by associating "mistakes" and "falling." The idea of making mistakes (falling) was reframed with the punchline: "Appreciate the pride in your legs for having the wisdom to stop you and with every fall the knowledge is increased about how to stand up the next time." This occurred in a simple and short anecdotal tangent which was taken in the midst of resource linking to forestall any objections she might manufacture in regard to the task being asked of her metaphorically. It thus became less possible for her to "find a reason" to not follow the directives offered. This added attitude-restructuring defused any resistance that might be built to block the examination of self-image scenarios being constructed.

S: And since she had been our client her unconscious mind knew something that was unknown to her conscious mind while you watch your reflection in that window doing new things with new feelings. That was a story we had told her about an old woman we had worked with who was afraid to walk by herself. *C:* And your hand just finding its own comfortable position to float in, and she said "I'm afraid to walk without my physical therapist because I might fall down." It was a great achievement that she was even walking at all but she did need to walk without that crutch. *S:* And so I told her: "You don't need a crutch to walk, I hope you do fall down, if you don't know how to walk. But really, you're only four and a half feet tall. How much damage do you think you could do to the floor falling down from only that height? And what kind of damage do you think could occur to your leg which is only about a foot and a half off the ground where the knee is located, two and a half feet high to the hip, it's only about three feet from the floor to your waist." *C:* She believed that in some ways but she still needed convincing. There was still some fear about what damage might be done from four and a half feet.

C: We reminded her that every child learns to fall down before it learns to walk so if you haven't got the knowledge in your unconscious mind of how to walk, I hope you do fall down quite a few times. Then we picked up a candlestick and dropped it from four and a half feet high, proving to both her conscious and her unconscious mind that it could just fall and bounce and sustain no damage, be just as good as before the fall. *S:* From then on she walked without her physical therapist. And that came to someone's unconscious mind while their conscious mind reviewed those fantasy rehearsals of the self complete with desired feelings and experiences that she didn't even know she could have in the context of roller skating.

As this phase of scenario building was ended, we used several pronoun alterations and indirect suggestions to help Kate relate as many of these ideas to her personal life as possible in the time allowed: for instance, ". . . is just a symbol for a lot of social activities that someone can engage in . . . and a lot of projects that you can undertake." Although poor grammar, technically, it is somewhat colloquially accepted when a speaker makes such minor errors in pronoun reference. The effect on the client may be a mild confusion or blurring between the realities of the story and actual life. Kate was free to take the message very personally and she was also free to take it as a story about someone else that did not apply to her.

C: And there's no telling how many fantasies flashed through her mind as she watched that reflection in that window. *S:* And roller skating is just a symbol for a lot of social activities that someone can engage in . . . *C:* And you know how in a dream . . . *S:* and a lot of projects that you can undertake. *C:* . . . so many things can be revealed in only a second it seems as if it's much longer. The learning and the impact is as if it were

much longer. *S:* And now your hand has moved down to your thigh. *C:*
And in those seconds of staring out the window the scenes flashed and
included all manner of activities important to her.

S: And I wonder if those learnings have moved down deep inside and undisturbed and unchangeable. *C:* And she didn't know it at the time but
she was going to have a lot of dreams in which you rehearse new activities and new projects at the conscious level while your unconscious
mind provides for you an association to that wisdom and knowledge.
And be very pleased about the way you interact in those fantasies.

We aimed for high goals in the final few paragraphs of the resource linking
phase in that the resolution of the story took the protagonist to a happy ending as a model for others. Voice tone shifting in the third paragraph to follow
created an interspersal induction-like effect for those items representing roles
a person might play while functioning as a model for others. These included:
"can learn from children," "be a room mother," "a scout master," "neighborhood children," "very nice parent," "important figure in her community,"
"her gifts."

References to dealing with children were likely to function as suggestions
for generative change. That is, Kate's changes and social adjustments immediately after therapy and in the months following therapy will be consistent
with a broader goal—being with children. Being with children presupposes
movement to include increased socializing, through dating, beyond commitment, to marriage, and finally, to having children. If such reference were pur-
sued in the current session or in subsequent sessions, Kate would develop a
framework that would actually bridge the gap from her current situation to
possible future situations. She would be encouraged to decide her degree of
interest and investment in having children. The meager reference to children
here did not provide sufficient map building for Kate to "come to grips" with
that important issue. However, it did put children in her map somewhere, if
only as a vague reference point. When and if she decides about children in the
future, some associative links have been created to feelings of emotional acceptance we helped her build in this session. Positive associations to thoughts
of having children were juxtaposed with attitudes conveyed by her parents,
thus preshaping positive perceptions she will have about children.

C: Now when the ambulance emerged from the tunnel, perhaps only a few
moments had passed or perhaps minutes. It's really hard to say. To her
it seemed like lifetimes. *S:* And for her it really was her lifetime, but her
life had changed in so many ways. *C:* Looking back on that time in the
ambulance, it was as if the death and the experience following it marked

a new beginning, a new life in some ways. *S:* And in her new life she found herself able to share something that she didn't fully understand and that was that the same experience that you know about by being touched so deeply and having those emotions accepted is something that you share with other people and touch them.

C: She, in fact, became a model for other people. It wasn't something that she ever expected she would actually be, a model in the sense of inspiration to others. *S:* But you can have that kind of alteration following the knowledge that was gained. *C:* And you can touch others, others in pain, providing a new measure of relief and comfort. She could also understand and touch those experiencing particular pleasures. *S:* She never would have thought before she died that she was going to become a symbol and a model for children of what they can achieve. *C:* She never thought she would demonstrate the strength that's revealed by showing weakness.

S: She didn't realize how much you can learn from children. It all started when she volunteered to be a room mother, which led to her becoming a scout master with the girl scouts and soon for her neighborhood children. *C:* And reflected in the face of children she learned a lot of things about the love that rested deep inside and had been available to her only when you become a very nice parent to very needing children. She eventually became a very important figure in her community. Many people knew her face. Many people knew of her gifts. *S:* Her unconscious never revealed to her conscious mind that learning to say nice things to children in the real world you learn to change the things that you say to yourself so that they are nice too. *C:* Some had experienced her gifts personally, directly . . . *S:* but her conscious mind did come to the realization that being a model for others was a great change in the way she thought her life would ever turn out and it was funny that it had turned out that way after she died. *C:* . . . and of course, that was the way that others experienced her gifts, indirectly and as a source of inspiration.

End Matching Metaphor

Returning to the metaphor about the man and his train marked the end of resource linking and the resolution of the initial drama that had been used to fixate her attention. There were several experiential associations we intended to make. The first involved her own name change. We reported that the boy had not been happy with just the name changed on his train, but needed to actually change the train too, bit by bit. This would mean overhauling every part of her that she really needed to alter instead of just pretending to have a new life. Sentences like "And you can exchange those parts that you desire" stated this clearly. We pointed out that his original thinking was not necessarily the best choice. The boy could have something that might even be better than the Lionel train and its status. The implication was that his purposes were the important ones and satisfying his purposes rather than the fantasies of others would bring the greatest satisfaction.

S: And as we spoke to the client he had a lot of thoughts about many things that were personal to him. He never asked us so we never explained why he was obsessed with thinking about how he had handled the incident with that train. C: He knew that he was very pleased with what solution he had finally decided upon. It was ingenious.

S: He really couldn't affort to lie all of the time, so he bought a Lionel transformer . . . C: and he just began to interchange and exchange those parts. He bought a Lionel coal car and a Lionel track switcher. S: He even found a place where he could buy the outside of a Lionel engine and put it over the original engine and frame that he had tried to hide from the public. C: And much much later he was able to actually buy the engine core and put it underneath the frame. S: Then he bought trees and pretty soon he didn't even care if they were real Lionel trees or not or Lionel mountains because he found out that you can pretend anything and master it.

C: And you can exchange in those parts that you desire, even choosing different brand names that are better than Lionel. S: And piece by piece he made all of the parts different until his imagination and fantasy conformed with reality and reality conformed with imagination. C: And he was so pleased that last day when he was finally able to add the Lionel caboose. That meant the train was completely exchanged and had become exactly what his heart always wished it could be. S: He didn't understand the symbolism in why his unconscious mind waited until the end to add the caboose but he was really pleased in the trance to realize that he had achieved in that childhood learning something that your unconscious knows and his unconscious knew and everyone's unconscious knows about how you take that creativity from childhood and use it in later life.

We had finished addressing that earlier association and had found a way to use the word "caboose" near the end just as she did in her idiosyncratic manner of stopping an ongoing conversation. She must expect to feel different when she changed. We knew that Kate was especially aware of her feelings. This was expressed in her symptom as well as her speech in discussing it. When changed in desired ways, she won't find the same familiar feelings and won't be able to guide herself appropriately by remembering how she felt before therapy. The issue is not a small one. Kate would feel differently about her ability to interact and to accept her body and she needed to expect to feel different and not be concerned if she had "funny feelings" after therapy. That experience was emphasized with the sentence: "You have to feel different when things have changed."

C: He had initially been so excited as a child when he realized that last piece had been exchanged. And yet an unexpected difficulty was his when he realized that even though he had the train that he had always wanted it somehow felt different and unfamiliar and he didn't quite know how to be comfortable with that new train and all of those new parts. S: He had never really believed that he was going to own that train and be able to compete with others who owned that kind of train.

S: And that was such a new feeling that it first seemed inappropriate to him. He thought he was going to wake up and suddenly lose all that he had worked so hard for. C: But reflecting back on his childhood learning really proved to him that you have to feel different when things have changed. And he spent a good deal of time playing with that new train and learning to be comfortable with that new feeling until finally it became very familiar and he was able to really enjoy having what he had always wanted. And watching it go round and round the track, going through the little tunnels, stopping at the little depots in the little towns he would imagine the people getting off of the train, going about their business, other people getting on the train and being transported to different cities, because in his imagination they could go anywhere, S: talk to anyone, C: do anything, S: become whole bases for learning about life that you live for a long time.

Finally, we wanted her to be free to keep her childlike qualities or to put them away and develop new experiences in adulthood that were not compared to her childhood. This final paragraph before reorientation suggested choice.

C: And you might expect that he kept that train even as a grown man. It was tucked away securely in the basement of the house where he lived. And from time to time he would sneak down the stairs and just be alone enjoying that train, symbolizing for his unconscious mind S: your ability to get on the right track with things in your life.

Reorientation

Reminders to have amnesia were included here, beginning with a suggestion to cover all possible alternatives. We assume that any vestiges of consciousness are alerted to attempt to remember when amnesia suggestions are made. This can be true no matter how subtle the suggestions might be. If an urge to remember something of the session is stimulated, we aid the client in forgetting the important work of the session by satisfying the urge to remember something. Kate was reoriented to the room noises and her feelings as a way to satisfy just such an urge. While she found herself wondering what to remember, we pointed out that she could remember the "bodily sensations," "noises in the room," "talking of other people," etc. Once the trance was terminated we switched the discussion to a topic other than what happened in the trance, a maneuver Erickson frequently encouraged to structure amnesia.

S: And I don't know what kind of knowledge he brought with him when he came out of trance because we suggested that he could either forget everything that we said or remember some of it or remember all of it, forget none of it, C: or he could forget some of it, remember most of it and enjoy discovering that which had been forgotten as time went on. S: He could even enjoy discovering that which had been remembered and you're someone who's been in trance thinking about of lot of things . . . C: And it's the same for everyone when they come out of trance . . . S: and you're able to remember a lot of things around you that are important, important ideas . . . C: those bodily sensations, those desires to adjust, S: noises, talking of other people, C: presence of other people, S: kicking of a chair or shutting of a door, C: the enjoyment you can have with those other people who are present, S: and the movement ahead, the ability to open ones eyes and keep yourself right where you are when you notice other people in front of you, staring with their sense of compassion, curiosity, C: understanding and acceptance. And you can continue to breathe comfortably even after coming out of trance.
S: So how long a time do you suppose that was? K: Seemed like forever . . . S: Very close. K: . . . and yet no time at all.

Kate's single session proved to be most rewarding for her. We asked her to return to our seminar the following day and make a presentation on a subject we chose. She did return and, having prepared well that evening, she gave a 15 minute report on Erickson's article about posthypnotic suggestion. She spoke calmly with noteworthy accuracy and clarity to an audience of 60 professional psychologists, social workers, and psychiatrists.

Several months after this immediate indicator of therapy effectiveness, our follow-up revealed noticeable gains she had made in several areas. She had shared feelings and even her tears for the first time with various associates on a few occasions. She had no anxiety about regulating her diet (which proved to be extremely beneficial in light of a subsequent diagnosis that she had diabetes). She reported many instances of assertiveness which she believed she would have never accomplished prior to the therapy session. And last, but certainly not least, she reported that she did not feel responsible for the difficulties she experienced as a child, although she had felt that way prior to therapy. She said that she actually had a sense of forgiving her parents, which was quite a shift from the attitude that led her to change both first and last name prior to seeking help.

In summary, these three cases represent minor variations of the multiple embedded metaphor pattern. Each hypnotic session may be structured in a manner that varies only slightly from this general theme, regardless of the number of sessions, weeks or months that the therapy may require. Illustrated in these cases is the basic logic of the therapeutic usage of hypnotic trance in five steps:

1) Engage the conscious and unconscious attention of the client.
2) Retrieve and help build the necessary experiential resources.
3) Direct hypnotic work at the core of the neurotic bind.
4) Link the resources to the immediate social and practical concerns in the client's world.
5) Facilitate generative change by associating the changes to perceptions and images which the client will encounter in the next stage of social development beyond that in which s/he is currently engaged.

8 SELF-IMAGE THINKING: THE ANTICIPATION FRAMEWORK

ERICKSON'S EMPHASIS ON SELF-IMAGE

"In all its phases, the Self is expressed symbolically" (Progoff, 1956, p. 181). Self-images are maps of the world and symbols of the self. They elaborate the associations a person expects to experience in various situations. They may be simple residual images of people and events from childhood, objective images of equipment and machines with motor programs attached, or they may be thoughtfully organized scenarios ("I could do it like that," or "I should have said that," or "Next time I'll do it that way") with associated emotional, postural, and verbal expectations conditioned to occur. In any case, they methodically serve as conscious or (primarily) unconscious guides for performance. They are learned in families of origin and are shaped by interactions with other minds and objects. Fortunately, they may be enhanced, changed, reshaped, and relearned when necessary.

A study of Erickson's work reveals many cases in which he helped clients build and shape positive self-images and anticipate real life situations in which they would enact those updated self-images. This emphasis was so frequent, in fact, that we suggest it was a central theme in his therapy. We begin this chapter, therefore, with a brief review of several of these cases in order to emphasize this recurring theme, as well as the variety of ways in which it was creatively addressed by Erickson. This variety, a hallmark of Erickson's style, was often as baffling as it was inspiring; consequently, his unique interventions and dramatic results seem difficult to recreate in systematic fashion. For this reason we have included in this chapter a systematic, recreatable method of building, shaping, and updating self-images and related scenarios. This method was derived from observation and analysis of typical features in many of Erickson's cases.

In a case involving a young woman referred for severe premenstrual cramps, Erickson noticed that she was pretty but was not confident about being pretty. She indicated this lack of confidence by "working too hard at it." Erickson outlined a course of treatment, summarizing:

In brief psychotherapy one of the important considerations is the body image. By body image I mean how does the person look upon herself? What sort of image do they have of themselves? . . . It is so tremendously important to have a good body image. A good body image implies not only the physical self, as such, but the functional self, and the personality within the body (Haley, 1973, p. 95).

He continued with questions which, when shared with the client, would focus awareness and shape perception necessary to create an accurate and positive self-image:

Does she know that it is all right to know that she has very pretty eyes? Does she know that it is all right for her to be aware of the fact that her chin is too heavy? Is it all right for her to have a pretty mouth, but to have her ears set unevenly? Does she know that the individuality of her face is the thing that gives her individual appeal? (Haley, 1973, p. 95).

Erickson stated simply that one of the first things which needs to be done in brief psychotherapy is to find out what the person's body image is. He used various methods in ascertaining body image, such as asking a person in a straightforward manner what his or her best features were, much as a doctor might conduct a physical examination, and indirectly making a person conscious of the body with statements like, "As you sit there . . ." (which focused awareness on what a person sits on and what kind of body is desired). He would sometimes request that a client produce a self-portrait; other times he might engage clients in a challenge as to whether or not they would recognize their own nude body if the head were not visible, thus forcing an intimate visualization and examination of the body.

Often the ascertaining of a body image and the process of changing it were integrated in a series of related assignments. For example, an unkempt 35-year-old woman who was "more than pleasingly plump" came hesitantly to therapy and primly explained her frustration at even getting a date, much less getting married and having children. Erickson's preliminary observation revealed her to be "obnoxiously dirty," cold, impersonal, seclusive and yet desperate in her need to get therapy. He offered her rapid therapy if she could tolerate a "shocking" experience. She agreed and was thereupon presented her first assignment, a mirror, tape measure, scales, and weight chart. Then, for over three hours Erickson led her through a "comprehensive, completely straightforward critique of her weight and appearance, with all possible proof to back it up. Each fingernail was examined and the amount of dirt described in detail—her fingernails were in mourning. Holding a mirror I had her describe for me the dirt on her face and neck . . . her dirty ears . . . uncombed hair, ill-fitting dress, the clashing colors . . ." (Haley, 1973, p. 92). Assessment completed, the process of change was begun with Erickson handing her a washcloth and instructing her to wash only one side of her neck and to contrast it with the unwashed side.

She arrived "remarkably well groomed" for her next appointment and was given her next assignment. She was informed that thereafter she would never be able to forget "something" which was apparent to everyone but which she had previously failed to notice. Leaving the session she was told: "You are never going to be able to forget again that you have a pretty patch of fur between your legs. Now go home, undress, get in the nude, stand in front of a mirror, and you will see the three beautiful badges of womanhood. They are with you always wherever you go, and you cannot forget them ever again."

In the subsequent session she was instructed to systematically alter and "fine tune" remaining aspects of her appearance and social skill, including consulting with a beauty counselor for grooming and fashion supervision, taking dancing lessons in preparation for an upcoming dance, and sewing a special gown for that occasion. Finally, she was to come to her next appointment on her way to the dance three weeks later. Erickson reported that on that evening she walked in really well dressed, embarrassed, blushing, animated, vivacious and "charmingly self-conscious." We like to add, with a touch of humor, that, as with many of Erickson's clients, she married shortly thereafter and eventually had four children.

Another individual seen by Erickson was "Harold," a young migratory laborer who considered himself to be a "dumb moron," was depressed, suicidal, phobic of women, and, according to his own assessment, homosexual. Erickson worked with Harold for several years, accomplishing what Haley described as character revision of the young adult (Haley, 1973, p. 120). We suggest that central to this long-term character revision was a systematic self-image enhancement that eventually resulted in Harold's graduating from college with social skills sufficient to actively pursue his newly recognized preference for women.

When Harold first came for therapy he was poorly groomed, extremely awkward, living in a shack, and bathing only infrequently in irrigation ditches. He had a self-image which dictated that he had no right to even hope to enjoy anything other than his "feebleminded, twisted up" existence. Of course, Erickson met him at this model of the world by agreeing with him and assuring him that "under no circumstances would he be given more than his rightful share of happiness" and that it was necessary for him to accept "all the happiness that was rightfully his, no matter how small or large a portion it was." Haley explained, "Throughout the case, when Erickson requests a change it is defined . . . as an extension, really quite a minor one, of the way he already is" (1973, p. 124). The relationship was defined as one in which "no attempt at real change" would be made; Harold would merely be helped to continue as a feebleminded moron—only happier and a better worker. Thus, self-image building could proceed in very small, almost imperceptible, component bits, especially emphasizing goals of career and social upgrading.

An entry point with Harold was a discussion about important, albeit menial labor, performed by the feebleminded such as himself. As explained by Erickson, ". . . unnoticeably, unobtrusively, there was an increasing emphasis on recognizing the coordination of the muscles with the senses and a respect and admiration for the reality around him as well as his part in that reality" (Erickson in Haley, 1973, p. 127). Since Harold was at least proud of being a good worker, Erickson metaphorically detailed what is expected of a good worker and the care necessary to maintain good "equipment" such as a tractor:

> . . . a piece of farm machinery unsuited for anything except manual labor. Then I pointed out that a tractor needed the right kind of care. It needed to be kept oiled, greased, cleaned, and protected from the elements. It should be properly fueled with the right kind of oil and gas, . . . and the valves should be ground, the spark plugs cleaned, the radiator flushed out, if the tractor was to be a useful manual laborer (Erickson in Haley, 1973, p. 129).

In this way Harold was indirectly encouraged to take care of himself, in specific, though unmentioned ways which would be consistent with his existing self-image while simultaneously enhancing it. He subsequently upgraded both his living conditions and grooming habits.

A number of activities were prescribed to Harold during the several years he was Erickson's client. Each one facilitated the development of a certain learning or skill through Harold's active participation in that situation. Eventually, of course, he amassed quite an assortment of social and professional skills. Still, Erickson overtly honored the "agreement" between them that Harold was only a feebleminded moron just trying to get along a little better and his self-image was not "updated" to include the many new skills (and their collective effect on him) until he could comfortably and convincingly accept it.

One of the prescribed activities was for Harold to meet "Joe," an invalid acquaintance of Erickson's and "learn well and thoroughly" from frequent visits to him. Just what Harold was to learn was unspecified but Erickson knew Joe's ingenious, determined, cheerful nature and that, despite the fact that Joe had not finished high school (or perhaps because of it), he could serve as a behavioral and attitudinal role model for Harold. Another assignment involved going to the library and studying cook books so as to become a competent cook, something "even a woman could do"; therefore, it wouldn't be beyond Harold's meager capabilities. A similar assignment was given for writing, something even children could do.

As the "agreement" between Erickson and Harold did include learning to be happier, it was within legitimate bounds for recreational pleasures to also be prescribed. Having a radio was rationalized as a means by which Harold could begin to exercise, not just his body as a good workman should, but also his "eyes and ears and total physical self." He was systematically instructed to first enjoy certain songs, then remember them, later beat time to music, hum an accompaniment, and finally sing along. He eventually was persuaded to take weekly piano lessons from an elderly woman who needed help with her yardwork in exchange. As Erickson explained, "Harold . . . did not recognize that he was placed in special contact with a woman, a contact that placed him both in a learning role in relation to a woman and also in a position where he could enact the role of a competent male" (Erickson in Haley, 1973, p. 132).

Harold also was maneuvered into swimming and dancing classes by careful justifying, rationalizing, and relabeling by Erickson. Dancing skill prepared him for an important assignment which dictated that Harold only:

> . . . visit public dance halls and observe carefully the number of young men who wished to dance but were too bashful and fearful to even try to learn how. Then he was to note the young women, the fat girls, the homely girls, the skinny girls, the wallflowers who looked about hopefully for a partner or desperately danced with each other while eyeing the young men who were shuffling about too embarrassed to dance (Erickson in Haley, 1973, p. 139).

Erickson had previously prepared Harold, via posthypnotic suggestion, to help a "limited number" of unhappy people who hope someone will help them, so at the dance Harold surprised himself by resolutely dancing with each of a half dozen discouraged "wallflowers." He later reported to Erickson: "That experience sure taught me that I ain't half as bad as I thought. I ain't afraid to do things" (Erickson in Haley, 1973, p. 140). So Harold himself had begun to redefine the "agreement" that he was a hopeless fool and his framework was altered by his own experience. Erickson followed up on this newly created resource feeling of "capability" by having Harold use time distortion in trance to review:

. . . who he was, what he was and what he would like to be and what he could do. Additionally, he was to review his past in contrast with his future, his actuality as a biological creature with emotional as well as physical forces, and his potentialities . . . (Haley, 1973, p. 141).

We would describe this series of instructions as creating a central self-image and rehearsing desired scenarios of the present and future. He was then challenged to enroll in college and finally to grapple with the most threatening learning of all—women. He succeeded in both categories and only then fully accepted an updated image of himself as worthwhile, capable, deserving, likable, and even above average.

With many clients, of course, a positive self-image and scenario "maps" of desired behaviors in specific situations can be much more quickly and easily achieved. The case just described required a good deal of preliminary experience and skill-building prior to mental rehearsal about how to use those skills in the future. This preliminary phase was necessary due to Harold's social retardation and impoverished background; nevertheless, an enhanced self-image and expanded map of behavioral, cognitive, and perceptual options seem to have been the ultimate goal throughout the lengthy preparation phase.

In another case known as the "February Man," the client was an educated and experienced woman; however, she saw herself as emotionally impoverished to the extent that she feared having children because she really did not remember anything good about childhood and did not feel capable of parenting her own children in a way that would make them happy. Basically, she had no role model for effective parenting and therefore no map to follow, and she had no personal experience from her own childhood of emotional satisfaction, well-being, or real "belonging" which she wanted to eventually impart to her children. Her therapy took place over several months in a series of hypnotic sessions for which she had spontaneous amnesia.

In her first session she was regressed to approximately four years old and "introduced" to the February Man, who was described as someone waiting to see her father on business. She talked to him in trance as would a lonely little girl who liked him and enjoyed his attentions. As she "grew up" in subsequent sessions, she continued to visit with her February Man and share her various interests, accomplishments, fears, etc. Erickson wrote this about the visits:

As I came to learn more about her, I was able . . . to regress her back to that age (of a specific memory) and appear a few days before . . . and join in her anticipation of it. Or perhaps I would join her a few days later and reminisce. . . . It was possible to interject into her memories a feeling of being accepted and a feeling of sharing with a real person many things in her life, . . . extrapolating into her memories of the past the feelings of an emotionally satisfying childhood (Erickson in Haley, 1973, p. 182).

As a result of this psychological level self-image building, the client, despite her amnesia for the sessions, began to evidence less and less concern about her ability to be an adequate parent. She now had a role model about how to stimulate emotional well-being in a child, as well as personal feelings of emotional satisfaction, well-being, and belonging. She described her change as a new "feeling of confidence that she would know how to share things properly with children of any age" (Haley, 1973, p. 182). Again, we would describe it as her building a self-image which included feelings of confidence, and mentally rehearsing that self-image through a variety of scenarios related to caring for children.

Another case involves a 17-year-old girl who was withdrawing pathologically due to her lack of breast development. Erickson's work with her demonstrates, as he once told another client, "You can pretend anything and master it" (Lustig, 1975). In her first trance he suggested heightened awareness of bodily sensations which were subsequently to be localized in the breast area, "making her continuously aware of the breast area of her body" (Erickson in Haley, 1973, p. 113). Later he asked her to periodically visualize herself in highly embarrassing situations involving her breasts and to feel the resulting physical sensations "first in her face, and then, with a feeling of relief, she would feel that weight of embarrassment move slowly downward and come to rest in her breasts . . . in a most bewildering but entirely pleasing way" (Erickson in Haley, 1973, p. 113).

By having her repeatedly use visual images of herself to stimulate previously unpleasant sensations of embarrassment and then have these sensations reinforce a new "entirely pleasing" awareness of her breasts, Erickson helped her develop what we call a "habit pattern" or automatic self-image thinking. After consciously making an association several times, the learned connection tends to become automatic, or relegated to unconscious functioning, such that sensations which previously signaled a "problem" instead trigger (automatically) an availability of resources or other therapeutic responses.

Subsequent to this hypnotic groundwork, the girl was instructed to entertain herself and the other students in her college by wearing tight sweaters over an interesting assortment of various sized "falsies" which she was to change frequently and randomly. This "pretense" would begin when she entered college in September. By May, she visited Erickson to report that she was no longer pretending because she had "grown her own" and in fact she requested his assistance in "making them stop" since they had reached a size she enjoyed. Erickson could not be certain whether any aspect of his hypnotherapeutic interventions had been a factor in her breast development. However, research has shown that images do guide performance and in this case the girl's visualized images resulted first in heightened awareness and stimulation of her breast area and secondly in self-images depicting desired outcomes. And she did, in fact, "master" what she had first only pretended.

And finally, a woman suffering to a phobic extreme from excessive modesty came to therapy for help at her husband's suggestion. Despite 12 years of generally good marriage she compulsively engaged in a bedtime ritual each evening which required her undressing in the dark in another room only after her husband had gone to bed. She would then don two layers of sleepware and join her husband in bed. Erickson's "direct work phase" with this woman was preceded by induction and retrieval of resource feelings such as restfulness, comfort, warmth, and "utter" helplessness to resist forthcoming instructions. Then she was directed to visualize a large mirror in which she would see a vacant room with a door that looked vaguely familiar.

With the stage thus set, Erickson directed her to watch the door open and reveal her own face wearing an

> . . . unexpected mischievous smile. . . . Look behind your face until you see your whole head, and now you can't believe it . . . your neck and shoulders are bare, your chest is uncovered, your body is naked, you are standing there horribly in the nude, you feel so paralyzed in such a peculiar, comfortable way . . . you can't stop looking—looking. And watch—watch carefully—you are beginning to dance—ballet dancing—with a wild wild rhythm of joyous abandonment . . . Kicking high, you stand frozen there on one foot, slowly turning your head to see . . . somebody is coming . . . sounds like a man. Slowly the mirror turns—slowly the man comes into view—it is your husband and he is laughing—he is clapping his hands—he likes your dance. You become unfrozen and you dance and dance with wilder abandon until you collapse in utter exhaustion and your husband picks you up . . ." (*CP* IV, p. 360–361).

Having survived one "showing" of this mental movie, Erickson instructed her to "watch, watch, watch" it all happening again until she had seen it five times from beginning to end.

Direct work completed, he then linked this scenario via posthypnotic suggestions to specific times and circumstances in her upcoming week. Amnesia was carefully suggested to provide a protective seal for the benefit of her conscious mind, which was not yet ready to incorporate the "shocking" new self-image. But her unconscious mind had been equipped with a very detailed new map to follow, complete with timetable and posthypnotic cues. After enacting the scenario as "rehearsed," she did remember the session and was able to keep the new self-image both consciously and unconsciously as she left her phobia in the past.

RESOLUTION OF UNCONSCIOUS EMOTIONAL CONFLICT

We have seen in the previous cases a wide variety of approaches to enhancing the self-image. Erickson's approach was aimed at resolving neurotic conflict and structuring associations of mental mechanisms to facilitate adaptation, growth, and development. Before elaborating the steps in a specific model of self-image thinking, we will briefly address related issues of conflict in psychoanalytic and ego-psychology theories. We want to address the issues about which part of the person builds the self-image and why it works.

Experience has demonstrated that there are more dynamics than merely those conforming to the Oedipal conflict. Likewise, there is far more to the dynamics of psychopathology and interpersonal problems than merely repressed emotion. The psychoanalytic conception of personality revolves around the theoretical theme of repressed emotion seeking expression. Conflict between genetic desires and social constraints gives rise to defense mechanisms (repression, suppression, denial, undoing, rationalization, projection, introjection, etc.). The inhibited impulses form various experiences of anxiety, love, sexual desire, anger, hate, jealousy, or aggression.

These repressed mental turbulants and conflicting emotions express themselves and in turn exert a highly disturbing effect on conscious experience and behavior. The effect of such psychodynamics can be seen as neurotic affect, physical and mental symptoms, dreams, fantasies, daydreams, antisocial and criminal behavior (Guntrip, 1973).

The Creative Unconscious

There was more to Erickson's conception of human functioning than the psychobiological metapsychology suggested by Freud. Because of that fact, he drew from a larger analysis than that of coping and conflicts to explain various psychological problems. He was not constrained by presupposed limitations created by the Oedipal conflict or sphincter related learnings of the preverbal infant.

Erickson's idea of the unconscious and conscious mind, as already stated, corresponds closely to dichotomies between the dominant and nondominant brain hemisphere functions. His ideas about dynamics of psychological pressure and influence were not restricted to the psychoanalytic view. In fact, he was rarely favorable to the strict and limiting conception of motivation referred to in the above summary. He emphasized, instead, a positive drive toward adjustment and creativity involving a wholistic-type inclusion of all facets of human experience.

Transpersonal psychologist Roberto Assagioli (1965) has offered a framework for understanding the variety of healthy, creative, inspiring, mystical, and religious phenomena that can be experienced. We take from his conjecturing a conviction that relatively loosely organized "positive" images existing in each person's history exert an organizing influence on experience. That influence can be as important as the loosely or more highly organized "negative" images and associated emotion created by trauma. These images may, in fact, stimulate ideomotor and ideosensory workings of the brain in the service of achieving desired goals. Those goals may be formed as a result of the positive symbols and conscious awareness working in harmony. The self-image concepts, images, and emotions that become unconscious guides for each of us can be said to be formed by this creative and essentially positive force.

Speaking of what eventually comes to be learned, automatized and then stored in the unconscious, we might ask: What part of the person does the organizing? Is the person conscious of this organizing and learning? Can the person be conscious of it? Is the conscious awareness of such organizing intermittent, constant, epiphenomenal, or sufficient and causal to create behavioral change? Is it necessary or is it unhelpfully intrusive to have awareness of learnings that are "best" carried out by the unconscious?

The organizing mechanism of the unconscious seems to operate in a manner such that a person can have conscious awareness of it. That is, a person can be aware of much of the organizing dynamics of the unconscious. This organizing by the unconscious seems to precede normal conscious experience. So automatic patterns of the unconscious framework (apprehending and associating) influence, a priori, what is noticed consciously about the "real world" in moment-to-moment experience. If one does have awareness of ongoing experience, then unique combinations of ideas and symbols, perceptions and meanings can be easily noticed as they first occur. In that case, consciousness can have a guiding hand in the experiences that come to function unconsciously. One may be said to "will" or "decide" upon what associations are allowed and hence become part of the belief system, perceptual system, and emotional life of the personality (Goulding, 1972, p. 107). This is precisely the case in building self-image thinking structures.

Both positive and negative bundles of experience can be organized with awareness before being relegated to the unconscious. We refer to the organizing aspect of personality as the creative unconscious. Assagioli extended the creative unconscious into increasingly arcane experiences, such as the variety of peak experiences described by Maslow and Lilly, and named the entire range of experience the higher or upper unconscious. His theory recognized not only the conflictual pressures of the id and its plight with the social world but also the positive organizing effect of meditations, affirmations, music, symbols, hero biographies, pilgrimages, willed acts, religious attitudes, and peak experiences.

Assagioli's theory is consistent and compatible with the various associational networks that Erickson called the unconscious. Although Erickson did not favor the mystical or supernatural explanations of experience into which Assagioli poked, we expect that he would agree with the positive balance of human nature which Assagioli presented. And he certainly would have agreed with implementing positive steps to focus conscious as well as unconscious mechanisms to form "bundles" of associated images and emotions. These networks become maps to channel therapeutically released mental and physical energy into desired behavior.

Since it is well-known that subliminal learning does not require conscious awareness, we cannot suppose that the conscious mind is at all times aware of the events that precede and constitute "learning." We have stated earlier that it is the psychological level of communication, rather than conscious insight, that determines the transactional outcome. The notion that part of the ego is conflict-free and synthetic in functioning has given rise to ideas about healthy, autonomous, integrative aspects of ego functioning (Hartmann, 1958). It is perhaps that portion of experience we, as therapists, condition our consciousness to notice when operating within the framework presented here.

Our awareness is atuned (as Erickson's seemed to be) to notice combinations of behaviors in the here and now which recapitulate themselves in other areas of the client's life. As such, they provide an illumination of the client's unique map of the world. The client's expression of a symptom is thus revealed as a metaphor for his or her life in general. For example, a trainee in supervision in our office explained that there was a pregnancy in his family and, as he did so, he placed his hands over his head "in passing." His gesture, although brief, distinctively resembled the gesture of one who pulls out or at his own hair. He was, in fact, balding in the front and top of his scalp. When we responded, "Some people have difficulties with their marital decision-making and actually feel like pulling their hair out," he sighed heavily and shook his head vigorously. We had noticed his metaphoric statement of the map of the world that influenced his self-image about adapting to having children. It was, of course, no surprise that the case he had brought for supervision concerned a client of his who was having violent thoughts about the new firstborn child in his family.

Bound Energy

"Residual images" is a term we use for the group of non-adaptive, coherent, and relatively organized images referred to by object relations theorists and ego psychologists when they observe the bulk of everyday mentation. They are archaic self-images. For example, Eric Berne observed, "It may now be said that the reminiscences may take the form of primal images and that the context which is repressed may consist of a complex of ideas and feelings embodied in a highly cathected set of such images" (1977, p. 80). Metaphorically speaking, if an associated bundle of images is broken, energy is released. That energy which has been bound up in the "highly cathected associations of images" can be said to be freed.

Therapeutic change, however, requires more than merely breaking bundles of images and freeing bound energy. That is, one cannot simply leave the process of productively using freed energy to serendipity. Neither can it be left up to the unconscious. We believe it is our therapeutic responsibility to help the client consolidate and direct the newly available energy by enhancing "self-image thinking." In the multiple embedded metaphor structure, one or more patterns to free bound energy are typically used in the central portion designated for "direct" work and then followed by some form of self-image thinking to specifically direct the freed energy.

A residual image is a memory that the person represents as a feeling associated to the picture or sound of some event. For example, the "hair pulling" trainee whose wife was pregnant recalled images associated with the pregnancy that produced his baby brother. He automatically experienced an unpleasant feeling in response to that residual image. The residual image did not allow him any choice. Every time some portion of that image was remembered, his feelings and behavior were influenced to some degree. Many memories are stored in this way as unexamined combinations of feelings hooked to markers in a person's experience. These residual script-like images interfere with thinking because, when the person is associating to various images needed to "think" with, these emotion laden feelings are likely to take him or her on tangents, bias observations and promote decision-making based on limits of the past. Since residual images from all ages of a person's past are stored in the memory, conditioned unconscious choices often lack the wisdom of the more mature and capable self. These residual images, with conscious and unconscious proportions, are the core of the neurotic complex which Erickson considered the target for his direct work interventions.

Let's further examine this core of residual images. As the senses apprehend some external stimulus, a search process occurs, as we have mentioned previously. The person may search for meaning in any sensory channel. A residual image consists of the previous image(s) and synesthesia associations conditioned to anxiety, tension and discomfort. The person's outward expressions and behaviors are modulated and guided by the image. This residual thinking is so conditioned that it often fails to reach the threshold of excitation necessary to gain conscious attention and the person is therefore "unable" to exercise choice about his or her conduct or feeling state.

There are, as well, "practical" residual images which are primarily task or equipment oriented and the behavior conditioned to them is not interpersonal. These images guide behavior related to the task or equipment and do not guide a person's feelings, attitudes or interactions with others. Since practical images are about things and tasks, they have continuity when "things" operate as they did during learning or as they did when rehearsed. Consider practical images which guide a pianist in playing the piano. During practice these images may adequately guide the pianist to play the piece, but during a recital any residual images associated with performance anxieties could easily disrupt these practical images, as well as the recital presentation.

Cognitive Change

Erickson considered hypnosis to be a modality for communicating ideas and understandings. That is, the client, hearing the words and delivery by the hypnotist, begins a line of thought and forms associations. Each set of associations is then further linked and associated to new ideas, understandings and potentialities. Bypassing or breaking conditioned bundles of residual images and helping the client construct a new map of reality facilitate cure. "It is this experience of reassociating and reorganizing his own experiential life that eventuates in a cure . . ." (CP IV, p. 38).

Initial changes in the map (images, perceptions, predispositions, associations of images, associated motoric learnings, and associated emotional affects) were considered by Erickson to be the factor that resulted in change, as we have mentioned repeatedly. In the course of induction the intent of the hypnotist is to create heightened awareness of inner experiences, including "the manner and the sequence in which those thoughts flash through their mind" (Erickson & Rossi, 1981, p. 5).

Erickson proposed that a person can break out of "limiting preconceptions to a broader understanding of our human possibilities" (Erickson & Rossi, 1981, p. 26). Again, he was not referring to overcoming Oedipal dynamics or merely resolving conflicts created by highly charged repressed emotions. He referred to experiential change in the client's map of the world which organized a new framework to guide subsequent belief, action, and feeling.

We can see evidence of this belief in cases reviewed at the beginning of this chapter, as well as in his moment-to-moment interview management. Reframing is a notable example of the latter. The notion of reframing, a conception of learning with many facets, has appeared many places in the recent literature of change (Lankton, 1980b; Lankton, Lankton, & Brown, 1981, p. 296; Mellor, 1980; Watzlawick, Weakland & Fisch, 1974; Zeig, 1980, p. 15). It is a primary tool for influencing cognitive change and permanent resolution of emotional conflict.

We have shown how positive interpretation of a previously negative behavior can be created with paradoxical splitting, as well as with metaphoric frame change. A short tangent can illustrate reframing as it occurred in the context of interview management.

The case involves a man whose opening remarks to Erickson consisted of a characterization of all psychiatrists in very vulgar terms. Erickson's response was typical of meeting the client at his model of the world; he replied, "You undoubtedly have a damn good reason for saying that and even more." Whereupon, the client did say much more; with profanity, obscenity, bitterness, resentment, contempt and hostility, he related his difficulty and his inability to get help through psychotherapy. Now, a typical response might be to consider this client resistant and proceed from that belief. Erickson, by contrast, reframed this presentation by saying, "Well, you must have had a hell of a good reason to seek therapy from me." Here, then, is a wonderful example of turning "seemingly uncooperative forms of behavior into good rapport" with reframing. (Erickson, Rossi, & Rossi, 1976, p. 59).

Erickson commonly used such reframing in managing moment-to-moment interactions. The client's customary conception of his or her world was reframed to reveal a positive aspect of life. "In both his hypnotic and his family work [he] tended to emphasize what is positive in the behavior of the person" (Haley, 1973, p. 34). His emphasis on the positive was not just a ploy to befuddle the existing framework of the client, as is evident in the cases of self-image enhancement at the beginning of this chapter. We now turn to a detailed discussion of self-image thinking as a way to visually emphasize positive options in a person's life, thereby expanding his or her map of the world in a very literal fashion and directing any energy "freed" by resolving conflicts which had produced unconscious emotional pressure.

SELF-IMAGE THINKING

The "self" has been discussed in the literature of psychology and psychotherapy since the inception of these fields. However, rigorous scientific investigation of concepts related to the self diminished after the historical theories of John Watson attempted to translate conscious thought, emotion, and feeling into behaviorally observable behaviors (such as laryngeal movements). Or, as Skinner described it: "A self is a repertoire of behavior appropriate to a given set of contingencies" (1971, p. 199). This definition is in distinct contrast to the definition of nonbehaviorist Progoff, who wrote:

> The Self is, on the one hand, the primal factor that is the basis of all psychological development; and, on the other hand, the Self is actually the final product of Individuation as the fulfillment of what is potential in man. The Self is thus both the raw material and the guiding purpose, the source and culmination of human life and of all psychological endeavor (1965, p. 181).

The current historical mood regarding acceptable graduate research and investigation makes it unfashionable to seriously consider the "self" as an area of psychological reality. Perhaps someday the subject will regain the thoughtful scientific study it deserves. Research and heuristic approaches to studying the self present many difficulties. Nonetheless, we discuss the concept of the self but reduce the complexity of the subject to mental representations of the self.

Our concept of the self-image includes a continuum of experience ranging from social experience on one end to biological experience on the other. In between these apparent polarities we include personality traits, feelings, and audition to the extent that these aspects are used to define for the person a range of comfortable behaviors and feelings.

About the self, George Herbert Mead wrote: "The self, as that which can be an object to itself, is essentially a social structure, and it arises in social experience . . . it is impossible to conceive of a self arising outside of social experience" (1965, p. 204). Jung commented about the biological end of the "self" continuum when he wrote that instincts themselves do not operate amorphously. He theorized that instincts from biological and genetic material inherited by the person must be channeled by images or they do not function. The instinct must have an image attached. "If any of these conditions is lacking, the instinct does not function, because it cannot exist without its total pattern, without its image" (Jung, 1959, p. 71). Self-perceptions are developed and shaped as the result of interactions. Thus, we link the biological act of perception to images of self-operation and finally to acts of social interaction and speculate that a causal relationship exists. Remembered social interaction shapes the self-image.

"Self-image" is a term often used loosely and seldom made explicit with even vague reference to imagery systems. However, as we use the term and as Erickson used the term, the self-image is any way that people record themselves or remember themselves mentally. The act of remembering oneself, of course, occurs both consciously and unconsciously and may include any type of mental representation. For example, "I can't stand coffee" is a self-image, as is feeling nauseous when thinking about someone else drinking coffee (but not consciously thinking the above statement in words).

Most people use archaic thinking to build self-images. They think of themselves in archaic inner dialogue or feeling states or fleeting visual images. Often the conscious imagery is actually of other people. When daydreaming of a person about whom one is pleasantly disposed, for instance, the imagery of that person's face or voice or touch may be all that is in consciousness and the memory of the self (feeling pleasant) may not be the object of consciousness. In that case the self-image is far removed from conscious deliberation and the image of the other person defines a part of the comfort zone and is therefore a self-image. Thus, the daydreamer may think of going to a meeting or a party because the other person would go to a meeting or a party. The image defines a range of activity of the self via a type of role modeling. A pleasant feeling is available through the memory of the other person and so the image of another person is operating as a self-image. The self-image may also be an actual visual representation of the person's own body and an auditory representation of the voice.

It is surprising that people seldom choose visual imagery to depict themselves and their own behavior since things are remembered faster when remembered visually. A picture *is* worth a thousand words! The visual matrix is the building block of the most delicate and sophisticated information. Music notation is displayed visually; blueprints for buildings are visual guides; maps for air and space travel are visual; and computers have been designed to give visual readouts to maximize information provided to the user. Yet most people, according to our investigation, do not use visual imagery to depict their own behavior and feelings. They do not use willful thinking to plan and objectify their own lifestyle and their interpersonal self-expression, though they can easily accomplish such thinking when it is suggested and systematically presented to them. People have not been encouraged to think in that way. In fact, cultural injunctions often endorse exactly the opposite. For example, "Think of others and don't think about yourself so much." As a result, people are far too passive in their own thinking and the use of their own images. Self-training in visualization skills and goal oriented fantasy makes possible objective thinking about the self and "imagineering" solutions.

The necessary foundation for self-image thinking is a rich array of imagery and an ability to direct it. Every time a person sees, hears or feels something that can later be recalled, a sensory-based image of that event has been recorded. Memory is comprised of an incredible number of operations that seem to reproduce images through complicated mental mathematics which are as yet unknown. However, each image is associated to others and these networks of associations are what guide behavior. The images may be less important guides than the mental operations that produce them, but for the sake of convenience we will refer to this entire set of operations as "images."

Many sets of images are unconscious, not mysteriously, but simply so conditioned and so automatic that they have receded from the threshold of excitation necessary for consciousness to occur. These "habit patterns" are many and varied. They include opening doors, buttoning shirts, shaking hands with acquaintances, looking at watches, eating, grooming and even such processes as ruminating over events that leave the thinker feeling depressed, sad, lonely, angry, etc. And again, once a group of images has been learned, related and associated together, the entire process can drop into an unconscious mode of operating. Then, "thinking" about those images proceeds in a habitual and automatic fashion. Such out-of-awareness "thinking" is responsible for the majority of neurotic emotional affect, behavioral difficulties and family disturbances that bring people to psychotherapy, but can also be the basis for the creative skills of the unconscious which Erickson utilized in the process of psychotherapy, as well as for purposeful self-image thinking.

Our model of self-image thinking consists of four parts: the central self-image, scenarios, habit patterns, and emanated images. The central self-image (CSI) is the most important. When it is complete, it consists of a person seeing in the mind's eye an accurate replica of the self and another person. The self is visualized with all the desired qualities that the person wants to have available as characteristics. These may be retrieved, one at a time, from the client's own memories and then "mirrored" by the therapist so that behaviorally specific visual clues for each quality can be added to the unembellished picture of the self. Or they may be elicited, as Erickson did in the case of the woman and her "three badges of womanhood" or in the case of the woman with "phobic modesty."

After "putting into the picture" the various desired qualities (i.e., confidence, charm, sense of humor, kindness, flexibility, etc.), another person is added who would support or enhance the client's having those desired traits. This can be seen explicitly in the previously cited case of the woman with "phobic modesty." It will be remembered that Erickson asked her to methodically construct a visual image of herself in an imagined mirror and then watch the mirror turn until a man came into the picture with her. The man Erickson described was her husband laughing in an accepting and friendly manner. Adding to the visualization of the self a "soundtrack," feelings and a supportive other person makes it complete.

There are several goals accomplished with the CSI. First, motor connections are built to the images. The CSI is a visual stimulus which represents, symbolizes and actually associates the person to desired feelings and behaviors whenever it is remembered in the present or future, either consciously or unconsciously. Secondly, the CSI is interpersonal. The presence of the other person in the picture insures that the CSI will not foster narcissism. Instead, it allows a person to imagine a valued goal and work toward it while maintaining interpersonal values as a guideline throughout the time spent attaining the goal. The interpersonal aspect of the image implies or presupposes that behavior occurs in a social field. Thus, the CSI shapes "means values." Furthermore, the presence of the other person prepares the thinker for the more complex mental gymnastics to follow in the subsequent stages of self-image thinking.

The outstanding features of the CSI include an interpersonal visual representation, related audition, associated desired feelings, the self-image as part of the picture, and resulting influence as this image guides the response of the person picturing it. Feelings and sounds are added to the image until the person is satisfied with the imagined self-expression reflected. The person constructing the image watches, as an observer, some imagined interaction between the self and the other person. S/he intermittently merges with the image to build associations to feelings by actually feeling the qualities. This feedback constitutes a checking of sorts to insure that the imagined qualities are actually desirable to the person.

After the CSI is constructed it is systematically rehearsed in visual fantasy through several pleasurable, routine, and anxiety-producing scenarios or "cope operas." As the name suggests, these scenarios become visual maps of available behavioral options which have been thoughtfully and carefully designed by the client to satisfy his or her desired qualities and values. Scenarios are added to the CSI by changing the background to allow various scenes to unfold in which the client watches the self interacting. The first scenarios should be pleasant. They serve as preliminary mental practice for the complex task of visualization.

Later the scenarios may deal with situations that would have been anxiety-producing to varying degrees. The rationale for such successive approximation is that initially the client is training the ability to fantasize and at that stage of learning will proceed more effectively without entertaining anxiety-producing images. So, to maximize the client's ability to keep the desirable feelings constant for the more difficult scenarios, the task of visualizing scenarios is practiced with successive approximations and positive reference scenes.

The visualized interactions must, at all times, reflect the qualities inherent in the desired self-image as it is maintained throughout the changing scenes of both pleasant and anxiety-producing situations. Adding an appropriate dialogue is equally important in reinforcing a positive image or modifying a negative one. Doing so not only begins to break any "negative" or traumatic residual associations, but also builds new associations to the desired feelings and skills which remain constantly in the picture. Thoughtfulness and mindfulness necessary to use one's self and talents in various "tough" spots are thus objectified and strengthened. Meichenbaum, using a very similar procedure, has shown that this type of thoughtfulness does increase the likelihood of a person's acting in accord with personal values, even in unexpected situations that somehow parallel the rehearsed fantasies. His results showed:

> . . . that the cognitive modification treatment program was significantly more successful in reducing test anxiety, as assessed by several self-report and performance measures, than a conventional systematic desensitization treatment procedure of the same length" (O'Neil, 1978, p. 64).

The habit pattern stage of the complete self-image thinking structure consists of the client's learning to use the slightest indicator of stress as a sign to engage conditioned, goal directed scenarios and attached feelings stemming from the central self-image. The habit can be conditioned in steps while strengthening all aspects of self-image thinking by first building the CSI and several scenarios and then purposefully recalling a stress moment. At the first signal of building stress (tight throat, muscles tense, "butterflies" in stomach, shortness of breath, etc.), thinking is then consciously directed to the CSI and previously established scenarios. Repeating this process for six to ten different pairings with the anxiety signals and scenarios is suggested.

For example, one man's CSI looked like himself when he felt most confident and enthusiastic. He saw his features constantly reflect these traits as he watched a realistic but imaginary scene in which he was buying a ticket at the airport during rush hour. He imagined interacting with other people, and since confidence and enthusiasm were associated to that picture, he thought of several possible options that he may have never tried before to sustain those qualities during adversity.

As he built the habit pattern, he remembered an anxiety situation without using self-image thinking and, as soon as he was aware of the beginning of his anxiety indicator (clenched teeth), he immediately switched to the positive visualization and sustained it. Repeating this process several times built a habit pattern such that any indicator of tension or anxiety became a valuable feedback mechanism. It signaled him that he was not acting like his picture or the image was not in keeping with his potential and intention. Therefore, the same feedback indicator of tension or anxiety became an ally of sorts or an associational device to remind him both consciously and unconsciously of his central self-image, scenarios, and available options.

Even encountering novel stress (is there any other kind?), people automatically begin to switch to visualized options of themselves handling the situation with the qualities they desire, possess and value. To repeat, performance is guided by imagery. Therefore, performance increasingly approaches that which is imagined, valued and expected (Jones, 1977). We follow our maps. This type of self-image mapping can become as conditioned as any residual imagery had been. It becomes automatic and unconscious, freeing the conscious mind to enjoy the resulting experience or give attention to other important details.

The emanated imagery stage of the self-image thinking structure occurs when we direct a client to "step inside" a picture of himself or herself enjoying the desired goal and have another fantasy which "emanates" from the first one. This special form of visualization can be used very beneficially to teach clients how they will experience the world when they meet their goals. This technique shapes perceptual readiness and aligns skills and resources with "end values."

This stage begins after the client has rehearsed a scenario of a desired outcome in the future. The next step is to merge with the central self-image within the imagined future, "pretending" that the future pictured as a desired goal has actually arrived. In the "present tense" of the future the client is directed to really enjoy the associated feelings of accomplishment, pride, intimacy, etc., which are present, and then to "fall into a daydream" and look back at all those steps taken in arriving at this "dream come true" (see the case of Florence in Chapter 4 [p. 93] and Dorine in Chapter 7 [p. 258]), keeping the pleasant feelings constant just as if the desired goal really had been reached. This emanated image shapes perception to look, listen, and apprehend data that are relevant to reaching the desired goals. The emanated image is an imaginary way to "look back" from the fantasized future and learn something important about making that dream come true.

DIRECT WORK PATTERNS

In the transcripts in earlier chapters we have used several sets of interventions to disrupt or change bundled associations, create cognitive change, or free "bound energy." These are by no means exhaustive of interventions possible in the multiple embedded metaphor structure but they do provide a range of treatment choices applicable to a variety of problems resulting from unconscious emotional conflict and residual images. We will highlight a few of them and elaborate important aspects of each to make them more available to the reader. Although they may be most frequently employed at the direct work phase, they will often be quite useful at other stages throughout the entire structure. This is also the case with self-image thinking, related scenarios, and emanated images.

Punchlines

"Punchlines" is a term we have used frequently to refer to directives embedded within a metaphor. They frequently occur within quotes to the protagonist in a metaphor so that the client actually hearing them may choose to take them personally or ignore them. Of course, as with indirect suggestions, punchlines should always be in the best interest of the client. Punchlines clearly request of the client a desirable or therapeutic behavior or attitude. This directive can be said to motivate the new behaviors which will later be detailed via self-image thinking or elaborated in a therapeutic outcome metaphor.

The punchline approach is a way for the client to save face and reduce the probability of defensiveness or resistance that might be encountered if the directive were given more directly. When a punchline is given in the context of trance and metaphor, the client's conscious mind can simply discount the applicability to himself or herself if the punchline is irrelevant or too relevant for comfort, while at the same time his or her unconscious mind can be expected to generate a therapeutic response.

In Chapter 7, "Dorine" was the complaining client who wouldn't let go of her grievances of the past in order to do those things in her best interest which she knew to do in her current life. Embedded within a metaphor about another client and within quotes of what Milton Erickson would have told that client, Dorine was told: "You're a damn fool if you don't do those things which you know are good for you . . . and Erickson would tell you that you're a disgrace to the trust that can be placed in a human being if you don't do what's good for you, but I wouldn't tell you that and I don't know how you'll get the message." When Dorine emerged from the trance she was cheerful and pleased. This response would obviously have been unlikely if that message had been delivered in any way that prevented her from saving face. That is a graphic example of protection provided for the client in the framework of the multiple embedded structure. Yet, the message was still shared with Dorine—she had to get in gear and use her skills to change. But punchlines are seldom so derogatory.

Kate's situation (see Chapter 7) was somewhat similar. We could not tell her to "compete with herself" without creating the risk of possible defensiveness, rationalizations, and excuses from her. But that was exactly what we did tell her in the context of embedded direct work. This was also the modality for speaking about highly sensitive material, such as the enhancement of her body image. We recommend embedding punchlines for any direct work dealing with sensitive sexuality issues, with admonishing or chastising, or with advice that the client's conscious mind is likely to directly oppose.

Another use of punchline interventions involves grief reactions that are not consciously contracted by the client. Rarely does a client ask for help to grieve more completely or more appropriately. That is, when clients have suffered loss but have not grieved sufficiently to prevent aberrant symptomatic reactions, they may contract to remove the symptom itself or diminish the problems created by the symptom. These clients frequently have "goodbyes" they need to say, either to deceased loved ones, divorced loved ones, parts of the self, children becoming independent, jobs that must be left, etc. When that is the case we typically relate a story we borrowed from Erickson in which the repeated punchline "say goodbye" appears.

The original story involved Erickson's mother when they had to leave the farm on which she had lived most of her life. As the story goes, she did not want to leave but circumstances dictated the necessity of her leaving. Since she loved the farm so much and had so many memories invested there, it was important that she very carefully and thoughtfully "say goodbye" to it in the way that he directed.

We begin the goodbye story by mentioning that we knew an old woman who was in the process of leaving her farm and we had her first face the south 40 acres and "say goodbye" to the fertile fields, all the crops, and all the labor that went into bringing those crops to fruition: "Say goodbye." Then, we explain that we had her go to the north 40 and "say goodbye" to the trees planted as a windbreak. Then go to the west, "say goodbye" to the stream flowing there and to the stone fence built by carrying each of those stones up from the stream. We metaphorically direct the client to "say goodbye" to the stream and "say goodbye" to the fence. And "say goodbye" to the view beyond and all those sunsets she had watched there.

Eventually, we explain that we take her into the house. We suggest that she "say goodbye" to the fireplace in the heart of the house; "say goodbye" to the kitchen stove. We mention that the woman was to go up in the attic where we asked her to make three piles: a large pile of things she's going to discard, a medium sized pile of things she's going to give away and a smaller pile still of things she's going to keep. Then we tell her to "say goodbye" to each pile: "Goodbye." "Goodbye." "Goodbye."

Finally, we mention that we led her out of the house. On her way out of the house to leave, she commented that the bushes by the steps needed pruning. We say that we reminded her to "say goodbye" to them as well. The story ends when we add that some years later she had occasion to pass by that farmhouse again and her comment was: "My goodness, look what they have done to their bushes. They've cut them down to nothing." Then we summarize that "Those weren't her bushes anymore. She had said her goodbyes."

We have found, as Erickson did, that this story has almost universal applicability since nearly every client has something or someone to say goodbye to. Frequently, clients will sob quietly as they listen to this metaphor and say personal goodbyes with tears flowing silently over their cheeks. Energy which has been bound in grieving over losses or in futile attempts to recreate the past is thus freed to create the desired present and future. If the client does not apply this learning personally, there is no resistance, no loss of rapport, and no hard feelings.

There are many themes for punchline metaphors that will be universally useful for most clients. Among these are metaphors that deal with the unique worth and value of the individual, sexual development metaphors, and rites of passage metaphors. We suggest that therapists gather or construct several such punchline metaphors in each of those categories.

Scramble

"Scramble" is a confusion technique which deals directly with confusing the occurrence of a symptom. The desired outcome of a series of directives about the order in which to review the five phases of the problem is that the client will find thinking about the problem more trouble than it's worth and simply forget about it, associating instead to the relaxation of trance or other resources. Due to the scrambled order of reviewing the problem, it is likely that in the future, remembering any part of the problem will result in a bit of confusion that can most easily be resolved by following the associative link to desired feelings. Consequently, the energy that was bound producing the symptom, analyzing it, or worrying over it can be redirected to resources and the business of living.

Erickson occasionally did a "scramble," as we call it, with such symptoms as bedwetting. In one case he sent an adult military selectee to a hotel room for three days in an attempt to cure him of bedwetting. The man was sent to the room with a deliberately constructed confusion regarding the occurrence of his problem. Although the strategic therapy in this case suggested instructions to change the problem by altering the context in which it appeared, the planting of certain ideas in his mind in the session prior to the sojourn to the hotel constituted the hypnotic aspect of the treatment:

This idea would make no sense to him, and he would become so confused and bewildered by it that he would be unable to straighten out his mind. Instead, the idea would run through his mind constantly, and soon he would find himself miserably, helplessly, and confusedly speculating about his shame, anxiety, and embarrassment when the maid discovered the dry bed instead of the wet bed he had planned (*CP* IV, p. 154).

With a complicated reassociation of simple resources, including confusion, Erickson was able to inhibit the occurrence of the problem. The client was disoriented with respect to the location in which the problem was to occur and disoriented with respect to the proper sequence or order of the problem. Erickson's therapeutic interventions, such as this, were frequently so creative that others are reluctant to attempt a simulation. To "standardize" this stylistic Ericksonian approach as a specific technique, we have formed a protocol for creating such confusion around the client's presented symptom.

The primary design of our scramble technique involves a confusion about the order of events leading up to and following the onset of the symptom. That is, we help the client get befuddled about the sequence of indicators that s/he had been using to gauge the onset or end of the problem. Specifically, the directives involve reminding clients that, while they may have thought about an episode of the problem having a beginning and an end (and if they had not before, they do then because of indirectly focused awareness), they may not have thought about its also having a middle. Furthermore, between the beginning and the middle there is a distinct phase which we label Phase Two. The middle is Phase Three, and between the middle and the end is yet another distinct phase which we label Phase Four. So, we systematically help the client recognize five phases that are the onset through the termination of the problem. With this arrangement thus set up and under our direction, we are ready to scramble or confuse the order of the occurrence.

We "help" the client review these, first in order from one to five, by recounting the steps slowly and allowing sufficient time between numbers to get a head nod or other ideomotor sign from the client indicating accomplishment at each phase. Thus prepared, we then suggest that there is no reason to continue to notice the problem in the same old way of beginning to end, so why not begin the review this time by first noticing Phase Three, then Phase Two, now Phase Five, Phase One, and finally Phase Four. We continue, using double binds and indirect suggestion to offer reasons for examining other possible orders. For example, perhaps remind a client that "your unconscious mind can learn something new while your conscious mind follows the instructions to examine the order, or maybe it will be your unconscious mind which automatically directs the order, allowing your conscious mind to participate in learning something new; but this time begin by first noticing Phase Five, then Phase Two, Phase Four, One, and Three." Such reordering is continued through various permutations and combinations of the numbers one through five.

After reviewing the problem in many different orders, the client will probably manifest some ideomotor sign of tension as s/he diligently tries to follow the somewhat tedious and confusing directives. When we notice moderate tension we suggest that "since it's so much trouble keeping up with all these different orders, why not just forget about it entirely and feel the relaxation instead." This suggestion is usually responded to with an audible sigh of relief, an automatic deepening of trance, and relaxation of musculature.

"David," discussed in Chapter 3 on diagnosis, presented the problem of a stomach ulcer. His sensations regarding his symptom were advantageously "scrambled" in the above manner and then he was led through self-image thinking to develop an automatic "triggering" of desired, rehearsed "scenarios." The scenarios and concomitant feelings of adequate functioning were linked to the confusion so that at the occurrence of any sensation previously connected with the ulcer, regardless of which "phase" of the problem it represented, he would be able to switch to the new map of conduct.

Reframing

"Reframing," as we mentioned earlier, endorses the idea that people can "break out of limiting preconceptions to a broader understanding of human possibilities" (Erickson & Rossi, 1981, p. 26). Specifically, it refers to the process of helping the client to identify a different framework for understanding and responding to a problem. Watzlawick et al. (1974) have mentioned that the essence of brief therapy is the gentle art of reframing. They suggest that "any successful suggestion [that] puts our patients' reality into a different conceptual and emotional frame" is reframing (Watzlawick, 1982, p. 153).

The purpose of altering the client's negative framework into a positive framework is to allow the subsequent therapy to accomplish one or more of several goals:

1) establish or identify motives, needs, desires or intention of both current and past behaviors and label them "positive" to eliminate apparent resistance;
2) discriminate between the motive and the self-defeating behaviors so that new and more effective means to satisfy the actual needs of the client system can be developed;
3) restructure the experience so that a set of new learnings and desirable

experiences are created in place of the problematic behaviors, feelings, and thoughts.

Reframing is especially useful for treating clients who have problems they consider to be out of their control, problems that, for any reason, require "re-understanding" or what Watzlawick et al. (1974) term "second-order change." In practical reality that includes most clients.

Many examples in the preceding transcripts can be cited. In the case of Dorine, for instance, we reframed her childhood difficulties as normal behavior for a child trying to help reduce difficulties in a family. Thus, we established ourselves as nonjudgmental about her acquisition of problems. Simultaneously, her need for defensiveness and resistance was reduced and she was offered a way to forgive herself for the misery she had created. This is an example of the first goal of reframing. Of course, subsequent therapy would hold her responsible for her actions in the future, but the reframing gave her a clean slate from which to begin.

Another example of reframing can be found in the case of pelvic pain. Rose was asked to use the first signal of the pain as a way to signal the age regressed resource of delight from walking. While reframing with Dorine was done to accomplish the first of the goals named above, it was used with Rose to accomplish the third goal. In Dorine's case, therefore, it was necessary to label and name the motive but with Rose the reassociation did not require conscious relabeling. The reframing was a matter of making the occurrence of the symptom a cue for the emergence of the necessary resource. By implication, then, the recognition of the symptom was no longer to be feared and avoided; it belonged to the new and positive framework.

The second goal for reframing listed above was exemplified in the earlier case of the child abuser. In his situation the act of abuse was reframed as his intention to control his daughter's behavior because he loved her and wanted to be certain she had appropriately learned values that were good for her. This reframing was only the first step in his therapy. Subsequent interventions were designed to teach him to control in a tender and more abstract manner and to recognize that she did possess qualities he could be proud of. The reframing, however, made it possible for him to stay in therapy and maintain a nondefensive manner while new learnings were being conveyed. The new framework became the holding force of the relationship between us, so that therapy could proceed to resolve the unconscious emotional conflict that led to the abuse.

It may be remembered that paradoxical splitting was the device that created this important alteration in frameworks. In fact, any case of paradoxical splitting will accomplish reframing that satisfies the second goal above. We find this type of reframing in all of Erickson's cases of symptom prescription in which a slight split was made to separate the undesirable behavior from the positive interpretation that accompanies it. In the earlier case of interview management, for instance, Erickson told the man using vulgarities that he must have had a good reason to say that and even more. The implied prescription of the resistance—"say more"—and the positive interpretation that he must have a good reason to feel that way placed the client in a positive therapeutic framework and there was no further resistance of the original type.

As noted, reframing is a useful intervention for both interview management and for establishing therapeutically consistent belief systems. Relabeling and reframing, however, are best used by those therapists who can really consider the client's behavior his or her "best choice." If the therapist cannot respect the client's behaviors and regard him or her as a unique and special individual, then reframing will be a hollow and transparent lie designed to manipulate the client for the therapist's own benefit. Reframing, paradoxical prescription, and metaphoric frame changing, like any of Erickson's interventions, should occur within the ethical framework previously explained. The therapist should use them sincerely and congruently or not at all.

Dissociative Reviewing

Dissociative reviewing is created by a series of directives which allows the client to stay comfortable while examining previously traumatic memories or displacing physical pain. It is appropriate to use when there are many limiting images related to a particular map of experience or when the active discomfort of pain prevents the retrieval of other resources.

An extensive use of dissociative reviewing can be found in the transcript of Tracy in Chapter 6. In that case dissociation was culminated with Tracy reviewing herself from a distance. The safe and comfortable distance allows the client to review almost any trauma and learn something therapeutically relevant in the process. The process of retrieving resources for dissociation with trance phenomena has already been explained. Basically, it can be structured through indirect suggestion once necessary resources have been elicited. It may also be structured more directly in deep trance, as it was in the Monde case when Erickson stated:

> In other words, would you like to see your adult body sitting in that chair over there? And you unconscious mind over here, but your body's over there? Tell me the position in which you're sitting (Lustig, 1975).

In either instance, the client is first directed in retrieving desired resources which may have been unavailable at the time of the traumatic experience. Then, optimally fortified and "protected" by healthy parts of the personality which are organized and mobilized for change, the client might be asked to maintain the mature, relaxed, detached, or confident resources as s/he observes a younger self in the distance. Therapeutic applications of the dissociative reviewing may include having the client simply watch the earlier scene, reframe the beliefs developed at the earlier age, detach the negative feelings once associated to the trauma, or scan the scene to identify some desired positive resource that needs to be identified.

Reciprocal Inhibition

Reciprocal inhibition of images is an intervention which allows immediate alteration or "editing" of sensory components of memories which consistently produce pain, confusion or anxiety. One specific subcategory of this has been described as "collapsing anchors" (Lankton, 1980a). Reciprocal inhibition is especially useful when a specific interfering image or group of associated images can be identified. The interfering image is changed by reciprocal inhibition (Bandura, 1969; Wolpe, 1948) so that it no longer automatically triggers the undesirable and limiting emotional experience. The process can be conceptualized as a method to "trim" disrupting experiences "down to size." It can be systematically accomplished in each sensory channel. A client identifies a "negative" residual image—Experience B. The therapist guides the client to identify an incompatible experience—Experience A. The therapist then directs that the incompatible portion of Experience A be superimposed onto the undesirable portion of Experience B. If necessary, all aspects of B may be edited by systematic superimposition such that a new arrangement of images will be created. The resulting map of experience with its edited portion will mean something different and allow the client different feeling, behavioral, and cognitive associations, despite continued memory for the original (now edited) experience. The following example clarifies the use of this intervention in editing an image which, although just outside of awareness, had limited the client's range of options.

A middle-aged man asked for help in overcoming chronic "attacks" of angina. He was healthy and physically fit otherwise. He was asked in the direct phase of the multiple embedded metaphor to mentally "recreate" the beginning of a typical attack. He was then assisted in identifying a precipitating event. The precipitating event in his experience was a previously unconscious image of a photograph. The photo showed his father and six uncles, all of

whom had died of heart attacks. Subsequently, he remembered having studied the photograph at the funeral of the last uncle to die.

The image had been incorporated long ago, possibly to serve as a reminder
of the faces of those he loved. It had long since been "forgotten," that is,
removed from conscious awareness, but its occurrence in unconscious memory continued to be a precipitating event, or the final development in the sequence of events that stimulated his angina. It seemed to automatically stimulate anxiety and physical ramifications, perhaps those associated with the
funeral home in which the memory was formed.

Reciprocal inhibition therapy, then, required finding a way, either metaphorically or directly, to make his memory of the photo and an incompatible
memory occur simultaneously or in close proximity, with the incompatible
image occurring last in the sequence. In this case the client was simply asked
to select a desirable visual scene which was incompatible with the residual image. He was then reminded to begin experiencing that desirable picture (playing tennis) just as he began to see the visual image of the photograph. Thus,
the visual memory of the photograph was inhibited or edited. It was altered
by the simultaneous presence of another, incompatible visual memory. We
include the use of metaphorically retrieved images to expand upon Wolpe's
original method, but the theoretical and procedural aspects still remain those
of Wolpe.

An example of editing from one of Erickson's training sessions illustrates
this pattern's broad range of application, as well as a metaphoric and creative
way to accomplish it. All who knew Erickson tended to love him and to look
forward with dismay to his inevitable death. Recognizing this problem, he
would frequently edit by first sharing delightful anecdotes such as one about
his habit over the years of sending "get well" cards signed "The Easter Bunny"
to hospitalized children at all times of the year. After telling the story, he
would add the visual stimulus of himself smiling broadly and chuckling
slightly.

Then, he would focus awareness on his death (and the anxieties associated
with its anticipation) by saying, for example, "When I die . . ." and then
pausing for the listener to focus on the thought of his death. He would continue and complete the reciprocal inhibition in this way: ". . . I'm going to
die with a smile on my face remembering all those cards I sent signed 'The
Easter Bunny'." Thus, the incompatible images of "Easter Bunny" and Erickson smiling were paired with the image of his dying. The paired images were,
in a sense, posthypnotically projected into the future.

Another example of this pattern is available in the case used to demonstrate indirect suggestions in Chapter 5. Therapy with that client was necessarily brief. Therefore, metaphorical resolution ("tie up loose ends," dream-

ing the benzine ring as a device to find order in a complex set of data, etc.) was facilitated by reciprocal inhibition. Images associated with "being at the heart of the matter," with the label "compulsive character," and with "realizing his original problem" were each paired to positive feelings created in trance and associated to images of "a warm furry cocoon." Here, for instance, is a line from that transcript: ". . . And the ball of yarn which could be so perplexing to the compulsive character became a warm, furry cocoon to support and soothe him while he looked out from inside." It might be important to underscore that when using reciprocal inhibition and juxtaposing positive and negative images, it is most effective to conclude with the positive image rather than vice versa.

Redecision

"Redecision" is a term we have borrowed from Bob and Mary Goulding (1979). It refers to securing from the client, while age regressed to the original scene, agreement and determination about a new course of conduct. It may involve age regressing a client to an early experience in which a decision about lifestyle and belief system was made and then providing an opportunity to establish a more useful framework based on different circumstances, learnings and guidance from the therapist. Erickson's case of Sandra W. (*CP* IV), for instance, illustrates how he elicited the resource of time distortion for a psychotic client and helped her discover how she could control her symptom with the resource. He commented that "An agreement to this effect was reached," demonstrating his policy of including the client's agreement in the therapy (*CP* IV, p. 74).

Nonhypnotic regression and redecision are often accomplished through such means as gestalt double chairing and frequently release considerable amounts of "bound" energy. It is typically a cathartic "insight" approach and the old decision is expected to be abandoned in light of the insight and newly available energy. However, in any nonhypnotic work, just as in Ericksonian hypnotherapy, the resources needed by the client are best established prior to the reassociation phase. If the means and mechanisms of enacting new decisions are not somehow represented in the client's map of the world, s/he will encounter considerable difficulty actually behaving in accordance with the new intention, even though new energy is available. That energy must be systematically directed in component bits which together create the larger "decision." Self-image thinking is especially useful following an insightful redecision in order to provide the necessary "hows" associated with the new decision to "be close" or "be assertive," etc.

Life Mazes

The term "Life mazes" is a collective term for directives, usually given in trance, which send a person on an imaginary journey through various doorways to other time orientations both past and future. This was seen in the case of Dorine in Chapter 7. It allowed elements of both dissociative reviewing and reliving of the past. In so doing it allowed several experiences to be created or retrieved from a chronically unpleasant past. Simultaneously, it allowed her to disengage from the past due to a confusion similar to that in "scrambling."

The client, as may be recalled from Dorine's case, is metaphorically directed to stand in front of several doorways and to pass through each of them, first systematically and then randomly. The doorways to the past are marked: "past as it really happened," "past much worse than it really happened," and "most ideal, wished for past." For the client who feels bitter or handicapped by the past as it was experienced, this activity accomplishes a reframing by vividly "reminding" him or her of a much worse past. Energy is released as elements of the "real" past are redefined.

Experiencing the ideal past creates an opportunity to "get" positive resources from the past which were either forgotten about or not there at all but would have been a natural part of that "ideal" past. Next, there is a fourth door which opens into a maze in which all pasts are combined randomly. Each "step" results in suddenly being in a different one of the three "pasts" just experienced individually. The steps into the past may be regulated by fantasized stepping stones or other devices and may represent months or years depending upon the specific client's personal situation.

As a client follows these suggestions, the lines of "reality" become blurred and it becomes difficult for the client to tell one past from the other or to understand the importance of doing so. Any energy bound by "hanging on" to grudges, resentments or learned limitations of the past can be freed as a result. The client is then ready to proceed through the last door to the future, in which self-image thinking and "map building" can occur or results of behaviors in the future can be examined.

Creating a Social Interface

Creating a social interface is the final pattern we wish to discuss in this array of interventions to enhance the multiple embedded structure. We have seen that work following the direct phase deals with social situations the client is likely to encounter—first the immediate social situation and then the next likely stage of social developoment to which the client will need to adjust. Erickson's creation of a social interface was a phenomenon that bridged the apparent gap between his hypnotic work and his strategic therapy work with whole families. He preshaped the context, perceptions, and expectations of the client for social involvement that was consistent and supportive of the therapeutic goals.

In many cases Erickson created interactions where none would have otherwise occurred: the client for whom he arranged a "double date" and whom he accompanied to a restaurant; the woman who, encouraged by him to "spit" a stream of water through her teeth, made contact with the man who frequented the water cooler; the woman he helped to act, groom, and dress to be socially attractive and then sent to an employees' dance; the puritan husband and wife who were shocked into having sexual fantasies and urges for one another; and from this book, George who was encouraged to listen for his wife's nasty words and to think about vulgar and assertive responses he might make in return. Erickson used this technique frequently and creatively; yet we find that there are a few elements in common in his cases. In summary, these are: 1) creating a context for the client to come together with the other person; 2) creating a consistent and therapeutic expectation of the other person that the client can use to interpret the other's behavior; and 3) preshaping perceptions of the other person so that the client will notice social cues that can, in fact, trigger attitudes or expectations which Erickson had designed and which would stand as "proof" or confirmation of the therapeutic attitude held by the client.

Assessing the client along the lines of the diagnostic framework outlined in Chapter 3 includes an observation of the sensitivity and flexibility that members of the social system have for each other. This can be methodically assessed in the areas of perception, cognition, and behavioral/emotional flexibility. It is this set of dimensions that needs to be considered in the creation of a social interface.

For example, with a family in which the father and daughter seldom talked we sent the daughter to the front porch with the expectation that if she saw her father there she might think to look for signs of stress on his face and ask him if he felt all right. We simultaneously sent the father to the porch for a "breather" from the family problems. Knowing that the daughter would be on the porch and knowing that she would likely ask about the father's feelings, we suggested that the father be alert to his daughter's true purpose in starting conversations. When the father encountered the daughter in the context created by us, he showed the concern that the daughter had come to expect due to her preshaped perceptions. But instead of noticing the concerned face and thinking it signaled anger, as she usually would, the daughter thought of it as an opportunity to ask about the father's feelings. Likewise, the father, expecting the daughter to be elsewhere, was surprised by her presence and provided the necessary look of concern. When the father heard the daughter ask about his feelings, his therapy had prepared him to take her seriously and to talk to her instead of shutting her out, as he might previously have done. Thus, the context, expectations and necessary sensory observations were suggested in the office to create a social interface in the real world outside the office. This is generally the goal of linking resources to the social network and the purpose of concluding the matching metaphor.

In summary, we have discussed several intervention patterns which are, of course, enhanced by the microscopic interventions of indirect suggestion, binds, tonal shifting, paradox, and metaphoric framing. Each of them can be easily organized within the macroscopic framework of the multiple embedded metaphor modality. Most of the interventions are aimed at the resolution of unconscious emotional conflict while respecting the broad parameters of the diagnostic framework. But beyond that goal, the "bottom line" of much of this work is an emphasis on enhancing the client's self-image, on helping the client develop self-management skills for personal resources and the ability to comfortably extend his or her sense of self into new areas of interaction and accomplishment.

9 THE FORCE OF CLOSURE

TERMINATING THERAPY

The termination of a therapy session, as well as the termination of the entire therapy relationship, has special meaning to clients. The underlying philosophy of a session will be crystalized in the client's mind as the session ends. We have already discussed how the client's social network is addressed in the final stages of the multiple embedded metaphor. In doing that, the therapist orients clients away from dependence on therapy to the interdependence of their social network. But individual coping styles and mechanisms for frustration tolerance will determine just how clients consciously anticipate their adjustment. Consequently, in their adjustment to the possibility of being left with the resources created in therapy clients can be hindered or helped by their conscious interpretations. They will draw upon areas of self-image thinking that may not have emerged in the treatment to anticipate their independence; as they do so, they form opinions about the usefulness of the therapy received.

Clients will often have their own unique transference responses based on previous separations they have experienced. There may be any number of separation "issues" that unconsciously affect the client's attitude at the time of termination. These will be most apparent in the final termination, of course, but careful observation can reveal signs of these difficulties in the moments of termination that hail only the end of a single appointment. These may indicate previous traumas, abandonments, repressed symptoms, fears of leaving home, fears of relating, and fears of inadequacy.

The business of other unfinished "goodbyes" may be revived. These may have nothing to do with the expressed purpose of the therapy but nevertheless be stimulated by the parallel situation. For example, the death of a friend from college may have had nothing to do with the marital therapy sought by the client. Yet, at termination, the client or therapist may find the need for adequate adjustment to this past situation stimulated by the end of the session or the therapy. This is often typified by negative emotions, tensions, "dead" spots, internal dialogues with deceased loved ones, unexplainable preoccupations, or unexpected delayed stress reactions from involvements in, for instance, the Vietnam War.

Although problems with "rekindled" business may frighten clients into temporarily believing they are not ready to terminate, a brief extension of therapy to address the unfinished business is often sufficient. Other problems, however, may crop up as a sign that therapy is, in fact, not finished and that the client has not been appropriately treated. In those cases, reevaluation of the diagnosis and further treatment planning may be necessary.

In the context of completing multiple embedded metaphors, however, the "force of closure" provides clients with a framework which often associates any termination concerns with new personal resources which can be used to resolve them. We refer to this process as "retroactively framing the therapy." The final transactions of a session will influence the way the bulk of therapy as a whole is perceived and remembered. Termination of a session or series of sessions implies: "This is what it meant; this is all there is." It forces the client to accept that to everything there is a beginning and an end. If termination is done "weakly", with doubt or incongruity, it diminishes the importance of the work that preceded it, just as a poor ending to a movie tends to ruin the entire drama that preceded it.

There are several aspects of termination for which the hypnotherapist needs to be prepared. The first involves appropriate endings for the metaphoric frameworks begun in the session. It is the therapist's responsibility to respect the needs and expectations of the client's conscious framework. As we have mentioned before, stories which were initiated earlier in the session can be resolved in many ways, often with positive, happy, or logical endings, while the real value of the metaphors is derived from those portions which were detailed within the embedded structure. The ending is less important for stimulating change than what was detailed and how it was sequenced within the story. However, regarding the client's conscious memory of the session, the ending may be most important.

There are occasions when a story's outcome is left to the client, just as there are occasions when stories do not end at all. For example, for a client who is deciding whether to divorce or remain married, the story may end with the protagonist reaching a decision which is not stated to the client. The protagonist of the story may come for therapy and be subjected to multiple tangents designed to increase the ability to judge the necessity of having his or her own needs recognized, to value relationships, to keep commitments, and to recognize the logic of ending things when ending is appropriate. But the "resolution" of the story may be that the protagonist knows exactly what to do and does not state that to the therapist. Hence, the therapist does not share it with the client, and ultimately, the client must decide about his or her own life with an increased awareness of important factors but without the option of copying a solution that fit someone else's life.

Sometimes a story may end in an abrupt or negative manner. This is occasionally the case when the urgency of the client's situation calls for prompt action on his or her part, such as when medical help, child care, or legal assistance is needed. Or, in one case, when the client needed to begin caring for herself and enjoying her role as a mature adult, the protagonist in the story postponed taking hold of life's responsibilities and embracing the joys of adulthood until a number of tasks were accomplished. The metaphoric description of these tasks provided the major vehicle for education in the therapy. But when the story itself came to an end, the expected happy ending was cut short by the untimely death of the protagonist. The point in such a tragic ending was, for the conscious mind, that the client, knowing how to proceed with her life, had better do so before it was too late.

Stories in the metaphoric framework usually end on an up beat. The final closure provides the conscious mind with a sense that the time taken for the multiple tangents was worthwhile. Next, the trance itself must be terminated, which will bring into the foreground those final, parting interactions with the hypnotist, who shifts into a role somewhat different from that which existed when the client was in trance. The hypnotist must deal with immediate comments, interactions, and topics at the end of the session. Erickson typically discouraged discussion of the therapy or trance after a session. When the therapy is not immediately discussed, the likelihood of amnesia is improved and the therapist respects the client's unconscious wisdom about what to remember and what to therapeuticaly "forget."

After the trance and metaphoric frames have been closed, some clients demonstrate an eager desire to discuss the trance. The session is not complete just because the multiple embedded metaphor has been resolved. In those cases, good manners and respect for the client's communications call for some response. The most vague comments, indirect suggestions, and binds are often useful. If clients insist that they were not in trance because they remember everything that was said or because of some other inappropriate reason, the hypnotist needs to remember the importance of "face-saving" for the client. A simple statement of sincere concern such as, "I'm sure that's the way you feel now, yes," may be enough. It is altogether inappropriate to worry along with the client and lose one's sense of confidence. When the hypnotist fears that therapy has failed, the client is signaled. If the therapy was brilliant but the hypnotist discounts it in the final minutes, the value of the work may be lost—along with the relationship with the client. A client's statement about trance will only be the conscious mind's report on the matter and, as such, it may be highly metaphoric or symbolic of the work done. A hypnotist would do well to consider these comments from the client as metaphors and remember to be metaphoric and symbolic in response.

At termination, it is time to orient clients to a framework related to leaving therapy and to the independence that comes with taking this step. For most clients it may be relevant to mention the possible use of amnesia upon reorientation and termination. Although we would not consider clients to be resistant meddlers in the affairs of their unconscious, we do respect possible doubts their conscious mind might entertain as to whether or not trance was accomplished and whether or not they need to develop an amnesia. We include here an example of typical reorienting remarks that we sometimes say in the final moments of the session after official trance has been concluded. Whether the client is "officially" in trance or out of trance is not particularly important, however.

We have mentioned amnesia and a person often wishes to recall everything as soon as the suggestion for forgetting is given. In fact, no one would be at all surprised if you really attempt to remember what you have learned. You may remember everything we said, or some of it, or only a part of it, or perhaps you will come to remember nothing of it at all. It might be that you will remember part of what we said and part of what you thought about when you heard us speak. Our words were only stimuli for your own thinking and you may remember only what you thought about and forget only what we communicated. You probably will search to recall just which you will remember and what is the difference between what we said and what you thought.

While we have been communicating you have learned a great many things. You may already have known some of those things. Many other things you will soon discover you have learned. Other things that you have learned you will never come to realize consciously. Sooner or later you will come to realize learnings you have gained and you might credit us for them. But many of those you learned by yourself and the credit is yours. Other things you may correctly credit to our stimulation of your thoughts. But most of what we communicated is still to be learned. You will discover that in your own particular way, perhaps in dreams at night, or at exactly those moments when you least expected but most desired it.

You may sense that you know more than you did when the session began and that is good. It is pleasant to know that you learned. So we hope that you did not learn everything that we have had to teach because in that way you can look forward to something you can yet discover again. But then too you may find that you learned much at different levels. What your unconscious learned is so very important for your subsequent living, though your conscious mind couldn't begin to articulate those learnings. Your conscious mind, however, has also learned and can enjoy its understandings. Perhaps you can consciously recall all of what your conscious mind thinks it learned but often your conscious mind can only speculate about the learnings of your unconscious mind. Perhaps your unconscious will allow your conscious mind to discover later, perhaps gradually, or maybe suddenly. You may only know at the right time and at the proper moment the precise learning you need or think you need.

And as we said, whether in trance or out of trance everyone tries to recall something when the subject of forgetting is presented. You may be considering your own thoughts and memories even now. And what is there to remember? You can remember the sounds around you. You can remember the breathing, the shuffling, the sounds outside the room, the temperature of your body. Maybe you can recall a slight breeze, some of your muscle movements and bodily stimuli. You can recall what you intended to do next and what you plan to do. And you can recall your unconscious learning of how to do it well and enjoy doing so.

Finally, the therapist needs to deal with countertransference feelings that may occur as a result of rapid and strong rapport built in the session. These feelings may include love, devotion, caring, narcissism, anger, disappointment, or possessiveness and may negatively influence clinical judgment. We recall a comment from Erickson that hypnosis does not hurt anyone, but rather the personality of the hypnotist may. There is no substitute for a therapist's involvement in training, supervision, and psychotherapy to insure the personal development which is so crucial. Hypnotists need to consider their own motivation as professionals at all times and abide by the codes of conduct set by the professional organizations to which they belong.

One timely signal of countertransference that is worthy of special mention is when a therapist, by whatever rationalization, claims that s/he does not need to prepare for the treatment sessions or does not operate from a treatment plan. We perceive such therapists as "flying by the seat of their pants" and allowing their own unexamined unconscious organization to dictate the flow of their clients' imagery and associations. A good solution to such rationalization is to seek supervision and psychotherapy. But that is a topic removed from our present concerns.

In this volume we have shared much of our understanding of Ericksonian hypnotherapy. On the subject of termination, we are reminded that Erickson believed change to be discontinuous. That is, change does not happen constantly. Sometimes people are in a position to change a great deal and sometimes they are at a plateau, so to speak. Brief therapy, short-term therapy, and family therapy are logical ramifications of such an understanding. Likewise, when clients terminate therapy, the door remains open for any number of return visits that may be useful in the months or years to come. Returning to an Ericksonian therapist for new approaches to various life situations is something even the most well adjusted and talented clients do. It need not be interpreted as a sign of dependency or a sign of symptom substitution.

Although resources and answers lie within, they may be greatly facilitated by an external instruction or stimulation to retrieve or recombine them in particular ways. For example, one of Erickson's sons shared with us that as he grew up he occasionally approached his father for solutions to then-current problems. Never once was a specific answer suggested, he said, until he had first followed the invariable instruction he later learned to expect: "Climb (Squaw Peak)." And, of course, the problem always changed (or was solved) as a result of the meditative climb and the psychological and literal change of perspective (Personal communication, December 1980). Ericksonian hypnotherapy is similar in that clients are directed to find their own solutions to changing situations as a result of being directed to alter their customary framework long enough to think globally and make new associations. Anne Morrow Lindbergh metaphorically described a changing of framework when she wrote: " . . . here on the beach the breathlessly still ebb-tides reveal another life below the level which mortals usually reach. In this crystalline moment of suspense, one has a sudden revelation of the secret kingdom at the bottom of the sea . . . " (1978, p. 109).

Many people are familiar with the experience of returning to the ocean periodically for the refreshing peace of mind that can be found there, perhaps as a result of the white noise sound created by the surf or the awesomeness of the ocean as it reflects the sunlight and stretches out to meet the horizon. Similarly, we returned to Dr. Erickson repeatedly for refreshing learnings, to have our familiar thoughts and memories stimulated in new ways. It was not that we were unable to create such learnings on our own, but that there was a special treat in store when we visited Erickson. It was not unlike the special treat that we expect when we visit the ocean again and again. Expect some clients to return because of their firm successes.

The ocean and the beach change daily. Like people, the ocean can seem to have a problem one day—for example, it can be green with thick algae—but be perfectly clear and sparkling the very next day. People also go through cycles. Erickson was a teacher. He taught people to look deeper than the surface in order to determine their true natures and the true nature of their problems. He taught people to change emotional and interpersonal realities by changing their presuppositions about the nature and meaning of their problems (Haley, 1973).

Learning, like change, is cyclical. We have written this volume to offer readers a total gestalt of information and now we must soon bring it to an end. There was much more to Erickson and his work than the entire group of his students, colleagues, friends and family is ever likely to share. Much of what each of us received from Erickson was personal, private, not for public consumption. Much of it defies articulation. For instance, he would sometimes conclude sessions by beginning a story like the following: "I saw four teachers from the midwest and I told them to climb Squaw Peak at sunrise. I mentioned that they should climb slowly and carefully, go more deeply into trance with each step until reaching the top, and there—be alone with me. See only me and talk over your life with me. Ask any questions you want and be very satisfied with my answers" (Personal communication, June 1978). We became excited about the possibility that he was about to induce a profound trance such as the one implied in the story. In fact, we hoped the others would not be able to hear what we said to him while in trance atop Squaw Peak. Then, as we prepared for him to offer the suggestions that would be necessary to develop the trance, he predictably surprised us with his final words for the day: "Now, get out of my office!" It was over again.

MOUNTAINS AND ELEPHANTS

Erickson was a genious. He will eventually rank in history with other greats and his work will come to be recognized increasingly in social sciences and perhaps even in other fields. His work was stamped with individual creativity. It might have seemed that his work was to be studied and appreciated but not imitated. Yet, as we have illustrated, Erickson's approach is learnable. It was intended to be shared by professional clinicians.

His attitude and philosphy toward people and problems contained principles of value to change agents in other contexts. It is not only possible but also likely that an understanding of his attitudes and principles of approach (though not necessarily his techniques) will become widespread.

Erickson's intention was consistently geared to help individuals locate and use the various psychological experiences within themselves to live in the world successfully, creatively, and enjoyably. He modeled the role of the professional, not of days gone by, but in many ways the professional of the future. The professional's role, as he played it, was that of a catalyst. He was not a permissive overseer, such as the catalyst in ultra liberal education, but rather an informed expert who actively helped point the way to strategic uses of inner resources.

The term "co-creation" highlights the mutual involvement between the professional and the client-system in the cycle that develops and induces personal resources. Erickson was a creator and a co-creator. The giving that

Erickson's work exemplifies is about shared growth and a love for humanity. He placed his highest value on the development of the individual and conceived of an individual as someone who was always in relationship to others. He never altered that opinion even in jesting. For instance, we asked him once if he thought he could solve the international political difficulty involving the Iranian hostage crisis of 1979. He replied, "I could solve it . . . but they are over there and I'm over here . . . if you want me to solve it, you'll have to bring them to me . . . then, I could solve it" (Personal communication, December, 1979). There was, even in this humorous statement, a feature of Erickson's work that remains important: Personal contact between the therapist and the subject must occur. Ericksonian hypnosis is, therefore, fundamentally different than that which can be produced and sold on prerecorded audiotape. In a real sense it must be live.

We have taught a number of things about Erickson's work that operate at various levels. We have used a variety of illustrations, cases, and explanations to convey those ideas. We have highlighted things that are as vague in scope as the attitudes behind his approach and have discussed such specifics as voice tone shifting. We have illustrated his use of language and the formulation of indirect suggestions and binds. We have shown how these can be combined in patterns that are still larger protocols for conscious/unconscious dissociation inductions, metaphors, and the production of trance phenomena. We have systematically related those components to the broader framework of diagnostic assessment and treatment planning. Finally, we have illustrated the multiple embedded metaphor framework as the still larger modality to contain the interventions and enact the treatment plan within the therapy session.

We have also talked about a great man who, as Buddha said, can, like a mountain, be seen from a distance. There have been many who broke away from the usual path to climb the mountain that was Milton Erickson. And there are many and various paths to Ericksonian approaches as a result. Each offers a representation of Erickson, and yet any representation of him is destined to be a misrepresentation. We are reminded of the Sufi story about the three blind men.

> Beyond Ghor there was a city. All its inhabitants were blind. A king with his entourage arrived nearby; he brought his army and camped in the desert. He had a mighty elephant, which he used in attack, and to increase the people's awe.
>
> The populace became anxious to learn about the elephant, and some sightless from among this blind community ran like fools to find it. Since they did not know even the form or shape of the elephant, they

groped sightlessly, gathering information by touching some part of it. Each thought that they knew something, because they could feel a part.

When they returned to their fellow-citizens, eager groups clustered around them, anxious, misguidedly, to learn the truth from those who were themselves astray. They asked about the form, the shape, of the elephant, and they listened to all they were told.

The man whose hand had reached an ear said: "It is a large, rough thing, wide and broad, like a rug."

One who had felt the trunk said: "I have the real facts about it. It is like a straight and hollow pipe, awful and destructive."

One who had felt its feet and legs said: "It is mighty and firm, like a pillar."

Each had felt one part out of many. Each had perceived it wrongly. No mind knew all: knowledge is not the companion of the blind. All imagined something, something incorrect. The created is not informed about divinity. There is no Way in this science by means of the ordinary intellect (Shah, 1970, pp. 25–26).

There are many ways of knowledge and skill yet to be developed. This book is but one way. Perhaps it is a personal power that has inspired this and the other existing interpretations of Erickson. Perhaps it is born of our questions. But Erickson would be quick to add that all of one's questions only serve to stimulate the answer within.

BIBLIOGRAPHY

Adler, A. *Social Interest: A Challenge to Mankind.* London: Faber and Faber, Ltd., 1938.

Albrecht, K. *Stress and the Manager.* Englewood Cliffs, NJ: Prentice-Hall, 1979.

Alexander, F. & Selesnick, S. *The History of Psychiatry: An Evaluation of Psychiatric Thought and Practice from Prehistoric Times to the Present.* New York: Harper & Row, 1966.

Assagioli, R. *Psychosynthesis.* New York: Viking, 1965.

Bandura, A. *Principles of Behavior Modification.* New York: Holt, Rinehart & Winston, 1969.

Bateson, G. *Steps to an Ecology of Mind.* New York: Ballantine Books, division of Random House, 1972.

Bateson, G. *Mind and Nature.* New York: Dutton, 1979.

Beck, A. *Depression: Clinical, Experimental and Theoretical Aspects.* New York: Hoeber-Harper, 1967.

Berne, E. *Principles of Group Treatment.* New York: Grove Press, 1966.

Berne, E. Primal images and primal judgment. In P. McCormick (Ed.) *Intuition and Ego States.* San Francisco, CA: TA Press, 1977.

Bernheim, H. *Suggestive Therapeutics: A Treatise on the Nature and Uses of Hypnotism. (1895).* Westport, CT: Associated Booksellers, 1957.

Braid, J. *The Power of the Mind over the Body.* London: Churchill Press, 1846.

Burton, A. *Operational Theories of Personality.* New York: Brunner/Mazel, 1974.

Campos, L. Using metaphor for identifying life script changes. *Transactional Analysis Journal*, 1972, 2, 2: 75.

Cartwright, D. & Zander, A. *Group Dynamics: Research and Theory.* New York: Harper & Row, 1968.

Cirlot, J. E. *A Dictionary of Symbols.* New York: Philosophical Library, 1962.

Charny, J. Psychosomatic manifestations of rapport in psychotherapy. *Pschosomatic Medicine*, 1966, 28, 4: 305–315.

Cheek, D., & LeCron, L. *Clinical Hypnotherapy.* New York: Grune and Stratton, 1968.

Cohen, A. The delinquency subculture. In R. Giallombardo (Ed.) *Juvenille Delinquency: A Book of Readings.* New York: Wiley, 1966, pp. 103–118.

Cornuelle, R. *Demanaging America: The Final Revolution.* New York: Random House, 1975.

Erickson, M. H. *The Collected Papers of Milton H. Erickson on Hypnosis. Volume I: The Nature of Hypnosis and Suggestion; Volume II: Hypnotic Alteration of Sensory, Perceptual and Psychophysiological Processes; Volume III: Hypnotic Investigation of Psychodynamic Processes; Volume IV: Innovative Hypnotherapy.*

Ernest L. Rossi (Ed.). New York: Irvington, 1980. (This is referred to in the text and the rest of this bibliography as *CP*.)

Erickson, M. H. The use of symptoms as an integral part of hypnotherapy. In J. Haley (Ed.) *Advanced Techniques of Hypnosis and Therapy: Selected Papers of Milton H. Erickson, M.D.* New York: Grune & Stratton, 1967, pp. 500–509.

Erickson, M. H. & Cooper, L. *Time Distortion in Hypnosis.* Baltimore: Williams and Wilkins, 1959.

Erickson, M. H. & Erickson, E. Concerning the nature and character of posthypnotic behavior. In *CP* I, pp. 381–411.

Erickson, M. H. & Cooper, L. Time distortion in hypnosis: II. In *CP* II, pp. 231–265.

Erickson, M. H., Hershman, S., & Secter, I. *The Practical Application of Medical and Dental Hypnosis.* New York: The Julian Press, 1961.

Erickson, M. H. & Kubie L. The successful treatment of a case of acute hysterical depression by a return under hypnosis to a critical phase of childhood. In *CP* III, pp. 122–142.

Erickson, M. H. & Rosen, H. The hypnotic and hypnotherapeutic investigation and determination of symptom-function. In *CP* IV, pp. 103–123.

Erickson, M. H. & Rossi, E. L. *Hypnotherapy: An Exploratory Casebook.* New York: Irvington, 1979.

Erickson, M., & Rossi, E. The February man: Facilitating new identity in hypnotherapy. In *CP* IV, pp. 525–542.

Erickson, M. & Rossi, E. The indirect forms of suggestion. In *CP* I, pp. 452–477.

Erickson, M., & Rossi, E. Literalness and the use of trance in neurosis. In *CP* III, pp. 100–101.

Erickson, M. & Rossi, E. Two level communication and the microdynamics of trance and suggestion. In *CP* I, pp. 430–451.

Erickson, M. & Rossi, E. Varieties of double bind. In *CP* I, pp. 412–429.

Erickson, M. & Rossi, E. Varieties of hypnotic amnesia. In *CP* III, pp. 71–90.

Erickson, M. & Rossi, E. *Experiencing Hypnosis.* New York: Irvington, 1981.

Erickson, M. H., Rossi, E. L. & Rossi, S. *Hypnotic Realities.* New York: Irvington, 1976.

Erickson, M. H. & Zeig, J. K. Symptom prescription for expanding the psychotic's world view. In *CP* IV, pp. 335–338.

Erikson, E. *Childhood and Society.* New York: Norton, 1963.

Fenichel, O. *The Psychoanalytic Theory of Neurosis.* New York: Norton, 1945.

Framo, J. Symptoms from a family transactional viewpoint. In C. J. Sager & H. S. Kaplan (Eds.) *Progress in Group and Family Therapy.* New York: Brunner/Mazel, 1972.

Framo, J. A couples group demonstration. Brookline, MA: Boston Family Institute film library, 1980.

Freud, S. The interpretation of dreams. In A. Brill (Ed.) *The Basic Writings of Sigmund Freud.* New York: The Modern Library, 1938, pp. 181–552.

Goleman, D. Perspectives on psychology, reality, and the study of consciousness. *The Journal of Transpersonal Psychology,* 1974, 6, 1: 73–85.

Goulding, M. M. & Goulding, R. L. *Changing Lives Through Redecision Therapy.* New York: Brunner/Mazel, 1979.

Goulding, R. L. New directions in transactional analysis: Creating an environment for redecision and change. In C. J. Sager and H. S. Kaplan (Eds.) *Pro-

gress in Group and Family Therapy. New York: Brunner/Mazel, 1972, pp. 105–134.

Guntrip, H. *Psychoanalytic Theory, Therapy and the Self*. New York: Basic Books, 1973.

Grinder, J., DeLozier, J., & Bandler, R. *Patterns of the Hypnotic Techniques of Milton H. Erickson, M.D.* (Vol. 2). Cupertino, CA: Meta, 1977.

Haimowitz, M. & Haimowitz, N. "Mary," a film produced by the American Counseling and Guidance Association. Evanston, IL: Morris Haimowitz, 1975.

Haley, J. *Strategies of Psychotherapy*. New York: Grune & Stratton, 1963.

Haley, J. (Ed.) *Advanced Techniques of Hypnosis and Therapy: Selected Papers of Milton H. Erickson, M.D.* New York: Grune and Stratton, 1967.

Haley, J. *Uncommon Therapy: The Psychiatric Techniques of Milton H. Erickson, M.D.* New York: Norton, 1973.

Hart, W. Symbiotic invitations. *Transactional Analysis Journal*, 1976, 6, 3: 253–254.

Hartmann, H. *Ego Psychology and the Problem of Adaptation*. David Rappaport (Translator). New York: International Universities Press, 1958.

Horney, K. *The Neurotic Personality of Our Time*, Vol. 1 & Vol. 2. New York: Norton, 1937.

Hull, C. *Hypnosis and Suggestibility: An Experimental Approach*. New York: Appleton-Century, 1933.

Jones, R. *Self-Fulfilling Prophecies: Social, Psychological and Physiological Effects of Expectancies*. New York: Wiley, 1977.

Jung, C. G. *Man and His Symbols*. C. Jung & M. L. von Franz (Eds.). New York: Dell, 1964.

Jung, C. G. On the nature of the psyche. In *The Basic Writings of C. G. Jung*. New York: Random House, 1959, pp. 37–104.

Khayyam, O. *Rubaiyat of Omar Khayyam*. E. Fitzgerald (Translator). Garden City, N.Y.: Garden City Books, 1952.

Kopp, S. *Guru: Metaphors From a Psychotherapist*. Palo Alto, CA: Science and Behavior Books, 1971.

Korzybski, A. *Science and Sanity: An Introduction to Non-Aristotelian Systems and General Semantics*. Lancaster, PA: The Science Press Printing Co., 1933.

Kris, E. *The Psychology of Caricature: Psychoanalytic Explorations in Art*. New York: International Universities Press, 1934.

Kroger, W. *Clinical and Experimental Hypnosis in Medicine, Dentistry, and Psychology*. Philadelphia: Lippincott, 1977.

Laing, R. D. *The Politics of Experience*. New York: Ballantine Books, 1967.

Laing, R. D. *The Politics of the Family*. New York: Ballantine Books, 1972.

Lankton, S. "Violet," audio supervision, 1975.

Lankton, S. *Practical Magic: A Translation of Basic Neurolinguistic Programming into Clinical Psychotherapy*. Cupertino, CA: Meta, 1980.(a)

Lankton, S. Experience chains: Change at a higher level. In J. Cassius (Ed.) *Horizons in Bioenergetics*. Memphis, TN: Promethean, 1980, pp. 56–72(b).

Lankton, S. Varieties of Ericksonian hypnotic suggestion. A videotape. Phoenix: Milton H. Erickson Foundation, 1981.

Lankton, S. The occurrence and use of trance phenomena in nonhypnotic therapies. In J. Zeig (Ed.) *Ericksonian Approaches to Hypnosis and Psychotherapy*. New York: Brunner/Mazel, 1982.

Lankton, S., Lankton, C., & Brown, M. Psychological level communication in transactional analysis. *Transactional Analysis Journal,* 1981, II, 4: 287–299.

Lazarus, A. *Multimodal Behavior Therapy.* New York: Springer, 1976.

Leary, T. *Interpersonal Diagnosis of Personality: A Functional Theory and Methodology for Personality Evaluation.* New York: Ronald Press, 1957.

Lindbergh, A. M. *Gifts From the Sea.* New York: Vintage Books division of Random House, 1978.

Lowen, A. *Bioenergetics.* New York: Coward, McCann and Geohegan, 1975.

Lustig, H. S. The Artistry of Milton H. Erickson, M. D., Part I and Part II. Haverford, PA: Herbert S. Lustig, M. D., Ltd., a videotape, 1975.

Maslow, A. *The Farther Reaches of Human Nature.* New York: Viking, 1971.

Mead, G. H. *On Social Psychology: Selected Papers.* Chicago: University of Chicago Press, Phoenix Books, 1965.

Mellor, K. Reframing and the integrated use of redeciding and reparenting. *Transactional Analysis Journal,* 1980, 10, 3: 204–212.

Moreno, J. *Psychodrama: First Volume.* Fourth Edition with Introductory Notes. New York: Beacon House, 1972.

Murray, E. J. A content-analysis method for studying psychotherapy. *Psychological Monographs,* 1956, 70 (13, Whole No. 420).

O'Hanlon, B. The use of paradoxical interventions in therapy: A practical model for clinicians (unpublished paper). Blair, NE: Bill O'Hanlon, 1981.

O'Neil, H. Jr. *Learning Strategies.* New York: Academic Press, 1978.

Ornstein, R. *The Psychology of Consciousness.* New York: Viking, 1972.

Patton, M., Fuhriman, A., & Bieber, M. A model and a metalanguage for research on psychological counseling. *Journal of Counseling Psychology,* 1977, 24, 1: 25–34.

Perls, F. *Ego Hunger and Aggression.* New York: Vintage Books division of Random House, 1947.

Prince, M. *The Unconscious.* New York: Macmillan, 1929.

Progoff, I. *The Death and Rebirth of Psychology: An Integrative Evaluation of Freud, Adler, Jung and Rank and the Impact of Their Insights on Modern Man.* New York: McGraw-Hill, 1956.

Putney, S. & Putney, G. *The Adjusted American: Normal Neuroses in the Individual and Society.* New York: Harper and Row, 1964.

Richardson, F. Behavior modification and learning strategies. In H. O'Neil (Ed.) *Learning Strategies.* New York: Academic Press, 1978.

Rogers, C. "Gloria" in "Three Approaches to Therapy." Orange, CA: Psychological Films, Inc., 1969.

Rogers, C. *On Becoming a Person.* Boston: Houghton Mifflin, 1961.

Rosen, H. *Hypnotherapy in Clinical Psychiatry.* New York: Julian Press, 1953.(a)

Rosen, H. The dangerous effects of hypnosis (when utilized by unskilled, inept, untrained or emotionally sick hypnotists). Paper read at the Fourth Annual Meeting of the Society for Clinical and Experimental Hypnosis, September 26, 1953.(b)

Rossi, E. Indirect approaches to symptom resolution. In *CP* IV, pp. 97–98.

Satir, V. "Perception." Brookline, MA: Boston Family Insititute tape library, 1980.

Satir, V. Personal Communication. February 20, 1981.

Scheflen, A. *Communicational Structure.* Bloomington: Indiana University Press, 1973.

Selvini Palazzoli, M., Boscolo, L., Cecchin, G., & Prata, G. The treatment of children through brief therapy of their parents. *Family Process,* 1974, 13: 429–442.

Shah, I. *Tales of the Dervishes*. New York: Dutton, 1970.

Skinner, B. F. *Beyond Freedom and Dignity*. New York: Alfred Knopf, 1971.

Soper, P. & L'Abate, L. Paradox as a therapeutic technique. *International Journal of Family Counseling*: 1977, 5, 1: 11–21.

Speck, R. & Attneave, C. *Family Networks*. New York: Random House, Pantheon Books, 1973.

Tart, C. *Altered States of Consciousness*. New York: Wiley, 1969.

Tart, C. *States of Consciousness*. New York: Dutton, 1975.

Toffler, A. *Future Shock*. New York: Random House, 1970.

Truax, C. B. Reinforcement and nonreinforcement in Rogerian psychotherapy. *Journal of Abnormal Psychology*, 1966, 71: 1-9.

Upham, F. *Ego Analysis and the Helping Professions*. New York: Family Service Association of America, 1973.

Watson, J. *Behaviorism*. New York: Norton, 1924, (Revision, 1930.)

Watzlawick, P. *An Anthology of Human Communication*. Text and Tape. Palo Alto, CA: Science and Behavior Books, Inc., 1964.

Watzlawick, P. Erickson's contribution to the international view of psychotherapy. In J. K. Zeig (Ed.) *Ericksonian Approaches to Hypnosis and Psychotherapy*. New York: Brunner/Mazel, 1982, pp. 147–154.

Watzlawick, P., Beavin, J. & Jackson, D. *Pragmatics of Human Communication*. New York: Norton, 1967.

Watzlawick, P., Weakland, J. & Fisch, R. *Change*. New York: Norton, 1974.

Weakland, J., Fisch, R., Watzlawick, P., & Bodin, A. Brief therapy: Focused problem resolution. *Family Process*, 1974, 13: 141–168.

Weisman, A. Nature and treatment of tics in adults. *Journal of Neurology and Psychiatry*, 1952, 68: 444.

Weitzenhoffer, A. Unconscious or co-conscious? Reflections upon certain recent trends in medical hypnosis. *American Journal of Clinical Hypnosis*, 1960, 2: 177–196.

Whitaker, C. Hypnosis and family depth therapy. In Zeig, J. K. (Ed.) *Ericksonian Approaches to Hypnosis and Psychotherapy*. New York: Brunner/Mazel, 1982, p.491.

Wolpe, J. *Psychotherapy by Reciprocal Inhibition*. Palo Alto, CA: Stanford University Press, 1948.

Zander, C. Group aspirations. In D. Cartwright & A. Zander (Eds.) *Group Dynamics: Research and Theory*. New York: Harper and Row, 1968. pp. 418–429.

Zeig, J. K. *A Teaching Seminar with Milton H. Erickson*. New York: Brunner/Mazel, 1980.

Zeig, J. K. *Ericksonian Approaches to Hypnosis and Psychotherapy*. New York: Brunner/Mazel, 1982.

Zukav, G. *The Dancing Wu Li Masters: An Overview of the New Physics*. New York: Bantam Books, 1979.

INDEX